This study addresses the question of why ideas of ancestry and kinship were so important in nineteenth-century society, and particularly in the Victorian novel. Through readings of a range of literary texts, Sophie Gilmartin explores questions fundamental to the national and racial identity of Victorian Britons. What makes people believe that they are part of a certain region, race or nation? Is this sense of belonging based on superstitious beliefs, invented traditions, or fictions created to gain a sense of unity or community? As Britain extended her empire over foreign nations and races, questions of blood relations, of assimilation and difference, and of national and racial definition came to the fore. Gilmartin's study shows how ideas of ancestry and kinship, and the narratives inspired by or invented around them, were of profound significance in the construction of Victorian identity.

Sophie Gilmartin is Lecturer in English Literature at Royal Holloway, University of London. She works mainly in the fields of Victorian literature, art and cultural studies.

CAMBRIDGE STUDIES IN NINETEENTH-CENTURY
LITERATURE AND CULTURE 18

ANCESTRY AND NARRATIVE IN
NINETEENTH-CENTURY BRITISH LITERATURE

CAMBRIDGE STUDIES IN NINETEENTH-CENTURY
LITERATURE AND CULTURE

GENERAL EDITOR
Gillian Beer, *University of Cambridge*

Editorial board
Isobel Armstrong, *Birkbeck College, London*
Terry Eagleton, *University of Oxford*
Leonore Davidoff, *University of Essex*
D. A. Miller, *Columbia University*
J. Hillis Miller, *University of California, Irvine*
Mary Poovey, *New York University*
Elaine Showalter, *Princeton University*

Nineteenth-century British literature and culture have been rich fields for interdisciplinary studies. Since the turn of the twentieth century, scholars and critics have tracked the intersections and tensions between Victorian literature and the visual arts, politics, social organization, economic life, technical innovations, scientific thought – in short, culture in its broadest sense. In recent years, theoretical challenges and historiographical shifts have unsettled the assumptions of previous scholarly syntheses and called into question the terms of older debates. Whereas the tendency in much past literary critical interpretation was to use the metaphor of culture as 'background', feminist, Foucauldian, and other analyses have employed more dynamic models that raise questions of power and of circulation. Such developments have reanimated the field.

This series aims to accommodate and promote the most interesting work being undertaken on the frontiers of the field of nineteenth-century literary studies: work which intersects fruitfully with other fields of study such as history, or literary theory, or the history of science. Comparative as well as interdisciplinary approaches are welcomed.

A complete list of titles published will be found at the end of the book.

ANCESTRY AND NARRATIVE IN NINETEENTH-CENTURY BRITISH LITERATURE

Blood Relations from Edgeworth to Hardy

SOPHIE GILMARTIN

PUBLISHED BY THE PRESS SYNDICATE OF THE UNIVERSITY OF CAMBRIDGE
The Pitt Building, Trumpington Street, Cambridge CB2 1RP, United Kingdom

CAMBRIDGE UNIVERSITY PRESS
The Edinburgh Building, Cambridge CB2 2RU, UK   http://www.cup.cam.ac.uk
40 West 20th Street, New York, NY 10011-4211, USA   http://www.cup.org
10 Stamford Road, Oakleigh, Melbourne 3166, Australia

© Sophie Gilmartin 1998

This book is in copyright. Subject to statutory exception
and to the provisions of relevant collective licensing agreements,
no reproduction of any part may take place without
the written permission of Cambridge University Press.

First published 1998

Printed and bound in Great Britain by Biddles Ltd, Guildford and King's Lynn

Typeset in 11 on 12.5 Baskerville [VN]

A catalogue record for this book is available from the British Library

Library of Congress Cataloguing in Publication data
Gilmartin, Sophie.
Ancestry and narrative in nineteenth-century British literature: blood relations from
Edgeworth to Hardy / Sophie Gilmartin.
p. cm. – (Cambridge studies in nineteenth-century literature and culture: 18)
Includes bibliographical references and index.
ISBN 0 521 56094 2 (hardback)
1. English fiction – 19th century – History and criticism. 2. Genealogy in literature.
3. Edgeworth, Maria, 1767–1849 – Knowledge – Genealogy. 4. Dickens, Charles,
1812–1870 – Knowledge – Genealogy. 5. Domestic fiction, English – History and criticism.
6. Family in literature. &. Narration (Rhetoric) I. Title. II. Series.
PR868.G354G55   1998
823'.809355 – dc21   CIP

ISBN 0 521 56094 2 hardback

For Daniel and Shirley Gilmartin

Contents

List of illustrations	page x
Acknowledgements	xi
Textual note: the novels	xii

Introduction	1
1 Oral and written genealogies in Edgeworth's *The Absentee*	23
2 A mirror for matriarchs: the cult of Mary Queen of Scots in nineteenth-century literature	54
3 Pedigree, nation, race: the case of Disraeli's *Sybil* and *Tancred*	102
4 'A sort of Royal Family': Alternative pedigrees in Meredith's *Evan Harrington*	130
5 Pedigree, sati and the widow in Meredith's *The Egoist*	163
6 Pedigree and forgetting in Hardy	195
7 Geology and genealogy: Hardy's *The Well-Beloved*	226
Conclusion	246

Notes	252
Bibliography	267
Index	276

Illustrations

1. Daniel Maclise, *The Marriage of Eva and Strongbow* (*c.* 1854). Courtesy of the National Gallery of Ireland. *page* 26
2. Frontispiece to the 1812 edition of Maria Edgeworth, *The Absentee*. 49
3. Joseph Severn, *The Abdication of Mary, Queen of Scots*, *c.* 1831. Courtesy of the Victoria and Albert Museum. 79
4. Richard Westall, *The Departure of Mary Queen of Scots to France When a Child*, probably *c.* 1794. Courtesy of the Victoria and Albert Museum. 84
5. Richard Westall, *The Flight of Mary Queen of Scots into England*, probably *c.* 1794. Courtesy of the Victoria and Albert Museum. 84
6. William Hennessy, illustration to Charlotte M. Yonge's *Unknown to History*, *c.* 1892. 95
7. 'New Crowns for Old Ones!' cartoon from *Punch*, 15 April 1876. 116
8. 'Empress and Earl, or One Good Turn Deserves Another', cartoon from *Punch*, 26 August 1876. 117
9. Edwin Longsden Long, *The Babylonian Marriage Market*, exhibited at the Royal Academy, 1875. Courtesy of Royal Holloway College. 176
10. Richard Redgrave, *Preparing to Throw Off her Weeds*, exhibited at the Royal Academy 1846. Courtesy of the Victoria and Albert Museum. 183
11. E. K. Johnson, *A Young Widow*, 1877. Courtesy of the Print Room, the Victoria and Albert Museum. 191
12. Henry Alexander Bowler, *The Doubt: 'Can These Dry Bones Live?'*, exhibited at the Royal Academy 1855. Courtesy of the Tate Gallery, London. 208

Acknowledgements

I would like to thank Gillian Beer and Tony Tanner for their advice and support during the research and writing of my doctoral thesis, which was an early draft of this book. I have also benefited from the help and guidance of Josie Dixon and Linda Bree at Cambridge University Press. I am very grateful to J. Hillis Miller for his support and encouragement over the years. My sisters, Clare, Emma and Bethan, have always been down the end of a phone when I needed them and are very good listeners. Various friends have offered invaluable commentary, emergency computer aid and emotional support, and I would particularly like to mention Joanna Lewis, Malcolm Smith, Clive Marsland, Gareth Noon and Rebecca Ferguson. I want to thank my step-daughters, Luśka and Zuza, for their affectionate and persuasive demands that I have fun with them rather than work. My husband, Rod Mengham, has been unfailingly supportive, and this project has benefited enormously from discussions and holidays with him. I wish to dedicate this book to my parents as a small token of thanks for their love and support.

A part of chapter 8 of this book has appeared in the journal *Victorian Literature and Culture* (25)1 (Spring 1997)

Unfortunately, Tess O'Toole's *Genealogy and Fiction in Hardy* (Macmillan, 1997) was published too late for Chapters 6 and 7 of this book to engage with her arguments.

Textual note: the novels

Editions of the novels which are the focus of this study are as follows:

Chapter 1

I have used the 1832 edition of Maria Edgeworth's *Tales and Novels* rather than that of 1812. Edgeworth revised the later edition of her works considerably, and this is particularly the case with *The Absentee*. I have, however, compared the two editions to explore the significance of Edgeworth's revisions. (*The Absentee, Novels and Tales*, vols. 9 and 10, London, 1832).

The edition used of Sydney Owenson, Lady Morgan's *The Wild Irish Girl* is a facsimile of the first edition of 1806 (*The Wild Irish Girl*, 1806; New York and London: Garland, 1979, 3 vols.).

Chapter 2

Charlotte M. Yonge, *Unknown to History: A Story of the Captivity of Mary of Scotland*, 1882; London, Macmillan, 1898.

Scott, Sir Walter, *The Monastery*, and its sequel, *The Abbot*, both originally published 1820 in 2 vols. each. This edition (Roxburgh), Edinburgh, 1885.

Chapter 3

The 'Hughenden edition' of Disraeli's novels is a reliable edition of his collected novels, based upon an earlier edition overseen by the author which was also published by Longman (*Novels and Tales of the Earl of Beaconsfield with Portrait and Sketch of His Life*: vol. 6, *Coningsby*; vol. 7, *Sybil*; vol. 8, *Tancred*, London, 1881).

Chapters 4 and 5

I have consulted the Standard Edition of George Meredith's works, published by Constable:
Evan Harrington, 1861; 1914
The Egoist, 1879; 1915
Celt and Saxon, published posthumously, 1910; 1919.

Chapters 6 and 7

I have used the 'New Wessex' edition in hard cover of Hardy's complete novels, published by Macmillan in the 1970s:
Far From the Madding Crowd, ed. Christine Winfield; intr., John Bayley, 1975.
Life's Little Ironies and *A Changed Man*, ed. F. B. Pinion, 1977.
A Pair of Blue Eyes, ed. and intr. Ronald Blythe, 1976.
Tess of the D'Urbervilles, ed. and intr. P. N. Furbank, 1975.
The Well-Beloved, ed. Edward Mendelson; intr. J. Hillis Miller, 1975.
In chapters 6 and 7 I have discussed a number of Hardy's poems, and here I have used *The Complete Poems of Thomas Hardy*, ed. James Gibson, London, Macmillan, 1976.

Introduction

In July of 1993, rather early for the journalistic 'silly season', a polite fracas broke out in the newspapers over Jeremy Paxman's family tree. Mr Paxman, the well-known British journalist and host of *Newsnight*, wrote, 'The *Jewish Chronicle* has introduced me to ... "an amateur genealogist now living in Torquay", who wants to claim me as one of the chosen race.'[1] The *Evening Standard* ran the exclusive: 'Debate has raged since the *Jewish Chronicle* raised the question: is Jeremy Paxman Jewish? Here he gives his definitive answer'. Paxman's answer was that as far as he could tell he was not Jewish. He admitted to some uncertainty, however: 'The problem is that, like most of the British, I simply have no idea of my family history further than a generation or two back.'

To this admission, Auberon Waugh responded with shock and 'existential anxiety' in the *Daily Telegraph*:

Can it be true that most Britons have no idea of their own ancestry? Do they have no family Bibles or records? To what purpose did their great-grandparents go to all the trouble and expense of bearing and rearing children, only to be forgotten in two generations? How can people be sure they exist until they have established their antecedents?[2]

Raising the emotional stakes in this exchange of journalistic badinage, Bernard Levin responded in *The Times* to Waugh's reaction; *his* ancestry could be traced back only one generation on his father's side and two on his mother's. His mother's parents, escaping the Russian pogroms, came to England with the clothes on their backs, a mortar and pestle and a samovar – no documents and certainly no pedigree. Levin accompanied his article, 'Pedigree, what pedigree?', with a childhood photograph of himself, presumably to prove to himself and his readers that he actually does exist. As he says, 'it is almost literally true that I am my own ancestors'. Bernard Levin proudly stresses the orally transmitted history of his family which may have no written pedigree, but does have samovars and stories:

No documents, but much reminiscence. As a child I sat hypnotised as my grandparents spun the stories of life in the Pale – real stories, that is, with real characters, real brutality and real comforting. Bron's autobiography ... cannot provide anything like my grandparents' world; what is the calm of the Waugh archives to the thunder of Cossack hooves, for all that I have not a scrap of paper to back up my memories.[3]

The following chapters study the relation of family lines and the family tree to nineteenth-century narrative. This may seem a far remove from the journalistic musings outlined above, but the fortnight's fracas over Jeremy Paxman's pedigree serves to introduce and to show the connections between many of the issues which I shall address. The articles reveal tensions over pedigree which I focus upon in their nineteenth-century guises, but which are still evident in Britain today in diluted or convoluted forms. There is the privileging of the old, and usually noble or upper-class English pedigree (Levin presents this as Auberon Waugh's ancestry: 'there can be no doubt that his ancestors robbed churches for Charles I, and possibly for Cromwell too'); the privileging of written over oral pedigrees; and the association of orally transmitted pedigrees with minority elements who have experienced, or are experiencing, an uneasy assimilation into Great Britain.

Levin demonstrates the facility of the imaginative move from a consideration of pedigree to an involvement with narrative. He stresses that he may not be able to prove the existence of his ancestors with a written pedigree, but that they have left him an oral genealogy based upon stories of their kin and their native Russia. It is the importunate note in Levin's repetition that these are *real* – 'real stories, with real characters, real tragedies, real brutality', etc. – which repercusses through my chapters on Edgeworth, Scott, Disraeli, Yonge, Meredith and Hardy. These chapters deal in part with pedigrees, and with the stories which accompany or are inspired by pedigrees, many of which are in danger of being lost or forgotten. Levin emphasises the reality and validity of his undocumented pedigree. Confronted with Waugh's family records (and an ancestry which has amply documented itself) Levin questions the inevitable authority of the written, English upper-class genealogy, and the idea that one may not actually 'exist' without the pedigree to prove it. Nevertheless, Levin translates the oral records of his family into a written record when he documents his family history in that most traditional of English newspapers, *The Times*. As a journalist, Levin is fully invested in a written culture; he preserves his pedigree and proves its existence to a wide readership by writing it down.

'Existential' anxieties inspired by the lack of pedigree are not limited to a modern sensibility. Because a family pedigree can be seen as the first element in an expanding series – pedigree, tribe (or region), race, nation (or: nation, race) – an individual's definition of self, his or her assertion of social existence, begins with the family tree. It is a first step in placing his or her identity in the context of the other elements in the series. In the following chapters I address the questions of what constitutes belonging, and of what makes people believe that they are kin, or part of a certain region, race or nation. Part of the answer to these questions lies in the constructions of narrative around pedigree, the stories which people accept, or indeed create around their ancestry. I investigate the relations of family lines and the family tree to nineteenth-century fiction, focussing upon how the family line/tree, working within the novel's plot, reflects class, regional, racial and national tensions within Britain at the time. I do not use the terms family line and family tree interchangeably; these two constructions of ancestry produce very different interpretations of who is kin and who is not. I shall clarify these terms as I go on, but at this point I should state that in the following chapters 'pedigree' and 'family tree' will be used interchangeably, as both evoke a multilinear model as opposed to the family *line*. I shall employ the terms 'pedigree' and 'family tree' when I am referring to ancestry or genealogy in general, because these terms include the family line.

Chapter One traces the incommensurability of Irish oral and English written pedigrees in the aftermath of Union of the two islands, as this is presented in Edgeworth's *The Absentee* (1812). Chapter Two explores the 'cult' of Mary Queen of Scots in nineteenth-century fiction and painting, and particularly in two novels: Walter Scott's *The Abbot* (1820) and Charlotte Yonge's *Unknown to History* (1882). Mary Stuart was perhaps the most charismatic of a line of royal women who served as role models for many nineteenth-century women, including Queen Victoria. This line of queens and princesses together constituted a 'matriarchal mirror' in which women could see reflected not only a number of the functions expected of them as women, but also roles which were supposedly outside their 'proper sphere'. Chapter Three, on Disraeli's *Sybil* (1845), and *Tancred* (1847), looks at the family tree *as* fiction; the genealogist Baptist Hatton bestows social and political power upon his clients by 'inventing' pedigrees for them. In *Tancred*, Disraeli glorifies his own Jewish pedigree and places it (and therefore himself) within an expanding imperialistic vision of England's future.

My fourth chapter, on George Meredith's *Evan Harrington* (1860), returns to the theme of Celtic versus Saxon pedigrees; although Evan is noble according to his ancient Welsh pedigree, in England he is merely a tailor's son. The decision to suppress part or all of this family tree has in this novel (and in Meredith's own life) class and nationalist implications. Chapter Five looks at Meredith's *The Egoist* (1879), and at how the expected unilinear narrative which follows the main line of the family tree is disrupted by matrilineal narratives and 'besieging cousins'. I argue also that the novel reveals Meredith's culturally comparative stance, far advanced for his time, through the 'oriental' metaphors in the novel, particularly the metaphors of sati and the Hindu widow. In Chapters Six and Seven, Hardy's *A Pair of Blue Eyes* (1873) and *The Well-Beloved* (1897) both reveal an anxiety over the manner in which genealogical and geological time scales can lead to the erasure of the record of the individual human life. Following a consideration in previous chapters of 'peripheral' Celtic elements and of Jewish elements which represent separation and difference within Britain, few things could seem more quintessentially English than Hardy's 'Wessex'. But I argue that the regional can present England itself as divided from within. The intensive inbreeding on Portland in *The Well-Beloved* gives the inhabitants of the 'island' a common pedigree, and makes of them, according to Hardy, a 'separate race' from mainland England. Regional difference, represented by an obsessively repeated pedigree in these novels, divides Great Britain as effectively as the separate pedigrees of the Celtic nations or the Jews.

An exploration of the fictions or myths which surround pedigree, and of pedigree's place *within* fiction, reveal much about Britain's anxieties over, and defence of itself as a unified nation. In recent years, there has been much interest in the role of narrative and the imagination in the construction of national identity.[4] Benedict Anderson, for example, defines a nation as 'an imagined community – and imagined as both inherently limited and sovereign'.[5] Harriet Ritvo and Jonathan Arac write that this envisioning of the nation as spatially and culturally limited was especially disturbed in the late eighteenth century and throughout the nineteenth century in Britain:

The established European powers found their traditional self-definitions challenged by the imperatives of capitalism and empire. That is, expansion – incorporation of the alien, either territorially or economically – was necessary to maintain preeminence, but that same expansion could diffuse or undermine the common culture on which the sense of shared nationality ultimately depended. The resulting strain may have been particularly acute in Great Britain, threatened externally by Napoleon as well as by its own internal dynamics.[6]

In these chapters, a concentration on the internal dynamics within Britain, and a focussing upon the imaginative and fictional constructions around pedigree, become involved with, and are an important key to understanding, the imaginative constructions of Britain as a cohesive, unified nation. A pedigree easily leads out into the internal dynamics of regional and national difference within Britain, and while it is important that these issues surrounding the expanding elements of the series do not inundate or confuse the study of pedigree, it is essential to locate the areas where pedigree crosses and elucidates the racial, regional and national tensions which threatened to fragment Britain's image of herself as unified and insular.

Despite, or perhaps because of, the pressures of imperial expansion, and the accompanying incorporation of alien peoples and cultures, England saw herself as an island nation which was unified, marked out both spatially and racially from other nations. English pedigrees were presented from about the 1830s on as an ancient mixture of the Anglo-Saxon and the Norman, and many Anglo-Saxonist historians and ethnologists considered the Norman contribution to be negligible: the strength of Anglo-Saxon blood had won over 'weaker' strains. The Celtic elements in these pedigrees were either suppressed or ignored. This, however, had not always been the case. According to Grant Allen, writing in *The Fortnightly Review* in 1880:

Fifty years ago everybody spoke of the 'Ancient Britons' as our ancestors ... The fashion for ignoring the distinction between British and English, a fashion derived from the Tudor kings and strengthened by the Union, led the whole world to talk of England as if it were in reality Wales. But during the present generation a great reaction has set in. Mr. Freeman[7] has never ceased to beat into our heads the simple fact that the English people and the English language are English, and not Welsh, or like any other thing.[8]

While Grant Allen claims that 'fifty years ago everybody spoke of the "Ancient Britons" as our ancestors', a hundred years previously a number of scholars and antiquarians had been asking whether Englishmen were not in fact of ancient Jewish origin. Howard Weinbrot argues that while 'the tale of Brutus the grandson of Aeneas as founder of Britain remains attractive through much of the seventeenth and eighteenth centuries' some rejected this ancestral narrative because it tended to make Britain 'an appendage of Rome' and also because it associated Britain's empire-building with the cruel and violent methods of classical empire expansion.[9] The 'Ancient Britons' or Celts, according to some scholars, endowed Britain with an even nobler and more ancient pedigree than that of Aeneas; according to Weinbrot, 'the Celts in general, and the Scots in particular, were often associated with the Jews':

> According to a widely held theory, the great Celtic peoples were offspring of Noah's grandson Gomer, who ... peopled all of Europe and parts of Asia Minor. They of course spoke Hebrew, which gradually evolved into Celtic. These nations were guided by the Druids and their Bards, a learned, legislating, and oral priestly class especially distinguished in Britain ... Alternatively, the first settlers in Britain included the Phoenicians who came to trade for tin in Cornwall and stayed to establish their own great eastern culture in western and central Britain. This semitic people may have been Jews and certainly spoke Hebrew. Whether on divine or secular schemes British Celtic ancestry was Hebraic, unclassical and often anti-classical.[10]

These myths of origin bring together Britain's genealogical tree with the most ancient and authoritative genealogies of Genesis:

> Now these are the generations of the sons of Noah, Shem, Ham and Japheth: and unto them were sons born after the flood ... By these were the isles of the Gentiles divided in their lands; every one after his tongue, after their families, in their nations. (Genesis 10: 1 and 5)

The genealogical tree is also juxtaposed with another 'tree' of origins – the linguistic tree: a sign that the British are a pure and chosen people lies in the above theory that Hebrew is the original language of the British, and that the Celtic languages are derived directly from the Biblical language. Hebrew was thought to be the one language spoken before the building of the Tower of Babel; it is therefore the holy and God-given language, a suitable tongue for God's chosen people in the British isles. By the nineteenth century, as Grant Allen states, it was no longer the fashion to speak of the Ancient Britons (the Welsh) as the ancestors of the English people, so the myths of origin which saw an unbroken genealogical and linguistic line between the Celts and the Jews were no longer gratifying to those of an Anglo-Saxonist persuasion. Indeed, at least one work of prophetic history in the nineteenth century, William Carpenter's *The Israelites Found in the Anglo-Saxons* (1874), aimed to identify the English with the Hebrew people. The powerful authority and sanction granted by ancient pedigree, and especially by those of Genesis, is evident in the various claims made in the history of Britain, and by the various nations within Britain, to those particular myths of origin. For the Celtic nations – especially after Culloden and the breaking up of the clans – in time of famine and massive emigration, a blood tie to the wandering tribes of Israel may have helped to explain and to give a moral, spiritual authority to the displaced and wandering state of their own tribes and nations.

Howard Weinbrot comes to an optimistic conclusion at the close of his long study, *Britannia's Issue*, about the contribution of the (supposedly related) Celtic and Hebrew strains in British culture:

Each [the Celtic and Hebrew] embodies those values in a non-English culture nevertheless essential for England. Each supplies a body of myths eminently adaptable to sublime and effective poetry that becomes a part of the nation's religious and emotional consciousness. Each contributes to the English assumption of a polyglot synthetic culture.[11]

Even if Weinbrot is using the word 'polyglot' in a Bakhtinian sense, it has an odd and disturbing ring at the close of a study which focusses particularly upon Scotland and (as discussed above) upon the linguistic tree. For, after all, if some eighteenth-century scholars held that the Celtic languages were purely derived Hebrew dialects, and therefore were languages which preceded the polyglot conditions after the Tower of Babel, then it is also true that the eighteenth and nineteenth centuries saw a fresh drive in the centuries-long campaign on the part of the English to reverse the Tower of Babel: those centuries saw a powerful political and cultural impetus on the part of England to eradicate the polyglot, to suppress the Celtic languages within Britain, making, through English, 'the whole earth of one language, and of one speech' (Genesis 11:1).

Weinbrot's study argues that James Macpherson's Ossian 'suggests how Britain was able to cope with apparent expansion into varied psychic worlds, and how, in current lingo, the "Other" was rendered oneself'.[12] While a study of Ossian does involve to some degree an exploration of Celtic poetry and oral traditions (even if in this case at least partly an 'invented tradition') it is also important to remember that Macpherson's poems are 'translations' from Erse into English. While *Fingal* (1762) and the other popular Ossianic poems made England and Europe aware of a (romanticized) ancient Celtic culture, strictly they did not contribute to Britain as a polyglot society. It may seem pedantic on my part to take 'polyglot' in its literal linguistic meaning here, but I do so because in a consideration of origins, the linguistic tree and the family tree are closely related. As Rod Mengham points out in his *The Descent of Language* (1993) the linguistic tree and the family tree are never far apart; they both exist within and are affected by 'social frameworks and historical phases' and language is partly like 'family history ... a social concept that can be repressively insisted on or subversively challenged with the possibilities of innovative change'.[13] I stress the problems in Weinbrot's optimistic conclusion that Britain is a 'polyglot, synthetic' nation because it erases the Celtic languages from the linguistic and genealogical trees of the British isles. To erase those languages from the linguistic tree is to obliterate the family trees, ancestral narratives and cultural traditions which were recorded in those Celtic languages. The linguistic trees and family trees were lost together, and although Weinbrot's book, this book and all the works discussed in this study are written in English, there are traces of ancestral narrative which cannot be recovered from Celtic culture, because the oral lines of transmission were broken. If these genealogical stories were recoverable, then Weinbrot's claim that Britain is 'polyglot' would be less difficult to swallow, and this study of genealogy in Britain would be a much fuller work.

Grant Allen's title for his 1880 article, 'Are We Englishmen?', hints at a society less at ease with the concept of Britain as cosily polyglot and synthetic. This question was a controversial and anxious one through the greater part of the nineteenth century. Some of the confusion surrounding this question lay in England's 'split personality'; the island nation defined itself not only as 'England', but also as 'Great Britain', comprising England, Wales, Scotland and Ireland.

Much of England's political anxiety at this time, and particularly in relation to Ireland, centered around the question of assimilation versus difference. (Ireland may have been particularly difficult to assimilate into a nation which had this schizophrenic definition of itself as both an insular and sea-defended nation and an archipelago of 'British isles', because it was an island unto itself). Were the Celtic elements within Great Britain assimilated provinces, or were they separate, different entities – nations in their own right? Grant Allen concludes his article by claiming that, 'though the British nation of the present day is wholly Teutonic *in form*, it is largely and even preponderantly Keltic *in matter*.'[14] This was a decidedly unpopular view; the majority in Britain regarded England as the central, dominant power which was Anglo-Saxon in its origins, and the Celtic elements as conquered and marginal. One of the few to concur with Grant Allen's conclusions was, as L. P. Curtis has noted, George Meredith.[15] His attitude to his own Celtic ancestry, and to the question of marginal/Celtic and central/English tensions within Britain, is discussed in Chapter Four.

The image of the family tree, and the etymology of 'pedigree' serve to construct the pervasive metaphors of this study. 'Pedigree' is derived from the Old French *pied de grue* or 'crane's foot', which resembles the multiple and connected lines of a family tree.[16] The picture of the crane's foot, with its claws branching downward, differs from that conjured up by the term 'family line'. The latter image ignores those tiny ligaments which represent collateral families who can be traced back to the common ancestor with as much validity as the primogenitive heir who is directly 'in line'. Each scion (a word also derived from the Old French, meaning shoot or twig) can serve as a cutting either to be grafted on to by another family line, or planted to become the progenitor, the origin of its own family line, with its own history and stories of origin. Before becoming too involved, however, in the metaphors of crane's toe and twig, the point I wish to make is that both these images of tree and crane's foot conceptually lead away from the direct linear descent of the family line which carries down from father to son. Instead these terms provide a view of multiple kinship lines spreading across the page of the pedigree, representing cousins removed, daughters married, younger sons and spinster aunts.

Lord Illingworth, in Oscar Wilde's *A Woman of No Importance* (1893), describes the Peerage as, 'the best thing in fiction the English have ever done'.[17] The pedigrees of noble families, both fictional and non-fictional, have always inspired story-telling. These stories may consist of the pedigrees themselves, as in the account at the beginning of Chronicles in the Old Testament, or may relate the battles and manipulations of a royal head to keep the dynastic line going, whether in Shakespeare's history plays, or in gossip about the royal family in today's tabloids. Lord Illingworth is referring not so much to these pedigree-inspired stories as to the dependence, in a society which is structured upon a system of primogeniture, upon the virtue of the females who give birth to the heir to the estate. It may be the 'fictions' or lies of these mothers which perpetuates the peerage; the heirs may be illegitimate, but the mothers will not say so, and all the fathers can do is trust the word of their wives. It is upon that trusted word that the peerage (and therefore much of the nation's rule), and the system of primogeniture relies.

Lord Illingworth, himself a fictional aristocrat, associates the nobility with fiction. Many popular novels of the eighteenth and nineteenth centuries followed the career of a noble or upper-class protagonist. With the introduction of the noble hero or heroine at the beginning of the novel, the reader has certain expectations concerning the ensuing narrative pattern. The adolescent Jane Austen plays with the reader's expectations in her two-page-long 'Novel in Twelve Chapters' entitled *The Beautiful Cassandra*. She introduces her heroine:

Chapter the First

Cassandra was the daughter and the only daughter of a celebrated milliner in Bond Street. Her father was of noble birth, being the near relation of the Duchess of —'s butler.

Will this 'novel' follow the narrative patterns which we expect for a noble protagonist, or (as she is a milliner's daughter) will it follow our expectations of the picaresque? In the second and third chapters of *Cassandra*, Austen holds the reader in suspense over these questions; the narrative shows signs of following the fortunes of the picaroon and signs of following the fortunes of the 'gentle' heroine.

Chapter the Second

When Cassandra had attained her sixteenth year, she was lovely and amiable, and chancing to fall in love with an elegant bonnet her mother had just completed, bespoke by the Countess of —, she placed it on her gentle head and walked from her mother's shop to make her fortune.

Chapter the Third

The first person she met was the Viscount of —, a young man no less celebrated for his accomplishments and virtues than for his elegance and beauty. She curtseyed and walked on.[18]

In chapter two we pause in expectation after the phrase 'chancing to fall in love with—', and in chapter three, after her meeting with the attractive Viscount. If she is a noble, 'gentle' heroine we expect her to fall in love with the Viscount and finally to marry him. Instead she falls in love with a bonnet and walks unconcernedly past the Viscount. Her future career includes stealing 'three ices' and knocking down a pastrycook. Cassandra's actions are often those of the picaroon, but the language of sensibility used to describe her, and the manner in which her pedigree is produced in chapter one, lead us to expect a 'traditional' narrative concerning a gentle-blooded heroine.

I describe this linear narrative which traces the career of the noble hero or heroine as 'traditional' because the expectations which are raised by this type of narrative predate the novel. These expectations of the narrative pattern, which Austen subverts in *The Beautiful Cassandra*, are powerful and compelling partly because they belong to an old, even ancient, tradition of story-telling with which many readers are familiar from the fairy-tales told to them in childhood. As in many fairy-tales, the reader expects that at birth the hero or heroine will be set apart in some way as unique or superior to others, that the plot will involve him or her in some fall from economic or psychological well-being, and that the narrative will conclude either with the protagonist's return to prosperity and happiness through marriage or the restoration of his or her estates, or both.[19]

Jane Austen took delight in subverting the traditional expectations of linear narrative in *The Beautiful Cassandra*. Many of the novels I discuss in the following chapters also undermine in various ways these narrative expectations. Several characters who gain narrative precedence in the works discussed would usually have been associated with the picaresque or have been relegated to a stereotyped role in a subplot; these characters are Jewish, Irish or Welsh, tailor's sons and poor relations. Some are from minor branches of the family tree, or, as in Charlotte Yonge's novel, are noble but for political reasons denied a place on the family tree, remaining 'unknown to history'.

Thomas Hardy's writing is perhaps more readily associated with stories of characters who either have no written pedigree, or whose noble pedigree, like Tess Durbeyfield's, has been lost or disassociated from her name. Yet Hardy is fascinated by old families, and in the Preface to his Decameron-like group of short stories, *A Group of Noble Dames* (1891), he clearly outlines a relationship between pedigree and narrative:

The pedigrees of our county families, arranged in diagrams on the pages of county histories, mostly appear at first sight to be as barren of any touch of nature as a table of logarithms. But given a clue – the faintest tradition of what went on behind the scenes, and this dryness of dust may be transformed into a palpitating drama. More, the careful comparison of dates alone – that of birth with marriage, of marriage with death, of one marriage, birth, or death with a kindred marriage, birth, or death – will often effect the same transformation, and anybody practised in raising images from such genealogies finds himself unconsciously filling into the framework the motives, passions, and personal qualities which would appear to be the single explanation possible of some extraordinary conjunction in times, events, and personages that occasionally marks these reticent family records ... Out of such pedigrees and supplementary material most of the following stories have arisen and taken shape.[20]

Often the intricacies of the family tree reveal or become the crises of plot and subplot; problems of inheritance, younger brothers, arranged marriage, adoption, illegitimacy, misalliance, the need for an heir – these become the driving force of plot, and are centered in the family tree and the will to keep the family line going.

Many eighteenth-century picaresque-type novels, such as *Tom Jones* and *Joseph Andrews*, follow the fortunes of heroes and heroines who appear to be of humble lineage. Often, however, by the end of the novel it has been discovered that there has been a swapping of babies, or an abduction of the baby by gypsies, and that the mysterious infant was in fact heir to the estate. Dickens, for example, uses a similar formula in *Oliver Twist* (1837-8). Pedigree is often restored retroactively, and this formula is repeatedly employed in eighteenth and nineteenth-century novels. In two novels discussed in the following chapters – Edgeworth's *The Absentee*, and Disraeli's *Sybil* – the heroine is discovered at the end of the novel to be of gentle birth, and the way is then cleared for her to marry the aristocratic hero. Proof of blood relies upon written documentation in both cases; Edgeworth's heroine must find her parents' marriage certificate to escape the taint of illegitimacy, and Sybil's pedigree is battled for, as it lies hidden in the muniments room of an old castle. In Charlotte Yonge's *Unknown to History*, evidence of the heroine's true birth is actually written on her body; the sign of her royal genealogy is branded into her flesh at birth. Yonge reverses the narrative conventions by making it impossible for the heroine to marry the man she loves unless she *denies* her royal blood.

By the end of the nineteenth century realist novelists such as George Moore, Arnold Bennett, and Gissing were confronting social wrongs, and following, instead of the narrative of the noble hero, the careers of proletarian or lower-middle-class protagonists who had previously been consigned to the subplot (as was often the case in Dickens's novels) or to the picaresque. A very different writer, Oscar Wilde, refusing to confront the gloomy facts of social realism, kept to the world of high society in his drama. But his writing often seems to parody the excesses of the Silver-Fork Novels, or those novels in which a lost baby is discovered to be a lost lord. His ridicule of their emphasis on pedigree and on the importance of being able to document one's origins is evident in *The Importance of being Earnest* (first performed in 1895). Jack, attempting to gain the hand of Gwendolen, wrestles with the difficult question of his mysterious origins with Gwendolen's mother, Lady Bracknell; he explains that, when a baby, he was found in 'an ordinary hand-bag':

LADY BRACKNELL In what locality did this Mr. James, or Thomas Cardew, come across this ordinary hand-bag?
JACK In the cloak-room at Victoria Station. It was given to him in mistake for his own.
LADY BRACKNELL The cloak-room at Victoria Station?
JACK Yes. The Brighton line.
LADY BRACKNELL The line is immaterial, Mr. Worthing.[21]

But of course the line, the *family* line, is *not* immaterial, and Lady Bracknell advises Jack to 'acquire some relations as soon as possible, and to make a definite effort to produce at any rate one parent, of either sex, before the season is quite over.'[22] Wilde parodies the formula whereby the baby of mysterious origins is retroactively ennobled, clearing the obstacles to marriage in the finale. Jack's ancestry is discovered; he is found to be the heir to an estate, and is ecstatic to find that his pedigree is not that of a hand-bag, and that Gwendolen will not have to 'marry into a cloak-room, and form an alliance with a parcel.'[23]

Many of the novels I discuss in the following chapters concern pedigrees which are at risk of being lost, forgotten or invalidated. This risk may exist for various reasons: because the pedigrees belong to those who are collateral to the main line of inheritance, whose relation to this line is considered too peripheral to record; because they are the pedigrees of marginalized Celtic nations whose ancestry has been dismissed; because they are illiterate, or working class, or because they are women (a woman's name is literally lost upon the family tree when she marries and takes her husband's name); because they are from a distinct, matrilineal Jewish pedigree; because a recognition of their place on the family tree is a threat to royal succession. The novelists in this study attempt to reinstate these forgotten or ignored pedigrees, and often question the ascendancy of the English upper-class or noble pedigree in the novel and in society.

The ambivalence and difficulty over Celtic pedigrees is explored in Chapter One and Chapter Four. The English often regarded the traditional Irish pedigrees as mythological and 'absurd'; this was partly a defensive reaction against their possible subversiveness. The Irish could claim to trace their ancestors back to the 'kings of Ireland', and for England at the time of Union (1800), and throughout the parliamentary debates on Home Rule later in the nineteenth century, there could be only one possible king (or queen) of Ireland, and he or she resided in London. The English and Irish pedigrees were therefore incommensurate. The paradox, therefore, in the idea of the 'Union' of England and

Ireland (and indeed at other times with Scotland and Wales) was that Anglo-Saxonists wanted no union with (or, as they saw it, adulteration by) the Celtic pedigrees through marital unions of the English and the Celts.

This attention to Celtic pedigree and the Celts as a race adumbrates the connections between the preoccupation with the genealogical tree in the nineteenth-century novel, and the rising concern over race in the mid- to latter part of the century. The French ethnologist Ernest Renan made the connection between pedigree and race when attempting to defend the 'Celtic Races' from the popular Anglo-Saxonist assessment of them as decidedly inferior. Renan published his treatise *La Poesie des Races Celtiques* in 1854. While purporting to study Welsh, Irish, Cornish and Breton poetry, Renan in fact used the opportunity to try to rehabilitate the racial image of the Celts. Among his sweeping statements of their redeeming qualities he also found faults; he writes for instance of the Irish:

Ireland in particular (and herein we perhaps have the secret of her irremediable weakness) is the only country in Europe where the native can produce the titles of his descent, and designate with certainty, even in the darkness of prehistoric ages, the race from which he has sprung.[24]

Usually, the further back a pedigree can be traced, the more noble it is considered to be. In this case, long lineage works against Ireland, because it serves as a link to her presumably 'primitive' prehistoric ancestors. Renan also seems to imply that Ireland's pedigrees are not 'historical' in his terms; they can be traced back, but to ancestors who are *pre*historic – outside his view of what constitutes valid history.

Matthew Arnold's four lectures at Oxford in 1866, which were published under the title, 'On the Study of Celtic Literature' in *The Cornhill Magazine*, were given partly to encourage the establishment of a chair of Celtic studies at Oxford. In these lectures Arnold, like Renan, used the subject of literature as an entrance into a discussion of the racial qualities of the Celts, and to compare these qualities with those of the Teutonic or Anglo-Saxon. Arnold was rebelling to a degree against his father's extremes of Anglo-Saxonist prejudice. His father insisted that there was an 'impassable gulf' between the Celts and the English, and that they were, as he quoted Lord Lyndhurst, 'aliens in blood'. An understanding of Celtic literature, Arnold argues, is essential to the understanding of a people with whom the English are politically joined. Arnold also puts forward the possibility that there may be strains of the

Celt in the modern Englishman. However, even if there is no blood-relation between the Celt and the English, an understanding of literature will bring a sort of kinship between them:

But it reinforces and redoubles our interest in Celtic literature if we find that here, too, science exercises the reconciling, the uniting influence of which I have said so much; if we find here, more than anywhere else, traces of kinship, and the most essential sort of kinship, spiritual kinship, between us and the Celt, of which we had never dreamed.[25]

Although Arnold supports the study of Celtic literature and language, it is interesting to note that he by no means sees this as a perpetuation of the Celtic languages within modern Britain: 'I must say I quite share the opinion of my brother Saxons as to the practical inconvenience of perpetuating the speaking of Welsh.' While this dismissive attitude may have been inspired partly by witnessing a rather unsuccessful *eisteddfod* in the rain in Llandudno, Arnold nevertheless invests in the idea that for Britain to be fully unified these strains of difference must die out:

The fusion of all the inhabitants of these islands into one homogeneous, English-speaking whole, the breaking down of barriers between us, the swallowing up of separate provincial nationalities, is a consummation to which the natural course of things irresistibly tends; it is a necessity of what is called modern civilisation, and modern civilisation is a real, legitimate force ... For all modern purposes, I repeat, let us all as soon as possible be one people; let the Welshman speak English, and, if he is an author, let him write English.[26]

The Celts may gain a chair for the study of their culture and literature, but they are advised not to produce any more Celtic literature to be studied. In effect, the chair at Oxford is a way of fossilizing Celtic culture; it is presented as about to die, if not already dead. The language of the above passage reveals Arnold's inconsistency of attitude about the 'Celtic genius' which he had intended to explore and to a certain degree, to champion, in these lectures. Some of the language evokes a gentle, consenting union: 'one whole', 'one people', a 'consummation'; while other phrases bespeak a more violent 'fusion': 'Breaking down barriers', 'swallowing up', 'a real legitimate force'. The terms of marriage and of a violent conquest or rape are both inscribed in this passage. Will the Celtic peoples assimilate naturally and quietly through intermarriage, a mixing of their pedigrees and racial strains? or will they continue to see themselves as separate, with their own pedigrees and stories, written in their own language?

One historian at this time who was less keen than Renan, and less ambivalent than Arnold, about 'redeeming' the Celtic races was the respected Anglo-Saxonist historian William Stubbs, Bishop of Oxford. He writes in a letter to a friend:

If the Jews are on their way back to Palestine, could not the Irish be prevailed upon *antiquam exquirere matrem* and emigrate in search of Scota, Pharaoh's daughter?[27]

Stubbs refers to one of the myths of origin in the pedigrees of the ancient Irish annals, which I discuss in Chapter One. In this passage, he compares the Irish and the Jews in England. This is no random comparison; within nineteenth-century England the Irish and Jews form the most clearly-demarcated, marginalized subgroups.

The Irish and the Jews inspire different aspects of Anglo-Saxonist anxiety in the mid- to late nineteenth century. Bishop Stubbs seems less worried about the Jews; they are a fairly stable population compared with the Irish who are emigrating to England in multitudes, fleeing famine and poverty. In the above quotation, Stubbs is not speaking of the return of landed Irishmen to their estates, as Edgeworth was encouraging in *The Absentee*; he wants the return of poor and dependent Irish to their homeland, where they cannot mix racially with the English. As Daniel Pick writes: 'when commentators spoke in alarmist terms of the state of affairs in England, Ireland was cast as a kind of infectious malady, afflicting the hitherto healthy English body.'[28] Many Englishmen would have liked to place the Irish poor in a type of quarantine on their own island, where they could not affect England economically by taking jobs that English workers wanted, or racially by 'adulterating' English blood through intermarriage.

What of that second 'subgroup', the Jews? If, as Stubbs writes, some were leaving England for Palestine, it certainly was not a mass migration. One English Jew who visited and was inspired by Palestine was Benjamin Disraeli, and in my third chapter I continue to look at the connections between pedigree and race by focussing upon his 'Young England' trilogy. In *Tancred* (1847), the last of that trilogy, Disraeli glorified the Jewish race and his vision of its role in saving England from spiritual decline. Yet the hero of this novel, who seeks spiritual rejuvenation in the East, is not Jewish, but a young nobleman possessing one of the most ancient pedigrees in England. Even Disraeli balked, as his peers most certainly would have done, at depicting the spiritual saviour of England as Jewish, and I shall explore the tensions arising in his novels between his own Jewish pedigree which he considered 'naturally aristocratic' and the English aristocracy which he so often portrayed.

With the rise of the British Empire, various racial 'outsiders', foreigners and 'primitive' peoples suddenly became the Queen's subjects. The concomitant rise of scientific societies such as the Ethnological Society (1843), and the Anthropological Society of London (1863), institutionalized a range of responses to the expansion of British territory which varied from a humanitarian goal to protect and defend primitive peoples, to a project of studying them and recording their history, to a great concern and fear over the mixing of races and the consequent dilution of Anglo-Saxon blood. Many felt that it was necessary to increase the strength, both in numbers, and in 'purity' of blood, of Anglo-Saxons, so that they would be able to populate and secure the new lands of the Empire.[29] The ethnological theories put forward by the French orientalist Count Arthur de Gobineau in his influential *Essay on the Inequality of the Human Races* (1853) compounded the anxieties of many Englishmen over the intermarrying of Celt and Saxon within Britain, and over the new possibilities of intermarriage with foreign immigrants coming from lands which were now part of 'Greater Britain'. L. P. Curtis writes of Gobineau: 'he did insist that the large scale migrations and emigrations of the working classes from all over Europe, including Ireland, posed a serious threat to the purity, and therefore to the ascendancy of the Anglo-Saxon race.'[30]

After the publication of Darwin's *On the Origin of Species* in 1859, consideration of the family tree inevitably brought one face to face with very early ancestors; the proverbial monkey, or even earlier, the trilobite. For many, this was a confrontation to be avoided. Rather than the pedigrees evoked by the geological timescales of Darwin or Lyell, this study focusses upon the human pedigrees of the less daunting genealogical timescale, and the manner in which many kept the monkey ancestor at bay by a concentration upon the political, class, regional, national and racial repercussions of their particular family lines. Nevertheless, while I have attempted, like many Victorians, to stave off the Darwinian in this study, there are many occasions when it impinges upon the smaller scale concerns of the family tree. Traditionally, the further back a pedigree can be traced, the more noble it is considered to be. Part of the anxiety over pedigree after Darwin was a haunting sense that a pedigree could possibly be traced back too far; when do those ancestors, considered noble through the mists of time, suddenly reveal themselves, through a little clearing in the mist, to have primitive, or even simian features? Ernest Renan's comment about the Irish, that they were the only people in Europe who could 'designate with certainty' their ancestors from 'the darkness of prehistoric ages' may carry with it a rather sinister note; we may not want to be too certain of those prehistoric forebears. The Irish in particular had a long tradition of being viewed by the English as 'primitive' or 'barbarous', from Spenser's famous description of them as crawling on hands and knees out of the bog, to the numerous *Punch* cartoons in the nineteenth century which portrayed the Irishman as having distinctly ape-like features and stance, and often wielding a club. Since the contemporary Irishman was so often depicted as primitive in the popular press at this time, the imaginative leap from genealogical human pedigree to the pedigrees of geological time scales is got over with alarming speed. Gone is the Romantic adulation of the 'noble savage'; these 'primitive' men are threatening and dangerous.

At a time when Britain was spreading her rule over what she saw as barbarous peoples, scales of space and of time became involved or confused with each other. Britain ruled over 'primitive' peoples who were geographically distant, yet part of the Empire, and who were distanced upon a timescale because they could perhaps represent a throwback to an early British type, a disturbing mirror of what the rulers may have been like many generations ago.

An anxiety over primitive or non-human ancestors is evident before Darwin's *Origins of Species*: in Disraeli's *Tancred* (1847), the noble hero moodily proclaims, 'I do not believe I ever was a fish'.[31] This remark was inspired by Chambers's unscientific, but controversial and influential work, *Vestiges of the Natural History of Creation* (1844). (In *Tancred*, Disraeli gives it the title *The Revelations of Chaos*). Hardy's character, Henry Knight, in *A Pair of Blue Eyes* finds a confrontation with an even earlier ancestor than the fish quite unavoidable. Having slipped off the edge of 'the Cliff without a Name' he is brought face to face with a trilobite as he hangs on for his life. The creature's eyes 'dead and turned to stone, were even now regarding him.' The horror of the confrontation with the 'ancestral' trilobite, and with the cliff of no name, lies in their impersonality, their seemingly absolute disconnection from the human. This horror is exacerbated by the knowledge that science claims a genealogical connection between man and the fossilized creatures of the cliff and of former seas, with whom we can have no human understanding or converse. Pedigree-hunting, the tracing of one's origins, becomes a risky pastime, plagued perhaps by the awareness that one must not take the generations back too far. Gillian Beer writes of a common response to Darwinian theory:

> One of the persistent impulses in interpreting evolutionary theory has been to domesticate it, to colonise it with human meaning, to bring man back to the centre of its intent. Novelists, with their particular preoccupation with human behaviour in society, have recast Darwin's ideas in a variety of ways to make them single out man.[32]

A concentration upon human pedigree, upon whether one's ancestors came over with the Norman invasion, were Celtic princes, or (as in one of Disraeli's many claims) were friends of the Queen of Sheba, is a comforting project in a Darwinian age. Rather than 'recast(ing) Darwin's ideas ... to make them single out man', the study of human pedigree may be a way to avoid Darwin's ideas. An historical rather than prehistorical pedigree, with its accompanying fictions and social implications, has a blinkering effect and provides limits to how far back those ancestors can be traced. The work of the ensuing chapters mimics in a sense these efforts to place man and human pedigree back at the centre, by exploring the implications of historical (rather than prehistorical) genealogies.

Just as there may be fear over tracing the family line back so far that it ceases to be 'civilized', or at least human, there may also exist a sense of alarm at the possible spatial infinitude of the pedigree. A drawn pedigree or family tree spreads out upon the page of the family Bible or legal document, but it has limits as to how far it is extended – even if those limits are only the edges of the page. Benedict Anderson has written of the limits which must define the 'imagined community' of the nation:

> The nation is imagined as *limited* because even the largest of them, encompassing perhaps a billion living human beings, has finite, if elastic boundaries, beyond which lie other nations. No nation imagines itself as coterminous with mankind. The most messianic nationalists do not dream of a day when all the members of the human race will join their nation.[33]

'No nation imagines itself as coterminous with mankind', and equally no pedigree imagines itself as coterminous with the entire human family. To do so would negate its meaning; it must have limits to provide definition, order. These limits are often arbitrary. It is true that if all the 'collateral kin' to which I have been referring were written onto the family tree, if all women kept their maiden names upon marriage, and all the cousins removed and other 'minor branches' of the family tree were recorded in the family Bible, a pedigree would multiply itself into a chaos, and eventually into meaninglessness. Nevertheless, there is nothing that has given a system of ordering based upon primogeniture, or upon the patrilineal rather than matrilineal, or upon English rather than Celtic, an absolute sanction as the sole way to proceed in the representation of genealogy. The narratives in the following chapters, by providing various alternatives to or perspectives on the traditional ordering of pedigree, reveal the arbitrariness of this accepted ordering, and by extension question the inevitable authority of the institutions which the traditional pedigrees uphold.

Some limits, and a chosen pattern or ordering, are necessary to the construction of pedigree, and equally to the construction of narrative. In his preface to *Roderick Hudson* (published in book form in 1876), Henry James writes of the necessity of limiting the potential boundlessness of 'relations' within narrative:

Really, universally, relations stop nowhere, and the exquisite problem of the artist is eternally but to draw, by a geometry of his own, the circle within which they shall happily *appear* to do so ... We have, as the case stands, to invent and establish them, [he refers to the 'simplification' or limits of what should be included] to arrive at them by a difficult, dire process of selection and comparison, of surrender and sacrifice.[34]

Referring to this quotation in her analysis of George Eliot's late novels, Gillian Beer comments on unlimited relations or associations: 'this infinite implication or infinite extension is perceived as at once alluring and yet artistically and existentially threatening'.[35] In pedigree, as in narrative, relations must stop somewhere. But James's claim that the 'selection' of relations is a process of 'invention', points to the role of the imagination in ordering a set of relations. If this ordering is partly established by 'invention' in narrative then a similar claim could be made upon the social ordering of relations which follows the patrilineal, or the primogenitive pattern. Indeed the narrative and social ordering of relations are allied when the narrative follows a dynastic pattern, focussing upon the career of the heir to the estate. The social and narratological relations are both based upon an act of invention or of the imagination. They are in a sense both arbitrary orderings. Obscuring this arbitrary quality is the presentation of the patrilineal and primogenitive pedigree in much eighteenth- and nineteenth-century fiction as a coherent, 'natural' institution, as the inevitable foundation of society which has always been in place. In her book *Uneven Developments*, Mary Poovey explores another institution which also presents itself as 'natural', inevitable, and as a foundation of society; that is, the binary construction of gender in mid-Victorian England:

> To describe an ideology as a 'set' of beliefs or a 'system' of institutions and practices conveys the impression of something that is internally organized, coherent and complete ... Yet it is one of [her book's] tasks ... to reveal the other face of this ideology – the extent to which what may look coherent and complete in retrospect was actually fissured by competing emphases and interests.[36]

My project, in this study of pedigree in nineteenth-century literature, is to expose the 'fissures' and discrepancies which pull apart the concept of the family line, and which disturb the certainty that this patrilineal, primogenitive and, in these cases, English construction is a necessary and inevitable foundation of British society. Mary Poovey has described the argument of her book, *Uneven Developments*, as 'closer to a fabric than a line of narration'. An exploration of the connections between pedigree and narrative, and of pedigree within narrative, necessarily resembles a 'fabric' or web of relations rather than a 'line of narration'. This is because a pedigree, like the relations it describes, is expandable into the further series which I have mentioned, of tribe/region, race, and nation. It is always shadowed by that ultimate expansion of relations into the entire human family. Like James's narrative, this study has undergone that 'difficult, dire process of selection'; it has had to limit its discussion of these possible expansions of pedigree into so many institutions. The overarching theme of the book is the question of assimilation versus difference; which pedigrees are assimilated or included, which seen as alien or excluded, in a nation's definition of itself and in a narrative's structure?

In *Beginnings*, Edward Said writes of Hardy's novels:

> if narrative is to be mimetic as well as productive, it also must be able to repeat as well as record the 'fathering-forth', the 'over-and-overings' (the phrases are Gerard Manley Hopkins's) of human life, the essence and image of which are biological self-perpetuation and unfolding genealogy.[37]

An opposing view of the relation of time and narrative is that of Louis Mink, a philosopher of history:

> To say that the qualities of narrative are transferred from life to art is a *hysteron proteron*. Stories are not lived but told. Life has no beginnings, middles or ends;

there are meetings, but the start of an affair belongs to the story we tell ourselves later, and there are partings, but final partings only in the story. There are hopes, plans, battles, and ideas, but only in retrospective stories are hopes unfulfilled, plans miscarried, battles decisive, and ideas seminal. Only in the story is it America which Columbus discovers, and only in the story is the kingdom lost for the want of a nail.[38]

Said views the connection between narrative and life (and specifically the generations of life, the 'unfolding genealogy') as mimetic; Mink on the other hand sees this connection as invented, fictitious. Perhaps somewhere in between these two views lies Wordsworth's statement in his 'Essay Upon Epitaphs' that, 'Origin and tendency are notions inseparably co-relative.'[39] Wordsworth is referring to birth and death, but the statement could also be applied to one's genealogical origins, and one's 'tendency' or path in life. People often see their family origins, their pedigree with all its class, racial and national implications, as partly defining them, and therefore as influencing their life's tendency or narrative. Whether this genealogical perspective determines an individual's life narrative, or does so only imaginatively, as Mink states, is less important than people's belief in a myth of origin, belief that their pedigree has partly defined them. These chapters explore pedigree in the nineteenth-century novel both as an invented or imagined construction in itself, and in its often related role as a catalyst for the invention of narrative.

CHAPTER ONE

Oral and written genealogies in Edgeworth's 'The Absentee'

George Meredith opens his unfinished novel, *Celt and Saxon* (published posthumously in 1910) with the chapter 'Excursion in a Celtic Mind' – in the mind, that is, of Patrick O'Donnell, a young Irishman travelling in England. Patrick muses on the English attitude which holds that Irish noble blood is inferior to that of the English:

> a question of blood would have fired his veins to rival heat of self-assertion, very loftily towering: there were kings in Ireland: cry for one of them in Uladh and you will hear his name, and he has descendants yet! But the youth was not disposed unnecessarily to blazon his princeliness. He kept it in modest reserve, as common gentlemen keep their physical strength.[1]

A century before, ten years after the 1800 Act of Union of Ireland and England, William Playfair's immense *British Family Antiquity* included a 'Baronetage of Ireland', and a 'Conclusion to the Irish Peerage'. An English genealogist, Playfair dedicated his work to the King – for him, the only possible king – of England. Those 'kings of Ireland' are to him an 'absurdity':

> The history, short as it is given here of Ireland, subsequent to its invasion by Henry II will enable the reader to understand better the situation of individual families than he otherwise would do; but as some of the families have a sort of traditional pedigree previous to the time of Henry, it is necessary to say something of that subject, and to speak of the fabulous history of that country, to which, notwithstanding its complete absurdity, some persons very bravely pretend to give credit.[2]

The language of the Act of Union of 1800 reveals no consciousness of these 'traditional pedigrees'. Its First Article states:

> that the said Kingdoms of Great Britain and Ireland shall, upon the First Day of January which shall be in the Year of Our Lord One Thousand eight hundred

and one, and for ever after, be united into One Kingdom, by the Name of The United Kingdom of Great Britain and Ireland; and that the Royal Stile and Titles appertaining to the Imperial Crown of the said United Kingdom and its Dependencies ... shall be such as His Majesty, by his Royal Proclamation under the Great Seal of the United Kingdom, shall be pleased to appoint.[3]

The First Article refers to two 'kingdoms', one of Great Britain and one of Ireland. They will be united to form 'One Kingdom' bearing the seals, armorial bearings, etc. that 'His Majesty ... shall be pleased to appoint.' Before the Union, the peoples of the separate 'kingdoms' had been aware of only one king, His Majesty of England. The kings of Ireland had been conquered in the twelfth century, although their descendants continued to wield influence over their territories long after that. Centuries of invasion, conquest and plantation under Norman, Elizabethan and Cromwellian rule had intervened since the Irish kings had held any great power, and it is perhaps understandable (and certainly politically expedient) that the language of the Act contains no trace of awareness that the 'kingdom of Ireland' pertains to any other king than the English one. The language of the Act has no memory, no resonance, of any other royal dynasty.

But the kings of Ireland and their noble lineages were not so utterly eradicated from memory or the popular imagination as the Act of Union would seem to imply, as is clear from Meredith's 'Excursion in a Celtic Mind' above. Eighteenth-century plays and novels, for example, often included the stock Celtic character who would enter, reeling off a long royal pedigree. In Smollett's *The Expedition of Humphry Clinker* (1771), the fiery Irishman introduces himself:

'My name (said he) is Master Macloughlin – but it should be Leighlin Oneale, for I am come from Ter-Owen the Great; and so I am as good a gentleman as any in Ireland.'[4]

The MacLochlainns and O'Neills were the ruling families of Ulster and Tyrone, and the heads of these ruling families had once been entitled 'kings of Ireland'. Smollett's Welshman in *Humphry Clinker*, Squire Matthew Bramble, is a great-nephew of ' "Matthew ap Madoc ap Meredith, esquire, of Llanwysthir in Montgomeryshire ... a gentleman of great worth and property descended in a straight line by the female side from Llewellyn prince of Wales." '[5] (In chapter Three I discuss another Meredith's claim to a royal Celtic pedigree when I focus upon George Meredith's ambivalence over his own Welsh 'princely' family tree.) These ancient Celtic pedigrees had been a popular joke of long tradition, certainly since Shakespeare's characterization of the Welsh captain Fluellen in *Henry V*.[6] But this alternative royalty was not always treated as a merely humorous matter; the 'Celtic Revival' in literature, which began about 1750, saw a great interest in the bardic poetry, and the history and customs of the Celtic peoples.[7] This revival, which continued well into the nineteenth century, rediscovered and sometimes invented a national history and literature for the Celt. Numerous poems about Celtic kings, princely heroes and heroines were inspired by or translated from Celtic examples, the former being the case in, for example, Thomas Gray's Pindaric ode, 'The Bard'. In Gray's poem, the bard, traditionally the figure who transmitted through memory and song the oral history and genealogy of the family and tribe, curses the English conquerors of his people, and prophesies the reinstatement of a Celtic royal lineage (in this poem, the House of Tudor!). Gray's poem in turn inspired other poets and painters within a Romantic tradition such as William Blake who produced engravings to illustrate Gray's poem, and John Martin with his famous painting of *The Bard* which depicts a powerful figure of the last of a dying 'race' lamenting under a lowering, suitably sublime sky.

The Celtic Revival of the eighteenth and early nineteenth century was both influenced by and influential upon the Romantic movement. However, literature and painting which took ancient Celtic themes as subjects did not go out of fashion with the ebbing of interest in the sublime. More than fifty years after the Act of Union, the Irish painter Daniel Maclise was asked by the Fine Arts Commissioners for the Painted Chamber at Westminster to paint one of the set subjects for the chamber, *The Marriage of Eva and Strongbow* (c. 1854, see fig. 1). This large canvas belongs less to Romantic tradition than to a Victorian school of painting which strove for historical realism and authenticity. In theme, however, it has a kinship with eighteenth-century poems and paintings of the bard; Maclise's bard, though defeated, sympathetically represents a noble culture of compelling aesthetic power. The historical subject concerns the marriage of the daughter of the King of Leinster to Richard de Clare, the Norman conqueror of Ireland in the twelfth century. Such a subject, destined for a chamber in the English centre of power and rule, could not fail to underline Ireland's position as conquered nation, subsumed into 'One Kingdom'. The marriage union symbolizes the Union of England and Ireland, but as Richard Ormond and John Turpin write, Maclise's painting depicts a marriage brought about by force rather than inclination:

Figure 1 Daniel Maclise, *The Marriage of Eva and Strongbow* (c. 1854).

Maclise chose to depict the marriage as a sacrificial event, illustrating ... the subjugation of a free people and the destruction of an ancient culture. In the centre, Strongbow, garlanded like a Roman general, tramples a cross underfoot, after his successful siege of Waterford ... Dermot MacMurrough, the treacherous King of Leinster, gives away his daughter Aoife or Eva, as part of his pact with Strongbow. She is attended by maidens in white carrying palms, like a row of virgin martyrs.[8]

Apart from the central figure of Eva, depicted as a sacrificial bride, the viewer's eye is drawn to the other figures upon which the light of the composition is concentrated: Eva's virgin train and, moving diagonally from these figures towards the left foreground, the group comprising the mother weeping over her dead child (as John Turpin notes, her stance is reminiscent of depictions of the massacre of the Innocents)[9], the woman mourning over the body of her lover, and the aged, defeated bard leaning on his harp. The portrayal of grief and love in the woman's embrace of her dead Celtic warrior is placed directly below the figures of Eva and Strongbow. Eva's unwilling stance before the conqueror (her father's hand pushing her toward him) is contrasted strikingly with the union of love in the figures of the native Irish below. Maclise's painting is weighted heavily towards sympathy for the conquered Celts.

Those who saw Maclise's painting exhibited in the Royal Academy in 1854 would have remembered the Irish MP Daniel O'Connell's agitations for repeal of the Act of Union which were concentrated in 1830 and again in 1841–6. O'Connell's work for repeal gave way later in the century to agitation for Home Rule, led by Parnell. The Union of England and Ireland was the source of political and popular debate throughout the nineteenth century. *The Marriage of Eva and Strongbow* presents a forced union, and this painting was proposed for the halls of the English Parliament. Within those halls and without there were many Irishmen who wished for a divorce from that centre of political power.

A marital union may be seen as both a point of origin for a family, and a continuation of the family line. The union of England and Ireland, symbolized by the marriage of Anglo-Norman and Celtic in Maclise's painting, gave rise to a metaphorical language of family relations to describe the political relations between Ireland and England. Although the language of the Act of Union itself is legalistic and unmetaphorical, the terms in which the debates over Union were couched were tellingly familial. For instance, Edward Cooke, arguing for Union in 1798, depicts Ireland as a difficult son:

> If any person has a son uneducated, unimproved, and injured by bad habits, and bad company; in order to remedy these imperfections, would it not be his first endeavour to establish him in the best societies, and introduce him into the most virtuous, the most polished, and the most learned company?[10]

The 'best societies' of virtue, polish and learning exist in England, and Ireland will be improved by England's example, according to Cooke. At another point in the same pamphlet, Ireland is no longer a profligate son, but a friendly sister; there will be an amicable 'Union of Sister Kingdoms'. Pemberton Rudd, however, writing in 1799 against Union, sees the 'sisterly' relationship in a different light:

> what Irishman would snatch the staff from the hand of Hibernia, scarce yet able to stand erect, or walk alone; to place it in the grasp of a sister, older, richer, greater and stronger?[11]

Writing in support of Union in 1798, William Johnson also sees Ireland and England as 'sister kingdoms'[12], but Ireland is clearly the younger sister in need of instruction. In his article he describes the Irish people as having, 'all the ardour and inconsiderateness of youth'. According to Johnson, 'moral causes' which are the effects of 'a long continuance of chastisement and affliction', have 'absolutely prolonged Ireland's infancy as a nation.'[13]

These familial metaphors, used to describe the Union of England and Ireland at the time of the Act, continued to be employed throughout the nineteenth century, as Repeal and Home Rule, among other Irish issues, were debated in Parliament and in the press. Popular metaphorical language in favour of Union presented England and Ireland as becoming one family. But it becomes clear from the few examples given here from eighteenth and nineteenth-century literature and painting that tensions existed within this 'family' of the United Kingdom/s. An exchange between Meredith's Irish hero and an Englishwoman in *Celt and Saxon* is evidence that these 'familial' tensions were equally prevalent a century later:

> She spoke reproachfully: 'Have you no pride in the title of Englishman?'
> 'I'm an Irishman.'
> 'We are one nation.'
> 'And it's one family where the dog is pulled by the collar.'[14]

The Union was supposedly intended to promote 'fraternal' relations between Ireland and England, but Ireland was uncertain whether its family position was that of brother, prodigal son, unwilling bride, infant, or the family dog.

After the Union, and throughout the nineteenth century, the language that is most evocative of the tensions existing between Ireland and England is that which describes family relations. Terms of blood relationship could be employed metaphorically, as already indicated, or literally and metaphorically together, as in the opening of Trollope's 1860 Irish novel, *Castle Richmond*; to the English public, Trollope admits, 'Irish cousins are regarded as being decidedly dangerous'.[15] There had been a tradition in eighteenth-century plays and novels of Irish cousins considered dangerous because of their propensity for stealing English heiresses away from needy Englishmen. The Irish fortune-hunter was a stock theatrical and common comic literary type in the eighteenth century; one example is Smollett's 'Master MacLoughlin' quoted above. The playwright Richard Sheridan and playwright/actor Charles Macklin, both expatriate Irishmen, attempted to exculpate the character of the Irish fortune-hunter; 'Sir Lucius O'Trigger' of Sheridan's *The Rivals*, for example, is a comically deluded and quick-tempered fortune-hunter who is nevertheless brave and honest. Maria Edgeworth in her novel, *The Absentee* (1812) takes the defence of the amorous Irishman abroad a step further; the Irish hero of her novel refuses to propose to an English heiress because he is in love with his Irish cousin. Not only is Edgeworth's hero decidedly not a fortune-hunter, but he allies himself with an Irishwoman whom he believes to be penniless. In an Anglo-Irish novel which is very much concerned with the effects of the political union of England and Ireland, it is significant that the marriage foretold at the novel's finale does not represent an amicable political union through the metaphor of a marital union of Irish and English lovers, as the conclusion of Lady Morgan's *The Wild Irish Girl* published six years earlier had done. Irish absentees return to their estates and Irish hero and heroine are to be married at the close of Edgeworth's novel. Not only does the hero marry his Irish countrywoman, he marries a woman who comes from a branch of his own family tree as well. Such Irish insularity, as opposed to English insularity, reveals that Edgeworth's attitude to the Union of England and Ireland was complex; it should not be as readily assumed as sometimes it has been that she was without reservation pro-Union.

Even those Irish who came to England from within the English Pale of Ireland were eyed warily for their uncouth, 'semi-barbarous' manners which seemed to threaten subversion.[16] Although these alien, foreign Irish cousins may have been related to English families from as far back as Norman settlements in Ireland or from the days of Elizabeth's or

Cromwell's plantations, their claims of kinship with their English cousins were often looked upon unfavourably. By the eighteenth century they had been assimilated, or had even 'gone native' and had regarded themselves as decidedly Irish for centuries. English cousins had trouble acknowledging, despite political Union of 'sister nations', that such foreigners from a 'primitive' land, could belong on their family tree.

The 'traditional pedigree' of the Irish families which Playfair ridicules in *British Family Antiquity* was based originally upon oral tradition, and of this he comments:

Nothing, in fact, is so absurd and ridiculous as attaching credit to oral tradition, or the songs of bards ... We all know, from our own experience, that, so far from oral accounts being to be depended upon, a recital varies every time it is repeated; and until a narrative is committed to writing, nothing is so subject to change: it is the very nature of tradition to alter relation as it proceeds ... We must therefore give very little credit to the accounts respecting Ireland previous to the era of authentic history, which began with the invasion of Henry II.[17]

In this chapter I shall consider the way in which the Anglo-Irish novelist Maria Edgeworth, in her novel *The Absentee*, writes about Irish genealogy based upon oral tradition, as opposed to the English genealogy of the kind to which Playfair, writing at the same time as Edgeworth, gives so much credence.

The tension between oral and written evidence pervades *The Absentee*. When the novel's young Irish hero, Lord Colambre, returns to Ireland after his years of education in England, he seeks to gain a true picture of that country which many English, as well as his Irish absentee mother, have so much maligned. Colambre finds that his parents, who are living as absentees in London and neglecting their Irish estates, are now in debt; his mother, Lady Clonbrony, spares no expense in her parties, equipage and dress, because these are essential weapons in her campaign to be accepted in London society. Colambre returns to Ireland to discover for himself whether his mother's distaste for her native country is founded in reason. Much of the novel is concerned with his attempts to discover a true picture of Ireland; will the evidence he relies upon be oral, written, or based upon the deeds, the actions of the Irish he is among?

In a Dublin coffee house, shortly after arriving in the city, Colambre makes the acquaintance of Sir James Brooke, an enlightened Englishman who advises Colambre that the best way to gain a fair view of the state of Ireland is first to read the various written accounts of the country which differ in historical context and perspective. Colambre's journey through Ireland, and his journey to a mature assessment of his native country is the dominant theme of the novel; this journey begins with an encouragement to rely upon written evidence. The main plot of the novel, which follows Colambre's travels through Ireland, opens therefore with a list of books that he should read; indeed *The Absentee* is littered with literary references. This chapter maps the tension between oral and written genealogies onto the treatment of oral and written evidence more generally in the novel. This is not to remove the sphere of interest from genealogy; in this moment of Irish and English relations – twelve years after Union, and at the beginning of a century which would feel numerous strains pulling this Union apart – it was important to the dominant, centralizing power of England to invalidate the separate, independent claims to power, government or royalty issuing from its margins. This invalidation was effected partly through a dismissal of oral culture and tradition in general. When Playfair states that, 'until a narrative is committed to writing, nothing is so subject to change', he discounts all oral culture, not only the Irish genealogies which have their foundation in oral tradition. Two years after Playfair's enormous work on the British nobility, Maria Edgeworth makes a connection similar to his; she also places oral genealogies within a wider oral tradition. I would argue, however, that there is submerged in *The Absentee* a conclusion quite different from Playfair's. Edgeworth's narrative is certainly 'committed to writing', but within her novel a pressure is brought to bear upon written evidence which tends to question its reliability, and the assumption of its inevitable validity. This questioning of the written is involved with the question of the validity of Irish oral culture, and of the claims to existence of an inherently Irish nobility (or even royalty), separate from the noble or royal families of England.

One subplot of the novel that is crucial to a questioning of the reliability of written evidence, and which provides a defence of Irish genealogy centres around the attempt to prove legitimate the birth of Grace Nugent, Colambre's orphaned cousin who lives with his parents in London. Colambre has fallen in love with Grace, but must find the marriage certificate which proves her legitimacy before he will consider marrying her. He requires written proof, but in the novel it is the tradition of oral praise represented by the figure of the Celtic bard which is endowed with a power and authority to defend Grace's name; this authority precedes and in a sense, supersedes, the authority of the written word. By naming Grace after a famous and popular song of the harpist Turlough O'Carolan (1670–1738), Edgeworth seems to suggest that in an oral tradition, Grace's name would have been amply defended: the verses, originally sung in Gaelic, praise the beauty and virtue of 'Grace Nugent'.[18]

In this novel, Grace, an unwilling absentee from Ireland, is defended indirectly by the 'songs of the bards' which Playfair, among other English genealogists and historians, either ignored or dismissed. The oral traditions of the bards are given an authority by Edgeworth which is reminiscent of the power bestowed upon the images of defeated bards in paintings such as Daniel Maclise's and John Martin's, discussed earlier. The bards bestow upon Grace an oral genealogy, which far from being unreliable and 'subject to change' proves in fact more reliable than one which is 'committed to writing'. In the novel, oral accounts, given both by bards and by the Irish antiquarian, Count O'Halloran, have always recognized the truth of Grace's character and birth, and Edgeworth gives her sanction to oral traditions and genealogies by proving them to be true of Grace Nugent.

Influenced greatly by her father, a free-thinking landlord of a large estate in County Longford, Maria Edgeworth's education was a combination of Enlightenment rationality and empiricism with vaguely radical enthusiasms. One might expect her to adhere to Playfair's dismissal of the 'absurdity' of Irish oral tradition and the 'mythologies' it produced. Indeed, in her *Essay on Irish Bulls*, which she wrote with her father in 1802, she does mildly ridicule Irish antiquarians and genealogists who trace the Irish people back to the early Scythians and Milesians. But her response to oral tradition is more complicated than a mere dismissal; through the contrast between Irish oral and English written genealogies she is also commenting on topics which range from the political relations of Ireland and England and their differing national sensibilities, to more general issues such as repetition and scandal, varying ideas of truth, and of the spirit versus the letter of the law.

Pieces of paper, whether leases, marriage certificates or written genealogies, are materials which may fall subject to misconstruction, loss, or erasure. It is dangerous to rely upon them absolutely, and Maria Edgeworth, living in a troubled and unsettled Ireland, knew this at first hand. Although she wrote in the *Essay on Irish Bulls* that she was 'more interested in the present race of [Ireland's] inhabitants, than in the historian of St. Patrick', and the speculations of 'rusty antiquaries',[19] she was herself a good genealogist who took great care of the book of her family history written by her grandfather, which the family referred to as 'The Black Book of Edgeworthstown'. This book traces the history of the family from the close of the sixteenth to the middle of the eighteenth century. Two of Maria's twentieth-century descendants, Harriet Jessie Butler and Harold Edgeworth Butler, edited the 'Black Book' and other family memoirs for publication in 1927. They attest that Maria, who had written a continuation to the family history, 'regarded [the 'Black Book'] with something like veneration' and that she 'records that it had proved of great value in establishing the title of the family to various portions of the estate.'[20] A reliance upon written evidence for land title proves hazardous in the case of the poorer Irish, however, as *The Absentee* demonstrates: the Widow O'Neil trusts that a pencilled memorandum from Colambre's father, entitling her to a renewal of the lease on her cottage, will be upheld. But this memorandum has been erased by the villainous land-agent Raffarty in the lord's absence, and this negates the truth of the written document and puts the poor widow on the street. Like the Widow O'Neil's lease, Maria's coveted 'Black Book' both told stories of, and became itself involved in situations where written evidence was at risk of destruction or misconstruction. It includes an account of how Maria and her family were forced to flee from their estate to the protection of Longford gaol during the rebellion of 1798. In haste to escape before the rebels arrived they buried the 'Black Book' in a box in the garden; presumably the Edgeworths felt it needed safekeeping because it was in part the written record of their English ancestor's appropriation of Irish land to which the rebels would claim they had no right. On the six mile journey to Longford Richard Edgeworth, who was the captain of a small corps of local men, realized that he had left,

> on his table a paper containing a list of his corps, and that, if this should come into the hands of the rebels, it might be of dangerous consequence to his men. He turned his horse instantly and galloped back to the house. His absence seemed immeasurably long, but he returned safely, after having destroyed the dangerous paper.[21]

Returning home after the rebellion, the precious 'Black Book' was unearthed from the garden, already showing signs of disintegration from the damp. Thus the family history was in danger of being stolen, and then of destruction through natural causes, and Richard Edgeworth effectively risked his life for another paper which, had it fallen into the wrong hands, could have been positively life-endangering to his men.

The English genealogist Playfair may have written that oral accounts cannot be depended upon, and 'until a narrative is committed to writing, nothing is so subject to change', but Maria's own experiences at this time in Ireland were evidence of the possible unreliability of written documents. The damp-marks on the pages of the 'Black Book', her father's return at a crisis point to destroy a dangerous paper; whether or not these facts consciously inform her writing in *The Absentee*, they serve to underline the possibility of misconstruction or abuse and the potential mutability of the written document. Although Maria Edgeworth has often been compared with her contemporary Jane Austen, the immediacy of Maria's experiences of rebellion, danger and instability in Ireland are an important reminder that the environments from which these writers came were very different. Austen's family papers were probably lodged quietly in the family lawyer's safe or in her father's library; it is difficult to imagine her wielding a spade in the back garden at Steventon. Perhaps the often unsettled political environment from which Edgeworth wrote influenced the representation of the written document in *The Absentee* as frequently subject to unstable and arbitrary conditions.

SENSE AND SENSIBILITY: MARIA EDGEWORTH AND LADY MORGAN

Nevertheless, the instability of the text remains a subtext in *The Absentee* in the same way that political instability and rebellion are never as overtly present as they are, for example, in her contemporary Walter Scott's Scottish novels. The extent to which Edgeworth represses the instability of the text as synecdochic of national instability is evident upon comparison with Sydney Owenson, Lady Morgan's novel *The Wild Irish Girl*, published six years before *The Absentee*. Mortimer, the hero of Morgan's novel is, like Colambre, the son of an absentee lord travelling incognito in Ireland. The guest of an impoverished Irish Catholic prince in a Romantic crumbling castle on the edge of the sea, Mortimer studies Irish language, antiquities and history. But, unlike Edgeworth, Morgan directly addresses the instability of the written document in Ireland through her hero's question to his Irish hosts. It is a question which Edgeworth's novel represses: '"how is it that so few monuments of your ancient learning and genius remain? Where are your manuscripts, your records, your annals, stamped with the seal of antiquity to be found?"'.

A priest, loyal to the prince and his daughter, replies to Mortimer;

'Manuscripts, annals, and records, are not the treasures of a colonized or a conquered country ... it is always the policy of the conqueror, (or the invader) to destroy those mementi of ancient national splendour which keep alive the spirit of the conquered or the invaded.'[22]

As Maria Edgeworth knew from her own experience in 1798 it is the restless and violent state of a country in rebellion against conqueror or invader which leads to situations in which the written documentation of the nation's past is destroyed. Ironically, in Edgeworth's case it was the 'Black Book' – a genealogical, historical record of her conquering or invading ancestors – which was at risk. Her own Ascendancy family experienced the difficulty of holding on to the records of the past, which would have documented their property rights to the land which their ancestors had conquered and invaded, while Lady Morgan stresses that this was precisely the problem facing the native Irish.

Lady Morgan's hero learns to appreciate and admire Irish antiquities, poetry and culture mainly through the instruction of Glorvina, a Celtic princess, the beautiful daughter of the Prince of Inismore. While in Edgeworth's novel Colambre learns to understand some of the oral traditions and the dialect of the 'lower Irish', Mortimer takes his study of oral culture much further, learning the Irish language itself – not just its translation into a dialect of English – and debating at great length (and a great many pages) such antiquarian/nationalist issues as whether or not the Irish or the Scots can lay claim to the Gaelic hero Fingal (the epic poem *Fingal* which renewed this debate had been translated/invented by James Macpherson in 1762 and was an important contribution to the Celtic Revival). Lady Morgan 'proves' through oral evidence that Fingal was an Irish epic hero, thus refuting Macpherson's written translations of an ancient Scottish epic: the old nurse at the castle of Inismore can, according to Mortimer, run through 'the whole genealogy of Macpherson's hero which is frequently given as a theme to exercise the memory of the peasant children' (vol. 2, pp. 78–9). In a country where invasion has led to the loss of 'manuscripts, annals and records' of its history and genealogies, the oral genealogy is highly valued, and Macpherson's apparent literary invasion and appropriation for the Scots of an Irish mythological genealogy is therefore particularly unwelcome. Genealogy, memory and oral tradition come together also in the Prince of Inismore's reply to a conciliatory offer of land from Mortimer's father (Lord M—): Lord M—'s ancestor had killed the Prince's ancestor and confiscated his lands during the Cromwellian wars, and ancestral memory is passed along the generations as the Celtic prince responds to the absentee English lord, ' "The son of the son of the son's son of Bryan Prince of Inismore, can receive no favour from the descendant of his ancestor's murderer" ' (vol. 1, p. 122).

As in Walter Scott's treatment of the Jacobite cause, Morgan sympathises with the old Gaelic order as represented by the Prince of Inismore, but only to the extent and with the knowledge that his royal line will die out or be rendered innocuous when romantically appropriated (as was the Stuart line) by the English. (Morgan outlines this type of appropriation of Celtic culture and royalty by English royalty: 'Nor is it now unknown to them [the lower orders of the Irish] that in the veins of his present Majesty, and his ancestors from James I, flows the Royal Blood of the *three* kingdoms united' (vol. 3, p. 68).) As Terry Eagleton has written of Mortimer's marriage to Glorvina:

> What takes place is a symbolic trade-off: Mortimer ... 'restores' Glorvina's property by marrying her, thus conveniently retaining it for himself ... The Anglo-Irish are buying into mythology in order to buy off a disaffected tenantry; and the strategy of Morgan's novels is to regulate this inequitable exchange between cash and culture, power and prestige.[23]

Terry Eagleton's assessment of Lady Morgan's description of an Ascendancy 'tactic' is persuasive. If the Anglo-Irish are buying/marrying into native Irish mythology, then Lady Morgan regulates the 'exchange' by making sure that the problematic areas of Irish culture are fictionally rendered innocuous. Catholicism, for example, will simply fade away. As Glorvina, a Catholic, assures her future husband to his 'surprise and delight', 'all are not devoted to its [the Church's] errors, or influenced by its superstitions'. She predicts of Irish Catholics that, 'the limited throb with which their hearts now beat towards each other, under the influence of a kindred fate, will then be animated to the nobler pulsation of universal philanthropy' and, 'once incorporated into the great mass of general society, their feelings will become as diffusive as their interests'(vol. 3, pp. 58–9). Defused through its diffusion into a Rousseauistic 'universal philanthropy', Catholicism is just one of the many aspects of Irish culture which are regulated in Morgan's fiction. Catholic 'superstitions' belong to the Irish lower orders, as does the Irish brogue, apparently ... Glorvina, who is 'born for Empire!' according to Mortimer, does not speak with an Irish accent even though she has never left the shores of her country. As he writes to his English correspondent:

> You ask me if I am not disgusted with her brogue? If she had one, I doubt not but I should; but the accent to which we English apply that term, is here generally confined to the lower orders of society. (vol. 2, p. 148)

So Mortimer negotiates the difficulty of an unpalatable Irish brogue for his English readership, and one begins to wonder about speech in a novel which stresses the importance of oral tradition in a culture which has lost its written records; what does the oral sound like? The content of Glorvina's speech is a mixture of quotations from French and Italian poetry, Shakespeare and Goethe, and the *sound* of this language of sensibility is apparently free of any trace of that 'disgusting' Irish brogue. While Maria Edgeworth's Irish novels are important to the history of the genre partly because of her careful and attentive rendering of the speech of the 'lower Irish', this brogue is almost unheard in Morgan's novel. Although the priest and Glorvina speak of ancient Irish genealogy and mythology – inheritances from an oral tradition – they do so in a language of Enlightenment rationality or Romantic sensibility, leaving the 'lower Irish' silent. This silence points to a lacuna in Morgan's telling of Irish history and culture: the Irish literally have no voice, no sound: the princess of Inismore sounds like any English or European 'woman of feeling' whose accents have been diffused, like her Catholicism, into a tone of 'universal philanthropy'. Mortimer may take lessons in the Irish language but he had better not speak it with an Irish brogue, and we hardly hear the voices of the lower Irish at all. Paradoxically, it becomes very difficult to hear the oral in a novel which stresses that the few available cultural records were transmitted through oral tradition. The linguistic tree and the family tree, for all the antiquarian etymologies and genealogies discussed in the novel, are under threat from a suppression of the voice. And it is at this juncture of language and genealogy that Lady Morgan's 'strategy', as Eagleton puts it, of exchanging between 'cash and culture' begins to unravel, for if the oral culture is impossible to hear, and if the written culture has been destroyed, then Mortimer may well ask, where is the proof that Ireland ever had a culture or has one now?: ' "But granting that your island was the *Athens* of a certain age, how is the barbarity of the present day to be reconciled with the civilization of the enlightened past?" '(vol. 3, p. 20).

One solution to the lack of written evidence of an 'enlightened past' in Ireland would be to write it oneself, either in a Macpherson-like invention, or through the genre of historical fiction. Lady Morgan wanted to fill in the gaps in the Irish cultural record by writing historical novels, but for this Ascendancy writer the past was indeed a foreign country – a dangerous territory upon which English ancestors were fighting on Irish ground, fighting those native Irish who would have been the heroes and heroines of her novels, if she had been able to write them. She had originally set her novel *O'Donnel* in the past but brought the action forward to the present day; Terry Eagleton comments that, 'She had hoped to use history, so she remarks in the Preface to that work [*O'Donnel*], to "extenuate the errors" of the present; instead, she found herself uncovering a grisly sectarian violence which would merely scupper her project of conciliation.'[24] Underneath the urbanity of Mortimer's letters to his English correspondent in *The Wild Irish Girl*, there is hidden a desperate need on the part of the author to explain Ireland to the world, to fill in all the gaps in the 'manuscripts, annals and records', and to compensate for the silencing of oral tradition. Morgan's anxiety to get her views across, to be heard, is clear from the very structure of *The Wild Irish Girl*: it is a one-sided epistolary novel; Mortimer writes from Ireland but we never have access to the replies of his English correspondent. If Morgan cannot resort to historical fiction and if the written and oral records of Ireland's past are not available to her, how can she convince her readership that Ireland is not simply 'barbarous' as Mortimer believes? Continuing the long conversation with the priest and the Prince of Inismore on Ireland's culture or lack of it, Mortimer says, 'I have always been taught to look upon the *inferior* Irish as beings forming an humbler link than humanity on the chain of nature' (vol. 3, p. 21). At this point Morgan's need to prove Ireland a civilised nation causes her to overcompensate furiously for those lacunae in the written records: during this conversation Morgan's explanatory footnotes literally invade her own novel for several pages; two or three lines of text are encroached upon by almost full pages of footnotes. These footnotes are evidence of Morgan's frustration; she cannot write of the past through historical fiction so she writes over the lacunae in Ireland's cultural and historical records, patching them over with her own accounts of antiquities and genealogy.

While Lady Morgan tried to compensate for, fill or cover over the gaps in Ireland's historical record, Maria Edgeworth professes to be unconcerned with the researches of 'rusty antiquaries', as she terms them in her *Essay on Irish Bulls*. Like their contemporary Sir Walter Scott, both Edgeworth and Lady Morgan write their own versions of a 'national' novel; unlike him, neither write an historical novel because the past is still too much present in Ireland. Scott heard tales of the Jacobite rising as a child; by the time he writes of them those events have taken on an almost mythical status, distanced by time and change. But killing and rebellion are within living memory for both Edgeworth and Lady Morgan. Morgan attempts to distance sectarian violence in *The*

Wild Irish Girl by giving murder a long genealogy ('The son of the son of the son's son of Bryan Prince of Inismore, can receive no favour from the descendant of his ancestor's murderer' (vol. 1, p. 122)) and Edgeworth's distancing strategy is simply to ignore that violent past and its legacy in the present. To her mind, Ireland is entering upon a newly enlightened age; rationality and progress are therefore her concern. Both writers, however, remember the Fenian rising of 1798. The lacunae in the annals and genealogical records, the silences and evasions about Ireland's past and who is privileged to speak of it, reveal more about the legacy of the past in Ireland's present than any historical novel they may attempt to write; they indicate also the problems that these two Ascendancy novelists faced in their differing strategies of conciliation.

Maria Edgeworth and Lady Morgan, 'sister' Anglo-Irish novelists, may at first glance resemble another pair of novelistic sisters, Elinor and Marianne Dashwood of Jane Austen's *Sense and Sensibility*: Maria, resembling Elinor in her Enlightenment sense and moderation, looks to a progressive present and future for Ireland, while the more flamboyant Lady Morgan regards Ireland's present and past with the sensibility and Romantic susceptibility of a Marianne Dashwood; Ireland for her is a place full of sublime ruins, poetry and ancient harp music. But, as in Austen's novel, there exists less of an opposition between the sense and sensibility of the two sisters and more of an exchange or dialogue. For instance, W. J. McCormack notes that in Edgeworth's later novel *Ormond* (1817), her fiction posits a 'westward flight' to the imaginary Black Islands on the Irish coast where the Gaelic King Corny represents the ancient Irish order of tribe and oral tradition; like Morgan's Prince of Inismore, Corny is a difficult but sympathetic type of a dying order. But even in *The Absentee*, which is certainly didactic and schematic, there are elements which disrupt the 'deftly symmetrical diagrams of an Edgeworth', as Terry Eagleton calls them. The disruptions of her composed and orderly 'diagrams' for a new Ireland lie, I would argue, in the subtle championing of the oral over the written in *The Absentee*. Lady Morgan wrote that 'manuscripts, annals and records, are not the treasures of a colonized or a conquered country' (vol. 3, p. 16). Maria Edgeworth would have found such a statement too divisive in a novel aimed at conciliation; but her own experience during her family's removal to Longford at the time of the Fenian rising of 1798 is refracted throughout her novel in the various tensions between oral and written evidence. The written text is liable to destruction or misprision and may be unreliable; oral tradition in her novel does not lead to the 'absurd' stories and 'mythical' genealogies of which William Playfair wrote, but to the truth. Does this subtextual defence of oral over written evidence in *The Absentee* in any way champion native Irish oral culture, its history and genealogies? To further explore this question I now turn to a closer examination of *The Absentee*.

'THE ABSENTEE'

After a brief stay in Dublin, Lord Colambre sets out upon his tour of Ireland. For a time he travels in the company of the English Lady Dashfort and her daughter, Lady Isabel, both of whom consider Ireland a primitive land, and wish to convince Colambre that it is so. The Dashforts plot to marry Colambre to Isabel, intending that the couple should settle back in England. Part of Lady Dashfort's scheme includes sullying the name of Colambre's Irish cousin, Grace Nugent; Lady Dashfort has seen that Colambre is secretly in love with Grace, and she uses her own Dashfort genealogy to create a scandal around Grace's name:

> One day, Lady Dashfort, who, in fact, was not proud of her family, though she pretended to be so, was herself prevailed on, though with much difficulty, by Lady Killpatrick, to do the very thing she wanted to do, to show her genealogy, which had been beautifully blazoned, and which was to be produced in evidence in the lawsuit that brought her to Ireland. Lord Colambre stood politely looking on and listening, while her ladyship explained the splendid intermarriages of her family, pointing to each medallion that was filled gloriously with noble, and even with royal names, till at last she stopped short, and covering one medallion with her finger, she said, 'Pass over that, dear lady Killpatrick. You are not to see that, lord Colambre – that's a little blot in our scutcheon. You know, Isabel, we never talk of that prudent match of great uncle John's: what could he expect by marrying into *that* family, where, you know, all the men were not *sans peur*, and none of the women *sans reproche*.'[25]

Lady Dashfort obscures the crest of the St. Omar family, to which Grace's mother belonged. She tells Colambre that Grace's mother took the name of Reynolds, but hints that she had no legal right to do so. (We later learn that Grace's father, a young Captain Reynolds, died in battle before publicly acknowledging his marriage. The marriage certificate lost, Grace's mother was never acknowledged by the Reynolds family.) Lady Dashfort's 'great uncle John' believed in the innocence of Grace's mother, married her and adopted Grace who grew up believing that he was her father, and knowing nothing of the disgrace surrounding her mother, or of her own suspected illegitimacy. After Lady Dashfort's insinuations, Colambre feels it his duty to repress his love for Grace, because he 'had the greatest dread of marrying any woman whose mother had conducted herself ill' (vol. 9, p. 161).

The 'blot on the scutcheon' to which Lady Dashfort refers occurs not simply because of the alleged reproach upon the St. Omar women, but also because the St. Omars are an old Catholic family. The name St. Omar would have been easily recognizable as Catholic to Edgeworth's readership; St. Omer was a well-known Jesuit college in Northern France, to which many of the Irish Catholic nobility and upper classes went to study since, as Catholics, they were barred from receiving an education in Ireland. To Lady Dashfort, who has no tolerance for Irish traditions, an Irish Catholic family, even if noble, would indeed be a taint or blot on her pedigree. She considers the Irish to be, in a sense, all 'beyond the Pale':

'To say I was rude to them [the Irish], would be to say, that I did not think it worth my while to be otherwise. Barbarians! are not we the civilized English, come to teach them manners and fashions? Whoever does not conform, and swear allegiance too, we shall keep out of the English pale.' (vol. 9, pp. 143-44)

'Pale' which signifies a fence or enclosure, came to mean 'a district or territory within determined bounds, or subject to a particular jurisdiction'.[26] In Ireland, the 'English Pale' (known simply as 'the Pale') was an area of English jurisdiction which varied in extent at different times in the country's history of conquest and reconquest. The area that the term most commonly refers to is around Dublin. In a novel which partly concerns the union of the whole of Ireland with England, it is telling (and almost prophetic) that Lady Dashfort refers to a relatively small and delimited area as properly controlled by English rule. She says that those who do not conform will be kept outside the Pale, a plan which implies a certain failure of England's political unity with, and jurisdiction over, Ireland, if most Irish are 'beyond the Pale'.

EDGEWORTH AND THE POETRY OF THE SPOKEN WORD

W. J. McCormack and Kim Walker have written of the novel that, 'at its own level *The Absentee* might be described as an anti-romantic novel [in the tone, plot, morality, etc.] written in favour of romance and romanticism'.[27] The mixture of the anti-romantic, didactic strain with the romantic is present in the mixture of written and oral in the novel; the oral tradition represents an old Irish culture with its tradition of oral poetry, literature and genealogy, while the written signifies England with its emphasis on the validity of the written document. Oral traditions are often associated with 'primitive', backward cultures, and Ireland was no exception. One might expect Edgeworth, as a student of Enlightenment rationality and progress, to ignore Ireland's oral traditions, or to see them as a vestige of the country's backward state. But her attention to the spoken word, to the Irish dialect, demonstrates her appreciation of the 'natural poetry' of the language. The Romantic movement's fascination with the oral tradition, whether in ancient British poetry, or in the 'language really used by men', as Wordsworth phrased it,[28] clearly influences the following passage from Edgeworth's *Essay on Irish Bulls*;

The irish nation, from the highest to the lowest, in daily conversation about the ordinary affairs of life, employ a superfluity of wit, metaphor and ingenuity, which would be astonishing and unintelligible to a majority of the respectable body of english yeomen. Even the cutters of turf and drawers of whisky are orators; even the *cottiers* and *gossoons* [Gaelic *garsun*, from French, *garçon*] speak in trope and figure. Ask an irish gossoon to go *early* in the morning on an errand, and to express his intention of complying with your wishes; instead of saying as an Englishman in his civil humour might – 'Yes, master, I'll be up by times,' he answers poetically,
'I'll be off at the flight of night.'[29]

With her friend Sir Walter Scott, Maria shared an interest in the collections of ancient oral or orally-derived poetry, ballads, and medieval poetry made popular by Scott's own *Minstrelsy of the Scottish Border* (1802–3), the poetry of MacPherson's 'Ossian', Percy's *Reliques of Ancient English Poetry* (1765), and Chatterton's forgeries, to name but a few. Edgeworth also shared with Scott a belief in the importance of dialect in her 'regional' or Irish novels. From the age of fourteen, she acted as her father's assistant on the family estate, helping with work that she would take on by herself in later life. She claimed that many of her stories were gleaned from visits to her tenants; reaching home she would write down what she had heard. (One is reminded of a similar aural spying at the other end of the nineteenth century: Synge listening through the floorboards to cottagers' talk in the West of Ireland). The written is dependant upon the oral which has preceded it in these examples.

Recording and disseminating the words of the Irish natives necessitates a fixing of the oral into the written. Maria Edgeworth's purpose in the Irish novels is partly to preserve the oral, and to justify it to English readers as worthy of record, containing its own beauty, poetry, validity.

Clearly, she regarded this as an important project; as well as her own work *Castle Rackrent*, which is one of the first novels to be written in dialect, and the meticulous reproduction of dialect in *The Absentee* and *Ormond* (1817), she writes in support of the Irish dialect in the preface to Mary Leadbeater's *Cottage Dialogues* (1811). Edgeworth claims that Leadbeater's is a 'useful work' because it 'contains an exact reproduction of the *manner of being* of the lower Irish, and a literal transcript of their language ... the thoughts and feelings are natural.'[30] Edgeworth concludes *The Absentee* with a letter from one of the 'lower Irish'; Larry Brady, Colambre's trusty Irish coach driver, writes to his brother Pat in London, giving an account of the triumphant return of Grace Nugent, Colambre and his parents, to their Irish estates. In a novel which is punctuated with literary references and formal written documents, this letter stands out as a union of the oral and written; Larry's style of writing is spoken language on the page, complete with Irish spellings and idioms which disclose their Gaelic derivation. He writes to his brother with the immediacy of speech, almost forgetting that Pat is not there to hear him; 'Now, cock up your ears, Pat! for the great news is coming, and the good. The master's come home, long life to him! and family come home yesterday, all entirely!' (vol. 10, p. 49). In allowing Larry Brady to tell the novel's conclusion, giving him the last word in this odd union of oral and written, Edgeworth privileges his oral and Irish form of story-telling. This privileging of the oral style indirectly supports the claims of oral genealogies which are the 'subtexts' of this very textual novel; the Irish annals and genealogies, although latterly written documents, originated from the oral traditions of poetry, history and story-telling of the bards. Irish claims to aristocratic continuity with the remote kings of Ireland are thereby potentially authenticated. Edgeworth's sympathy with the claims of oral tradition, with the 'songs of the bards', informs both her treatment of the subplot to clear Grace Nugent's pedigree of its taint, and her treatment in general of oral/Irish as opposed to English/written versions of the truth.

'AN INSULATED BEING': GRACE NUGENT'S TAINTED PEDIGREE

Lady Dashfort's pedigree, because it is written and emblazoned, carries an air of validity about it, as if it could be proven and substantiated by English law. She subverts the Irish oral tradition of praise, represented in the harpist O'Carolan's song 'Gracey Nugent', which could serve to defend Grace's name during her absence, by using the apparent material truth of a written document to corroborate her own spoken rumours and lies about Grace's pedigree. Playfair so ridiculed Irish genealogies because, 'Bards, in all ages, seem rather to have intended to flatter the chiefs, or amuse the people, than to give them true information.'[31] The marvellous, almost mythical pedigrees which the bards traditionally related are one kind of fiction, but Lady Dashfort corroborates her own blend of oral genealogical fictions, based upon insinuation, with the 'evidence' of English written pedigree. Her intention is to use a mixture of oral and written not to 'flatter' but to taint an Irish noble line.

As both cousin and admirer of Grace, Colambre should be able to speak in her defence, but the combination of written and spoken evidence from Lady Dashfort silences him. As a prelude to her attack on Grace's name, Lady Dashfort tries to establish the family connection between the St. Omars and Colambre. Because he knows little of Grace's background, he does not realize that her mother was a St. Omar. So, when Lady Dashfort asks him, 'Are you, my lord Colambre, or are you not, related to or connected with any of the St. Omars?', he replies, 'Not that I know of, but I really am so bad a genealogist, that I cannot answer positively' (vol. 9, p. 158).

The main plot of *The Absentee* is concerned with Colambre's travels to his family estates in Ireland, his gradual enlightenment and education in the state of Irish affairs, and his desire finally to cease being an absentee. W.J. McCormack writes of the plot around absenteeism:

Absenteeism, as the tale's plot, does not simply monopolize thematic concerns; the plot operates as emblem also, for the essence of the absentee's dilemma is that he denies connection, connection between place and person, community and individual, present and past.[32]

Of the subplot involving the clearing of Grace's name, Marilyn Butler writes, 'It is not relevant to the theme of absenteeism, and indeed can scarcely be made intelligible without reference to *Patronage*.'[33] I would argue, however, that this subplot crucially underlies the plot of absenteeism; Colambre must cure himself of being, as he calls himself, a 'bad genealogist', if he is to make the connection between place and person, present and past. Grace's name must be cleared before she herself can cease to be an absentee and return to her place in Clonbrony Castle and, if Colambre wishes to marry her, the future of his pedigree depends upon the past of Grace's pedigree. Colambre must look into Grace's mother's past to study and restore the pedigree from the collapse implied by the doubt cast upon the virtue of its female line.

A learned Irish antiquarian, Count O'Halloran, helps Colambre to make the necessary connections to become a 'good genealogist'. The Count's title is not English, but continental; he served in the Austrian army, and was probably a descendant of one of the 'Wild Geese'.[34] Now an old man, he has returned to Ireland and wishes to see a dignified understanding between his country and England. He rejects the Jacobite implications of his name to such a degree that later in the novel he personally delivers his maps and military charts to the government ministry in London, papers which may be of help to England in the French wars. The fact that these papers must be personally delivered emphasises the possible risks and dangers surrounding written documents if they are misconstrued or, as in this case, are lost or fall into enemy hands. Again, this is significant in a novel which is full of textual references to other books, and whose plot so often relies on the recovery of written documents.

Count O'Halloran is an eccentric whose interests range over Irish antiquities, genealogies, military plans and tactics, and fishing. It is likely that he is at least partly based upon a Sylvester O'Halloran (1728–1807), a doctor who wrote on surgical subjects before turning to antiquarian research.[35] In his *General History of Ireland* (1774), Sylvester O'Halloran defends the validity of ancient Irish history, stating that because Ireland, unlike England and continental nations, has not been invaded by the Romans, the ancient Irish annals and other documentation of the country's early history are trustworthy, having been preserved intact. He writes:

Sequestered in a remote island, giving laws to neighbouring states, and free from foreign invasions for the certain space of 2060 years, they [the Irish] had time and leisure to attend to their history and antiquities; and they certainly exceeded all nations of the world in their attention to these points![36]

In the conclusion to *An Essay on Irish Bulls* (1802), Sylvester O'Halloran is the subject of the Edgeworths' light raillery. The essay's tone seems to partake of the same feeling expressed in the opening preface to *Castle Rackrent*, which writes of ancestry, that, 'Nations as well as individuals gradually lose attachment to their identity, and the present generation is amused rather than offended by the ridicule that is thrown upon their ancestors.'[37] *Castle Rackrent*, published in the year of Union, and the *Essay* two years afterwards, are both forward-looking, both wishing to put old habits and difficulties behind Ireland, as if the nation has been suffering in a late dark age, and the Enlightenment Edgeworths want to bring it out into the light, partly through a connection with England. In *Essay on Irish Bulls*, Maria Edgeworth and her father mildly ridicule national historians of Sylvester O'Halloran's ilk:

> we profess to be attached to the country [Ireland] only for its merits; we acknowledge, that it is a matter of indifference to us whether the Irish derive their origin from the Spaniards, or the Milesians, or the Welsh: we are not so violently anxious as we ought to be to determine, whether or not the language spoken by the phoenician slave in Terence's play, was irish; nay, we should not break our hearts, if it could never be satisfactorily proved, that Albion is only another name for Ireland.[38]

A change of attitude towards the past occurs between the writing of *Castle Rackrent* and the *Essay*, and the writing of *The Absentee*. Genealogy in *Castle Rackrent* is absurd, with its long line of unhappy marriages for money, lack of children, and literally toss-of-the-coin decisions as to who the heir will marry and what will be the fate of the estate. The optimism for the future of Ireland exhibited in the preface to *Castle Rackrent* and the *Essay* is not possible in *The Absentee* without Colambre taking genealogy seriously, and linking past and present by clearing Grace Nugent's name. W. J. McCormack quotes Burke's *Reflections* in relation to *Castle Rackrent*, but Burke's declaration that 'people will not look forward to posterity, who never look backward to their ancestors', is even more germane to *The Absentee*. This is supported by the portrayal of Count O'Halloran, who, far from eliciting the Edgeworths' mockery of 'rusty antiquaries' like Sylvester O'Halloran, is presented as one of the most dignified and respected characters in the novel.

It is in Count O'Halloran's study that Colambre sees a book open at the title of a chapter, 'Burial Place of the Nugents'. Noticing the hero's interest in the Nugent family history, the Count offers an urn to Colambre which he had found in an old burial ground of that family. Lord Colambre accepts it from the count, saying, 'It would be highly valuable to him – as the Nugents were his near relations' (vol. 9, p. 173). Here, Colambre first begins to establish his connection between past, present and place. He declares his own connection with the Nugents, to the discomfiture of Lady Dashfort who had supposed that she had successfully sullied their name in his eyes with the St Omar-Nugent scandal of illegitimacy. The Count's genealogical and antiquarian studies of the Nugents offer an alternative to Lady Dashfort's blazoned genealogy. This opens Colambre's eyes to a study of pedigree which is Irish and based originally upon oral tradition, instead of Lady Dashfort's combination of written pedigree and scandalous rumour intended to blacken an Irish history. Still, Colambre will not consider marriage to Grace until all blemish has been removed from her name by tangible, printed evidence; the discovery of this evidence occurs later in the novel, and the manner in which he finds it presents a mixture of oral and written validation which helps Colambre to become a 'good genealogist'.

In London, returned from his Irish travels, Colambre considers fleeing both Ireland and England to enlist in military service on the continent, because he cannot trust himself to live in close proximity to Grace Nugent; he fears his love for her will overcome his moral objections to the taint upon her name and background. Count O'Halloran, who has come to London at the request of the English government, visits Colambre and they talk into the night of the Count's military stories, after Colambre has asked him for advice about a career in the service. It is in the midst of these stories that the Count mentions a brave young officer named Reynolds who had died in his arms on the battlefield. Colambre makes the connection between this name and the name that Grace's mother claimed as her husband's upon returning to England without proof of her marriage. Reynolds had been secretly married to Grace's mother, and in his death throes had entrusted his marriage certificate to the Count. The certificate was lost when the Count passed it on to the English ambassador in Vienna who was then returning to England. Unbeknownst to the Count, the ambassador failed to deliver the certificate to the Reynolds family, hence the inability of Grace's mother to prove that she had been married, and the shadow over Grace's birth. The plot turns from a search for a true picture of Ireland to a hunt for this important certificate, but the two quests are related. Colambre searches among the now-deceased ambassador's disorganised papers and finds the certificate by chance as it is about to be thrown out, wrapped in old copies of the *Vienna Gazette*. He finds the written, authorized version of Grace's legitimacy that he needs, but to do so he must draw on an oral tradition of storytelling and praise which belongs to an old Irish genealogist like the Count. Indeed, the evening of the Count's revelatory story-telling had begun with an encomium to the St Omars, praise which directly opposes Lady Dashfort's previous slur on their name and crest ('all the men were not *sans peur*, and none of the women *sans reproche*'): as the Count tells Colambre; 'Such a family to marry into; good from generation to generation; illustrious by character as well as by genealogy; "all the sons brave, and all the daughters chaste"' (vol. 9, p. 318).

Now that he has removed the taint from Grace's pedigree with written proof, Colambre's next step is literally to connect the present with the past by finding Grace's grandfather and, with the marriage certificate, to force him to acknowledge her. Mr. Reynolds's two sons (the eldest being Grace's father), have died. He is left, as he says, 'childless, without a single descendant, or relation near enough to be dear to me! I am an insulated being!' (vol. 10, p. 13). Without the discovery of a bit of paper buried in old newspapers, Reynolds, Grace Nugent and Colambre would have been 'insulated beings'. Reynolds declares, 'Rather have no descendant than be forced to acknowledge an illegitimate child' (vol. 10, pp. 2–3), and to Colambre and Grace the uncertainty surrounding Grace's birth is an 'invincible obstacle' to their union.

The Absentee becomes burdened with an alarming sense of the arbitrary. Colambre is attempting to make connections through genealogy, and through experience in his native land of the links between 'place and person, community and individual, present and past.'[39] But these attempts at connection are seriously threatened by the arbitrary forces of chance and coincidence. At the end it seems only by *deus ex machina* that the necessary connections for a happy ending are discovered. Many examples of this dangerous randomness involve the spoken word against the written. An important subplot, connected with the subplot of Grace's legitimacy, and demonstrating the opposition of the oral and written, is centred around the difficulty over the Widow O'Neil's lease. This subplot impinges directly upon the main plot's theme of the effects of absenteeism, but its concern with lost writing, with lost written proof, connects the theme of absenteeism with the subplot of the lost marriage certificate and Grace's legitimacy, and therefore with the theme of oral versus written genealogies.

Travelling *incognito* through his father's estates, Colambre stays in the Widow O'Neil's humble cottage where she lives with her son and a young woman who was named at birth in honour of Grace Nugent. Grace's cottier namesake is engaged to the widow's son but the marriage may have to be cancelled if the lease cannot be renewed, as the son will then be forced to emigrate through economic necessity. Before leaving Ireland with Lord and Lady Clonbrony Grace had taken a great interest in the widow and her family; she ensured that Lord Clonbrony – when actually on the stair of the carriage which would take him away

Figure 2 An illustration from the 1812 edition of *The Absentee* catches a moment from the novel in which oral and written evidence hang in the balance. In this scene depicted from chapter 13 Colambre rushes into his father's study to halt the validation of the false lease documents. The literal centrality of the written papers here, and their immediate undermining by oral evidence depict an opposition which is repeatedly at stake in *The Absentee*.

from his estates for many years, wrote a memorandum on the back of the lease for its renewal if it were to expire while he was absent. Unfortunately, this was written in pencil, and the dishonest land-agent Raffarty, who wants the cottage, erases it. This effectively puts the widow on the street and prevents any marriage between Grace and the widow's son, making both Graces dependent upon a piece of paper before they can marry. Were Grace Nugent available to give oral evidence for the widow, her word would be trusted, but, as it is, Grace's reluctant absenteeism means that the falsification of a written document holds legal power. Colambre, who is travelling in disguise, opportunely reveals his identity and steps in to save the day for the widow and the cottier Grace. Unlike his keeping silent over Lady Dashfort's use of her written genealogy to slur Grace's family name, Colambre takes Grace's part this time. He defends Grace's intentions, and in the person of the cottier Grace, defends Grace's namesake.

Numerous 'portfolios of letters, and memorials, and manifestoes, and bundles of papers of the most heterogeneous sorts' bury the marriage certificate from view (vol. 10, p. 1), written documents in this case obscuring the truth. But for Grace's grandfather and Colambre the print of the genealogy and the marriage certificate is indelible and essential to their faith in legitimacy and virtue. Edgeworth reiterates the importance of virtue in the female line, and seems to applaud Colambre's sense of the importance of Grace's mother's chastity. However, the obvious arbitrariness and risk surrounding pieces of paper like the marriage certificate, the widow's lease, and the leases that Lord Clonbrony almost signed to the great detriment of his tenants (see fig. 2), undermine the rigour and severity of Colambre's and Reynolds's position over Grace's birth. This rigour lies in their absolute dependence upon written proof, as opposed to a generous trust in the oral evidence of Grace's virtue and the virtue and honour of her family line.

In telling contrast with Colambre's heavy reliance upon written proof of virtue in the woman he loves is the tale of John Nugent, the man Grace Nugent was brought up to believe was her father. Lady Clonbrony tells the tale in a letter to Colambre earlier in the novel:

> She [Grace's mother] brought an infant to England with her, and took the name of Reynolds – but none of that family would acknowledge her: and she lived in great obscurity, till your uncle Nugent saw, fell in love with her, and (knowing her whole history) married her. He adopted the child, gave her his name, and, after some years, the whole story was forgotten. (vol. 9, p. 177)

This brief sketch is a love story of passion rather than prudence. It is a story which has perhaps more dramatic potential than Colambre's determination to reject Grace while there is doubt over her mother's virtue. However Edgeworth clearly sanctions Colambre's prudence; 'Lord Colambre had the greatest dread of marrying any woman whose mother had conducted herself ill. His reason, his prejudices, his pride, his delicacy, and even his limited experience, were all against it' (vol. 9, p. 161). While Count O'Halloran advises Colambre:

'In marrying, a man does not, to be sure, marry his wife's mother; and yet a prudent man, when he begins to think of the daughter, would look sharp at the mother; ay, and back to the grandmother too, and along the whole female line of ancestry.' (vol. 9, p. 319)

Count O'Halloran, however, defends the virtue of the St Omar women 'along the whole female line of ancestry' without written evidence.

Colambre's prudent love story pales beside the passionate one of John Nugent. Within the novel's moral and didactic framework Edgeworth supports Colambre's sense and prudence, but finally, Grace must be allowed the dignity of not appearing too easily won by her careful lover. Near the novel's conclusion Grace hears her mother's history, and of the discovery of the marriage certificate which proves her legitimacy, for the first time. Although Grace realizes that this marriage certificate removes what Colambre saw as the 'invincible obstacle' to their union, the possibility of marriage is far from her thoughts as she hears the tale of her mother's disgrace; she can only repeat, 'in tones of astonishment, pathos, indignation – "My mother! – my mother! – my mother!" ... For some time she was incapable of attending to any other idea, or of feeling any other sensations' (vol. 10, p. 40).

John Nugent adopted Grace and 'gave her his name'; he gave her the right to a place on the St. Omar pedigree, with its motto of 'sans reproche'. He reproaches neither Grace nor her mother, but Colambre will not give his name to Grace or risk sullying his family tree with illegitimacy. Perhaps there is a sense that Grace, if not positively wronged by Colambre's caution and lack of trust in her character, has at least been subjected to a love which is certainly reserved in its prudence. John Nugent's belief in his bride's virtue, unsupported by written proof, is contrasted with Colambre's determination not to marry Grace without it, in spite of the oral evidence in her favour; the novel is full of spoken praises of her by Count O'Halloran, the widow and her family, and Colambre's own parents who have raised her since she was orphaned. We see no marriage ceremony at the novel's finale. Instead we leave Colambre assiduously wooing Grace, which is perhaps fortunate; otherwise we might feel that he has been too richly rewarded after his rather mean if honourable prudence.

The novel ends instead with another type of prospective union, that of the brothers Pat and Larry Brady. As discussed earlier, Larry Brady writes to his brother in London telling him to come home as all is changed for the better since the return of the Clonbronys from English exile. *The Absentee* was written twelve years after the Act of Union, but the unions – marital, fraternal, or of landlord to the tenants of his estate – are all unions of the Irish with the Irish in Edgeworth's novel. Larry's letter closes the novel on a note of humour, generosity and sentiment. In Edgeworth's scheme of things, these are decidedly Irish qualities, as opposed to English sense, reason, prudence, and at times, cold-heartedness. Sense versus sensibility, written versus oral, rational versus irrational are a few of the dichotomies set in place in the novel, and they carry traditional connotations of English versus Irish national traits. Unlike the unpleasant Lady Dashfort, Edgeworth refuses to add to this list the most common, popular cliché of English 'civilization' versus Irish 'barbarism'. Instead she puts forward a case for what she regards as the best union possible; a union which is not, as Meredith's Patrick O'Donnell put it, 'one family where the dog is pulled by the collar', but a union of sense and sensibility, prudence and generosity of spirit, reason and imagination. These qualities, allocated to the English and Irish respectively, are stereotypes which continued throughout the nineteenth century, and which indeed occur to a certain degree even today.

The novel may intend to present the best formula for an amicable political and cultural union of Ireland and England, but this union of nations is not represented in the novel by the common metaphor of marital union; Colambre marries not an English heiress, but an Irishwoman from his own family tree. For all its prudent didacticism, the novel ends with a celebration of Irish 'sensibility' and ancient tradition; upon Grace Nugent's return to Clonbrony Castle, from among a crowd of cheering, loyal admirers, 'the blind harper, O'Neil, with his harp ... struck up 'Gracey Nugent'' (vol. 10, pp. 51–52). Grace, who will soon be married to Colambre, is now surrounded by those who welcome her without need of written proof of her virtue, or her right to a place among them. Rather than the defeated bard depicted in Maclise's *The Marriage of Eva and Strongbow*, the harper O'Neil celebrates the future marriage of Colambre and Grace. The harp is the traditional instrument of the bards, with which they sang flattery to their chiefs, as well as stories of genealogy and history. Now singing Grace's praises, the harpist is in this case proof against William Playfair's statement that nothing is 'so absurd and ridiculous as attaching credit to oral tradition or the songs of bards'.[40]

CHAPTER TWO

A mirror for matriarchs: the cult of Mary Queen of Scots in nineteenth-century literature

> 1604–5. March 1. – ... In the matter of the tomb [of Queen Elizabeth], his Majesty made difficulty saying he had not been made acquainted with it. But I showed him the smallness of the sum and that you had bargained with a workman already, which I thought you had not done without Acquainting his Highness with it. So he passed it but with this addition, that he hoped when there was more store of money others should be remembered, which you may guess whom he meant.[1]
>
> (Sir Thomas Lake to Viscount Cranbourne (Robert Cecil), concerning permission from James I to build Queen Elizabeth's tomb)

Shortly after taking the throne James I of England, VI of Scotland, was negotiating, financially, politically and perhaps emotionally, between the memories of two formidable dead women – his dynastic predecessor for the English throne, Queen Elizabeth, and his dynastic predecessor for the Scottish, his own mother Mary Stuart, Queen of Scots. In the above extract James only hints darkly at that other tomb which he would soon commission to be designed, the tomb for his mother. Early in his reign, negotiations over the memorialising of these two women were bound to be tricky, not only because the English queen had ordered the execution of the Scottish queen in 1587, but also because, as an infant, James had been placed upon his mother's rightful throne while she was imprisoned at Lochleven, her first prison of many before her execution nineteen years later. Nevertheless, in 1607, Mary is in the words of James 'our late dearest mother, of famous memory, Mary, Queen of Scotland'. The letter James wrote upon the transferral of his mother's headless corpse from Peterborough to Westminster Abbey reveals the tangle of dynastic, national and familial genealogy involved in the negotiations over Elizabeth's and Mary's tombs. He had ordered his mother's tomb to be made in Westminster Abbey, 'in the place where the kings and queens of this realm are commonly interred', that the 'like honour might be done to the body of his dearest mother, and the like monument be extant of her, that had been done to his dear sister, the late Queen Elizabeth.'[2] After her death, he may call his mother 'Queen of Scotland' – during her life he had not recognized her as such. Having united the crowns of England and Scotland in his own kingship, he may bring his mother, as a 'queen of this realm' to be buried in the aisle opposite to the recent tomb of that English queen who had been haunted by the fear that Mary would indeed become queen of *her* realm. And while James calls Mary, 'mother' and Elizabeth, 'sister', in their time Mary and Elizabeth had often addressed each other in letters as 'Your good sister and cousin'. Of course Mary and Elizabeth were indeed related, through Henry VIII's sister, Margaret Tudor, but the ironies and incongruities of the familial terms with which James, Elizabeth and Mary refer to each other are still striking. Certainly they were so to the Victorian courtly biographer and historian, Agnes Strickland, who was the first to edit the letters of Mary Queen of Scots in English translation in 1844. One of the letters which Strickland includes is that of Elizabeth to James six days after the execution of his mother; she addresses it to 'My dear brother', signing herself (as she had so often signed letters to Mary Stuart) 'Your most assured loving sister and cousin'. Finally, Miss Strickland is unable to contain her indignation, and when Elizabeth writes, 'I would you knew (though not felt) the extreme dolour that overwhelms my mind for that miserable accident', the editor intervenes with a scathing footnote: 'Cutting off the head of his mother – by accident!'.[3]

Mother, sister, cousin, brother: the diplomatic, political necessity of these kinship terms in the dynastic negotiations of the sixteenth and seventeenth centuries is lost upon the Victorian lady-editor. What matters for Agnes Strickland is the sentimental, familial affection and loyalty which should, she implies, lie behind the relationships represented by these kinship terms – and that means a son should not claim kin with a cruel queen who has chopped off his mother's head. In this chapter I will focus upon the dilemma which exists between the public and private face of genealogy, when genealogy is both a dynasty which must be continued, and also family – those linked by blood and, perhaps, by ties of affection. In nineteenth-century Britain the popular fascination with the lives of royal women was partly inspired by the way these queens and princesses dealt with this genealogical dilemma: being both royal and female they inhabited both the public and private spheres, and their blood relations were both dynastic and familial. Linda

Colley has written that many women from the mid-eighteenth century on viewed their contemporary princesses and queens as role models. Watching the lives of these royal women as they went through the rites of passage in common with other women – birth, adolescence, marriage, the bearing of children or the loss of a child, widowhood – their royal subjects felt an affinity with them.[4] I would argue that it was not only contemporary royal women that fascinated British subjects (and in particular female subjects), but a matriarchal line of royal women from British history who were popularized in the literature, history and painting of the time to construct a 'genealogy' of women, a matriarchal mirror in which eighteenth- and nineteenth-century women could see their own lives reflected and refracted. Particularly in the Victorian period when the idealized woman, the 'angel of the hearth', kept to a well-defined private sphere, the fascination with royal women may have been in part due to the fact that whatever these women did within the private sphere of family was translated into the public sphere of dynasty: care of the husband was perhaps at the same time support of the king, and the nurture of children, the assurance of a healthy future dynasty. Reflected in royal women, their female subjects could see their own domestic roles on a grander scale, as a part of history, as services to Britain. While the importance of their domestic role in this matriarchal mirror was reaffirmed, women could also see that the genealogical dilemma between dynasty and family that these royal women faced often brought difficulty and even tragedy. As this chapter will argue, the popular depictions of royal women were often drawn so as to reassure British women that they were better off in the private sphere, and that those royal women who had become entangled in genealogical ambitions, emphasizing dynasty rather than family, often made a sad end.

Mary Queen of Scots is the royal woman at the center of this chapter because her immense popularity as an historical subject from the late eighteenth century and throughout the nineteenth century raises interesting questions about what her figure had come to represent. She is a queen who certainly had to contend with dilemmas of genealogy: Mary's closeness to the English throne made her the focus of plots to depose Elizabeth which eventually ended in the Scottish queen's imprisonment and execution, and the dilemma of dynasty versus family is clear in the separation of Mary from her son by the Scottish nobles who wished to place him on the throne, thereby gaining the power of regency over the infant king. This controversial royal woman, divided between the public and private spheres, was the subject of numerous history paintings in the eighteenth and nineteenth centuries. Indeed art historians have written of an actual 'cult' of Mary Queen of Scots in British history painting, a cult which coincided with and 'would have been inconceivable without the burgeoning of historiography in the mid eighteenth century'.[5] The cult surrounding this queen extended to other arts as well in the eighteenth and nineteenth centuries: Schiller's drama *Maria Stuart* (1800); Sophia Lee's novel, *The Recess* (1783–5) and Walter Scott's novel, *The Abbot* (1820); Donizetti's opera *Maria Stuart*, inspired by Scott's work; poetry by Burns, Wordsworth and Swinburne among others; works of fiction such as Harriet Martineau's 'historiette' *The Anglers of the Dove* (serialized in *Once A Week*, 1862) and Charlotte M. Yonge's historical novel, *Unknown to History* (1882) all give evidence of a fascination with the figure of Mary Stuart in this period. Later in this chapter Walter Scott's and Charlotte Yonge's novels about Mary Stuart will be discussed in detail. Both novels focus upon relationships between female characters, including Mary Stuart, who seem to mirror each other in various ways, and in this mirroring their lives are also held up for reflection by their nineteenth-century readers. Before turning to examples of the literature and painting which take Mary Stuart as their subject, however, I wish to consider the genealogical relations between the Scottish queen and a great English queen – not Elizabeth I, but Queen Victoria.

CLAIMING KIN: VICTORIA AND MARY QUEEN OF SCOTS

The young Princess Victoria had been brought up under the strict 'Kensington System' established by her mother and her mother's ambitious advisor, Sir John Conroy. Conroy predicted that there was a fair chance that Victoria would become queen while still a minor, therefore requiring a regent. He wanted that power, and set out from the time Victoria was very young to gain control over her thoughts and behaviour through a system of royal education which directed (and was the torment of) her public and private life as she grew up. Its rules dictated that she often show herself to the people of England, through public appearances and travels, but that she have no friends of her own age or indeed any intimates outside the small circle of her mother, governess and Conroy's family. She was never to be left alone, even at night, and was to read no works of fiction. If the emotional young princess ever had an adolescent rebellion, it was in 1837 when she both came of age and took the throne of England. Upon accession she promptly dismissed

Conroy and his Kensington System, and turned instead to the Prime Minister, Lord Melbourne, for advice and information upon her new role. Indeed such was Victoria's trust in and attention to Lord Melbourne's every word that the pages of her journals are punctuated with 'Lord M. said – ' and 'Lord M. advised – '. As Viscount Esher writes, Lord Melbourne saw her every day, 'but never appeared to weary of her society. She certainly never tired of his.' His 'potent influence over the mind and actions of the young queen ... was the natural outcome of the business relation between a very charming and experienced man of the world who happened to be her Prime Minister and a very young girl isolated in the solitary atmosphere of the throne.'[6] Victoria records in a journal entry from July 1839 a revealing conversation with 'Lord M.' which is an exception to her more habitual concurrence with his opinions. They have been talking, she writes, of 'poor Mary of Scots' execution'. Melbourne says severely of the Scottish queen, 'She was a bad woman, she was a silly, idle coquettish French girl', but Victoria writes simply, 'I pitied her'.[7] Perhaps the nineteen-year-old English queen, recently released from the monotony and constraint of the Kensington System, and in love with dancing and 'mirth' (as she calls it), did not feel that it was only 'French girls' who liked to be a bit 'silly, idle and coquettish' upon occasion. And since she had been forbidden to read fiction when growing-up, it would seem from her journals that the focus for her imagination and sense of romance was often upon historical figures rather than fictional heroes and heroines. In January 1840 she was reading Henry Hallam's influential *Constitutional History of England* (1827) which initiated another exchange with 'Lord M.' about Mary Stuart. She wrote in her journal:

> Talked of Hallam and my liking it so much; his giving an account of the persecutions in Elizabeth's reign; of Queen Mary of Scots and her innocence. 'All the ladies take Queen Mary's part,' Lord M. said, 'all those who reason like Hallam do quite admit her to be guilty, and all those who consult their feelings, do not.' Talked of Darnley's murder, which I maintained her not to have knowledge of, but which Lord M. says she *did* know of. 'I think she was quite right to have him knocked on the head,' Lord M. said funnily, which made me laugh. Talked of Rizzio's murder, and poor Mary's cruel fate.[8]

Victoria, like so many of her female subjects, seems to have regarded Mary Stuart as a romantic or tragic heroine. But, unlike other British women, Victoria also claimed kinship with the English-Scottish royal line that Mary Stuart had given birth to through her son James. If the terminology of 'sisterhood' used between Mary and Elizabeth I has seemed ironic and incongruous, Victoria's claiming of kin with the Stuarts is equally so. As she wrote in her journal during a trip to the Scottish Highlands in 1873:

Yes, and *I* feel a sort of reverence in going over these scenes in this most beautiful country, which I am proud to call my own, where there was such devoted loyalty to the family of my ancestors – for Stuart blood is in my veins, and I am *now* their representative, and the people are as devoted and loyal to me as they were to that unhappy race.[9]

Victoria's 'creative' interpretation of her family tree conveniently ignores those Stuarts still living in exile – the descendants of the deposed James II – who may still have considered Victoria as usurper of the Stuart right to the British throne. Victoria clearly found a satisfaction in her claim of kinship to that more romantic dynasty of Mary Stuart and Bonnie Prince Charlie, and would repeat the claim throughout her life.[10] This imaginative genealogical grafting of the Stuart line onto her own royal line was 'fictional' in more ways than one: fictional in that it was a claim only partly true (her view of herself as the latest 'representative' of the Stuarts requires an imaginative leap over history), and fictional because the claim was both directly and indirectly inspired by the literature of Sir Walter Scott. The precedent in Victoria's family tree for claiming kin with the Stuarts was her uncle George IV, whose much-feted royal excursion to Edinburgh in 1822 was entirely orchestrated by Walter Scott. Scott wanted to encourage the king to claim his Scottish blood, and was so successful in this endeavour as to reach deep into the king's psyche, to where it really counted – his wardrobe. George IV went to enormous expense to array himself as a kilted Highlander for the Edinburgh ball, and as Adrienne Munich has written of the later phenomenon of Victoria and Albert in their Scottish estate Balmoral, 'the charade of "tartanitis" ... performs a genealogy'.[11] Indeed it was after this trip to Scotland that George IV paid from his privy purse for the erection of Canova's monument to the Stuarts in Saint Peter's, Rome. This monument to the exiled descendants of James II is inscribed in Latin to 'James III, Charles III, and Henry IX, Kings of England', a genealogy and dynasty which his own existence as 'George IV' denied.

As with her uncle, and in common with so many of her subjects, Victoria's romantic love of Scotland and her sentimentalization of 'that unhappy race', the Stuarts, was heavily influenced by the poetry and novels of Sir Walter Scott. Victoria's journals from 'our life in the Highlands', published during her lifetime,[12] contain numerous references to Scott's works. Before and after Albert's death they are the constant companions of her Scottish travels, and the lens through which she views the history and landscape of Scotland, and her place in its history. But it is not only the Stuarts of Scott's *Waverley* novels, of the era of the '45 and Bonnie Prince Charlie, which capture the genealogical imagination of Queen Victoria (as was the case with her uncle): her Highland journals make frequent mention of Mary Stuart, as on her first trip to Scotland in 1842; 'Tuesday, Sept. 6 ... We passed Lochleven, and saw the castle on the lake from which poor Queen Mary escaped'. Mary's imprisonment and escape from Lochleven is the setting and main action of Scott's novel *The Abbot* (1820). As John Sutherland writes, the novel, 'had a huge influence in making Lochleven attractive to tourists – recalling the cultural impact of *The Lady of the Lake*. In the long term, *The Abbot* glamorized posterity's image of Mary Queen of Scots to the point where it can now never be deglamorized'.[13] Victoria was no exception to those nineteenth-century tourists who flocked to Lochleven, and her favourite guide-book, *Black's Picturesque Tourist of Scotland* ('far the best' she tells us) gives a long account of the escape from Lochleven, and various other crises in the life of, as *Black's* describes Mary, that 'unfortunate princess'[14]. Victoria both took a 'deep interest' in Mary Queen of Scots because she was herself, as she repeatedly claimed, of Stuart blood, but she also seems to have participated, to a degree, in the popular interest of her subjects in the Scottish queen. The contemporary literary, historical and painterly illustrations of Mary's life give evidence of the particular genealogical negotiations which I am exploring in the nineteenth century: that is, the negotiations between genealogy defined as the ties of the immediate close family; genealogy as dynastic, historical and national; and genealogy as a fictive or at least partly imagined construct. The ancestral negotiations which I will be discussing in this chapter place Mary Queen of Scots within a genealogical matriarchy – a history of queenship or of royal females which was very popular in this period. Victoria was both the latest matriarchal descendant of this genealogy and fascinated by it.

CULT OF THE ROYAL WOMEN

In her book *Britons*, Linda Colley discusses a 'gallery of royal females' which in the period she covers (1707–1837) led some Britons to refer to their nation as the 'Queendom'. Queen Charlotte, consort to George III; the spurned Princess Caroline, threatened with divorce by George

IV; the much-mourned Princess Charlotte who died in childbirth: in their various ways these royal women came to represent for their female subjects much about the role and status of women throughout the realm. Colley argues that these royal women, 'helped transform public attitudes to the British monarchy from the last quarter of the eighteenth century onwards, and ... influenced at the same time women's attitudes towards themselves'.[15] She concludes that 'the feminisation of the British monarchy ... was immensely important for all classes of women' as it 'provided them ... with a splendid edition of the universal facts of life that they themselves were likely to experience.'[16]

Rallying around these queens and princesses, their female subjects could feel more confident that their separate feminine sphere of domesticity with its emphasis upon the moral upbringing of children was of national importance. Their own queens reigned in a separate feminine sphere within the monarchy, and they, as British women, could also be 'queens' in Ruskin's sense of guardians of the hearth, those rulers over a moral household who wield 'the stainless sceptre of womanhood' as he described the role of woman in *Of Queens' Gardens*.[17]

Although Linda Colley includes Victoria in this cult of royal women, her study finishes upon the young queen's accession in 1837. While Queen Charlotte and Princess Caroline were consorts to the crown, and Princess Charlotte died before she could take the throne, Victoria was the first queen since Anne to rule in her own right. This fact was bound to unsettle to some degree the concept of 'separate spheres' because as both Queen of England and woman, Victoria had to combine those two spheres within herself. This was not an easy task in a society increasingly devoted to the distinct areas of public and private for men and women respectively, and Victoria's negotiation of her divided roles may have got her into a muddle: some of her subjects commented that she 'ruled her nation as a mother, and her household as a monarch.'[18]

The importance of Victoria's domestic role is very clear in Agnes Strickland's preface to her 1840 'history', *Queen Victoria from Her Birth to Her Bridal* (a book with which Victoria found much fault and which Miss Strickland promptly suppressed).[19] Written in the year of the Queen's marriage to Albert, Strickland's preface is almost dismissive of Victoria's three-year reign as a single woman, as it looks forward to the sound of pattering feet:

A more auspicious page, we trust, will, in due time, be added to the annals of Queen Victoria's life, in the accomplishment of those hopes which render our youthful sovereign so interesting to every class of her subjects. May we, ere long, behold her Majesty invested with those claims to our affection, which will cause the splendour of her maiden reign to fade before the sacred and endearing associations with which the throne will be surrounded when we hail her as the joyful mother of a hopeful reign of princes, in whom the mighty qualities of our ancient royal line of sovereigns may be blended with the milder virtues of the amiable and illustrious house of Saxe Coburg Gotha.[20]

This passage would suggest that dynastic and gender roles become entangled in a confusion over separate spheres when a woman rules: Victoria, who should exhibit the traditionally feminine 'mild' and 'amiable' virtues, instead inherits the more masculine 'might' from her genealogy. Albert, though 'illustrious', is the successor of a mild and amiable line. Still, Strickland puts hope in a 'hopeful race of princes', rather than princesses, which may be expected to sort out this gender/genealogy problem.

Her hope for a 'race of princes' is somewhat ironic when one considers that Agnes Strickland made her career writing about the British 'race' of queens and princesses. Indeed, Strickland's popular royal biographies and histories played a crucial role in the 'feminisation of the monarchy' which Linda Colley discusses for the century before, and were important in creating a genealogy of royal matriarchs. This matriarchy served as a mirror not only for female British subjects, but also perhaps for the latest queen in this female genealogy, Victoria herself.

Agnes Strickland's (1796–1874) first publication was a poem for the *Norwich Mercury* in 1817, 'Monody upon the Death of Princess Charlotte of Wales'. From that time on she wrote almost obsessively about the lives and deaths of female royalty in Britain, editing the 'Court Magazine', and then publishing volume upon volume of her very popular works: *Lives of the Queens of England*; *Lives of the Queens of Scotland and English Princesses Connected with the Regal Succession of Great Britain*; *Lives of the Last Four Princesses of the Royal House of Stuart*; a life of the young Queen Victoria and a separate edition of a biography of the queen to whose memory she was the most devoted, *The Life of Mary Queen of Scots*. These works, so familiar to a Victorian readership, create a genealogy which excises men from the dynastic tree. In this pedigree women succeed each other in part by reflecting each others' traditionally feminine experiences in the eyes of their nineteenth-century readership. Strickland frames Victoria within this mirror of royal matriarchs by making her in a sense the next in line not to William IV, whom she succeeded to the throne, but to Princess Charlotte. As she writes in the opening to the first chapter of her biography of Victoria:

The birth of the Princess Victoria of Kent appeared as if ordained by Heaven to console the British nation for the loss of the beloved and lamented Princess Charlotte of Wales. The people were disposed, for the sake of her on whom such fond hopes had been centred, to regard with peculiar complacency the prospect of the British sceptre reverting to a female hand.

Placed, then, within a sentimental succession of female royals in the hearts of the British people (according to Miss Strickland) Victoria becomes a Queen of Hearts, healing her subjects' grief for the death of Charlotte.

Strickland's numerous 'lives' of historical and contemporary females have an important place among the historical, fictional and painterly narratives of royal women which expand the matriarchal mirror far back into British history. Linda Colley's persuasive argument concerning the 'feminisation of the British monarchy' primarily limits itself to queens and princesses from the mid-eighteenth century to the accession of Victoria. In fact, the 'gallery of royal women' whom British women could look to as role models or as romantic heroines was far wider when Victoria joined its ranks than it had ever been.[21] Victoria, coping in her own life with the separate spheres and expectations of family circle and dynasty, hearth and Empire, not only served as another royal woman for her feminine subjects to focus upon, but also chose as they did a past royal woman for whom she felt a particular sympathy – Mary Queen of Scots.

By the time Walter Scott wrote *The Abbot* (1820) the historical, poetic, dramatic and painterly representations of Mary Stuart had made her an extremely popular and familiar historical figure. She was the perfect romantic heroine – beautiful, noble, tragic and ambiguous. As Scott writes:

Who is there, at the very mention of Mary Stuart's name, has not her countenance before him, familiar as that of the mistress of his youth, or the favourite daughter of his advanced age? Even those who feel themselves compelled to believe all, or much, of what her enemies laid to her charge,[22] cannot think without a sigh upon a countenance expressive of any thing rather than the foul crimes with which she was charged when living, and which continue to shade, if not to blacken her memory.[23]

The long painterly tradition surrounding Mary was given new life by Scottish painters such as Gavin Hamilton, David Allan, Sir William Allan and Sir David Wilkie,[24] the latter two being well-acquainted with Scott; Scott continues:

It is in vain to say that the portraits which exist of this remarkable woman are not like each other; for amidst their discrepancy, each possess general features which the eye at once acknowledges as peculiar to the vision which our imagination has raised while we read her history for the first time, and which has been impressed upon it by the numerous prints and pictures which we have seen. (vol. 2, p. 5)

The paintings render Mary Stuart's countenance 'familiar' to his readers and they are evidence, 'not merely of admiration, but of warm and chivalrous interest' which remains after the lapse of time.

It would seem that Queen Mary's was a familiar face also to Queen Victoria: various portraits of Mary were held in the Royal Collection and Victoria's attention to them was the source of what was perhaps her single contribution to nineteenth-century women's fashion. While she was given the rather affectionate title by some of her subjects as 'the worst-dressed woman in the world',[25] Victoria nevertheless instigated the fashion for the much-admired widow's head-dress – the 'Marie Stuart cap'. As Lou Taylor writes of this most popular style in nineteenth-century mourning wear:

Both indoor and outdoor caps shared one common feature and that was a V-point shaped down over the centre forehead and described always as the Marie Stuart style. This point was reintroduced by Queen Victoria on Albert's death in 1861, taken from the portraits of the widowed Mary Queen of Scots. The Queen wore it for the rest of her life and it was taken up by most of her widowed subjects.[26]

Wearing the Marie Stuart cap, a nineteenth-century widow's gaze into the mirror reflected in some ways her mirroring of her widowed monarch. But Queen Victoria was also participating in this mirroring of royal women: her gaze into the mirror presented an image partly inspired by her gaze at the portraits in her collection of Mary Queen of Scots. Entering upon her widowhood, Victoria framed herself within an 'ancestral' portrait of the romantic and tragic figure whom she regarded as her Stuart ancestor.

By the time of Albert's death, Queen Victoria was accustomed to dressing up in costumes from a royal past. In her book, *Queen Victoria's Secrets* (1996), Adrienne Munich argues that, helped by Albert, Victoria found a 'genealogy in her closet'. Albert's love of organizing costume balls gave Victoria and Albert the opportunity to 'masquerade as olden monarchs while ruling as new ones'.[27] Munich records that at the Plantagenet ball in 1842, Victoria and Albert dressed as Queen Philippa and King Edward III, and the Stuart (or Restoration) Ball in 1851 'honoured Charles II, the "Merry Monarch", and allowed Victoria and Albert to play out their inheritance of the Scottish throne'.[28] With the purchase of their Scottish estate, Balmoral, and their designing of their own personal tartans (first 'invented' as the mark of clan – of a Scottish genealogy – in the eighteenth century[29]) clothing again, according to Munich, 'performs a genealogy' for Victoria and Albert.

While Munich's entertaining argument for sartorial genealogies is convincing, she effectively closes the dressing-up box upon Albert's death. It is certainly the case that Albert was a tremendous influence upon Victoria's wardrobe – he often approved or vetoed what she wore, and was the instigator and designer of more imaginative dressing in the costume balls. But Victoria's choice of the Marie Stuart cap as the crowning point of her widow's weeds was in some way her own feminine creation of a genealogy through clothes, uninfluenced by Albert, and part of her participation in a matriarchal line of royal females. Already sentimentally attached to the Stuart line through her love of Scotland and the works of Walter Scott, Victoria chose its most romantic heroine as her sartorial model.

Of Victoria's widow's weeds, Munich comments that they 'became her, at least to those who could see her sorrows in her clothes and who used her dress to respond to her image as both unerotic and ordinary'.[30] While the image of the dumpy queen, crinolined in black crape, is certainly unerotic to most, and ordinary to her Victorian subjects, her widow's cap is evidence that the queen herself regarded her dress with something more of a romantic flair than Munich's assessment would suggest. Victoria was imitating another queen who was presented to the Victorians through contemporary paintings and novels as both extraordinary and erotic.[31] Antonia Fraser has argued that there were four perspectives on Mary which were put forward by historians, novelists and painters from the 'battle of the books' which began before her death and which continues to the present day. Each of these found support in the nineteenth century, and depending upon who was writing or painting, Mary was presented as the Dynastic Rival to Elizabeth; the Martyr Queen; the Scarlet Woman (often to a degree conflated with a view of her Catholic religion as the Scarlet Whore of Rome); or the *femme fatale*, who, as Fraser describes, 'was helplessly alluring, not responsible for those disasters which attended her, a patient of history, not its agent'.[32] To this list I would add Mary as Maternal Figure – a woman of strong motherly feeling who had her child wrested from her. I will be addressing this particular image of Mary, an image which became especially popular in the nineteenth century, with reference to Yonge's *Unknown to History* later in this chapter.

Of Mary's Victorian detractors, the most virulent was the historian J. A. Froude. To Froude's thinking, Mary Stuart seems to have been the Scarlet Woman and Scarlet Whore rolled into one:

She was the old Mary Stuart still, the same bold, restless, unscrupulous ambitious woman, and burning with the same passions, among which revenge stood out predominant. Hers was the panther's nature – graceful, beautiful, malignant and untameable.[33]

According to Froude, she was the weaver of a web of Jesuitical lies and plots. Like a Black Widow spider she lay at the centre of a web, the murderer of her second husband Darnley. Married three times, and according to those of the Scarlet Woman/Scarlet Whore school of thought, a husband-killer, Mary was hardly the best model, sartorial or otherwise, for the 'Widow of Windsor', that icon of the Victorian widow, faithful to her husband's ashes (a phenomenon which I discuss further in Chapter Five). Froude had written of Mary's first widowhood in France that 'she was speculating before the body was cold upon her next choice',[34] an assessment that was highly incongruous with Victoria's emotional state upon the death of Albert.

Interestingly, the opinions of eminent eighteenth- and nineteenth-century historians such as Froude who wrote against Mary took far less hold in the popular imagination than the views of her as Martyr Queen, as *femme fatale* or as Wronged Mother. In a study of the Scottish queen in British history painting Helen Smailes writes: 'This interdependence of painting and historical writing seldom resulted in a close correlation of treatment. Without exception the history pictures were favourable towards their subject even where their related literary or historical source was openly critical or tendentious.'[35] By the nineteenth century, however, and certainly after Scott's publication of *The Abbot* in 1820, the novels, poems and short stories about Mary Stuart were also, like the paintings, favourable to their subject. It may be that the narrative paintings and the literature influenced each other, as in Joseph Severn's 1850 painting of Mary's forced abdication, inspired by a scene from *The Abbot* (see fig. 3).

Scott presents the defence of Mary Stuart as a chivalric duty: he leaves it undecided whether or not she is guilty of the 'foul crimes' imputed to her. She is regal and beautiful, and therefore worthy of defence:

We know that by far the most acute of those who, in latter days, have adopted the unfavourable view of Mary's character longed, like the executioner before his dreadful task, to kiss the fair hand of her on whom he was about to perform so horrible a duty. (*The Abbot*, vol. 2, pp. 5–6)

As we have seen, Scott was certainly proven wrong in the case of Froude, and Agnes Strickland takes the defence of Mary away from the swords or pens of the chivalric male and places it firmly within the moral duty of women.[36] In her view, women throughout history have simply known by instinct that Mary was innocent:

If the favourable opinions of her own sex could be allowed to decide the question [of her guilt or innocence], then may we say that a verdict of not guilty has been pronounced by an overpowering majority of female readers of all nations, irrespective of creed or party. Is, then, the moral standard erected by women for one another lower than that which is required of them by men? Are they less acute in their perceptions of right and wrong, or more disposed to tolerate frailties? The contrary has generally been asserted. Yet, with the notorious exceptions of Queen Elizabeth, Catherine de Medicis, and the Countess of Shrewsbury, Mary had no female enemies. No female witnesses from her household came forward to bear testimony against her, when it was out of her power to purchase secrecy if they had been cognisant of her guilt. (Nor did) the ladies of her court.[37]

Repeatedly Strickland claims that Mary was never 'deserted by the high and excellent of her own sex'. Agnes Strickland's view of Mary belongs to the 'Mary as Martyr Queen' school, but popular portrayals of the Scottish queen, even when favourable to her, often contained other elements such as the erotic *femme fatale*, the strong queen and dynastic rival to Elizabeth, the maternal woman. As I have argued, Mary Stuart was one of that 'gallery of royal females' that eighteenth- and nineteenth-century women looked to, and while Strickland attributes the special relationship that women of past ages and her own age have with Mary to the queen's almost saintly femininity, her popularity may be based also in the mystery and ambiguity of her nature and in the many, and often conflicting, aspects of womanhood which are presented in her popular image. As a member of that matriarchal genealogy of queens and princesses, it is Mary Stuart who offered the greatest diversity of roles and aspects to which women could respond in their own self-representation and definition. As Roy Strong writes of the paintings of Mary Stuart:

although she was built up as a monument to the female virtues and as an instance of the inability of women to exert power and rule, there was always the lingering possibility that perhaps her defamers were right. Any defence of her virtues suggested an examination of the evidence for her vices – a dabbling into rape, sexual violence and outright murder. And this double image may have considerably increased her potency as a symbol to the suppressed womanhood of mid-Victorian England.[38]

Roy Strong reads the literary treatments of Mary Stuart as presenting her as a Gothic heroine, 'weeping' and 'overcome by faintness', and perhaps it is this interpretation which leads him to conclude that the Queen of Scots is portrayed in both the literature and painting as 'an instance of the inability of women to exert power and rule'.[39] This is hardly the case in two of the best-known fictional treatments of Mary in the early and late nineteenth century; Scott's *The Abbot* (1820) and Charlotte M. Yonge's *Unknown to History* (1882). However, the ambiguity of her character, to which Strong alludes, is evident in both novels. The image of Mary as a 'divided self', as a woman with many roles to play, will be the focus of the following study of Scott's and Yonge's fictional accounts of Mary's imprisonment at Lochleven and in England, respectively. In these novels the division of character and self-identity is brought about by genealogical conflict: as was the case with Queen Victoria, these nineteenth-century depictions of Mary Stuart see her divided between her genealogical role as the successor of a ruling dynasty, and her genealogical role as mother, this latter role itself divided between propagator of dynasty and maternal woman.

PRINCESS CAROLINE AND 'THE ABBOT'

Scott's Mary Stuart, like so many of his important historical figures, is introduced late in the novel and within a frame plot, which in this novel takes the form of the adventures of the orphan Roland Graeme. Roland has been sent from his home on the lake-isle of Avenel to the lake-isle of Lochleven to act as a page to the recently-imprisoned Queen of Scots. He soon becomes involved in a plot, designed by the noble George Douglas, to aid the queen in her escape.

George Douglas is the grandson of the Lady of Lochleven, Mary's gaoler, and when his plot to free Mary is discovered by his grandmother, the proud noblewoman laments the fall of her House:

'O ancient house of Lochleven, famed so long for birth and honour, evil was the hour which brought the deceiver under thy roof!'
'Say not so, madam,' replied her grandson, 'the old honours of the Douglas line

will be outshone, when one of its descendants dies for the most injured of queens – for the most lovely of women'. (vol.2, p. 183)

In 1820 Walter Scott was well aware of the market value of the combination of injured queen/lovely woman, because it was in this year that the scandals surrounding the Princess Caroline came to a crisis when she returned to England from the Continent to claim her right, as the consort of George IV, to be declared queen. Caroline and George had regarded each other with mutual loathing since their arranged marriage in 1795. They had had one daughter together (the Princess Charlotte) and had then gone their separate and scandalous ways. Like Mary Queen of Scots, Caroline had been denied access to her child, and, like Mary, she had been accused of an affair with her Italian secretary. On the day of the grand coronation of George IV, Caroline arrived in state at Westminster Abbey, only to be turned away at the door, denied her chance to be crowned queen. George IV began divorce proceedings against her under the 'Bill of Pains and Penalties' which meant that if her adultery could be proven the king could divorce her (if not execute her for treason, a penalty which was still a legal option under the Bill). The trial of the princess began in August 1820 as Scott was finishing *The Abbot*. Of Scott's timing, John Sutherland writes that it 'would have been hard for any moderately aware Briton reading *The Abbot* in 1820 not to think of Caroline – the most inconvenient queen in Scottish history since Mary of Scotland'.[40] Scott's friends wrote to him noting the parallels between the stories of the two queens, and Sutherland argues that, 'in a year dominated by hysteria on the subject of inconvenient queens, Scott's novel (whose composition and publication shadow the divorce proceedings almost to the day) was clearly topical and its topicality may have enhanced its sales.'[41]

Scott was on friendly terms with the Princess Caroline, and had been her guest in London upon several occasions. In 1806 he composed a poem for her father, 'Health to Lord Melville', and included a verse of chivalric defence of the princess:

> Our king, too – our princess – I dare
>   not say more, sir –
> May Providence watch them with
>   mercy and might!
> While there's one Scottish hand that
>   can wag a claymore, sir,
> They shall ne'er want a friend to
>   stand up for their right.

> Be damn'd he that dare not, –
> For my part, I'll spare not
> To beauty afflicted a tribute to give:
>   Fill it up steadily,
>   Drink it off readily, –
> Here's to the princess, and long may
>   she live!

Like the noble Douglas extolling 'the most injured of queens – the most lovely of women', Scott poetically springs to the defence of royal 'beauty afflicted'. As with the later fictional George Douglas in *The Abbot*, he regards it as his feudal and chivalric duty as a Scot to defend the Princess Caroline. Of course it was also Scott's duty as a writer and businessman to know his readership and market: it was not simply *The Abbot*'s topicality which may have enhanced sales in 1820, but also the fact that the novel arrived in a climate which, since the middle of the previous century, was sympathetically disposed towards its female monarchs and princesses. As Linda Colley has related, tens of thousands of working and middle class women across Britain 'had signed addresses in support of the Queen' (Caroline) in 1820. Scott must have been aware that he was writing a novel that was in effect concerned with not one but two 'injured queens' and popular heroines.

While the parallels between Mary and Caroline may hold in 1820, it is clear from John Sutherland's 1995 critical biography of Scott that these similarities may become dated and distorted: he writes, 'Granted that one was tragedy and the other ripe farce, there were obvious parallelisms between Caroline and Mary Queen of Scots – two adulterous women extremely vexatious to their sovereigns'.[42] Sutherland's comment ignores the fact that what was most probably adultery in the case of Caroline, is not proven to be so in the case of Mary Stuart (the extremely controversial Casket letters, supposedly written between Mary and her lover Bothwell, were the subject of enormous controversy in the nineteenth century, and have been acknowledged as fakes by most twentieth-century historians). And while Caroline was assuredly 'inconvenient' to her sovereign husband George IV, it is difficult to ascertain whom Sutherland means to be Mary's 'sovereign': if Elizabeth, then this ignores the fact that Mary, as both Scottish and a queen in her own right would certainly not have regarded Elizabeth as her sovereign; if he means Mary's son James then this does not acknowledge Mary's insistence that she was sovereign of Scotland, and that her abdication was illegal because obtained through force and threat of violence. Nevertheless, while Sutherland's comments expose the risk of becoming carried away by neat reflections and parallels between historical lives, they also indicate the seductiveness of these parallels to the popular imagination as they take the form of narratives, of fiction. To her subjects Caroline's troubles were the ongoing narrative in the papers of the day, a soap-opera with all the narratological surprises and suspense of fiction. Mary's life was, as Sutherland acknowledges, in the form of a tragedy, but in Scott's hands, it was also romance and adventure.

Perhaps what the 1820 readership of Scott's novel would have recognized as central to both Mary's and Caroline's stories was the plot of a woman struggling to be recognized as queen, and in this struggle confronting the genealogical dilemmas of dynastic succession and family disharmony. While Scott reflects Caroline in Mary, perhaps exploiting to a degree the popular interest in the lives of contemporary and historical royal women, he also sets in place within his novel a number of women whose lives offer parallels with each other and with the lives of contemporary readers. In their struggles with power, dynasty and genealogy they not only reflect the troubles of Mary Stuart, the novel's heroine, but also reflect a shared female experience in each other.

LADIES OF THE LAKE

The Abbot is the sequel to Scott's 1820 novel *The Monastery*. It takes up the story of young Roland Graeme, who had been an infant at the close of the earlier novel. Roland is a fairly typical Scott hero in that he is rash, impetuous and, like the hero of Scott's first novel *Waverley* (1814), a wavering, undecided youth. While Edward Waverley vacillated between the Jacobite and Hanoverian at the time of the 1745 Jacobite rising, Roland wavers between Catholicism and the new Reformed Protestant Church in the sixteenth century.

Towards the end of *The Monastery* the infant Roland was rescued from the arms of his dead mother as she lay over the body of his father, mortally wounded on the battlefield. At the opening of *The Abbot* Roland is not only an orphan but is believed to be illegitimate. As a child he travels with his itinerant grandmother, Magdalen Graeme, who is a proud and half-crazed pauper of noble family, secretly devoted to Catholicism and heavily involved in plots to overthrow the Protestant faith. In their travels, Roland is almost drowned in the Lake of Avenel. The childless Lady of Avenel, yearning for an infant of her own, saves the boy. Impressed by his innate grace and nobility, she offers to raise Roland in her island-castle. Magdalen agrees to leave her grandson with the Lady of Avenel not only because it leaves her free to pursue her plotting unencumbered by the child, but also because she believes that Roland, when he reaches manhood, will act as an important spy for the Catholic cause from within the Protestant household of the powerful Avenels. (Halbert Glendinning, the Lord of Avenel, was the peasant hero of *The Monastery*. He has raised himself through marriage and politics to become an important ally of the Earl of Murray, Mary Stuart's illegitimate half-brother and the most powerful man in Scotland). Roland Graeme grows up proud, difficult and the bane of the Avenel servants. Although he is devoted to the Lady of Avenel and loved by her, his adolescent misdemeanours force the Lady to banish him from her household. Through Halbert Glendinning he is introduced to the Earl of Murray in Edinburgh. The Earl has recently imprisoned Queen Mary in the island-castle of Lochleven, and he orders Roland to travel to Lochleven to act as Mary's 'page' (or in fact in Murray's plans, as a spy upon his half-sister). Partly through his susceptibility to the beautiful queen's charms and gentleness, and partly through his growing love for the noble Catherine Seyton, a young lady-in-waiting to the queen, Roland becomes devoted to the queen's cause and helps her to escape from Lochleven. In this, Roland is the fictional counterpart of the historical Willy Douglas, a young page of the Douglas family who in fact aided Mary's historical escape from Lochleven in 1568. The novel ends with Mary's defeat at the battle of Langside after the escape, and her fateful decision to leave Scotland for England and Queen Elizabeth's protection, rather than for France. Before she leaves Scotland for what would become her life-long imprisonment under Elizabeth, she brings together Roland and Catherine Seyton, a boy of unknown parentage and a girl of high nobility. In a very conventional device of plot closure, Roland's genealogy is discovered to be both noble and legitimate: he is heir to the Avenel estate where he was nurtured. Catherine and Roland are married 'spite of their differing faiths' in a union by which Scott would seemingly wish to foretell a united Scotland, no longer riven by religious difference.

According to John Sutherland, *The Abbot* is the first sequel novel in English, and as such 'tremendously influential' upon the sequels and dynastic series of novels which, like those of Trollope, Thackeray, and Charlotte Yonge we associate so readily with the nineteenth-century novel. The only sequel that Scott ever wrote, *The Abbot* was partly a response to the critical reception of *The Monastery* – an attempt to clarify and correct that earlier novel. While the form was new and Scott was never to repeat it, the *Monastery/Abbot* combination nevertheless follows the genealogical pattern which is so often associated with the serial form, with the consanguineous fictions and dynastic sagas which follow the fortunes of a family across the generations. The opening of *The Abbot* takes up the story of the Lord and Lady of Avenel, who were the young lovers of *The Monastery*. Mary Avenel was a young impoverished orphan of noble descent who took refuge during a border raid with the respectable but plebeian Glendinning family. She grows up in the Glendinning household, much loved by the two brothers of that family, but especially loving the younger brother, the impetuous Halbert Glendinning. The romantic plot of *The Monastery*, set against a Scotland divided by religious differences and at the beginning of the dissolution of the monasteries, is the conventional tale of a youth of noble soul but lowly stock in love with a girl of noble blood. At the end of the novel Mary and Halbert are married, both having converted from Catholicism to the Reformed Church.

Rather than the conventional happy union in the final page of the story, however, Halbert's brother (the 'Abbot' of the sequel novel) is impressed with the 'melancholy belief that the alliance of Mary with his brother might be fatal to them both'.[43] In fact no such fatality occurs in *The Abbot*, and Scott seems to have either forgotten the bodings of the last page of *The Monastery* or simply did not know what to do with that foreshadowed plot when he began writing the sequel. But if there is no 'fatality' in store for Mary Avenel or Halbert Glendinning, then it does seem at the opening of *The Abbot* that their union has been fatal to the Avenel line. The lady of Avenel, alone in her castle in the middle of the lake of Avenel, mourns her childlessness and the extinction of her line:

'But, alas! what avails the blood which Halbert has shed, and the dangers which he encounters, to support a name or rank, dear to him because he has it from me, but which we shall never transmit to our posterity! with me the name of Avenel must expire.' (vol. 1, p. 21)

The fact that this sequel, a form usually associated with genealogical continuity and succession, begins with childlessness and genealogical extinction indicates much about the problems of dynasty and pedigree with which this novel is concerned. Scott writes of the Avenels that 'two circumstances only had embittered their union, which was otherwise as happy as mutual affection could render it': the one, childlessness, and the other, 'was indeed the common calamity of Scotland, being the distracted state of that unhappy country, where every man's sword was directed against his neighbour's bosom' (vol. 1, p. 16). Not only against his *neighbour's* bosom, Scott might add, but against the bosom of his nearest kin: Scott's 'Scottish' novels so often record how national differences over religion, clan loyalty or political alliance divided father against son, brother against brother, both in the sixteenth-century setting of *The Monastery/The Abbot* and in the period of the Jacobite rising in the Waverley novels. As Darsie Latimer in Scott's *Redgauntlet* admits to his friend, the 'circle of consanguinity' in Scotland is very wide, 'extending to sixth cousins at least',[44] and (as Darsie's fate bears out) it is crucially bound up with personal and national identity.

Of the period of Scottish history in which *The Monastery* and *The Abbot* are set, Antonia Fraser writes of the ramifications of this 'circle of consanguinity' to the Stuart line and to the state of Scotland:

The many intermarriages, common to all Scottish noble families of this period, meant that by the 1540s there were descended from younger sons or daughters of the kings a number of rival Stewart families – the Lennox Stewarts ... the Atholl Stewarts, the Stewarts of Traquair, the Stewarts of Blantyre, and the Stewarts of Ochiltree. Even those dignitaries whose name was not actually Stewart often stood in close relationship to the crown through marriage or descent; throughout her reign Mary [Stuart, or Stewart] correctly addressed as 'cousin' the Earls of Arran, Huntly and Argyll, heads respectively of the clans Hamilton, Gordon and Campbell. Kinship as a concept was all-important in Scotland of the period.[45]

As Antonia Fraser points out, the English Tudors were far more 'prudent' than their Stuart cousins: they saw the benefits of pruning the family tree, accomplishing this through dynastic marriages, enforced celibacy, or execution. Scotland and England differed considerably therefore, in the workings of kinship structure surrounding the ruling family line, and this difference in genealogical alliances filtered through to those noble families close to the throne, and to the unity or disunity of the two nations – the greater the dynastic competition around the throne, the greater the disharmony among the noble families. In Scotland genealogy and nation were crucially 'related': family feuds divided the nation for centuries. As Scott's Mary Stuart 'imputes' to her rebel lords:

'your own turbulent, wild, and untameable dispositions – the frantic violence with which you, the Magnates of Scotland, enter into feuds against each other

... setting at defiance those wise laws which your ancestors made for stanching of such cruelty, rebelling against the lawful authority, and bearing yourselves as if there were no king in the land; or rather as if each were king in his own premises.' (vol. 2, p. 35)

Scott's novels, particularly the 'Scottish' novels, are steeped in the bloodiness of blood relations, relating tales of the fraught and complex connections between family lines and nation.

As if representing the state of the Scottish nation in microcosm, the lake-isles of Avenel and Lochleven (the main settings for *The Abbot*) are riven by genealogical problems of succession, dynastic loyalty, illegitimacy and family feud. In Scott's novel, the male heads of the family are absent from the islands, reflecting the view of a number of Scots at the time who were uneasy with a 'lassie' on the throne. In defiance of John Knox's *First Blast of the Trumpet Against the Monstrous Regiment of Women*, it is the women who rule on Avenel and Lochleven (while their men are away) and their handling of genealogical problems has both familial and national implications. Scott's 'ladies of the lake' include Mary Glendinning, Lady of Avenel, and on the island of Lochleven, both Margaret Douglas, Lady of Lochleven, and Mary Stuart, who is the prisoner of the Douglas family on the island-castle of Lochleven.

Arriving on the tiny island of Lochleven Roland Graeme feels that 'the ancient castle, which occupies an island nearly in the centre of the lake, recalled that of Avenel, in which he had been nurtured' (vol. 1, p. 355). Both islands and their ruling or imprisoned women reflect each other in a number of ways.

Whether Mary Avenel is ruler or lonely prisoner on the island of Avenel is left ambiguous in Scott's opening to *The Abbot*. Her husband, Halbert Glendinning, was 'perpetually summoned to attend his patron [the Earl of Murray] on distant expeditions, or on perilous enterprises and thus [was] frequently absent from his castle and from his lady' (vol. 1, p. 16). She has no children to 'occupy her attention' while deprived of her husband's society. Scott's description of a day in the life of Mary Avenel is not unlike the daily routine of the prisoner Queen Mary, described later in the novel, except that Queen Mary has indeed more society than the Lady of Avenel:

To superintend the tasks of numerous female domestics was the principal part of the Lady's daily employment; her spindle and distaff, her bible, and a solitary walk upon the battlements of the castle, or upon the causeway, or occasionally, but more seldom, upon the banks of the little lake, consumed the rest of the day.

But so great was the insecurity of the period, that when she ventured to extend her walk beyond the hamlet, the warder on the watch-tower was directed to keep a sharp look-out in every direction, and four or five men held themselves in readiness to mount and sally forth from the castle on the slightest appearance of alarm. (vol. 1, p. 19)

While the men guarding Avenel are protecting its Lady from what lies beyond the island's shores, and the men guarding Lochleven are keeping aid away from the queen, in both cases the women are trapped, circumscribed by their islands. The portrayal of the Lady of Avenel in her 'melancholy and solitary existence' is one of the most intensely bleak images of female loneliness that Scott ever wrote, and the Lady of Avenel blames her desolation upon her noble genealogy: remembering her freedom and happiness as a young girl in the unaristocratic Glendinning household she laments;

'Why was I not ... the peasant girl which in all men's eyes I seemed to be? Halbert and I had then spent our life in his native glen, undisturbed by the phantoms either of fear or of ambition.' (vol. 1, p. 21)

Halbert's ambition is to rise among the Scottish nobility so that he may be worthy of the title he has gained from his wife. Although Halbert acknowledges the advantages of a higher pedigree he is also subject to the 'jealous inconsistency' of moments 'in which he felt mortified that his lady should possess those advantages of birth and high descent which he himself did not enjoy, and regretted that his importance as the proprietor of Avenel was qualified by his possessing it only as the husband of an heiress' (vol. 1, p. 54).

The branches of Mary Avenel's family tree hedge her in from all sides, rendering her one of Scott's loneliest women: her husband stays away from her in his jealous ambition to prove himself independent of her pedigree; the 'pride of ancestry' in the ladies of the surrounding gentry prevents them from associating with Mary because she has married a 'peasant' ('she who marries a churl's son, were she a king's daughter, is but a peasant's bride' (vol. 1, p. 40) says Magdalen Graeme); she is both orphaned and childless ('with me the name of Avenel must expire' (vol. 1, p. 21)). Into this isolated existence comes the child Roland Graeme whom Mary decides to adopt. While the Lady of Avenel had once cried, 'I am doomed never to hear a child call me mother!' (vol. 1, p. 22), Roland, gaining consciousness after his rescue from the lake, 'Stretched his arms toward the lady, and muttered the word "mother", that epithet, of all others, which is dearest to the female ear' (vol.1, p. 21). Underlining the similarities in situation of Mary Avenel and Mary Stuart, Scott furthers the metaphors not only of solitude, but of imprisonment;

Young Roland was to the Lady of Avenel what the flower, which occupies the window of some solitary captive, is to the poor wight by whom it is nursed and cultivated, – something which at once excited and repaid her care. (vol. 1, p. 42)

While Walter Scott is hardly, in 1820, making a proto-feminist statement in his linking of a woman's domestic sphere with a prison, it is nevertheless the case that Scott's sequel to the romantic union of Halbert and Mary at the close of *The Monastery* pronounces a grim and desolate fate for the young bride. Scott's investment, in his own life and in his novels, in the 'circle of consanguinity' which he feels is so important in Scottish life, becomes even more important in the lives of his female characters. Without kin, a man may at least attempt to make his way in the world, through fighting, making allies, gaining the favour of a patron, as does Halbert Glendinning. But bereft of family and of the hopes of continuing her genealogy, Mary Avenel shadows the experience of many women whose circle of consanguinity has been broken – whether through childlessness, families divided by feud or religious differences, or simply by death. The island castles in *The Abbot* are both literal and figurative: they serve as strongly protected fortresses so necessary in a nation divided into rival clans; they are also a metaphor for the literal isolation of women whose lives are rendered desolate by the consequences of genealogy.

Scott further establishes the shared female experience of Mary Avenel and Mary Stuart through the figure of Roland Graeme. Employed as a page in turn to both women, he inspires their maternal yearnings, foregrounding their childlessness. While Mary Stuart has a son, she, like Mary Avenel, 'is doomed never to hear (him) call her mother'. (Mary Stuart's last view of her infant son occurred shortly before she was abducted to Lochleven. She never saw him again.) Both women then suffer the consequences of troubled genealogy: Mary Avenel produces no successor to the Avenel name, and Mary Stuart's infant son and successor is given the crown against her will when she is forced to abdicate at Lochleven. Maternal desires and dynastic dilemmas: both the intimate, personal and the wider more public problems of genealogy come together in these two women.

LOCHLEVEN

The removal of the novel's action from Avenel to Lochleven results in a very different matriarchal mirroring in the two ladies of Lochleven: Margaret Douglas and Mary Stuart. For complex genealogical and dynastic reasons, the Lady of Lochleven views her prisoner as a rival. Margaret Douglas had been a mistress of Mary's father, James V. Margaret's son by James, the Earl of Murray, is the most powerful man in Scotland but is nevertheless barred from the throne because he is illegitimate. This fact never ceases to rankle in the Lady of Lochleven's breast:

'Had James done to her,' she said in her secret heart, 'the justice he owed her, she had seen her son, as a source of unmixed delight, and of unchastened pride, the lawful monarch of Scotland, and one of the ablest who ever swayed the sceptre. The House of Mar, not inferior in antiquity or grandeur to that of Drummond, would then have also boasted a Queen among its daughters, and escaped the stain attached to female frailty, even when it has a royal lover for its apology.' (vol. 2, p. 2)

The Lady of Lochleven's secret musings lay just as much stress upon the matriarchal line – her family tree 'boast(ing) a Queen among its daughters' – as upon her ambition for her son to be king. Both Margaret Douglas and Mary Stuart are frustrated, thwarted monarchs, and, for want of a wider sphere, their dynastic battles against each other are translated into domestic battles. Scott makes this juxtaposition of the dynastic and domestic very clear in the following scene: Margaret Douglas is silently furious when she is kept standing in Mary's prison apartments. Mary recognizes this and infuriates her further:

'Nay, Lady of Lochleven, if you take it so deeply,' said the Queen, rising and motioning to her own vacant chair, 'I would rather you assumed my seat – you are not the first of your family who has done so.' (vol. 2, p. 166)

While Mary Avenel and Mary Stuart reflect each others' maternal desires – or their feminine nature, as Scott and his contemporaries would have seen it – Margaret Douglas and Mary Stuart reflect in each other what would have been viewed as the more masculine traits of competitiveness and ambition, leading to battles for dynastic succession. As Scott presents her, Mary is able to veil those 'masculine' characteristics which are essential to a ruling queen (as opposed to a queen consort) with a fascinating femininity. In Scott's interpretation Mary is alternately flirtatious, erotic, mischievous, coquettish, regal, dignified, haughty,

Figure 3 Joseph Severn's *The Abdication of Mary, Queen of Scots* is either a study for, or a version of, the larger painting exhibited at the Royal Academy in 1850. This exhibition's catalogue declared that the source for the scene was chapter 22 of Scott's *The Abbot*. Mary's seated figure surrounded by the towering, implacable men, her woeful, shaded face, the lute and delicate lace handkerchief, depict her as a depressed and wronged lady in distress, this being one of the popular and romanticized faces of Mary in the cult surrounding the historical figure of the Scottish queen.

powerful, maternal: these various masks render her an ambiguous figure – the reader is left uncertain as to what is her 'true nature' and what is merely play-acting. At times Scott's Mary is herself uncertain, as when she 'casts on Roland a glance which might have melted a heart of stone', commiserating with him, 'with a feeling partly real, partly politic' (vol. 2, p. 14). Scott's Mary recognizes that theatricality and the wearing of masks are essential to the role of a queen, and that she must become self – divided between feeling and acting, between maternal nature and dynasty, between roles and traits which were seen in turn as conventionally masculine or feminine. The 'savage tone' of Lindesay's voice, as he comes to force the queen to abdicate in chapter twenty-one of the novel, briefly reduces the Queen to 'hysterical agony' and she behaves as a conventional romantic heroine, weeping and swooning. However she immediately recovers her queenly nature: 'I am ashamed of my weakness, girls . . . but it is over – and I am Mary Stuart once more' (vol. 2, p. 12). Upon this declaration of identity she produces a *tableau vivant*, 'shaking down her tresses she arose from her chair, and stood like the inspired image of a Grecian prophetess'. Much later, at a crisis in the novel's action, the Abbot enjoins Mary to 'Be a Queen, madam . . . and forget you are a woman' (vol. 2, p. 331). But for Scott's Mary Stuart her femininity and the theatricality of queenship are inextricably bound up in her identity.

While Mary Stuart is a central figure in *The Abbot* (far more than the Abbot himself, for instance) the frame story follows the adventures of Roland Graeme, and his romance with Catherine Seyton. Both Roland and Catherine are fairly stock characters and in order to string along an interest in their story Scott provides us with the unnecessary and silly complications which take the form of a 'Shakespearian' sub-plot: Catherine has an identical twin brother, Henry, of whom Roland has no knowledge. Inevitably, Roland's and Henry's paths keep crossing and Roland thinks that his beloved is roaming the country, Rosalind-like, disguised as a swashbuckling and poniard-drawing boy. Frequent moments of 'almost-revelation' are equally inevitable, as when Roland questions Catherine about a time when, 'it pleased you to lay your switch across the face of my comrade, I warrant, to show that, in the house of Seyton, neither the prompt ire of its descendants, nor the use of the doublet and hose, are subject to the Salique law, or confined to the use of males' (vol. 2, p. 61).

This plot device grows increasingly exasperating with each occasion that Catherine, on the verge of understanding or explaining the fact that she has a twin brother, is interrupted: 'hark, the bell – hush, for God's sake, we are interrupted', etc. The division of Catherine, in Roland's mind, into male and female does however serve to echo the Queen's divided self. Roland interprets Catherine's 'masculine' nature/disguise in genealogical terms; the House of Seyton does not limit its 'prompt ire' or the 'use of the doublet and hose' to its male line. Women are not 'subject to Salique law', a law which inhibits women from taking the throne. But Catherine, unlike Mary, is not destined for monarchy, so her 'male self' must eventually be suppressed by Scott. The epigraph for chapter twenty-nine of the second volume is taken from *Henry VI* ('Pray God she prove not masculine ere long'), but this is an ill-founded fear in Scott's novel: Henry Seyton, the male twin, is killed in battle at the close of the novel, and it is proven that Catherine never wandered abroad looking for a fight, but was safely immured all the time in the domestic sphere, in the Queen's prison on Lochleven.

Now that Catherine has been found to be sufficiently feminine, the only obstacle to her marriage with Roland is based in pedigree; as Catherine tells her lover:

'You think not, that whenever I re-enter my father's house, there is a gulf between us you may not pass, but with peril of your life – Your only known relative is of wild and singular habits, of a hostile and broken clan – the rest of your lineage unknown ...'.
'Love, my dearest Catherine, despises genealogies.'
'Love may, but so will not the Lord Seyton.' (vol. 2, p. 269)

Finally the Queen intercedes with Lord Seyton to arrange the marriage between Roland and Catherine, proving herself in this instance a 'despiser of genealogies' through her maternal love and solicitude for her two young followers. After this display of a sentimental, maternal approach to genealogy rather than the dynastic approach of a ruling monarch, Scott himself intercedes by ennobling Roland (he is discovered to be heir of the House of Avenel). The result of these manipulations of gender and genealogy is to make Catherine feminine and Roland noble, enabling an entirely conventional novelistic conclusion.

Indeed the conclusion to the sequel novel *The Abbot* offers a far more conventional view of marriage than was seen at the opening of the novel. *The Abbot* began with the loneliness of Mary Avenel, and when one remembers that she was the young girl whose union to Halbert Glendinning concluded *The Monastery*, the marriage at the end of the sequel novel seems to be darkly shadowed by that of the earlier. Just as

Mary Avenel's isolation stems from her husband wishing to prove himself worthy of a high pedigree, so Catherine Seyton it seems, may suffer the consequences of that ambition in her own husband. Roland has said to her of his unknown lineage, 'my deeds shall control prejudice itself – it is a bustling world, and I will have my share. The Knight of Avenel, high as he now stands, rose from as obscure an origin as mine' (vol. 2, p. 270). In a novel in which the experiences of female characters reflect each other, the conventional happy ending of *The Abbot* may be shadowed by what we know was the result of the 'happy ending' of *The Monastery*. Catherine Seyton, like the Lady of Avenel, may pay a high price for her noble blood with a husband who cannot countenance receiving his title from the female line.

Mary Stuart's narrative in *The Abbot* ends with her decision, after escape from Lochleven and defeat at the Battle of Langside, to cross the Solway to England, rather than to seek protection in France. In Scott's later novel, *Redgauntlet*, Darsie Latimer is drawn inexorably to the Solway Firth wishing to make that same crossing to England, a country which he has been mysteriously forbidden from entering. Crossing the border of Scotland and England holds the clue to his genealogy – to his birth and nationality. In *The Abbot* 'crossing the water' has powerful consequences for Mary's national and personal future (and there may be echoes here of the popular Jacobite song, 'Over the water to Charlie', the Chevalier being another case of a dethroned monarch whose crossing the water could determine the fate of a royal line and the nation). Scott heightens the drama of Mary's decision to cross to England. As she steps into the English boat from the Scottish shore, Mary stands on the border of two nations: 'She had already placed her foot on the gangway, by which she was to enter the skiff, when the Abbot, starting from a trance of grief and astonishment ... rushed into the water, and seized upon her mantle.' The Abbot becomes an Ossian-like image of the Celtic seer as he foretells her doom;

'She [Elizabeth] foresaw it! – she foresaw it ... Blinded, deceived, doomed Princess! your fate is sealed when you quit this strand. – Queen of Scotland, thou shalt not leave thine heritage!' (vol. 2, p. 351, see fig. 5)

The Abbot sees Mary's choice of England rather than France as 'madness and ruin' because of the personal and dynastic clash between the English and the Scottish queens: 'A woman to a rival woman – a presumptive successor to the keeping of a jealous and childless Queen!' (vol. 2, p. 346). Mary, however, believes Elizabeth will give her protection and aid: in this, Mary puts her trust in a more sentimental interpretation of kinship and genealogy than that of dynastic competition; Elizabeth, she says, will 'extend her hospitality to a distressed sister' (vol. 2, p. 350).

Queen Elizabeth, that 'Royal Sister', is the last of the line of noble women in *The Abbot* whose problems over genealogy and matriarchy mirror one another. Elizabeth adumbrates the experiences of the Lady of Avenel, the Lady of Lochleven and of Mary Stuart: she is childless; she has, like the Lady of Lochleven's son Murray, been tainted with the accusation of illegitimacy; and while Mary has been usurped by her son James, Elizabeth is under threat of usurpation by Mary, and will, like Mary, be succeeded by James. Although she is rarely referred to in the novel, and never appears as a character, her presence looms in the background of this historical novel; she is the last woman in Scott's mirror of matriarchy.

NARRATIVE BORDERLINES

That moment of personal and national transition depicted in the scene discussed above as Mary crosses to England held a 'special fascination'[46] for the historical and figure painter Richard Westall. Indeed Westall (1765–1836) had made his name as a painter largely through the acclaim and attention he won for his series of paintings taken from the life of Mary Stuart. He became sufficiently well-known to become drawing-master to the young Princess Victoria, and perhaps it is not too much to conjecture that Westall's enthusiasm for the subject of the Scottish queen was at least one of the influences upon the princess which led to her life-long interest in Mary Stuart. Westall painted five subjects from the life of Mary Stuart, but his *The Flight of Mary Queen of Scots into England* received a number of treatments at his hands in watercolour and oil aside from the drawing shown here, which probably dates from 1794 (see fig. 5). Westall's *Flight of Mary* 'formed a pendant to a similar drawing of her embarcation for France in 1548' (see fig. 4).[47] These two paintings exhibited together depict moments of transition and crisis in Mary's story and in the history of Scotland. In Westall's painting of her embarcation to France, the five-year-old child has just stepped from her mother's arms onto the gangway of the boat (recalling Scott's literary depiction of her flight to England, above). Here, the child Mary is escaping to France to avoid the 'rough wooing' of Henry VIII. (Henry wanted to raise Mary in the English court as a bride for his son Edward).

84   *Ancestry and Narrative in Nineteenth-Century British Literature*

Figure 4 Richard Westall, *The Departure of Mary Queen of Scots to France when a Child* (c. 1794).

Figure 5 Richard Westall, *The Flight of Mary Queen of Scots into England* (c. 1794).

Westall's narrative paintings portray moments of literal and figurative transition: the crossing of a geographical, natural border, and also a border-point in the life of Mary (a literal *rite de passage*). These moments of transition carry tremendous narrative power, both in narrative history painting and in literature. Indeed, so many history paintings from the eighteenth and nineteenth centuries – the great period of British history painting – which take Mary Queen of Scots as their subject, pay tribute to the dramatic moments of transition and crisis which have made her life so suited to narrative treatment. Scenes such as the murder of Riccio; Mary's foot on the gangplank as she escapes across the waters from Lochleven castle; Mary's 'last look at France' in paintings by Frith and Herdman in which she watches the shores of France recede as she sails to Scotland; and numerous paintings of Mary, pen in hand, on the verge of signing her abdication: these moments of transition are narratologically effective because they raise conjecture on the part of the reader or viewer: what if ... she had refused to cross the water? turned back? gone to England instead of France as a child? or to France instead of England as an adult? thrown the pen to the floor and refused to sign the fateful document? These points of choice, of alternative paths, constitute what Roland Barthes referred to as the cardinal functions or the nuclei of narrative. Of their role he wrote:

cardinal functions are both consecutive and consequential. Everything suggests, indeed, that the mainspring of narrative is precisely the confusion of consecution and consequence, what comes *after* being read in narrative as what is *caused by*; in which case narrative would be a systematic application of the logical fallacy denounced by Scholasticism in the formula *post hoc, ergo propter hoc* – a good motto for Destiny, of which narrative all things considered is no more than the 'language'.[48]

The historical fact of Mary Stuart's execution at Fotheringhay in 1587 only increases the narrative force of these conjectures; knowing the tragic ending of the story, each moment of transition gains in retrospect a sense of crucial consequence, of fatality. In this sense, the inevitability of historical fact serves to make the fictive or artistic versions of Mary's life narratologically urgent and satisfying.

The narrative treatment of genealogy also produces powerful conjecture: what if ... the foundling is discovered to be the heir of –? the taint of illegitimacy is removed from the romantic hero or heroine? if marital alliance could bring harmony to warring families or nations? if the noble pedigree is discovered to be a fake? As will be discussed further in the final chapters, Thomas Hardy recognized the narrative impulse which a pedigree can bestow. For him, as for Walter Scott, the 'dry-as-dust' pages of an old family tree may be transformed into, as Hardy termed it, a 'palpitating drama' when the human stories of chance meetings, misalliance, orphans, or unhappy marriage are glimpsed beneath the antiquarian's scrawl. (This phenomenon is literalized in the case of Scott's fictitious correspondence with the antiquarian Dr Jonas Dryasdust in the prefaces to many of his novels). History, or in this case the history of a family, breeds imaginative conjecture – and for many nineteenth-century writers, that is a very short step away from fiction.

UNKNOWN TO HISTORY

While the narrative paintings discussed above are based upon single moments of transition which inspire conjecture, Charlotte M. Yonge's 1882 novel, *Unknown to History*, takes a genealogical 'what if?' and transforms it into 'palpitating drama'. The novel takes as its initial conjectural premise the question of what would have happened if Mary Stuart had secretly given birth to a daughter while imprisoned at Lochleven? As Yonge notes in the preface to the novel, the supposition is not entirely unknown to history. She refers her readers to Strickland's *Life of Mary Queen of Scots* and Burton's *History of Scotland*. Strickland writes:

The painful and dangerous illness which attacked Queen Mary in February [1568], being exactly nine months from the period of her compulsory abode in Dunbar Castle [with Bothwell, her third husband], has given a delusive colour to the tradition which nearly a century later was mentioned by La Laboureur in his notes and additions to Castelnau, – 'that she was brought to bed of a daughter at Lochleven, who, being privately transported to France, became a nun in the convent of Soissons'.[49]

Agnes Strickland dismisses this story entirely, explaining that Mary, 'a delicately organized Princess' was simply suffering the mental and physical stresses of imprisonment. Twentieth-century historians, however, have established that Mary was indeed pregnant by Bothwell by the time she was abducted to Lochleven. While imprisoned there she miscarried of twins, and was ill enough for those around her to fear she would die. It was, according to Antonia Fraser, a few days later, 'while the queen was lying in bed after her miscarriage, by her own account in a state of great weakness, having lost a great deal of blood, and scarcely able to move' that Lindesay and others came to force her signature on the abdication papers.[50]

Few of these traumatic medical details, however, enter the nineteenth-century legends surrounding Mary Stuart. Charlotte Yonge begins her story with the time-honoured plot device of a baby being found in a shipwreck by a worthy sailor. Following La Laboureur's account, Yonge assumes that Mary gave birth to a daughter at Lochleven and managed to smuggle the child away from the island to be taken to the protection of a French convent, Notre Dame de Soissons. In Yonge's version, a storm at sea wrecks the ship *St. Bride*, and the infant princess, Bride Hepburn, is the only survivor. The plot is set in place when we learn that the captain who saves the unknown baby is Richard Talbot, 'the second son of a relative of the Earl of Shrewsbury', and that his wife Susan, 'was a distant kinswoman of the famous Bess of Hardwicke': the Earl and his wife Bess of Hardwicke were the gaolers of Mary Stuart for the greater part of her nineteen-year imprisonment in England. Bride Hepburn is adopted by Richard and Susan and christened Cicely Talbot (for many years they are not aware of her parentage). She is brought up on the estate of the Earl of Shrewsbury where Mary is imprisoned. The growing girl admires the 'Queen of Sorrows' from a distance until the day an accident exposes the secret marks burnt into her back. These marks had been branded there when she was a baby so that she would always be able to be identified as of royal lineage. The discovery is kept a secret to all but Mary, her lady-in-waiting and the Talbot family. The Queen has gained a daughter, and if she chooses, an important player in the game of dynastic succession.

Both historical novel and *Bildungsroman*, *Unknown to History* follows Cicely's growth into experience as she learns to love her queen/mother, and also as she gains knowledge of what is expected of a royal woman as she observes the many roles her mother must play, and the many and conflicting facets of her nature. Cicely also grows into maturity with her gradual recognition of the worth of her foster-brother Humfrey. Prior to her knowledge of her lineage, Cicely and Humfrey had acknowledged their love for each other and were promised in marriage. Queen Mary however makes Cicely vow that she will never marry him as his lineage is no match for a princess. As the years go by, Cicely remains the queen's secret daughter, witnessing the dynastic machinations of Bess of Hardwicke, the Babington plot (Anthony Babington is in love with her), the plot's discovery, the trial of Mary Stuart and the preparations for her execution. Underlining the delight of narrative conjecture in the historical novel, Yonge has her heroine journey secretly to London where she has an interview with Queen Elizabeth to plead for her mother's life.

At this interview, a late scene in the novel, Cicely is surprisingly unafraid of Queen Elizabeth: the English queen reminds her of that familiar stern face from her childhood and adolescence – the face of Bess of Hardwicke. Cicely has the courage to offer herself to Elizabeth as a hostage for her mother's life, promising to live under the eye of the English court if her mother is allowed to leave for a convent on the Continent:

'Here am I, Bride Hepburn, ready to live in your Majesty's hands as a hostage, whom you might put to death at the first stirring on her [Queen Mary's] behalf.'

And later in the interview she declares,

'I give you my solemn word as a Queen's daughter that I will never wed, save by your consent, if my mother's life be granted. The King of Scots knows not that there is such a being. He need never know it.'[51]

Queen Bess reminds Cicely of another powerful Bess; she herself is willing to give her life for her mother's: in this exchange between Cicely and the English queen women are reflecting and 'standing in' for one another. As in Scott's novel of Mary Stuart, this mirroring of women's lives forms the essential structure of Yonge's historical novel. The novel's matriarchal framework contributes to a genealogy of women both historical and 'unknown to history' who share in a fund of female experience. Indeed, Cicely's promise to Elizabeth that she will remain a secret ward of the court and that she will 'never wed' without Elizabeth's consent would have instantly conjured up a 'gallery of royal females' for Yonge's Victorian readership: Cicely's proposed future reflects the actual fates of Lady Jane Grey, her sisters the Ladies Katherine and Mary Grey in the reigns of Mary and Elizabeth Tudor, and the tragic fate of Arabella Stuart in the reign of James VI of Scotland, I of England.

All these women suffered, like Mary Stuart, because their genealogy brought them too close to the English throne. The famous Lady Jane was declared queen for nine days after the death of Edward VI before she was executed by Mary Tudor.[52] Her sisters were effectively prisoners of the English court. Lady Katherine married secretly, and the childless Elizabeth, furious at the birth of a son to Katherine, had her marriage declared invalid and imprisoned both husband and wife in the Tower. Their children (they managed to have another son while in the Tower) were therefore illegitimate and no longer a dynastic threat. Lady

Mary Grey, also, was a life prisoner of the royal court: like her sister, she too married secretly and was imprisoned in 'The Chequers', the house and estate which in this century has become the Prime Minister's country seat. In Yonge's novel, Richard and Susan Talbot fear that the revelation of their foster-daughter's lineage will bring her a similar fate to that of the Ladies Grey. Richard tells his wife:

'A drop of royal blood is in these days a mere drop of poison to them that have the ill luck to inherit it ... it brings the headsman's axe after it.' (p. 100)

He fears that,

'they would be sure [to put Cicely in prison] sooner or later. Here has my lord [the Earl of Shrewsbury] been recounting in his trouble about my lady's fine match for her Bess [Bess of Hardwicke's marriage of her daughter to Charles Stuart; the issue of this union was the ill-fated Arabella Stuart], all that hath come of mating with royal blood, the very least disaster being poor Lady Mary Grey's! Kept in ward for life! It is a cruel matter'. (p. 101)

The infant Arabella Stuart is a minor character in Yonge's novel. Her history, with which Victorian readers were well-acquainted, shadows Cicely Talbot's possible fate in the realm of fiction. Arabella was the issue of Bess of Hardwicke's dynastic machinations. She was the child of Bess's daughter Elizabeth Cavendish, and Charles Stuart, younger brother to Darnley, Mary Stuart's murdered second husband. Arabella's royal lineage thrilled her ambitious grandmother, but pronounced a miserable fate for the child. Her proximity to the throne resulted in her becoming a ward of court, effectively prohibited from marrying. At the age of thirty she secretly married William Seymour, grandson of Lady Katherine Grey, but their plan to escape to the Continent collapsed at the last moment and Arabella was arrested and brought back to London. Her cousin, King James I, furious that she had married without his consent, placed her in the Tower, where she died insane in 1615. The fifteen-year-old Felicia Hemans published her first book of poetry *Records of Woman* in 1808, opening her prolific and precocious career with a long poem retelling the fate of the Lady Arabella. Stanza 9 is in the voice of the imprisoned Arabella:

> There went a swift bird singing past my cell -
> O Love and Freedom! ye are lovely things!
> With you the peasant on the hills may dwell,
> And by the streams; but I – the blood of Kings
> A proud unmingling river, thro' my veins
> Flows in lone brightness, – and its gifts are chains![53]

In her preface to the poem, Felicia Hemans writes that Arabella's 'affinity to the throne proved the misfortune of her life', because it 'shut her out from the enjoyment of that domestic happiness which her heart appears to have so fervently desired'.[54] Once again genealogy and domestic affection are set against one another, in an opposition which would be repeated throughout the nineteenth century in numerous records of women's lives.

The fate of these royal women hangs over Yonge's *Unknown to History*, and Mary herself expresses the importance of keeping her daughter's lineage a secret. As she explains to Cicely:

'Remember that did the bruit once get abroad, thou wouldest assuredly be torn from me to be mewed up where the English Queen could hinder thee from ever wedding living man.' (p. 190)

Of course Mary and Cicely cannot know that Mary's words pronounce the fate of the baby Arabella who sleeps in an adjoining wing of the castle, but Charlotte Yonge and her Victorian readers knew that the infant who was the focus of Bess of Hardwicke's ambitions would grow into this tragic fate.

The English royal family were adept at pruning their family tree, and all these women whose lives are depicted or adumbrated in Yonge's novel – the Ladies Jane, Mary and Katherine Grey, Arabella Stuart, Mary Stuart, and potentially the fictional Cicely Talbot – pay the consequences of being too close to the throne. Imprisoned, executed or forced into celibacy, their fates declare that they will not be allowed to propagate, to carry on a dynasty (Mary Stuart's son James is of course an ironic exception to this). Perhaps part of the fascination with these women for nineteenth-century readers lies in the fact that they are denied what in the popular view of the time were the cherished roles of womanhood – the roles of wife and mother. Because of their place upon a royal family tree, they are prohibited from enjoying what were seen as the naturally feminine joys of family life.

Charlotte Yonge probably based Mary Stuart's maternal relationship with Cicely Talbot upon the actual relationship between the historical Mary and Arabella Stuart. After her parents died, the infant Arabella was raised by Bess of Hardwicke, and consequently grew up a member of the household in which Mary was a prisoner. As Antonia Fraser writes of Mary's quasi-maternal relationship with her little niece, the queen:

enjoyed the innocent and touching companionship of the little girl, who with her royal blood and claims to two thrones [Scottish and English], so incongruous with the simple routines of infancy, may have reminded Mary of the child she had once been.[55]

Yonge emphasises the fictional Mary's motherly love for Cicely and her desperate need to be close to her child. In their first interview, after Mary has explained to Cicely the truth of her parentage, Mary, 'with sobs of tempestuous emotion' cries,

'Speak to me! Speak to me! Let me hear my child's voice.'
'Oh, madam –'.
'Call me mother! Never have I heard that sound from my child's lips. I have borne two children, two living children, only to be stripped of both. Speak, child – let me hear thee.' (p. 185)

There is much evidence for the maternal, affectionate nature of the historical Mary Stuart, but at this moment of *Unknown to History* Mary is a true Victorian heroine – the figure of the bereft mother fighting to be with her child. The pathos of her, 'Call me mother! Never have I heard that sound from my child's lips', is reminiscent of that catch-phrase of Victorian melodrama, 'Dead, dead, and never called me mother', from the stage version of Mrs. Henry Wood's best-selling novel *East Lynne* (1861). Indeed, it also echoes the lament of the Lady of Avenel in Scott's *The Abbot*, 'I am doomed never to hear a child call me mother!'.

In Scott's novel Mary's maternal affection for Roland Graeme and Catherine Seyton was reflected in the Lady of Avenel, and the regal, dynasty-building side of her character was reflected in the Lady of Lochleven. In Yonge's novel, a similar feminine triangle is in place: Mary's 'divided self' – the roles she must play as woman and queen – are mirrored in turn in the motherly domesticity of Cicely's foster-mother, Susan Talbot, and in the dynastic ambitions of Bess of Hardwicke.

Both Mary Stuart and Susan Talbot have had children 'taken from them'. At the opening of the novel, Susan is mourning the recent death of her baby daughter. Her husband returns from a long sea journey carrying the baby girl he found in the shipwreck. The infant Cicely's 'weak cry forcibly recalled the last hours of her own child' (p. 4). Later in the novel, Susan deliberates whether or not to reveal to Mary Stuart that Cicely is her lost daughter, emphasising not the national or dynastic importance of this fact, but the maternal:

'The only cause for which I could bear to yield her up would be the thought that she would bring comfort to the heart of the poor captive mother who hath the best right to her.' (p. 101)

Much of Yonge's novel focusses upon Cicely's relationship with her two mothers. The longer she lives with the Queen, growing in the understanding of her royal ancestry and its expectations, the more distant she becomes from her closely-knit foster-family. The reader's sympathy for the maternal feelings of Mary Stuart is mitigated by the observation of Susan's pain as her child gradually grows away from her.

Both Walter Scott's and Charlotte Yonge's depictions of Mary Stuart are highly sympathetic to the Queen, but both writers leave room for those ambiguities in her multi-faceted and theatrical persona which have led to such different interpretations of her character and history. The principal ambiguity of the queen's image in Yonge's novel is revealed in the plans she forms for her daughter's future: no 'despiser of genealogies' as in Scott's novel, she plans that Cicely will make an important dynastic alliance some day. But Mary is not the only character who imagines great alliances and royal sway for Cicely. Even the humble Richard and Susan Talbot are inspired by their foster-daughter's genealogy to create possible histories of national and religious importance. Debating whether or not to destroy the written proof of Cicely's birth, Richard says to his wife:

'Suppose it were the course of providence that the young King of Scots should not live, then would this maid be the means of uniting the two kingdoms in the true and Reformed faith! Heaven forfend that he should be cut off, but meseemeth that we have no right to destroy the evidence that may one day be a precious thing to the kingdom at large.' (p. 102)

Again genealogy breeds narrative and historical conjecture in Richard's 'Suppose it were ...'. Cicely's birth could change the state of both the Scottish and English nations.

Mary thanks Richard and Susan for understanding that Cicely must break her engagement with their son Humfrey. The royal daughter must make a dynastic marriage, for, as Mary says, 'as we all know but too well, royal blood should have no heart' (p. 201). Yonge presents us with this disturbing dichotomy within the queen, part of her essential ambiguity: she is maternal and loving – royal blood *with* a heart – but she would use her daughter as a pawn in the game of dynastic alliances. Within the novel, her plotting for Cicely is matched by Bess of Hardwicke's plans for Arabella Stuart. By 1882, the year of *Unknown to History*'s publication, the Victorian antipathy to arranged marriage had been widely established, as is evident in the novels and periodicals of the day, and in paintings such as William Quiller Orchardson's well-known *Marriage de Convenance* (Royal Academy, 1884) and its sequel *Marriage de Convenance – After!* (Royal Academy, 1886). Both Mary and Bess of Hardwicke would wish an arranged marriage upon the girls under their care. Considering the popular Victorian aversion to the custom (waiving the question of whether or not this was hypocritical) this mirroring of Mary in the ruthless Bess shows the Scottish queen in her least positive aspect in Yonge's novel.

The famous Bess of Hardwicke raised herself from obscure birth to become one of the most powerful and propertied women in England. She achieved this by marrying four times, gaining property and power with each widowhood. Her last husband, the Earl of Shrewsbury, gave her a title, but the Countess would not stop at mere nobility. Charlotte Yonge gives an account of Bess's genealogical ambitions, to be achieved through the infant Arabella. Even the child's name expresses a genealogy so old that it disappears out of the realms of history and into mythology and theology. Upon learning the child's name, Susan questions her husband:

'I never heard such a name. It is scarce Christian. Is it out of a romaunt?'
'Better that it were. It is out of a pedigree. They have got the whole genealogy of the house of Lennox blazoned fair, with crowns and coronets and coats of arms hung up in the hall at Chatsworth, going up on the one hand through Sir Aeneas of Troy, and on the other hand through Woden to Adam and Eve! Pass for all before the Stuart line became Kings of Scots! Well, it seems that these Lennox Stuarts sprang from one Walter, who was son to King Robert II, and that the mother of this same Walter was called Arnhild, or as the Scots here call it Annaple, but the scholars have made it into Arabella, and so my young lady is to be called.' (p. 114)

In naming the child Arabella, Bess reveals her matriarchal ambitions. Of low birth herself, she hopes that the fantastic antiquity of her granddaughter's royal pedigree will obscure her own origins. Bess effectively rewrites her own genealogy in 'blazoning' her granddaughter's, and the pedigree reveals that her ambition is the thrones of both England and Scotland. Many traditional English pedigrees and antique histories gave Aeneas of Troy as the founder of the English nation. The combination, therefore, of the ancient Kings of Scots with the very first of the English royal line in Arabella's pedigree makes Bess guilty of that ambition (for her descendants at least) for which Mary Stuart lost her head – to rule over both realms of England and Scotland.

Chapter fifteen of Yonge's novel is entitled 'Mother and Child', and it runs through the spectrum of Mary's maternal affection and dynastic ambitions for her daughter. The queen teaches Cicely that she must be, as she herself is, a divided being, 'two maidens in one – Cis Talbot by day, and Bride of Scotland by night'. By the end of the chapter Mary has learnt of Cis's childhood promise to marry Humfrey, and gives her a lesson in the duties of a royal woman:

'Princesses mate not with Yorkshire esquires. When the Lady Bride takes her place in the halls of her forefathers she will be the property of Scotland, and her hand will be sought by princes.' (p. 199)

As the years go by, Cicely learns to cope with her double existence, but secretly she still loves Humfrey. Mary tells her daughter, now a young woman, that she would be a 'perilous bride' for Humfrey because:

'They have made it treason to wed royal blood without Elizabeth's consent. No, no, for his sake, as well as thine own, thou must promise me never thus to debase thy royal lineage.' (p. 398)

When Mary goes to her death towards the close of the novel, all these heartless machinations have been disavowed by the queen and she comes close to fulfilling the role of 'Martyr Queen' in death. Her last words to Humfrey, to be passed on to Cicely, are; 'Give her my joy and blessing, and tell her my joy is come – such joy as I never knew before!'. Mary's transformation whilst awaiting death is reminiscent of Sydney Carton's as he anticipates the guillotine in *A Tale of Two Cities*. The prospect of her execution after nineteen years of fruitless plotting to escape her English prison helps Mary to transcend the schemes and ambitions which clouded the character of the good and loving woman in Yonge's treatment. Mary has realized that Cicely should marry for love and not be sacrificed in a political and dynastic alliance. She brings the lovers together: 'Wilt thou take her Humfrey, and with her, all the inheritance of peril and sorrow that dogs our unhappy race?' (pp. 552–3)

William Hennessy's illustration of this scene for the original Victorian editions of the novel depict a Queen Mary who bears an uncanny resemblance to Queen Victoria (see fig. 6). Seated in mourning dress and what would be known in the Victorian period as the 'Marie Stuart' mourning cap, it is only the crucifix at her side and the Elizabethan ruff

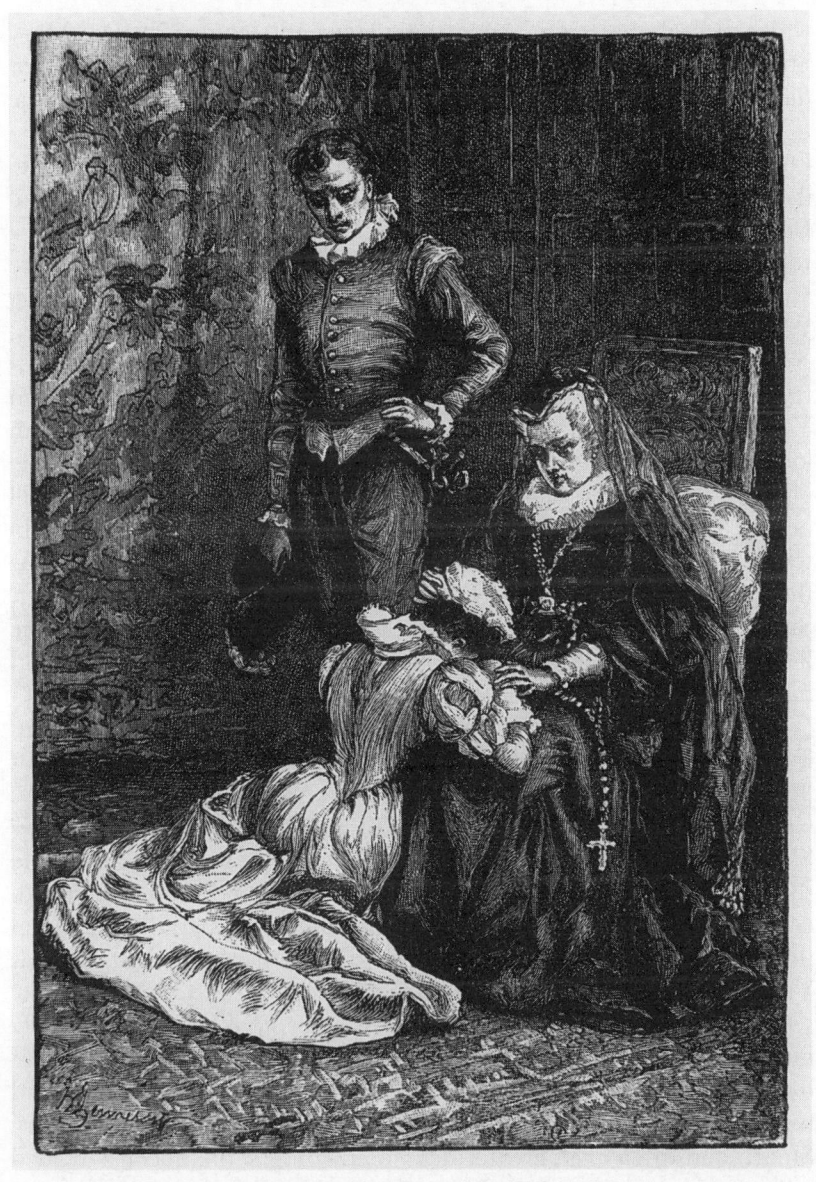

"O mother, how can you ask?"

Figure 6 William Hennessy, illustration to Charlotte M. Yonge's *Unknown to History*, c. 1892.

which reveal that this is not the nineteenth-century queen. Mary Stuart's face and figure appear fuller than in any other eighteenth- or nineteenth-century paintings of her, increasing her resemblance to the matronly figure of Queen Victoria. It is interesting to note that by 1882 Queen Victoria had for many years been witnessing, if not arranging, the dynastic marriages of her own children with the royal families of Europe. In 1881 her grandson Prince William married, and in April 1882 her son Leopold married Helen of Waldeck. Of course, these were always to be spoken of as love matches rather than political alliances. Whether or not the resemblance of Queen Mary to Queen Victoria is a conscious or deliberate one on the part of William Hennessy, it is certainly the case that both the illustration and the scene depicted in Yonge's novel represent Mary, if not *as* Victoria, then as the Victorian ideal of the good mother. No longer bent upon arranged marriages, she gives her blessing to a marriage based on love in which her daughter will be consigned to a man who will protect her and establish a home in which Cicely may rule in the domestic sphere, 'unknown to history'. As the queen admits to Humfrey, the influence of Cicely's foster mother, Susan Talbot, is indelibly marked upon her daughter's nature: 'She lived too long with thy mother to be aught save a homely Cis. I would have made a princess of her, but it passes my powers' (p. 553).

Writing of the public's response to their contemporary royal women in the eighteenth and nineteenth centuries Linda Colley writes that 'female royals, as the public liked to conceive of them, lent yet more weight and heroic stature to the idea of a separate women's sphere'.[56] She is referring to royal women who do not rule in their own right – the series of queen consorts in the mid-eighteenth and early nineteenth centuries before Victoria took the throne in 1837. As argued earlier in this chapter, the case of a queen who rules in her own right, such as Victoria, Mary Stuart, or Elizabeth I, complicated the notion of a safely separable womens' sphere. Separate spheres could not be so easily divided between the husband and wife, and the queen could become divided in herself between the roles of monarch and mother, and between her public and private personae. In Scott's novel of Mary Stuart, and to an even greater degree in Yonge's, the queen's divided self is made apparent through the manner in which she copes with the dilemmas of genealogy in her life: which will be more important, family or dynasty? the happiness of the child, or the assurance of the child's succession or noble genealogy? Yonge's novel moves from an emphasis on family, with the depiction of Cicely's happy life as a child in Susan

Talbot's domestic sphere, to an emphasis on dynasty as Cicely grows to understand the expectations of royal blood, and returns finally to an emphasis upon family at the expense of dynasty at the novel's close.

In the final chapter, set ten years after the execution of Mary, James VI of Scotland is 'under one of his many eclipses of favour' (p. 583) with Queen Elizabeth (James hopes to succeed Elizabeth to the English throne). This leads Elizabeth to remember the claims of Cicely Talbot, and to consider whether she should publicly acknowledge Cicely's lineage (which is still a secret) in order to frustrate James by using Cicely as a pawn in a game of succession.

Cicely had escaped to the continent upon marriage to avoid a fate similar to the Ladies Grey or Arabella Stuart. Wishing to determine Cicely's whereabouts, Queen Elizabeth calls Cicely's foster-brother to court, telling him:

'She is my kinswoman, if so be she is all she calls herself. Now, master Talbot, go not open-mouthed about your work, but tell this lady that if she can prove her kindred to me, and bring evidence of her birth at Lochleven, I will welcome her here, treat her as my cousin the Princess of Scotland, and, it may be, put her on her way to higher preferment, so she prove herself worthy thereof. You take me, sir?' (p. 586)

Elizabeth hints that she may pass the succession through a female line to Cicely, rather than to James. However when Diccon returns from The Hague, where Cicely now has her home with Humfrey, he must tell the English Queen that Cicely gratefully refuses the offer of prospective queendom; 'with deep and humble thanks ... She prays your Grace to leave her in obscurity in The Hague' (p. 587). Elizabeth is incredulous, demanding, 'what is her house to be preferred to mine?', but Diccon answers her by interpreting 'house' not as a genealogy, but as a 'home':

'Her house, madam, is one of those tall Dutch mansions with high roof, and many small windows therein, with a stoop or broad flight of steps below, on the banks of a broad and pleasant canal, shaded with fine elm trees. There I found her on the stoop, in the shade, with two or three children around her; for she is mother to all the English orphans there, and they are but too many. They bring them to her as a matter of course when their parents die and she keeps them till their kindred in England claim them.' (p. 588)

Diccon tells Elizabeth that, 'none knowing her true birth, she is yet well-nigh a princess' among the dwellers of The Hague. Cicely is childless, but as foster-mother to the English orphans she reinforces the maternal and domestic values which she learned from her own foster-mother, Susan Talbot. Refusing Elizabeth's potential offer of the English throne, Cicely rejects matriarchal dynasty for another type of matriarchal inheritance – her 'proper sphere' as wife and (foster-) mother. Remaining 'unknown to history' Cicely solves the problem of a 'divided self': she no longer has to act out the public and private personae of herself as Bride Hepburn/Cis Talbot. In a declaration reminiscent of Fanny Price's, 'I cannot act' in Austen's *Mansfield Park*, Cicely insists, 'I know I cannot feign' (p. 529).

It was Mary Stuart's supposed acting or feigning that J.A. Froude found so reprehensible. In his *History of England* (1856–70) he minutely describes Mary's behaviour at her execution, commenting that it consisted of the 'most brilliant acting throughout'.[57] Of her dress at execution – the white gauze veil, black velvet dress and crimson underskirts – Froude wrote:

The plain grey dress would have sufficed, had she cared only to go through with simplicity the part which was assigned to her. She intended to produce a dramatic sensation, and she succeeded.[58]

It is little wonder that Mary chose to play a different part than that 'which was assigned to her' since that part, chosen by her enemies, would have included confessing herself a murderess and betraying her religion. Instead it is clear that she assumed whatever control and power she could in her final moments in the public sphere, and directed her own chosen role – that of a wronged queen who dies for her faith.

As stated earlier, while some historical accounts of Mary Stuart were distinctly unfavourable, most of the literary and pictorial treatments of Mary's life were sympathetic. Both Walter Scott and Charlotte Yonge present Mary as an ambiguous, even controversial figure, but nevertheless as a woman to be admired. In both their novels, Mary's feigning, her theatricality, is an essential part of her regal identity and status. As she says to Cicely in Yonge's novel, 'when there is need to dissemble, believe in thine own feigning'. It is to Cicely's credit that she cannot learn this lesson, and the novel's values applaud the young princess's complete lack of duplicity which renders her fit for the domestic rather than the national realm. But Yonge and Scott both recognize that it is necessary for a woman in the public gaze to act many parts if she is to keep her identity whole. She must dissemble, and at times believe in her own feigning. Mary Stuart's belief in each of the different roles that she must play is a method of survival for a woman who cannot simply, in the words of Scott's Abbot, 'Be a Queen ... forget you are a woman'.

Scott's *The Abbot* and Yonge's *Unknown to History* presented their nineteenth-century readership with a mirror of matriarchy. The ways in which the gallery of women in both novels reflect and comment upon one another's experience gave nineteenth-century women a mirror in which they could view aspects of their own lives, and the various roles, public and private, that women could play. While Scott and Yonge both champion woman's role in the domestic sphere, the dignity and glamour of Mary Stuart would have offered a tantalizing glimpse into the life of a woman who had to live almost entirely in the public sphere, even while immured in Elizabeth's prisons.

SENTIMENTAL ROMANISM

In 1867 the Dean of Westminster organized an investigation of the tomb vaults under the Abbey, in order to ascertain precisely where the body of James I was buried. In his *Memorials of Westminster Abbey* Dean Stanley records how in their searches through various vaults they found the tomb of Mary Queen of Scots. Her coffin, in the Stuart vault, rested below that of Arabella Stuart, and it is perhaps fitting that the child who had provided Mary with an outlet for her maternal affection during her imprisonment, and who died, as she did, a prisoner, should be buried with her. Of Mary's tomb, Stanley writes that it was:

> revered by devout Scots as the shrine of a canonised saint. 'I hear,' says Demster, thirteen years after the removal of the remains from Peterborough, 'that her bones, lately translated to the burialplace of the kings of England at Westminster are resplendent with miracles.' This probably is the latest instance of a miracle-working tomb in England, and it invests the question of Queen Mary's character with a theological as well as an historical interest.[59]

Froude writes that after Mary's execution, 'Orders had been given that everything which she had worn should be immediately destroyed, that no relics should be carried off to work imaginary miracles'.[60] He dismisses any 'theological interest' that Mary may have aroused as 'imaginary':

> She was a bad woman, disguised in the livery of a martyr, and, if in any sense at all she was suffering for her religion, it was because she had shown herself capable of those detestable crimes which in the sixteenth century appeared to be the proper fruits of it.[61]

For Froude, the crimson of Mary's underdress (the Catholic colour of martyrdom) represents not martyrdom at all but his rendering of Mary as Scarlet Woman in the garb of the 'Scarlet Whore of Rome'. Charlotte Yonge has her fictional Mary defend the charge that she is proclaiming herself a martyr at her execution:

'Nay, sir ... I am not so presumptuous as to call myself saint or martyr; but though you have power over my body, you have none over my soul, nor can you prevent me from hoping that by the Mercy of Him who died for me, my blood and life may be accepted by Him, as offerings freely made for His Church.' (p. 513)

Perhaps part of the difference between Froude's and Yonge's version of Mary's faith is that Yonge was a follower of the Oxford Movement, while Froude *had* been a Tractarian, but had lost his faith when J. H. Newman converted to Catholicism in 1845. The bitterness against the faith that claimed Newman, whose charismatic leadership had influenced the young Froude, is perhaps a reason for the strong bias against Mary Stuart in his writing. Froude may have had a point, however, when he wrote that in his own time Mary had become 'a fitting tutelary saint for the sentimental Romanism of the modern world'.[62] If Mary's was the last tomb in England to be visited for its 'miracle-working' properties – a last vestige of Catholicism appearing in one of the most important churches of a post-Reformation nation – it could also be argued that in the nineteenth century Mary was to some Britons an historical version of the type of interceding saint or martyr which their own Protestant faith could not allow.

Linda Colley has argued that the fascination with contemporary royal women became 'a kind of substitute religion' in Protestant Britain:

In a Roman Catholic country, the cult of the Virgin Mary can satisfy some of this need for an idealisation of conventional female experience. But for the Welsh, the Scots, and the English, this consolation had been officially removed by the Reformation. The remarkable prominence of the female component of the British Royal Family from the end of the eighteenth century right down to the present day, a prominence that has coincided with a gradual decline in church attendance, can be seen in part as a kind of substitute religion, a strictly Protestant version of the cult of the Virgin.[63]

Although more than a 'strictly Protestant' version, I would extend this argument to the cult of Mary Queen of Scots in the eighteenth and nineteenth centuries. Indeed Scott frequently refers to Mary Stuart as 'Our Lady' in *The Abbot* and Yonge refers to her as the 'Queen of Sorrows', both titles for the Virgin Mary. For some women, the figure of Mary Stuart as tragic martyr may have helped to fill the role of the

Virgin Mary which had been lost to them in the Reformation – the figure who is at once familiar to them as a woman, but who may also transform womanhood into something idealized, transcendant.

Back in Westminster Abbey in 1862, Dean Stanley and his fellow investigators had penetrated the vault which contained the coffin of Mary Stuart:

> the presence of the fatal coffin which had received the headless corpse at Fotheringay was sufficiently affecting, without endeavouring to penetrate further into its mournful contents.[64]

They decide to leave the tomb undisturbed, an act of forbearance in a century in which so many attempts, historical and artistic, were made to penetrate further into the 'mournful contents' of her life. Opera, drama, painting, poetry, history and the novel: Mary Stuart is represented through all these genres, and in many guises. Whether as Scarlet Woman, 'tutelary saint', *femme fatale*, mother or queen, the Queen of Scotland was an important member of a genealogy of royal women, of a mirror of matriarchy for nineteenth-century British women.

CHAPTER THREE

Pedigree, nation, race: the case of Disraeli's 'Sybil' and 'Tancred'

> Fancy calling a fellow an adventurer when his ancestors were probably on intimate terms with the Queen of Sheba.[1]

> If the Jews are on their way back to Palestine, could not the Irish be prevailed upon *antiquam exquirer matrem* and emigrate in search of Scota, Pharaoh's daughter?[2]

The above quotation from Bishop Stubbs refers to one of the more fabulous pedigrees in the ancient Irish annals which traces the Irish back to an originating mother in Egypt. In Chapter One I was concerned with the return of the Irish absentees to their estates and ancestral roots – not in Egypt as Bishop Stubbs suggests, but in Ireland. Indeed for some Anglo-Irish absentees, England was a foreign country, and their ancestral origin there may have seemed as remote as the native Irish descent from 'Pharaoh's daughter'. The Ascendancy Colambres in Edgeworth's novel do make a successful return to Ireland with their Irish pedigrees intact and freed from taint. Bishop Stubbs facetiously links the Jews and the Irish as two groups in England whom he would like to see return to their homeland. (Of course in the case of the Irish he is thinking less of absentee landlords and more of the masses of Irish poor who came to England to escape famine.) This return would have been problematic indeed for members of the Diaspora at that time, who had no land to return to. Benjamin Disraeli is one person of Jewish descent who in his mid-twenties made a journey to find his ancestral roots in Palestine, but he then returned to England, eventually to become Prime Minister. Many years after his Grand Tour in the East, Disraeli had Queen Victoria proclaimed Empress of India. Isaiah Berlin has speculated that at this ceremony and in Disraeli's relationship with Victoria, 'the gorgeous trappings of empire, the elephants and the durbars, and all those eastern splendours' reveal something of Disraeli's 'genuine orientalism ... He did half genuinely see Victoria as a great empress and himself as her vizier; she was Semiramis and Titania, Empress of the East and Queen of the Fairies.'[3] In countering anti-Semitic attitudes, Disraeli claimed that his ancestors were 'on intimate terms with the Queen of Sheba'; as Prime Minister he could claim intimacy with the Queen of England and, presiding over her proclamation as Empress of India, he could imaginatively make her his own Queen of Sheba. Disraeli's imaginative conflation of two royal lineages, the modern English and the ancient Eastern, serves to introduce my discussion of two novels in Disraeli's 'Young England' trilogy which have been considered by most critics to be thematically quite disparate; I refer to *Sybil* (1845) and *Tancred* (1847). Robert Blake has written of the trilogy:

> It is probably best to regard the trilogy as expressing two distinct themes. *Tancred* is the vehicle for Disraeli's own highly idiosyncratic views on race and religion ... They really have little connection with the ideas in *Coningsby* and *Sybil*. It is in these two novels that Disraeli's theory of history and the doctrine of Young England are expounded.[4]

Although I would agree that *Sybil* and *Coningsby* do stand together, I would argue that there are stronger connections between these two novels and *Tancred* than is at first apparent. *Tancred* is an exotic tale set in the East, while *Sybil* (which I will be focussing on rather than *Coningsby*) is set in 1840s England at the time of Chartism and workers' unrest. The stories would seem to have little in common, but I shall argue that, as in the example of Disraeli's imaginative conflation of Queen Victoria and the Queen of Sheba, the Eastern and the English elements in these novels impinge crucially upon each other, and do so because of Disraeli's complex and often inconsistent views on lineage and aristocracy.

A common reaction of both Irish and Jews confronting a dominant English culture was to claim an aristocratic lineage anterior to (and therefore considered superior to) the aristocratic pedigrees of the English. As I have discussed in the Introduction and Chapter One, Irish antiquarians proclaimed their people's descent from the ancient kings of Ireland, or even from Pharaoh's daughter, or the Milesians or Scythians; these genealogies were alternatives to an alien English royalty which was claiming ascendancy over their nation. Similarly, Disraeli did not downplay his Jewish ancestry, but proudly proclaimed his descent from an 'unmixed Bedouin race, who had developed a high civilisation at a time when the inhabitants of England were going half-naked, and eating acorns in their woods.'[5]

In *Coningsby* (1844), the second novel of the 'Young England' trilogy, Disraeli further propounds his theories of his own pure and 'unmixed race', which he claims as 'naturally aristocratic'. In this novel the character Sidonia, a powerful, mysterious Jewish financier and philosopher, tells the hero:

The Hebrew is an unmixed race ... An unmixed race of a first-rate organisation are the aristocracy of Nature. Such excellence is a positive fact; not an imagination, a ceremony, coined by poets, blazoned by cozening heralds, but perceptible in its physical advantages, and in the vigour of its unsullied idiosyncracy.[6]

In his biography of Lord George Bentinck (1851) Disraeli writes that, 'The world has by this time discovered that it is impossible to destroy the Jews.' He goes on to argue that this fact 'proves that it is in vain for man to baffle the inexorable law of nature which has decreed that a superior race shall never be destroyed or absorbed by an inferior'. Disraeli then moves the Jews in Britain from their marginalised position to one of centrality; their racial energy and purity should serve as an example to the country:

Thus it will be seen that all the tendencies of the Jewish race are conservative. Their bias is to religion, property, and natural aristocracy: and it should be the interest of statesmen that this bias of a great race should be encouraged, and their energies and creative powers enlisted in the cause of existing society.[7]

Robert Blake has written of Disraeli's beliefs about his ancestry, and of the importance of his 'return' as a Jew to Palestine: 'It was natural that someone of his peculiar temperament – ambitious, egotistical, romantic and introspective – should seek some sort of compensatory myth. This was what he found in the east, above all in Jerusalem and Syria.'[8] However, Blake's description of Disraeli's myth-making as 'compensatory' raises the question of what Disraeli was compensating for. The above quotations from *Coningsby* and *Lord George Bentinck* give no indication that Disraeli felt a need to 'compensate' for his Jewish ancestry; rather than compensating, he seems to be explaining to an unenlightened English population that the Jews should be looked to as a source of racial inspiration and 'natural aristocracy'. Disraeli's 'myth-making' about Jewish ancestry was partly an appropriation of the popular eighteenth- and nineteenth-century orientalist vision of the East as a place of romance and exoticism. As a young man of Regency taste on his Grand Tour, Disraeli seems to have modelled himself specifically on

Byron's presentation of Eastern luxury and sensuality; imitating Byron imitating Eastern princes in his dress and manners. Although he never lost his taste for a touch of the exotic upon sober Victorian tailoring, Disraeli in later life employed these Romantic stereotypes about the East for more far-reaching ends, to make his Judaism more accessible and palatable to an English public as he progressed through political life. His self-identity as an aristocrat and a leader of men lay in his belonging to a race of ancient and pure genealogy which had 'live[d] in the desert and never mixe[d] its blood'.[9] In this chapter I shall refer to many of the stories concerning ancestral, national and racial origins as 'myths'. Myth has been defined as 'a kind of story ... through which a given culture ratifies its social customs or accounts for the origins of human and natural phenomena'.[10] Disraeli's 'myths of origin', both for the English and the Jewish peoples, rely upon his novelistic fictions, and upon his accounts of history and religion. Some of Disraeli's contemporaries may have believed his accounts to be fictional simply in the sense of 'untrue', but Disraeli himself, putting the political expedience of some of his views to one side, seems to have believed in his versions of political and religious history. It is beyond the scope of this study to untangle the facts from the fictions in Disraeli's myth-making; my concern is with the way in which myths of ancestral origin are used as foundations for myths of racial and national origin, and the way in which Disraeli brings the Eastern and English myths together in his own personal and idiosyncratic mythology.

Disraeli imaginatively traced his pedigree back to intimates of the Queen of Sheba, and to the tribes of Israel; later in this chapter I discuss how he also created certain myths or fictions about his own more recent family pedigree, by connecting his family tree with the semi-aristocratic and well-known de Lara family. Biographers have since found these claims to be unsubstantiated.[11] Disraeli's 'myth-making' not only pertains to his own pedigree and race but also interprets English pedigrees and historiography to create a revised English history in *Sybil* and *Tancred*.

SYBIL: BLOOD WILL OUT

Meeting for the first time in the ruins of Marney Abbey, Charles Egremont, the noble protagonist of *Sybil*, and the Chartist agitators Walter Gerard and Stephen Morley, discuss the troubled state of England. Egremont, who has much to learn, comments complacently:

'Well, society may be in its infancy ... but, say what you like, our Queen reigns over the greatest nation that ever existed.'[12] Egremont believes that England is 'the greatest nation'; her people are in a sense a 'chosen people'. In *Tancred*, Disraeli writes of a young Englishman's response to another chosen people – those of the Holy Land. The genealogies of the tribes of Israel in the Torah contribute to that people's definition of themselves as both a race and a nation. As Isaiah Berlin has written: 'All Jews who are at all conscious of their identity as Jews are steeped in history. They have longer memories, they are aware of a longer continuity as a community than any other which has survived.'[13] Disraeli was acutely aware of this need for a people to define themselves through a sense of their collective past, and in his writing he connects with the past through the family lines which can be traced back through the generations.

Questions of pedigree and its relation to race and myth-making in history and politics are common to both *Sybil* and *Tancred* and reveal much about Disraeli's fictions in his life and politics as well as in his novels. Indeed, in Disraeli's case, life, politics, novels and sense of history are extremely difficult to keep distinct. Christopher Harvie has suggested of Disraeli that, 'As a politician he was a cross between the epic narrator and entertainer, and both are callings which demand a belief – however fleeting – in what's being said.'[14] Epic narrators tell the stories of a race or nation which may then become traditional and accepted history, and faith in these stories is what gives a people a sense of nation. John Vincent writes that *Sybil* addresses the question of 'who ought to rule?', and *Tancred* the question 'what to believe?'[15] One question depends upon the other; to know who ought to rule one needs to believe in the story or history that this ruler presents to the nation, and to believe that this ruler deserves a place in that story. In *Sybil* the controversy over 'who ought to rule' is focussed in questions of who has ruled in the past, and why those pedigreed, aristocratic families who did rule then should still rule over a modern England. *Sybil* explores the workings of pedigree, as the following analysis demonstrates.

Sybil, the daughter of Chartist factory worker Walter Gerard, sees an 'impassable gulf' between herself – one of the people – and the noble Charles Egremont, who is the younger brother of the selfish and elitist Lord Marney. The obstacles which must be overcome before they are married at the end of the novel are Sybil's own prejudices against the aristocracy, and her fear that her marriage with Egremont would alienate him from aristocratic society and his own family. The novel moves through aristocratic country houses, Parliamentary machinations, Chartism, rick-burning and factory strikes, towards a breaking down of the prejudices and fear which separate the ruling classes and the people. This dismantling of the barriers between rich and poor is to be realized in the character of Sybil. After her father has been imprisoned for Chartist agitation, she sees that some among 'the people' had actually plotted against him, and she rethinks her own prejudices:

She had seen enough to suspect that the world was a more complicated system than she had preconceived. There was not that strong and rude simplicity in its organisation which she had supposed. The characters were more various, the motives more mixed, the classes more blended, the elements of each more subtle and diversified than she had imagined. (p. 335)

Her conviction that the aristocracy are the enemy is conveniently dispelled before the papers which unexpectedly restore her noble title and vast lands and fortune are discovered. The obstacles are removed from her union with Egremont, who, equally conveniently, has become Lord Marney upon the death of his elder brother.

The discovery of a will which restores title and riches to a poor protagonist, and leaves the way open to marriage and a happy ending is of course a familiar enough feature of eighteenth- and nineteenth-century novels. Nevertheless, Disraeli's inability to resist ennobling his supposedly working-class protagonists annoyed the writer and liberal reformer W. R. Greg in his review of *Sybil* in the *Westminster Review* (September, 1845). He notices 'with severe reprobation ... the low aristocratic feeling which has presided over the conception' of Sybil and Walter Gerard. Greg criticizes Disraeli for being unable to depict Gerard as a 'virtuous, educated Chartist-artizan without making [him] descend with an unbroken pedigree from a Norman baron, – by representing him as proud of his descent, – and as the rightful heir, – and ultimately the successful claimant to an English earldom!'[16] Disraeli also takes care that the good industrialists in *Sybil* – the Traffords – are also of 'gentle blood'. The Traffords run their mill along feudal, patriarchal lines – providing housing, education and places of worship for their workers. Their methods are an example of views promoted by Young England followers who believed that those who rule have duties and responsibilities to the people. Often these views would manifest themselves in a nostalgia for a time in English history before the dissolution of the monasteries. In Disraeli's novel, the Catholic Walter Gerard embodies this nostalgia for the Church's role in providing charity to the people, and the noble estate-owners' duty to care for their tenants in a feudal patriarchal system.

Presumably, industrialists may be the new patriarchs, and John Vincent sees Disraeli as promoting a sort of 'natural' aristocracy in his writings:

> Disraeli's point could not be clearer: there was nothing inherently aristocratic about the British aristocracy, no qualities of blood that might excuse their defects ... Aristocracy, therefore, is neither pedigree nor blood; it is a set of rules to be learned – it is the art of governing by consent, of uniting all hearts. It is a skill not a social position. Egremont, Lord Marney's younger brother, embodies the learning process.[17]

This interpretation of Disraeli's view of the aristocracy is understandable if one sees Disraeli as compensating for the fact that he himself is not of old English pedigree or blood; in that case claims for a meritocracy such as Vincent describes would be valuable to him. But, as I have argued, Disraeli had no need of an old English pedigree, as he believed that by virtue of being Jewish, from 'an unmixed Bedouin race', he was by definition aristocratic. As Isaiah Berlin writes of him; 'It was as fellow-aristocrat that he led the dukes and the baronets against the manufacturers and the Benthamites'.[18] But Vincent's analysis is also belied by the evidence in *Sybil* that Disraeli feels it necessary to ennoble those who seem naturally fit to rule. Long before Sybil's noble title is validated, the adoring village children, impressed by her noble bearing, call her 'the Queen', perhaps furthering the Young England contention that the monarchy should be stronger, because the People feel a closer bond and more immediate communication with the Queen than they do with Government.

Disraeli could not resist conferring nobility upon his favourites in *Sybil*, but what is usually considered a mere mechanism of plot – the discovery of the papers which prove the rights of inheritance – becomes a subplot of importance to the theme of the novel through the character of Baptist Hatton, the Catholic genealogist whose knowledge restores Sybil to her title and inheritance. Like Disraeli, Hatton can also confer nobility, and his method and approach as a genealogist reveal much about the relationship in Disraeli's writing between pedigree and fiction, and about Disraeli's views of pedigree and its place in English history.

If Sybil comes to believe that in this world 'the characters are more various, the motives more mixed, the classes more blended than she had imagined', then there can be no man more appropriate to restore her title and fortune than Baptist Hatton (p. 335). He is, like the Emir Fakredeen in *Tancred* whom I discuss below, an ambiguous and mixed character – scheming and sinister at times, but also imaginative and kind. His relation to Sybil and her father is from the beginning one of both deceit and benevolence. Years before the events referred to in the opening of the novel, Hatton had come into possession of the papers which were proof of Walter Gerard's rights to the lands of Mowbray and Mowbray Castle. Although Hatton had been a friend of Gerard's father, he did not know where the noble-blooded son could be found, and as a result Walter Gerard remained a man of the people, ignorant of the legal feasibility of his claim to inheritance. Hatton was at this time a poor man and his sale of these papers made his fortune, 'by allowing him to settle in the metropolis, pursue his studies, purchase his library and collections' and generally establish himself in business as a genealogical researcher for London society (p. 306). He sold the documents to the current possessor of Mowbray Castle, who employed Hatton to fiddle his pedigree so that with the papers he could then, in effect, buy the title of 'Lord de Mowbray' as well as ensure that this dangerous evidence of the Gerards' rights to the lands could be safely locked in the muniments room of Mowbray Castle. The current Lord de Mowbray is a *parvenu* aristocrat who wishes to veil his own pedigree as 'the son of a footman' by buying the title of lord to complement his lordly wealth and lands, and to clash less with the pedigree of his wife, the daughter of a Duke. Hatton eventually becomes the wealthy and powerful genealogist to the stars of London society. He creates and destroys peers with his genealogical researches; those who come to him are willing to pay well for a 'reworking' of a pedigree which will confer social advancement or inheritance.

Years after writing *Sybil*, Disraeli as Prime Minister would be deluged with claims for peerage. *Sybil* is populated by scheming characters who wait for the current administration to fall in hopes that their turn will finally come for the peerage and other forms of patronage. Disraeli mocks their self-serving tactics and the desperation of characters like Sir Vavasour Firebrace, who wishes Hatton to present his appeal to the crown that baronets have their rights of old restored – the right to wear 'dark green costume' and white plumage in their hats. Support for the party is partly managed by the manipulative Tadpole and Taper, who gather political support by promising (quite falsely) the Governorship of Ireland to the Duke of Fitz-Aquitaine, the Garter to Lord de Mowbray, and the Buckhounds (an office in the Royal Household) to Lord Marney. They all wait for the administration to fall, but as a journalist tells Stephen Morley, the Owenite radical who is in love with Sybil, it is Baptist Hatton who has the power; 'He has made more peers of the realm than our Gracious Sovereign ... and since the reform of parliament the only chance of a tory becoming a peer is the favour of Baptist Hatton' (p. 273). Pedigree becomes political; Hatton's genealogical research creates peers, and he places his clients among the rulers of the nation. This arbitrariness of who will rule as peer may be in part Disraeli's reflections upon Pitt, who created many peers, and as John Vincent puts it, 'diluted the peerage wholesale'.[19]

Charles Egremont's claim to nobility is the product of a 'mystification' or a process of fictionalizing pedigree similar to that employed by Baptist Hatton, except that Egremont's dates from the sixteenth century. The founder of the family, one Baldwin Greymount, was 'a confidential domestic of one of the favourites of Henry VIII'. As an Ecclesiastical Commissioner, he was employed in the taking and sacking of monasteries, by means of which he eventually became a wealthy and landed proprietor. Over the centuries a Greymount was elevated to the peerage, and in time:

The heralds furnished his pedigree, and assured the world that although the exalted rank and extensive possessions enjoyed at present by the Greymounts had their origin immediately in the great territorial revolutions of a recent date, it was not for a moment to be supposed, that the remote ancestors of the Ecclesiastical Commissioner of 1530 were by any means obscure. On the contrary, it appeared that they were both Norman and baronial, their real names Egremont, which, in their patent of peerage the family now resumed. (p. 12)

He writes of another of Hatton's clients: 'So that however recent was his date as an English earl, he might figure on the roll as a Plantagenet baron, which in the course of another century would complete the grand mystification of high nobility' (p. 307). In *Sybil*, Disraeli describes both this process of pedigree invention and the current account of English history as a 'mystification', and the invention of family history is crucially connected to national history:

If the history of England be ever written by one who has the knowledge and the courage, and both qualities are equally requisite for the undertaking, the world would be more astonished than when reading the Roman annals of Niebuhr. Generally speaking, all the great events have been distorted, most of the important causes concealed, some of the principal characters never appear, and all who figure are so misunderstood, and misrepresented, that the result is a complete mystification ... (p. 17).

Those who have pedigree, whether it is truly 'old blood' or that supplied by the creations of Baptist Hatton or the inventions of a new administration, are at this time often those who are involved in the politics of the nation. As policy-makers the peers help create the story which the nation will eventually call its history. In *Sybil*, pedigree, politics and history are all intrinsically connected, and they are symbolically and practically brought together in the genealogist Hatton.

Hatton is the great fictionalizer within Disraeli's fiction. Consulted by peers, politicians and lawyers, and living in the Inner Temple, he is very much at the centre of things. Yet he is presented as a cool, impassive observer of men's frenzied attempts to buy future ambitions from one who will provide them with a family past. Hatton is partly an outsider because he is a Catholic, but there is also an exotic, rather artistic quality about him. This is no dry-as-dust antiquarian, but a clever businessman who, like Disraeli, is romantically and imaginatively inspired by old pedigrees. Like the Whig historian whom Disraeli describes above, Hatton's profession at times requires that he distort great events, conceal important causes, and repress principal characters in his researches into pedigree. Like the biased historian, who manipulates the facts for his party line, Hatton manipulates the branches of a pedigree for the sake of his client. Often, as in the opposing claims of Lord de Mowbray and Walter Gerard, he may change the interpretation of his facts to suit the particular claim he is working on, perhaps reversing a former claim he defended. But is Hatton purely motivated by the money he receives for these distorted pedigrees, in the same way that the unscrupulous historian or politician is motivated by what is politically expedient? Hatton is a brilliant and artistic figure; the dry facts of a pedigree inspire him to create fictions for his clients, and he takes pride in his imaginative, inventive artistry. But he is never more inspired about his work than when he decides to reverse the claim that made his fortune years ago, and to prove that Walter Gerard is the true Lord de Mowbray. Hatton can be a sinister schemer, who laughs scornfully behind the backs of those *parvenu* aristocrats who have paid him for their titles. He works Gerard's claim for no recompense, because he is moved and inspired when he comes across a family which is truly of the 'old blood' and the 'old faith'.

Hatton is also moved by Sybil's beauty, and he plots a potential future for the Gerards which is a confused mixture of admiration for their old pedigree and a desire to himself figure in their family tree:

'Let me see – let me see. I could make her a baroness. Gerard is as much Baron Valence as Shrewsbury is a Talbot. Her name is Sybil. Curious how, even when peasants, the good blood keeps the good old family names! The Valences were ever Sybils ... Could I do more? ... What if my son were to be Lord Valence? ... To build up a great Catholic house again; of the old blood, and the old names and the old faith – by holy Mary it is a glorious vision!' (pp. 293–4)

After indifferently creating stories through pedigree for others, the combination of Sybil's beauty, the old faith and old family move Hatton to begin creating plots and stories around the future of his own pedigree. An old lineage such as the Gerards' combines both personal and national history; through the stories of individuals in this Catholic family, English history at least as old as the Crusades comes alive. This clearly strikes the imagination of both Hatton and Disraeli.

The destruction of the monasteries is a critical theme in *Sybil*. It is involved with Young England's vision of a country that would rediscover the central role of the pre-Reformation Church in society – in the form of landlords, educators, providers of refuge and charity for the poor – and it also related to Disraeli's ideas about the telling of history. For Disraeli, the Reformation was a crisis point when England had to change its story about itself as a nation, having to call its religious traditions, its Church and even its queen by a different name. For those among the old families who would not concur there was the threat of annihilation of their name and title through the loss of their lands. Disraeli looks back to this period of the Reformation – much further than the contemporary Whig historian he criticises – to reveal what he sees as the shams and destruction which the English people have been taught to believe is a proud national history. Walter Gerard explains this to Charles Egremont when they meet for the first time outside the ruins of Marney Abbey:

'And now 'tis all over', said the stranger, 'and travellers come and stare at these ruins and think themselves very wise to moralize over time. They are the children of violence, not of time. It is war that created these ruins, civil war, of all our civil wars the most inhuman, for it was waged with the unresisting. The monasteries were taken by storm, they were sacked, gutted, battered with warlike instruments, blown up with gunpowder; you may see the marks of the blast against the new tower here. Never was such a plunder ... nor has England ever lost this character of ravage.' (p. 74)

The monastery ruins, mellowed with time, are deceptive; like the gentler account of English history which has been sold to the nation, the ivied walls and grassy mounds of these ruins hide the violence and destruction, the gunpowder blasts and batterings perpetrated against them.

This version of history 'mystifies' or paints over the awkward facts in the national story of 'the greatest nation'. Like the mystifications of pedigree which Hatton performs, it is not a genuine history according to Disraeli; the ruins are a relatively new destruction, not the result of the gentle ravages of time, and the Egremonts were not Norman knights, but plain Greymounts employed as 'confidential domestics' as recently as the reign of Henry VIII.

Eric Hobsbawm and Terence Ranger have called this historical obfuscation the 'invention of tradition' in their edited anthology of that name. Eric Hobsbawm defines 'invented tradition' as:

A set of practices, normally governed by overtly or tacitly accepted rules and of a ritual or symbolic nature, which seek to inculcate certain values and norms of behaviour by repetition, which automatically implies continuity with the past. In fact, where possible, they normally attempt to establish continuity with a suitable historical past. A striking example is the deliberate choice of a Gothic style for the nineteenth-century rebuilding of the British parliament.[20]

The battered ruins of Marney Abbey place this building in what Hobsbawm describes as the 'assumed mists of time'; as with the Gothic style of the rebuilt parliament buildings, the ruins of Marney Abbey and the invented pedigrees of Baptist Hatton are given an aura of antiquity which they do not rightfully possess, and this assumed age corresponds with a 'suitable historical past'. Like a fake antique sold in the market, a biased and falsified history is being fobbed off on the English people as something old, when it is of quite recent date according to Disraeli. False antiquity has been used as a ploy to give this version of history the authority of age. Disraeli wishes to expose what he believes is a false national history.

Disraeli's character Baptist Hatton would also like to rewrite English history by restoring a Catholic family to the land they owned before the Reformation. Through *Sybil*, Disraeli reveals the strife and division of the Reformation which has, as he sees it, been excised from officially accepted accounts of English history. He then fictionally reconciles the two factions of this 'civil war' which resulted from the destruction of the monasteries, by uniting Egremont and Sybil; Egremont is a descendant of an Ecclesiastical Commissioner who made his fortune through confiscation of Catholic lands, while Sybil is a Catholic whose family lands had been confiscated at that very time.

It could be said that Disraeli and his creation Baptist Hatton are in somewhat similar positions. Both have 'stories' to weave around certain historical facts; Hatton weaves his fictions around certain facts of genealogy, and Disraeli around certain facts of genealogy and history. These inventive tactics are related to the processes of organising fiction itself. In fiction, and especially in the novel, plots and subplots contend, like the greater and lesser branches of a family tree or different versions of history, for supremacy. At times a minor character from a lesser branch of the family can rise to threaten or destroy the noble protagonist. Family skeletons-in-the-closet are suppressed, often springing out of the closet at awkward times in the novel's plot, just as in Hatton's researches; a lesser branch of a pedigree may threaten the title of the main branch because Hatton has chosen to promote the claim of the lesser through his research. Disraeli claims that the same is true of history:

> A remarkable feature of our written history is the absence in its pages of some of the most influential personages. Not one man in a thousand for instance has ever heard of Major Wildman: yet he was the soul of English politics in the most eventful period in this kingdom ... But he was the leader of an unsuccessful party. (pp. 17–8)

Major Wildman was a political figure ignored by the historians. In *Sybil* Disraeli writes his own revisionist version of England's history in which he privileges characters who may have gone unacknowledged before. The novel combines pages of Disraeli's reinterpretation of recent political history with the acknowledgement, through the fictional characters of Sybil and her father, of the ancestral claims of a marginalized Catholic family. He intends to write upon the pages of history both as a re-writer or re-interpreter, and as one who actively writes himself into a new history through his own political actions. He does not intend to become a Major Wildman, erased from written history. In writing *Sybil*, Disraeli was attempting both to give a Tory account of history, and to further his own political career – his own making of history – through his promotion of the Young England movement.

Disraeli is setting out to write a revisionist history within the form of fiction. His fictional creation, Baptist Hatton, is capable of revising history by re-introducing or even 'fictionalizing' the genealogies with which he works. There is a possibility that Hatton's creative genealogies might undermine the reader's trust in Disraeli's revisionist history; if Hatton can so easily manipulate the details of a pedigree to suit his business purposes, then should we trust the interpretation and manipulation of the facts of English history in the hands of Hatton's creator? A revised history gives a nation an alternative narrative by which it can partially define itself as a nation; but Hatton's work seems to imply that there can be a multiplicity of narratives from which to choose. Presumably, Disraeli believes that his alternative account of history is the true one, but the manipulations of Baptist Hatton within Disraeli's story introduce an element of the arbitrary and of possible alternatives which could undermine the author's version. Moreover, Disraeli is not consistent in his definition of aristocracy and of who should rule. Egremont expresses to Sybil his convictions concerning who ought to rule England; his impassioned eloquence in the following much-quoted passage seems to indicate that he functions as Disraeli's mouthpiece here:

'The People are not strong; the People can never be strong. Their attempts at self-vindication will end only in their suffering and confusion... The new generation of the aristocracy in England are not tyrants, not oppressors... as you persist in believing... They are the natural leaders of the People, Sybil; believe me they are the only ones.' (pp. 319–20)

If, as John Vincent writes, Disraeli 'could not be clearer' that aristocracy is something that can be learned and that 'there was nothing inherently aristocratic about the British aristocracy', then who are these 'natural leaders' of whom Egremont is speaking? Whether consciously or not, Disraeli as author is just as able to 'mystify' us about the identity of the English aristocracy as is Baptist Hatton or the Whig historian whom Disraeli denigrates. Like a good politician and tactician he exhibits a wonderful flexibility in his opinions on who the 'natural' leaders of England are. Obviously, he includes himself among those who should lead, and, as I have indicated, he interprets his racial background as aristocratic.

With the flair of a Baptist Hatton, Disraeli also 'interprets' his own more recent pedigree, and this version of his ancestry serves to introduce *Tancred* (1847), Disraeli's favourite novel, and the novel with which he seems to have identified most closely. The hero, who travels from England to the East, as did the young Disraeli, is a scion of one of England's oldest aristocratic families. Disraeli cannot endow himself with English blue blood, but he can write a novel about a young aristocrat who travels (as he did) to seek inspiration in the East, and who hopes (as he eventually did) to return to England with the authority and almost divine sanction to enter Parliament and to become a leader of the nation. While propounding his theories in *Tancred* of the Jewish people being 'naturally aristocratic', Disraeli also brings together the Eastern

Figure 7 'New Crowns for Old Ones!' cartoon from *Punch*, 15 April 1876.

Figure 8 'Empress and Earl, or One Good Turn Deserves Another', cartoon from *Punch*, 26 August 1876.

and English aristocracy in a similar fashion to the way in which he would, in later life, imaginatively conflate the Queen of Sheba and Queen Victoria.

As a number of critics and biographers have noted, the relationship between Victoria and Disraeli had an air of romance which Disraeli fostered and which the Queen clearly enjoyed; he was her knight, her vizier. The two well-known *Punch* illustrations included in this chapter satirically illustrate this romantic version of the relationship between the Queen and her Prime Minister. The cartoon entitled 'New Crowns for Old Ones!' (*Punch*, 15 April 1876, see fig. 7) which refers to Disraeli's long and difficult campaign to win for the Queen her much-coveted title 'Empress of India', indicates that a Victorian readership was very much aware of this romantic partnership. The fact that Disraeli's slogan ('New Crowns for Old Ones!') is an adaptation of the street cry of old clothes-men in the proverbially Jewish rag trade is obviously intended to work partly as a racial slur upon Disraeli and generally to diminish the worth of the Eastern crown upon which both Victoria and her devoted knight placed so much value. The slogan is also an allusion to the story of *Aladdin*, and perhaps on some level the cartoon is acknowledging Disraeli's Scheherazade-like power to create stories inspired by the East. Both of the *Punch* cartoons present Disraeli (however satirically) in the role of aristocrat: in 'New Crowns for Old Ones!' it is both Victoria and Disraeli who are holding crowns, and in 'Empress and Earl' a few months later (*Punch*, 26 August 1876, see fig. 8) Disraeli, who considers himself 'naturally' noble by virtue of his Eastern blood, is in the process of being crowned into an English aristocracy by the English queen to whom he recently gave an Eastern nobility.

In *Tancred*, English and Eastern aristocracies are joined in a romantic union when the English nobleman Tancred and the Jewish princess Eva fall in love. The projected union, racial, religious and romantic, of these noble lineages is the concern of the following analysis of this novel.

TANCRED: DISRAELI AS THE NEW CRUSADER

What is the use of belonging to an old family unless to have the authority of an ancestor ready for every prejudice, religious or political, which your combinations may require?[21]

In the preface to the collected edition of his father's writings entitled, 'On the Life and Writings of Mr. Disraeli by His Son', Disraeli gives a brief biography of his father. The account of Disraeli's nearest ancestor is detailed and we can assume, factual, but the biography's opening account of his more remote ancestors fades into mythical haze. Disraeli 'mystifies' or fictionalizes much of his pedigree, whether consciously or not. He claims that his family were descended from 'one of those Hebrew families whom the Inquisition forced to emigrate from the Spanish peninsula at the end of the fifteenth century'. They fled to Venice where, 'undisturbed and unmolested, they flourished as merchants for more than two centuries under the protection of the lion of St. Mark, which was but just, as the patron saint of the Republic was himself a child of Israel'.[22] (It is a very common gesture on Disraeli's part to remind his English audience that the fathers of Christianity, including Christ himself, were Jewish; I shall discuss this further below.) Disraeli writes that after his grandfather settled in England his family married into the families of the Laras and the Villa Reals; these were famous and venerable old Jewish-Portuguese families. As I noted at the beginning of this chapter, scholars have shown that this account is largely fictional. It was also important to Disraeli to stress that his family were Sephardic Jews rather than Ashkenazi. Of this Robert Blake writes:

There was in Disraeli's day, and long after, a notion that the Sephardi Jews were more 'aristocratic,' whatever that may mean, than the Ashkenazi who came from central and Eastern Europe. Disraeli was undoubtedly a Sephardi ... What matters is that he believed that his origins were highly aristocratic and the belief had no small effect on his political outlook and his political career.[23]

In discussing Disraeli, Blake is satirically uncertain of what constitutes 'aristocracy'. But Disraeli insists upon the inherent aristocracy of the Jews and particularly of the Sephardi, as in exchanges such as the following in *Tancred* between the hero and his Italian guide, Baroni. Tancred is surprised to learn that Baroni is Jewish:

'You do not mean that you, too, are Jews?'
'Pure Sephardim, in nature and in name.'
'But your name surely is Italian?'
'Good Arabic, my lord. Baroni – that is, the son of Aaron; the name of old clothesmen in London and of Caliphs at Bagdad.' (p. 336)

The extent to which *Tancred* is at times a deeply personal defence of the author is evident if, for instance, in reading the above dialogue one remembers that during election speeches hecklers had nicknamed Disraeli 'Old Clothes'. *Tancred* is a novel strangely divided between the English aristocracy, and the 'natural' or spiritual aristocracy which

Disraeli claims for Eastern peoples. The first part of the book is set, as are much of *Coningsby* and *Sybil*, in the country houses and smart London addresses of the English nobility. After leaving Oxford, Tancred Montacute, the only son of adoring parents, the Duke and Duchess of Bellamont, refuses to take up his expected place in Parliament and wishes instead to travel to the Holy Land. Tancred believes that this land has unique spiritual qualities because it is the only place where God has spoken directly with man, and where God assumed the form of man. As he explains to his father:

'Our castle has before this sent forth a De Montacute to Palestine. For three days and three nights he knelt at the tomb of his Redeemer. Six centuries and more have elapsed since that great enterprise. It is time to restore and renovate our communications with the most High.' (p. 55)

Tancred is descended from a Crusader knight and a member of the oldest English aristocracy but he feels that this is not enough to give him the right to enter Parliament to become one of the nation's leaders. In fact Tancred seems completely uninterested in entering Parliament. At a dinner party before he leaves for Jerusalem he meets Coningsby and Charles Egremont, brought together from the first two novels of the trilogy. They try to enlist him among their ranks – a fictional version of the Young England movement. But Tancred decides shortly afterwards to leave for Jerusalem, where he wishes to kneel at the Holy Sepulchre to ask, 'What is Duty, and what is Faith? – What ought I to do, and what ought I to believe?' (p. 55). Something is keeping Tancred from the ability to *do*, from the ability to participate in the active life of politics. His crusading ancestors had faith and that motivated them to act. Tancred believes that the creed of his family line needs restoration and rejuvenation before he can act as scion and representative of that noble pedigree.

Here Disraeli anticipates the works of later nineteenth-century novelists who were concerned with degeneration. Tancred's feeling that his family's faith and ability to act have become worn out is reminiscent of concerns in Hardy's writing. An example of this is Angel Clare's attitude to Tess in *Tess of the D'Urbervilles*, when he rejects her after her confession:

'I think that parson who unearthed your pedigree would have done better if he had held his tongue. I cannot help associating your decline as a family with this other fact – of your want of firmness. Decrepit families imply decrepit wills, decrepit conduct.'[24]

Sidonia, the wealthy Jewish financier modelled partly on Baron Rothschild, encourages Tancred to go to Jerusalem, giving him letters of introduction and credit. Sidonia believes that 'All is race; there is no other truth' (p. 149), and that a race will inevitably degenerate if it mixes its blood. In answer to a question about the degeneration of the Spaniards' power – 'The race is the same; why are not the results the same?' – Sidonia replies:

'Because it is worn out... Why do not the Ethiopians build another Thebes or excavate the colossal temples of the cataracts? The decay of a race is an inevitable necessity, unless it lives in deserts and never mixes its blood.' (p. 150)

With a mixture of Norman and Anglo-Saxon blood in his veins, Tancred may be from a pure aristocratic line in England, but he cannot hope for the racial purity of Sidonia. Sidonia has the energy of his unadulterated race – he is behind the political and financial dealings of Europe; like a 'spider in its web' he lies at the centre of things, quietly and crucially active. Tancred comes from a tired pedigree in a tired race. He can only hope that a pilgrimage to the Holy Land will restore a spiritual energy, and dispel, as Hardy later described it, 'the chronic melancholy which is taking hold of the civilized races with the decline of belief in a beneficent Power'.

Tancred travels in the Holy Land, and 'pours forth [his] passionate prayers at all its holy places' (p. 262), but he does not receive the sign from God that he had hoped for. As he is travelling to Sinai he is captured by Bedouins and becomes involved in a very complicated ransom plot fabricated by the arch-schemer of the novel, the young Emir Fakredeen, who;

possessed all the qualities of the genuine Syrian character in excess; vain, susceptible, endowed with a brilliant though frothy imagination, and a love of action so unrestrained that restlessness deprived it of energy, with so fine a taste that he was always capricious, and so ingenious that he seemed ever inconsistent. (p. 213)

Fakredeen claims that he is an Arab and a Christian. He has been brought up as foster-child to the Jewish financier Besso, who is the father of the beautiful and philosophical Eva, with whom Tancred falls in love. Fakredeen becomes devotedly attached to Tancred, for whose imprisonment he was responsible, and they eventually join forces with a plan to unite all Arabs in a great Arabian empire. Tancred declares, 'a man might climb Mount Carmel, and utter three words which would bring the Arabs again to Granada, and perhaps further'.

From our current political perspective, Disraeli's lack of discrimination between Arabs and Jews may seem odd, as for example when Tancred's guide Baroni proclaims that, 'The Arabs are only Jews on horseback' (p. 253). And in *Coningsby* Disraeli writes:

Doubtless, among the tribes who inhabit the bosom of the Desert, progenitors alike of the Mosaic and the Mohammedan Arabs, blood may be found as pure as that of the descendants of the Scheik Abraham.[25]

The Arabs are 'Jews on horseback' and the Jews are 'Mosaic Arabs'; the peoples who are today defined, still perhaps with some uncertainty, as Arabs and Jews are both, for Disraeli, desert tribes of 'unmixed' blood. This idea becomes more complex and fraught when considering Disraeli's 'great apparent earnestness', according to Edward Stanley, over 'restoring the Jews to their own land'. Stanley records that Disraeli outlined plans for a Jewish nation to him, confiding to him that, 'A man who should carry them out would be the next Messiah, the true Saviour of his people.'[26]

Unencumbered by twentieth-century knowledge of the 'Middle East Question', Tancred is inspired by the East to think politically, and for the first time to make active political plans. Having as yet received no sign from God, he explains to Fakredeen that he has passive, not active faith. But his trust that there is such a thing as faith, and that it truly originated among the Arab peoples, inspires the impressionable Fakredeen, at least momentarily. Tancred was unable to work towards a political goal in England, shunning the thought of his entry into the House of Lords. In the Holy Land, Fakredeen's almost unthinking love of action supplies Tancred with energy. But how is one to reconcile Tancred's tired pedigree, tired race and passive faith with his plans, like those of T. E. Lawrence years later, to fight in the desert and unite the Arab peoples? Disraeli's peculiar views on religion and race obviously needed some kind of escape clause or reasoning to make them palatable, both politically and religiously, to the English reading public. As a baptised Jew, Disraeli had an idiosyncratic and conveniently synthetic way of looking at the Church of England; 'For myself, I look upon the Church as the only Jewish institution that remains'.[27] This view lies behind Tancred's comment to Fakredeen:

'I am an Arab only in religion – but the consciousness of creed sustains me. I know well, though born in a distant and northern isle, that the creator of the world speaks with man only in this land: and that is why I am here.' (p. 260)

Elsewhere in this novel it is repeated that God has in the past spoken only to an Arab. Disraeli once said, 'I am the blank page between the Old Testament and the New.'[28] If so, then he is now writing his own Apocrypha in that blank page when, in *Tancred*, his hero receives a divine vision on Mount Sinai. In this miraculous vision, an 'angel of Arabia' tells Tancred that the earth is about to break forth into new multitudes, new generations, and that once again these spiritually and intellectually primitive people (Europeans) must take their spiritual philosophy from Arabia. He tells Tancred; 'Cease then to seek in a vain philosophy the solution of the social problem that perplexes you. Announce the sublime and solacing doctrine of theocratic equality' (p. 291). It is ideas that are divine and do not pass away, the angel instructs. Presumably, Tancred should now go forth and deliver these instructions to the degenerate and tired European races, but after descending from Mount Sinai and suffering an acute attack of brain fever, which the beautiful Jewess Eva cures (shades of Sir Walter Scott's Rebecca), he remains in the East, still planning a united Arabia with Fakredeen.

This is potent stuff. After *Coningsby* and *Sybil*, in which the respective heroes went through a learning process which prepared them to take their places as English rulers, we might expect the same for Tancred. The first third of the novel, set in England, would seem to augur that Tancred's journey to the Holy Land would eventually bring him back to England with some answers to his questions and with some new ideas about how to improve the so-called 'Condition of England'. Disraeli allows an Englishman a divine vision, and we expect him to return with it for the betterment of England. (Disraeli did not make Tancred a young *Jewish* Englishman; this might have seemed rather too transparent for his reading public.) However, rather than solutions, divine or otherwise, to England's troubles, the novel lacks closure, lacks any solutions that may be expected from an ambitious political author who has in previous works propounded his theories. *Tancred* has no conclusion as such, and the theme of pilgrimage and return is aborted. Rather than returning, Tancred is on the point of committing himself further to the Holy Land at the end of the novel, as he proposes to Eva and awaits her reply. Suddenly cries are heard, calling for Tancred, and the last sentence of the novel reveals that Tancred's parents, 'The Duke and Duchess of Bellamont had arrived at Jerusalem' (p. 487).

Critics of *Tancred* have often ridiculed this bathetic ending. It is a strangely abrupt and anticlimactic close not only to the novel but to the 'Young England' trilogy as a whole. But there are perhaps elements of the last chapter which hint at how this ending should be read. Tancred discovers Eva in the garden, and she tells him, 'sorrowfully':

'I have a vague impression that there have been heroic aspirations wasted, and noble energies thrown away ... Your feelings cannot be what they were before all this happened, when you thought only of a divine cause, of stars, of angels, and of our peculiar and gifted land. No, no; now it is all mixed up with intrigue and politics, and management, and cunning arts of men. You may be, you are, free from all this, but your faith is not the same. You no longer believe in Arabia.' (pp. 484–5)

Tancred vows to her that *she* is his Arabia, and that he believes in her, but that is hardly the answer that we, or Eva, expected to the grand questions with which Tancred came to the Holy Land – 'What ought I to do, and what ought I to believe?' While *Coningsby* and *Sybil* both end on confident notes, *Tancred* seems to admit a failure to keep firm ideological faith when trying to rule or 'manage' a nation politically. Tancred has very much returned to the world of men when he replaces the divine angel of Arabia with Eva. And if he cannot sustain that immediate belief in divine intervention and communication in the Holy Land, then we can scarcely imagine him translating it into Victorian English politics. Indeed, this is the greater part of the disturbing inconclusiveness of the novel's final sentence. It seems impossible that the Duke and Duchess of Bellamont could be in Jerusalem; their world of English aristocratic politics and Church of England values seems completely incommensurate with Eva's much more ancient, and as Sidonia would say, more racially pure 'aristocracy'.

It seems that Tancred's faith cannot be imported to England, and his desire to marry Eva is left unanswered because they come from two different worlds, and from incommensurate aristocratic lineages. Unlike the wedding of Sybil and Egremont, ostensibly a union of 'the two nations', the situation of Tancred and Eva is not converted into a happy union. Were they to be united, Eva's children would begin what Sidonia has described as racial degeneration. She would be mixing her blood not with 'Arabs of the deserts', but with a northern European. There seem to be no answers for Tancred, no possibility of his return with answers for English society, and therefore no possibility of closure for this strange novel, the last of Disraeli's trilogy.

It is interesting to conjecture about a possible connection between the lack of a marriage between Eva and Tancred and Disraeli's own marriage. Disraeli had been happily married to Mary Anne (formerly

Mary Anne Wyndham Lewis, the widow of Disraeli's former political partner) for eight years upon the publication of *Tancred*. Mary Anne was not Jewish, and Disraeli had been baptised into the Church of England as a child. But Disraeli's views about the racial purity of the Jews are never touched upon as regards his private life; he never refers to the question of race in his own marriage, or considers his marriage as exogamous. Mary Anne had no children by her first husband, and she and Disraeli were childless. If they had had children, these children would have been Christian, even if Disraeli had retained the Jewish faith, because Judaism is a matrilineal inheritance. Perhaps this was in Mary Anne's mind when, before travelling abroad with Disraeli in 1845, she rushed into the drawing room and into the arms of a disconcerted Charlotte de Rothschild, breathlessly explaining that she had written a will leaving all her property to Charlotte's six-year-old daughter Evelina. According to Charlotte, Mary Anne had confided to her:

'Disi and I may be blown up on the railroad or in the steamer, there is not a human body that loves me in this world, and besides my adored husband I care for no one on earth, but I love your glorious race ... I love the Jews – I have attached myself to your children and she is my favourite.'[29]

Perhaps the childless and romantic Mary Anne, inspired by her husband's Judaism, sought to bestow her own matrilineal inheritance upon a female Jewish child, passing something of herself down through Jewish blood lines. Was this her own 'compensatory myth' for the fact that she herself was a racial outsider to the 'glorious race' which her husband presented (and represented in his own person) as exotic, powerful and brilliant? This is necessarily conjecture, because nothing has been written about how Disraeli's concept of 'unmixed blood' figured in his and Mary Anne's private life. As I have argued, if Eva and Tancred were to marry, their children would be Jewish through a matrilineal inheritance, but no longer 'racially unmixed'; this quandary at the end of *Tancred* is left unresolved. To give the novel the closure which critics have so often demanded, Disraeli would have had to confront issues of exogamous marriage and racial purity. His resolution of these difficulties, when one considers the championing of unmixed Jewish pedigree throughout *Tancred*, would have been either inconsistent with the rest of the novel, or would have run the risk not only of hurting his wife, but also of offending his English readership.

Baptist Hatton, of *Sybil*, and the Emir Fakredeen, of *Tancred*, are both storytellers. Hatton makes genealogical fictions out of pedigrees, and

Fakredeen exhibits a similar manipulative flair with his pedigree, race and creed. This is necessary if he wishes to unite 'Arabia'; even his own family of Shehaab is divided into different religions, and the people he wants to unite are of numerous creeds. He wishes for some symbol which could serve to bring them together; as he says, 'the cross, the crescent, the arc, or an old stone, anything would do' (p. 258). Instead, he uses himself in place of a unifying symbol, to stand for whatever is politically expedient at the time. He tells Tancred that he is a Christian; Tancred relates this to Baroni and the phlegmatic guide replies, 'I have known a good many Shehaabs, and if you will tell me their company, I will tell you their creed' (p. 260). Disraeli exhibits a versatility and imaginativeness on the subject of religion which is in some ways similar to Fakredeen's, as for example when he declares the Church of England to be a 'Jewish institution'. In a letter, a draft of which he kept in his papers at home at Hughenden, he wrote, presumably to a clergyman:

For myself, I look upon the Church as the only Jewish institution that remains, and irrespective of its being the depository of divine truth, [I] must ever cling to it as the visible means which embalms the memory of my race, their deeds and thoughts, and connects their blood with the origin of things.[30]

And in his biography *Lord George Bentinck* Disraeli enumerates what Christians owe to Judaism:

The Saxon, the Sclave, and the Celt have adopted most of the laws and many of the customs of these Arabian tribes, all their literature and all their religion. The toiling multitude rest every seventh day by virtue of a Jewish law; they are perpetually reading 'for their example' the records of Jewish history and singing the odes and elegies of Jewish poets; and they daily acknowledge on their knees, with reverent gratitude, that the only medium of communication between creator and themselves is the Jewish race. Yet they treat them as the vilest of generations.[31]

In *Tancred*, Fakredeen's flexibility over questions of religion, race and family are an odd mixture of political expedience and genuine, if shifting, belief. Political expedience could have led Disraeli to play down his Judaism, but clearly he vaunted his ancestry. His views on religion were firmly grounded, unlike those of his fictional Shehaab. Disraeli's placing of Judaism at the centre of Christianity was certainly a clever (and politically tactical) move, but it was a perspective on his ancestry in which, as is evident from his letters, novels and his biography of Bentinck, he fully trusted.

As a politician and as a writer Disraeli believed in the power of storytelling. A nation needs a story in which it can invest itself imaginatively, and Disraeli wished to supply this to Britain, both through his novels' Tory interpretation of history and the future that they held out as possible for the nation. His narratives entered all parts of his life, from his own personal history, with his version of his pedigree, to the 'myth-making' over his race and creed. For the Jewish nation, the Torah's story of the tribes of Israel unites their pedigree, race, creed and history. Disraeli understood the power of this combination, and when he said, 'I am the blank page between the Old Testament and the New', he meant to write on that page a new history of England, with himself written into that history. The 'adaptability' or creativity of Hatton and Fakredeen, their ability to include or exclude branches of a pedigree or certain races and creeds at will, does make them ambivalent characters. But their artistic imagination is a necessary quality to lead a nation, and to create the stories which help the nation define itself as such.

In his essay, 'Nations and Novels: Disraeli, George Eliot and Orientalism', Patrick Brantlinger focusses upon the relationship between nation and narrative. His essay responds in part to work on the subject by Homi Bhabha, and by Jonathan Arac and Harriet Ritvo.[32] Of their work he writes:

The contributors to both express some version of the theme that modern nation-states are the main sites for the production of literatures, and that these literatures are therefore, whether explicitly or implicitly, consciously or unconsciously, imbued with nationalism. A corollary is that the development of the modern nation-state and that of the novel were not just simultaneous occurrences, but in some sense codeterminant.[33]

I would agree with Brantlinger that the nation's relationship with narrative may be more complex than this. One example of the complexity of nationalist novels is the case of Edgeworth's *The Absentee* explored in Chapter One; this novel covertly wrestles with the difficult question of which nation's nationalism we are reading – Ireland's or England's? Brantlinger describes this quandary as ' "conflicting nationalisms"; novels that express Scottish or Irish or Nigerian nationalisms involve more or less explicit critiques of English nationalism/imperialism.'[34]

The case of *Tancred* is yet more convoluted than this; Disraeli tells the story of Tancred and Fakredeen's attempts to unite the Arab peoples in one nation, but in this case narrative is not produced from the site of the modern nation-state, because the Jewish author of this narrative has no

Jewish (or, as he might term it, 'Arab') nation from which to write. From this perspective, Disraeli's *Tancred* can be seen as a critique of anti-Semitism in England, in its presentation of Jews as a superior race to, and of older lineage than the English. But Disraeli's novel, although it looks east and criticizes England for its lack of appreciation of the Orient (and, by inference, of its 'oriental' author) is certainly not a critique of English nationalism/imperialism. Such is the complexity of Disraeli's paradoxical narrative that what he writes, as a Jew, from a marginalised minority position in English society, is not as we might expect a criticism of nationalism/imperialism. Instead, he writes a nationalist narrative which uses his position of outsider as a way to inspire England to look east with imperialist intentions. Disraeli imaginatively appropriates the East for himself and for England; inspiration from the Orient will bring spiritual recovery from the land of one Chosen People to another.

In a letter from Disraeli the Prime Minister to Queen Victoria, acknowledging her approval of suggestions he had made for peerages, Disraeli exhibits that same skill of combination that Fakredeen needed to unite the Arab peoples;

> The programme he placed before your Majesty had been deeply considered; it consists in a great degree of representative men, and carried into effect by your Majesty's favour, it will gratify large bodies of your Majesty's subjects. Notably both Protestants and Catholics; the landed interest especially: the three Kingdoms all recognized, while Manchester is not forgotten.[35]

Eva tells Tancred that he is 'free of intrigue, politics, and management', and this is probably why, even if he did have the 'frothy imagination' of Fakredeen, and a vision for England, he would be unable to communicate it to the English people. *Tancred* cannot end with its hero's return, or a hopeful vision for the future, as did *Coningsby* and *Sybil*. Disraeli did return from the Holy Land in 1831, probably without having been granted a divine audience with the angel of Arabia, but nevertheless with the ability to communicate his vision for England in fictions which included stories of pedigree and race and their relation to history and politics. Indeed, Disraeli the politician in many ways surpasses the wild fantasies of his favourite novel, *Tancred*. The Emir Fakredeen had advised Tancred:

> 'Let the Queen of the English collect a great fleet, let her stow away all her treasure, bullion, gold plate and precious arms; be accompanied by all her court and chief people, and transfer the seat of her empire from London to Delhi.' (p. 263)

Between the wanderings of Fakredeen's 'frothy imagination' in this novel of 1847 and Victoria's elevation to Empress of India in 1876, lies an imaginative leap that Disraeli was able to make. *Tancred* failed to end with the union of the English and Eastern aristocracy in the marriage of Tancred and Eva, but Disraeli's relationship as Prime Minister with Queen Victoria was considered by him romantically, imaginatively and pragmatically as an alliance of his own eastern 'naturally aristocratic' blood with the most royal blood of England. Disraeli's stories or 'myths of origin' concerning his own Jewish lineage enabled him to position himself in English society and therefore, as both novelist and politician, to create defining narratives for the nation he was to lead.

CHAPTER FOUR

'A sort of Royal Family': Alternative pedigrees in Meredith's 'Evan Harrington'

> She was a pretty old lady, with bright black eyes, but she seemed proud. She came from Wales; and had had, a long time ago, an eminent person for an ancestor, of the name of Morgan-ap-Kerrig – of some place that sounded like Gimlet – who was the most illustrious person that ever was known, and all of whose relations were a sort of Royal Family.
>
> (Esther on Mrs. Woodcourt, *Bleak House*)[1]

Midway through Meredith's early novel *Evan Harrington* (1860), Rose Jocelyn, the 'Amazonian' young English heroine of the novel, plays with her dog and with the affections of her obtuse aristocratic admirer, Ferdinand Laxley. She feels confident and proud in her as-yet undisclosed engagement to the hero, the tailor's son Evan Harrington, and can afford to cast affectionate sops to Laxley, to whom she wishes to be kind, and also to keep under control. The dog, 'Pat', whom she is training is 'an Irish retriever-pup of the Shannon breed':

> Pat made a bolt. He got no farther than the length of the whip, and all he gained was to bring on himself the terrible word of drill once more. But Pat had tasted liberty. Irish rebellion against constituted authority was exhibited. Pat would not: his ears tossed over his head, and he jumped to right and left, and looked the raggedest rapparee that ever his ancestry trotted after. Rose laughed at his fruitless efforts to get free.[2]

In my earlier chapter on Edgeworth's *The Absentee* I quoted a conversation between Meredith's Irish hero Patrick and an aristocratic Englishwoman from Meredith's late unfinished novel *Celt and Saxon*. When Patrick stresses that he is an Irishman, she asserts that 'We are one nation', and he responds, 'And it's one family where the dog is pulled by the collar.'[3] Meredith uses the language of master and beast in reference to Ireland yet again in his article 'Concession to the Celt' for the *Fortnightly Review* in 1896. He writes in support of Home Rule for Ireland,

130

an issue being hotly debated in Parliament at the time, because he feels that England has so mishandled and neglected Ireland that efforts at appeasement will now be to no avail. His attitude to the Irish here is sympathetic and well-meaning but also condescending. Meredith's bestial metaphor for Ireland turns from the dog 'pulled by the collar' to the horse pulled by the rein; the Irish, he explains, do not hate the English – it is simply their 'nature to chaff at the bit'.[4]

If Rose's thoroughbred Irish retriever won't yet 'down-charge' to her command, her thoroughbred admirer will; Ferdinand Laxley falls to his knees in abject proposal. Within the little empire of her country estate, Beckley Court, Rose Jocelyn holds sway. Until she receives a blow to her self-assurance later in the novel, she is supremely confident that she can charm and manage her parents, her uncles, and the guests at Beckley. The image of Rose training the Irish retriever says much about what Meredith envisions as the extent of her control, and, as he calls it, her 'generalship'. The Irish dog will eventually be assimilated into the aristocratic sporting pursuits of an English country house, under Rose's training.

Rose is a true daughter of the Empire; she loves England and things English and dislikes the foreign, as is evident from some of her first words in the novel. Returning by ship from Portugal, she declares: 'I'm sure I smell England nearer and nearer! . . . I used to lie and pant in that stifling air among those stupid people, and wonder why anybody ever left England' (p. 31). Rose's dog is likened to a 'rapparee', a word from the Gaelic which came to refer to a seventeenth-century Irish rebel soldier. This language of conquest in training her dog reveals that Rose has all well in hand. With her confidence in things English, she conveys an impression that if she strode into any rebel or foreign country the natives would no longer 'chaff at the bit', but 'down-charge' immediately.

George Meredith was fascinated by what he saw as racial and emotional differences between Celt and Saxon. His own ancestry, as his father often reminded him as a boy, was Celtic – Irish on his mother's side, and Welsh on his father's. In fact both sides of the family had intermarried with local Hampshire families, a point which Meredith's father chose to ignore when entertaining his son with tales of his glorious and noble Celtic pedigree. Meredith's ambivalent attitude to this heritage is apparent in the shifting attitudes to the Celt in his writing; sometimes mildly satirical or condescending, sometimes awkwardly defensive, often grandly celebratory. In the case of his early novel *Evan*

Harrington, Meredith's ambivalence is evident in his giving the hero a Welsh pedigree, and then suppressing it as the hero makes his way into the English aristocracy.

Evan Harrington is probably Meredith's most autobiographical novel; many of the characters are closely based upon Meredith's relatives, and the heroine upon the upper-class Janet Duff-Gordon, with whom Meredith was in love at the time of writing. This chapter's consideration of pedigree and class warrants some attention to the autobiographical background, because in the writing of this his first novel for serialization in a London journal, Meredith is positioning himself with respect to London's literary society and the English class system. His hero's successful entry into the English upper classes reflects the author's project of wishing to write himself into the centre of the intellectual and social scene as a successful novelist and poet. For both the hero and his author, this entrance involves a wrestling with or suppression of pedigree. Pedigree here manifests itself in two forms; recent ancestors (father and grandfather) in the family business of the tailor's shop, and remote ancestors from a royal Celtic lineage regarded as certainly useless if not absurd in England. Meredith certainly attempted to obscure his tailoring background, and his attitude to his Celtic ancestry was vacillating and ambiguous. After his death, Meredith's friend Edward Clodd wrote that, 'Myths rarely accrete round men of note until they die, but Meredith's reticence about his parentage and birthplace gave rise to a host of legends during his lifetime, none of which he was ever at pains to dispel.'[5] So ready to repress knowledge of his family's past, he yet wrote a novel which exposed it to the public eye.

At times *Evan Harrington* exhibits the nervous symptoms arising from this repression. Allon White wrote of the way that Meredith coped, in his life and writing, with the shame and embarrassment resulting from his exposure to public gossip after his wife eloped with the painter Henry Wallis. Wallis had used Meredith as model for his famous painting *The Death of Chatterton*, and as the scandal of Meredith's wife's affair was making its way around London's literary and artistic circles, Wallis's painting portrayed the cuckolded husband sprawled, open and vulnerable, on a garret couch in the role of the failed poet Chatterton. Meredith as failed husband, and by association with Chatterton, failed poet, was exposed to the crowds which came to view Wallis's acclaimed painting at the Royal Academy. The intensity of his feelings of shame and humiliation were often expressed metaphorically in his work as the process of being 'stripped naked', as, for example, in describing Willoughby's sensations of the 'imps' of society tugging at the coverings over his naked and vulnerable self in *The Egoist*:

> they will hang on to us, restlessly plucking at the garments which cover our nakedness, nor ever ceasing to twitch them and strain at them until they have fairly stripped us for one of their horrible Walpurgis nights: when the laughter heard is of a character to render laughter frightful to the ears of men throughout the remainder of their days.[6]

Although Evan Harrington is better able to confront that terrible laughter of public ridicule than Willoughby Patterne, he nevertheless looks for the decent covering of gentility for his social self; to attain this social covering he does not turn to his pedigree, however. For centuries a Welsh pedigree had been considered scanty covering in English society; as Algernon Sidney wrote in his *Discourses concerning Government* (1683) of Henry VII, 'Who had no better cover for his sordid extraction than a Welch Pedigree, that might show how a tailor was descended from Prince Arthur, Cadwaller and Brutus.'[7]

His novel serialized in a popular London journal for the first time, Meredith's letters to his editor Samuel Lucas clearly indicate that he was anxious about what the public thought of each part of the serialization. A fear of exposure and possible failure before the public must have been greatly increased by the stress of keeping up with the numbers of the periodical. Meredith's repression of his own ancestry does result, in *Evan Harrington*, in a certain nervousness and bluster over issues of genealogy and class. These nervous symptoms exhibit themselves in the inconsistencies, ambivalence, and awkwardness surrounding the hero's genealogy. Not only are these symptoms personal to Meredith; they beset English society at a time when questions of pedigree and class are embodied in the opposition of the tradesman and the gentleman. This chapter explores various aspects of pedigree and class in Meredith's early novel: his use of his writing as an escape from his trade background; his relation to his Celtic ancestry; the formation of alternative or fictional genealogies for the hero of *Evan Harrington*, and a consideration of the 'naturally aristocratic' and healthy hero versus the degenerate 'diseased little heroine' of the novel.

CELT AND SAXON

But in spite of these wanderings racial pride was part of his make-up. 'Prove to me,' he would say in his grand voice and with a shout of laughter, 'that Shakespeare was not a Welshman.' (George Meredith to Viscountess Milner)

'As a child I was immensely tickled by the contrast between the tailor's shop and the princely family pedigree hanging in the back parlour.' (George Meredith to Viscountess Milner)[8]

In my chapter on Edgeworth's *The Absentee* I discussed the attempts of eighteenth- and early nineteenth-century English genealogists and antiquaries to discredit the traditional, ancient Irish pedigrees. As a conquered nation, Ireland could have no royal line of her own, and Irish pedigrees were dismissed as absurd lies and myths. The pedigrees of Wales, a country which had been conquered much earlier than Ireland, were subject to similar treatment. English ridicule of Welsh tales of origin is evident in Meredith's second comment to Viscountess Milner above, and in his treatment of Welsh pedigree in *Evan Harrington*; it is a long tradition which can be found in Shakespeare's treatment of the Welsh leader Owen Glendower, or in this passage from Sir John Vanbrugh's *Aesop* (1697), in which a Welsh herald named 'Quaint' explains his calling by the fact that his mother was a Welsh woman:

AESOP: A Welch Woman? Prithee of what Country's that?
QUAINT: That, Sir, is a country in the World's back-side, where every Man is born a Gentleman, and a Genealogist.[9]

Having origins in a country described as 'the world's back-side' is hardly the best recommendation for a gentleman.

In a sense, both Meredith and his fictional hero Evan Harrington must make the choice between being a gentleman *or* a genealogist. Both Meredith and his creation enter English aristocratic circles wishing to be recognized as gentlemen. Meredith comprehends the cringing embarrassment it would bring if he were to become a genealogist of his own line and proclaim himself a Welsh tailor-prince. He enters English society as a self-made man, concealing his origins, and relying upon his acceptance as a literary gentleman. One family who clearly welcomed Meredith on these terms were the decidedly upper-class Duff-Gordons. According to Lionel Stevenson, Lady Duff-Gordon 'was the centre of a devoted group of literary men, notably including Tom Taylor, A. W. Kinglake and Thackeray.'[10] Her sixteen-year-old daughter Janet Duff-Gordon had her own coterie of literary admirers, and Meredith was a favourite among them. Janet's appropriation of him as 'her poet' (a phrase she continued to use in old age) may indicate a touch of the condescension which her class afforded the literary figures of the day who hailed from lower or trading-class backgrounds; the kind of treatment, for example, which Charles Kingsley's 'tailor-poet', Alton Locke, finally rebelled against. But Meredith does not rebel; he conceals his tailor origins, and makes light of his Welsh pedigree when he feels it will make him vulnerable to ridicule in an English class system and the English literary world. This is especially the case at the time of writing *Evan Harrington* when Meredith was still on the margins of both these worlds – not yet securely established as an author and particularly sensitive over class differences because actually in love with Janet Duff-Gordon.

Commenting on the quotation from John Vanbrugh's *Aesop* the historian Prys Morgan writes:

The image of Wales was of a quaint back-of-beyond where gentlemen with hardly a shirt to their backs reeled off endless family trees going back to Aeneas from Troy, a land of unchanging backwardness, whose people had plenty of ancestry but no national history.[11]

By the time Meredith came to write *Evan Harrington* many attempts had been made to revise this image of Wales. In the eighteenth and early nineteenth century the interest in British folklore and customs, ancient poetry, oral traditions and legends was marked by such works as Bishop Percy's *Reliques of Ancient English Poetry* (1765), Scott's *Minstrelsy of the Scottish Border* (1802-3), and the celebrated fakes of Chatterton and James Macpherson ('Ossian'). This interest in ancient British culture extended itself to Wales and was actively taken up by both Welsh and English antiquaries and enthusiasts, such as Lady Charlotte Guest. As was sometimes the case with the rediscovered ancient Irish and Scottish poetry in this period, the translations of ancient Welsh poetry and legends were a curious mixture of the genuine and the invented, and constituted an effort to reclaim (and sometimes to fabricate) a recognized historical and literary tradition for Wales. Meredith's father-in-law, Thomas Love Peacock, had married a Welsh woman, Jane Gryffydh, the namesake of Meredith's first son, Arthur Gryffydh. Peacock's *The Misfortunes of Elphin* (1829), a prose version of the legend of the Welsh bard Taliesin, demonstrates his familiarity with the new translations of Welsh poetry and legend; the story of Taliesin was probably gleaned from Edward Davies' *Mythology and Rites of the Druids* (1809), and many of the songs in the novel are based upon those in Iolo Morganwg and

William Owen Pughe's the *Myvyrian Archailogy of Wales* (1801), which, with the help of his wife, Peacock translated from the Welsh originals.[12]

Living with Peacock in the early years of his first marriage, and admiring his father-in-law's writing, Meredith clearly took an interest in ancient Welsh legends and poetry. Leaves from his notebooks, dating from the 1850s, reveal that he was reading and taking notes on Charlotte Guest's translation of the Welsh legends. A poem published on 4th February 1860 in *Once A Week*, a week before the first instalment of *Evan Harrington* in the same journal, has its source in the mythology collected in Guest's *The Mabinogion* (1838–49). This poem, 'The Head of Bran the Blest', celebrates Welsh origins at the same time that he was writing a semi-autobiographical novel which suppresses these origins; this conjunction of the novel and the poem, and the content of the poem itself, disclose much of Meredith's ambivalence and unease over his Welsh ancestry.

Meredith wrote to Samuel Lucas, the editor of *Once A Week*, of the poem:

What are you going to do with 'The Head of Bran'? It is the best thing you have yet had of mine; but it is enough for me that you have to consider the multitude.[13]

Meredith was anxious to put this and another poem in the journal before *Evan Harrington* commenced serialization. The poem was published, accompanied by an illustration by Millais and a short foreword by Meredith explaining the history of Bran, and referring the reader to Charlotte Guest's translation of the Welsh legends:

He [Bran] was the son of Llyr, king of Britain, and said to be the first convert to Christianity in these islands. Hence his title, 'Benedigeid, the Blessed'. Taliesin, the bard, the 'radiant brow', was one of the seven princes to whom it was committed to carry the Head to its resting place. The Head was buried, looking towards France, in the Gwnvryn, or White Mount, site of the Tower of London.[14]

As recently as the seventeenth century the Welsh had referred to themselves as 'Brittains' by which they meant not that they were a part of the islands of Great Britain, but that they embraced the tradition, based upon the ancient pedigrees, that the Welsh were 'the earliest and prime people of the British isles'.[15] Nowhere in Meredith's poem are Wales and the Welsh referred to by name; instead 'Britain' is intoned repeatedly, as for example in the words of Bran:

> Glory to Britain!
> Death echoes me round.
> Glory to Britain!
> The world shall resound.
> Glory to Britain!
> In ruin and fall.
> Glory to Britain!
> Is heard over all

In mid-nineteenth-century England, 'Britain' did not refer to the land of the Welsh, but to a group of conquered Celtic nations clustered around England, the ruling centre. Meredith is interested in Welsh culture and in his own Welsh ancestry, but he is not about to take a stand as a peripheral Celtic nationalist when he is making his way to the centre of London society through the publication of his poems and novels in London journals. Meredith claims Welsh legend and myth for Britain as a whole – as had been the case for centuries with the more familiar Arthurian legends which had reached England long before through poets or redactors such as the medieval French Chrétien de Troyes.

While claiming Welsh mythology for all Britain – and for the London journals – Meredith stresses in the foreword to the poem that Bran's head was buried on the site of the Tower of London. No place could be a more clichéd venue for what is essentially English in the popular imagination. While playing down or obscuring his own Welsh background, and the fact that Bran was a Welsh prince, Meredith has nevertheless written in an English newspaper that the head of a Welsh prince once protected England from foreign invasion, sending out its defensive magic from the most historic and political site in the English capital. Meredith's appropriation of a Welsh king for Britain, and placement of that king at the heart of British history and mythology, gives a version of British history in which the Welsh are no longer marginal but quite literally at the centre. Whether conscious or not on Meredith's part, this placing of the Celtic 'severed head' (a symbol common in Celtic legend and ancient art) in London, at the hub of the Empire, serves as a metaphor for the desire of the ambitious young author to be at the centre of English letters and London's intellectual life. Meredith's novel *Evan Harrington*, to which I now turn, was a significant element in his campaign for that centre.

THE 'SNIPOCRACY'

Evan Harrington begins with the funeral of the 'Great Mel', a Lymport tailor and the father of the hero. The Great Mel, who is based upon Meredith's grandfather, had been a legend in his own time – a tailor who dined and rode to hounds with the county families. His familiarity with the county gentry lay partly in the fact that his chivalrous manners and fine figure made him very popular with the county wives, and partly because their husbands appreciated the fact that he rarely sent them a tailor's bill. Although Evan's father 'knew his place', he rode over the prejudices against his class and trade. He succeeded in this because he was bolstered by a confidence which arose not only from a belief in the 'natural aristocracy' of his appearance and manners, but also from the belief that he was in fact aristocratic – and probably from a more ancient line than the county families who condescended to know him. Of his pedigree, Meredith writes:

Now Mr. Melchisedec was mysterious concerning his origin; and, in his cups, talked largely and wisely of a great Welsh family issuing from a line of princes; and it is certain that he knew enough of their history to have instructed them on particular points of it. (p. 11)

Supported by this secret confidence in either a 'natural aristocracy' or a forgotten Celtic nobility, the children of both the fictional and real Great Mel (Evan's father and Meredith's grandfather respectively) had been brought up to greater expectations than the tailor's shop. The two sets of daughters, both those in the novel and Meredith's aunts, succeeded in their aspirations, all making socially good marriages which either raised them to a higher level amongst the trading classes, or as in the case of Meredith's aunt Louisa, out of the trading classes altogether and into the ranks of foreign nobility. Louisa married an English diplomat, and went to live in the Azores Islands. Bringing back the latest in Parisian fashions, and anecdotes of the foreign nobility amongst whom she mingled, she was the foundation of the fictional Louisa, the Countess de Saldar in *Evan Harrington*.

At the opening of the novel, Evan returns from Portugal by boat with his sister Louisa who has made a fortunate marriage with a Portuguese count. They are sailing together with a British diplomat, his wife and niece, all having been exiled from the Portuguese court because of a political coup. In Portugal Evan had acted as unpaid secretary to this diplomat, and had fallen in love with his niece, Rose Jocelyn. Louisa, the

Countess de Saldar, is desperate to keep her tailor origins concealed, even from her own husband. Evan does not intentionally conceal his background, but his relationship with Rose might be jeopardized by its revelation; thus he passively acquiesces in his sister's concealment of the family origins. Returning from Portugal, Evan is forced by his mother and his 'gentlemanly' code of honour to take on the huge debts left by the Great Mel. Instead of a career as a diplomat, which would place him among Rose's class, Evan must face his future prospects as a tailor. Devastated as he is by these prospects (which would mean giving up hope of Rose) Evan dutifully means to bear the burden, and the plot is driven by the many ways in which he is distracted from his purpose by the Countess and Rose. Evan is invited to stay at Beckley Court, Rose's family estate, and the delights and seductions both of her charm and of country house life help him to forget that he is a tailor, or 'snip'. The trials and tactics of the Countess as she tries to keep Evan out of the tailor shop and marry him to Rose, the tribulations of Rose as she learns to love Evan as a tailor, and Evan's struggle with his duty and the varying codes of the gentleman and the tradesman, are the catalysts of the plot.

THE 'DEMOGORGON' OF THE TAILOR'S SHOP

In 1904 Meredith told the Viscountess Milner of the reaction of his relations to *Evan Harrington*:

'My mother was Irish. My father's people were in a very small way in trade, but they were immensely proud of a long pedigree, which proved that they were princes! I made great fun of them and their pedigree in a book, and they and their descendants have never forgiven me! The women of the family were very remarkable. Born distinguished, many of them married well, one a Portuguese Cabinet Minister, one a wealthy brewer, and so on.'[16]

By 1904 Meredith was a successful and admired literary lion, visited in his home at Box Hill by the celebrities and young writers of the day. But the evasiveness over his background is as much in evidence in the above as it was in his early novel; he cannot actually name the family trade, he needs to joke about the family pedigree when many who knew him stated that he was obviously proud of his Celtic background, and finally he speaks of his aunts as 'born distinguished'. What does this rather vague phrase mean for Meredith? It is as ambiguous as the 'Nature's proof' of gentility or aristocratic bearing that the hero's aunt claims for Evan in the novel. Although Meredith mercilessly caricatures his aunts in *Evan Harrington*, they are the members of the family upon whom he focusses when speaking with Viscountess Milner. As the fictional Louisa's sisters cling to the thought of her marriage into the nobility (albeit foreign nobility) because it distances them from the 'Demogorgon' of tailordom, so Meredith chooses to focus upon his non-fictional aunts who married out of tailordom. The subtitle of *Evan Harrington* is 'He would be a gentleman'; clearly this is a title that the author also covets.[17]

In writing the novel Meredith adopted the rather condescending and satirical tone about a Welsh 'royal' pedigree which he perhaps felt appropriate for an English readership. Just as Disraeli was proud of the 'aristocratic' Jewish pedigree which he claimed for himself, but shied away from making any of his fictional heroes of Jewish lineage, so Meredith, although proud of his Celtic ancestry chose to make his hero ignore this heritage.

Critics have described the plot of *Evan Harrington* as in some respects a wish-fulfilment on the part of Meredith with regard to his love for Janet Duff-Gordon; Evan, the son of a tailor, is accepted as a gentleman and an equal by Rose Jocelyn's parents and wins her hand at the end of the novel. At the time of writing the novel, Janet became engaged to Henry Ross who was twenty years older than she and the head of a banking firm in Egypt. She was preparing to accompany him to Alexandria at the time of the novel's publication. Rose Jocelyn also leaves England at the end of the novel, to accompany her husband Evan who has become attaché to the Naples embassy. Writing to Samuel Lucas in September 1860, Meredith mulls over some of the problems with the writing of the novel, and anticipates with dread the final instalment; 'The ground was excessively delicate. This is too late to dwell upon; but I shudder at the thought of the last number.'[18] The 'excessive delicacy' of the novel's material has much to do with its autobiographical nature, which, unknown to the public, would be transparent to Janet Duff-Gordon and her family. Her imminent departure from England with a man very much from her own class must have left Meredith feeling exposed and embarrassed by that 'last number' which contains the happy ending for his fictional would-be self and Janet. In the same letter to Samuel Lucas quoted above, Meredith writes that he has, 'avoided making the fellow [Evan] a snob in spite of his and my own temptations'. Norman Kelvin comments on Meredith's careful treatment of his hero in relation to both his own and his hero's class position and Janet Duff-Gordon:

Since Meredith wished [Janet Duff-Gordon] to regard the novel [as her own], he was determined that it should not contain the image of an upstart aggressively pushing himself into a world in which he was not wanted: into her world.[19]

Fighting to gain the centre of English society, Evan has his battles fought for him by the Countess and Rose; he is a decidedly unaggressive hero. Both Rose and the Countess try to provide Evan with an alternative pedigree to that of the tailor shop; the Countess attempts to make a foreign nobleman of him by instructing him in the manners and dress of the Portuguese court, and Rose, by marrying him and suppressing his past, can offer him a future pedigree untainted by tailordom. George Meredith must fight his own battles by gaining the literary reputation which will open the doors of society for him. In *Evan Harrington* we can see the ambivalence of the author as he confronts, evades or pillories his family background. Although underplayed and eventually dismissed, the hero's Celtic ancestry is an important subtext in the novel, revealing Meredith's difficulty in positioning himself in English society and his fear of ridicule and marginalization. His first step in revising his family background, in exorcising it of embarrassing ghosts, is to turn to the generation immediately before him on the family tree; Meredith fictionally revises the life and character of his father. It is to this re-writing of the family history that I now turn.

RE-WRITING THE FATHER

In a conversation with Edward Clodd, Meredith briefly and brutally dispensed with his father; 'My father lived to be seventy-five. He was a muddler and a fool.'[20] If the marriage of Rose and Evan at the conclusion of *Evan Harrington* approaches a wish-fulfilment on the part of Meredith in his love for Janet Duff-Gordon, Evan's career can also be seen as a fictional alternative to the stunted, disappointed life of Meredith's father.

George's grandfather Melchisidec Meredith's ambitions for his children were partly satisfied by the socially successful marriages of his daughters. He also had higher ambitions than the tailor's shop for his son Augustus. Meredith's father was in training for the medical profession, but at Melchisidec's death it was found that the accounts of the tailoring business were in a state of confusion; much money was owed, and Augustus, although temperamentally unsuited for the task, inherited the tailoring shop and its debts.

The first seven chapters of the novel lead up to this crisis of Augustus Meredith's youth. Evan returns home from Portugal where he has been visiting Louisa – just as, according to Lionel Stevenson, it is probable that Augustus Meredith was staying with his sister Louisa in the Azores. As the ship comes into port, Evan hears of his father's death and rushes home to Lymport. Here fiction and the history of Meredith's father begin to diverge. Augustus Meredith had a difficult, frustrated life after having to take over his father's business and debt; the tailoring business went bankrupt and he was eventually forced to become a journeyman tailor in London. At this time, Meredith's mother having died, he married his young housekeeper, a union which Meredith seems to have regarded with contempt. The re-writing of his father's career in *Evan Harrington* exorcises the disappointment, disillusionment and hurt pride, both in Augustus Meredith's life, and in George Meredith's opinion of his father. Much as he dismissed his father as 'a muddler and a fool', Meredith did not know the Augustus who, against his gentlemanly inclinations and education, had to become a tailor at the age of seventeen. This turning-point came long before the author was born, and Meredith discusses how premature experience can shape the formless nature of youth – sometimes, disastrously. As he writes of Evan in the opening chapters:

Are you impatient with this young man? He has little character for the moment. Most youths are like Pope's women; they have no character at all. And indeed a character that does not wait for circumstances to shape it, is of small worth in the race that must be run. To be set too early, is to take the work out of the Sculptor who fashions men. (p. 50)

Meredith protects his fictional creation from the circumstances which in his own father's case may have 'set' his character too early; the plot is driven by attempts to escape the destiny of the tailor shop. In Evan's case the circumstances which save him from this destiny are fashioned by others; the desperate plots of the Countess and Rose are what remove Evan from the taint of trade.

Lionel Stevenson has written of Meredith's father that he,

absorbed the illusions of royal ancestry without the saving modicum of common sense that Old Mel had retained from his boyhood days as the apprentice tailor. Before long it was gleefully reported that when the slim dark young man was on a holiday in Bath his expensive raiment and courtly air gave rise to a rumor (which he did nothing to quell) that he was a foreign count travelling incognito. The nickname 'Count Meredith' stuck to him in Portsmouth as long as he lived there.[21]

Meredith appropriates this story for Evan's father in the novel. Evan himself, in his Portuguese cloak and dark moustache of foreign fashion, has the demeanour, in the eyes of his approving sister, of foreign nobility. But Evan has no desire to claim alliances with the 'foreign' nobility, whether Portuguese or ancient Welsh. Meredith saves his hero from the ridicule that his father was subject to as 'Count Meredith' when he claimed a royal Welsh lineage. Dismissing Evan's Welsh pedigree, Meredith brings Evan from the Celtic fringe by supplying him with an alternative and 'psychological' pedigree, and one which is important to English history; that is, the pedigree of the Percy family. A print of the Douglas and the Percy has hung on Evan's bedroom wall since childhood, inspiring a love of English history and chivalry. The scene in the print is of the English Percy taking the dead hand of the Scottish Douglas, whom he has just slain. Both the Douglas and Percy are noble soldiers, but the history depicted here is of an English bias; the unruly Celt conquered by the English soldier. Evan calls the Englishman 'Gallant Percy', and clearly sympathizes with the English conqueror rather than the dying Gael. Emotionally, psychologically, Evan aligns himself with the winning side of the English noble line of the Percys rather than with a conquered Celtic nation. The author of 'The Head of Bran' and 'Aneurin's Harp' suppresses Evan's true pedigree, and provides him with the inspiration of a noble English line, partly to save him from the ridicule of the class among whom he wishes to be accepted, and partly to make him an appropriate hero for Rose Jocelyn. She is the scion of a noble English line, and the war-like and courageous representative of a conquering nation. Although she is limited by her sex and the pursuits of a country estate, she nevertheless inspires the reader with confidence in her ability to conquer not only canine 'rapparees' as discussed at the beginning of this chapter, but the real insurgents as well.

DEBT, DUELLING AND THE DEAD HAND

After Evan's return from Portugal for the funeral of his father, Evan's mother takes him to his old room which has not been altered since he left. He studies the familiar print on the wall:

'The Douglas and the Percy: "he took the dead man by the hand". What an age it seems since I last saw that ... Gallant Percy! I know he [his father] wished he had lived in those days of knights and battles.'

He does not hear his mother's curt reply, 'It does not much signify whom one has to make clothes for' (p. 79).

Evan's mother has yet to inform him of the enormous debts his father has left behind, debts which accumulated largely because he seemed to think it beneath him to press his customers for payment. Evan goes to bed at the end of the chapter, this time in the knowledge that he will have to take on his father's debt and become a tailor himself. He again contemplates the print of the Douglas and the Percy. Here Meredith echoes the above quotation 'he took the dead man by the hand', with the 'dead hand' or mortmain of Evan's inheritance which takes the form of his duty to pay his father's debts:

There were the Douglas and the Percy on the wall. It was a happy and glorious time, was it not, when men lent each other blows that killed outright; when to be brave and cherish noble feelings brought honour; when strength of arm and steadiness of heart won fortune; when the fair stars of earth – sweet women – wakened and warmed the love of squires of low degree. This legacy of the dead man's hand! Evan would have paid it with his blood; but to be in bondage all his days to it! (pp. 86–7)

The 'dead man's hand' – that of the Douglas and Percy print, and of his father's legacy – signals how Evan is caught between two codes of honour – the aristocratic and the tradesman's. To preserve the honour of his father's name he must pay the debts, but in doing so he will have to become a tailor, and consequently lose any chance of marrying Rose or of obtaining a diplomatic appointment which would raise him into a sphere where a code of aristocratic gentility would apply. Evan's idealistic envisioning of this latter code of honour is evident in the above quotation. Robin Gilmour describes it rather differently:

'honour' in this unreformed sense meant paying one's gambling debts, but not the tradesman's bill; deceiving a husband, if need be, but not cheating him at cards; insulting a servant with impunity, but one's equals only at the risk of a duel.[22]

Because he cannot decide which of the dead hands he means to grasp, Evan is caught in a limbo between these two codes of honour, and his time at Beckley Court occupies an unreal liminal space in which he avoids declaring himself one way or the other. Evan's floating and undeclared identity confuses Rose's brother, Harry Jocelyn, and this confusion is focussed upon the place that debt and duelling hold in the aristocratic code described above by Gilmour. When Harry wants to fight a duel with Evan, to avenge his engagement to his sister, he is unsure how to go about it because he has borrowed money from Evan which he cannot repay. He cannot challenge him to a duel while he owes him money, and yet if Evan is not a gentleman, but only a tradesman, then it is not necessary for him to pay the debt in this aristocratic code of honour. By the same token, if Evan is not a gentleman then he should not fight a duel with him, as only gentlemen solve their disputes in such a way. Thoroughly confused, Harry characteristically ends up doing nothing.

With the exception of chapter six, 'My Gentleman On the Road', in which Evan suffers gallantly the embarrassment of not being able to tip a postillion sufficiently, Meredith is very protective of his hero, never letting him appear personally in debt. It could be said that Meredith is unusually sensitive about the figure Evan cuts; just as we never see him with a pair of shears in his hands, we never see him worrying over his linen, or the state of his gloves or hat. At Beckley of course he does not need to worry about paying for anything, and this keeps at bay the paradox he is living: that as a gentleman one should not be seen worrying over a thing as petty as a tailor's bill, despite the fact that unless he becomes a tailor and demands that gentlemen pay their bills to him, he will not be able to afford the clothes which are the outward sign of the gentleman. Behind all this is the fact (never directly stated) that Evan's bills have been paid by his brother-in-law, Andrew Cogglesby, who earns his money through trade as a brewer. Lulled by his acceptance as a gentleman, and the ease of life at Beckley Court, Evan risks falling into the alternative definition of 'gentleman' which Ruskin gave to 'a man of pure race'; he risks becoming 'a man living in idleness on other people's labour'.[23]

Anthony Trollope, with his close attention to the financial matters of all his characters, often deals with this phenomenon of 'country house credit'; as long as a man can establish the reputation and society of a gentleman, invitations to the homes of the wealthy should not be wanting. There he may live off little or nothing, surrounded by luxury. Such is the case with Burgo Fitzgerald of the Palliser novels, for instance; in his aunt's town house, Burgo 'was utterly a pauper. There was no pauper poorer than he in London that day. But, nevertheless, he breakfasted on *paté de foie gras* and *curaçoa*, and regarded those dainties very much as other men regarded bread and cheese and beer.'[24]

The Countess de Saldar, exiled and penniless with her Portuguese count, fully understands how to use this system of credit, and wishes Evan to take advantage of it. She has no doubts that he can be accepted as a gentleman on the country house circuit. What makes a gentleman is of course one of the key questions in the novel. Rose asks herself, 'whether it really was in Nature's power, unaided by family portraits, coats-of-arms, ball-room practice, and at least one small phial of Essence of Society, to make a Gentleman.' The views of the women in the novel are revealing; Rose Jocelyn, the Countess de Saldar, and Rose's cousin, the crippled and sickly heiress Juliana Bonner, all love Evan and are ambitious for him. Their responses to his predicament throw light upon their society's attitude to the pedigree, blood and 'breeding' of this tailor's son.

GOOD BREEDING AND SEXUAL SELECTION

As long as Evan keeps his family history hidden the Countess has no worries about his gentlemanly breeding; these signs of good appearance she considers self-evident both in herself and her brother. 'Surveying the field' of action open to her upon arriving at Beckley, she writes to her sister of Evan:

By the way as to *hands* and *feet*, comparing him with the Jocelyn men, he has every mark of better blood. Not a question about it. As Papa would say – *we* have Nature's proof. (p. 181)

'Nature's proof' of good blood, and the elegance and polish of manners that Evan acquires in the Portuguese court, are the qualities which the Countess believes will gain him title, money, or both, through 'the divine portal' of matrimony.

Like the Countess, Rose also believes implicitly that Evan is a gentleman of good blood. At first she is not aware of his origins in trade, which she abhors. There is an element of snobbery in her trust in Evan's breeding; if she likes him and regards him as a friend then it follows that he must of course be the 'right sort', one of her own class. Suspicions of his true pedigree in trade cause her growing unease and discomfiture. She is forced to come to terms with her own complacent belief in the superiority of her class, and her worry drives her at crisis points in the novel to test 'Nature's proof' of a gentleman rather than the proof of old blood, to which she is more accustomed among the country house guests at Beckley.

When Evan and the reader first hear Rose's voice after she has returned to her native soil from Portugal, it is full of the excitement and talk of competition and those 'healthy games' that Meredith admired as so characteristically English. Racing up on her horse to the cricket field, she says:

'Here I am at last, and Beckley's in still! ... We shall beat you. Harry says we shall soon be a hundred a-head of you. Fancy those boys! ... How I wish you had made a bet with me Squire.' (p. 163)

Here is Rose, 'the brilliant young Amazon, smoothing the neck of a mettlesome grey cob' (p. 163). A kind of Boadicea, she is ready to compete, to fight, and like her spirited horse, she has 'Nature's proof'. Of the heroism and bravery of Meredith's heroines, Allon White wrote:

Acts of physical courage in Meredith are the compulsive enactment of a victory over shame, they are the defence – particularly for women – against the scorn of the world.[25]

Rose is naturally courageous, and at the cricket match there is as yet no shadow of shame haunting her. However this natural boldness and competitiveness is intensified to the pitch of a desperate compulsion which is a 'defence against the scorn of the world' and against self-contempt, when, later in the novel, she considers what the world will say of her love for a 'snip', or tailor.

Rose's brother Harry and his friends suspect Evan's concealed tailoring background, and they deride both his trade and his aristocratic demeanour by labelling him a member of the 'snipocracy'. 'Snip' is a term which haunts Rose; her growing fear about the truth of Evan's ancestry causes her to respond viscerally to a label which she finds shameful and repugnant. Perhaps Rose's dramatic response to 'snip' lies partially in her unconscious acknowledgement of the word's connotations of castration. The common saying about tailors to which Meredith makes the occasional careful allusion in the novel is 'nine tailors make a man'; tailors were comically stereotyped as weak and desexualized, and the connotations of 'snip' would tend to underline this emasculation. Rose's desperation to prove Evan more 'manly' than the other men at Beckley Court reveals her drive to negate utterly the sexual implications of his family profession, and to 'sexually select' a healthy, virile mate.

Competitive herself, Rose instigates physical competitions between Evan and Ferdinand Laxley, her aristocratic suitor. The country estate becomes an arena for physical feats which Rose hopes will prove before all that the socially and sexually degrading reputation of tailordom may be dismissed with regard to Evan. The rivalry between Laxley and

Evan, which Rose encourages, comes to a crisis in chapter twenty, 'Break-Neck Leap'. The incidents of this chapter and their aftermath deal with courage in physical competition as part of 'Nature's proof' of pedigree, and connect the pedigree of animals with that of their masters.

The chapter opens with the guests of Beckley Court riding forth to watch an amateur steeple-chase, which Rose has suggested in bellicose response to Laxley's boasts of his horsemanship. She 'had backed herself, and Drummond and Evan to beat him' (p. 250). But it soon becomes clear that although Rose undeniably has the courage to compete in the race, her heroic propensities have by this point been displaced onto Evan. Because she loves him she has begun to bind her identity and self-love to his, and as she tells him later, after she has risked his life, 'I only wanted you to beat. I wanted you to be first and best' (p. 291). At the opening of the chapter her suspicions of Evan's background make her truly desperate to reassure herself that he has 'Nature's proof' of superiority, and is 'naturally' aristocratic, if not by pedigree then by prowess:

'Why Ferdinand, he can beat you in anything! . . .'.

But the truth was she was now more restless than ever. She was not more distant with Evan, but she had a feverish manner, and seemed to thirst to make him show his qualities, and excel, and shine. Billiards, or jumping, or classical acquirements, it mattered not – Evan must come first. He had crossed his foils with Laxley, and disarmed him; for Mel his father had seen him trained for a military career. Rose made a noise about the encounter, and Laxley was eager for his opportunity, which he saw in the proposed 'mad gallop'. (pp. 250–1)

In *On the Origin of Species*, published a few months before the first part of *Evan Harrington*'s serialization, Darwin writes on sexual selection:

The rock-thrush of Guiana, birds of Paradise, and some others, congregate; and successive males display their gorgeous plumage and perform strange antics before the females, which standing by as spectators, at last choose the most attractive partner.[26]

In his novel *The Egoist* (1879), Meredith echoes Darwin's language in Willoughby's philosophy and practice of courtship:

We now scientifically know that in this department of the universal struggle, success is awarded to the bettermost. You spread a handsomer tail than your fellows, you dress a finer top-knot, you pipe a newer note, have a longer stride; she reviews you in competition, and selects you. The superlative is magnetic to her . . . She cannot help herself; it is her nature, and her nature is the guarantee for the noblest races of men to come of her. In complimenting you, she is a promise of superior offspring. Science thus – or it is better to say – an acquaintance with science facilitates the cultivation of aristocracy.[27]

Like the Social Darwinists of his day, Willoughby appropriates Darwinian theory to support his own beliefs and purposes; for him 'the noblest races of men' are, as a matter of course, those of his own English aristocracy. (I discuss this passage further in the next chapter.) In *Evan Harrington*, Rose has unthinkingly concurred in this assumption, until she falls in love with someone rumoured to be the son of a tailor. While keeping a full consciousness of this fact at bay, Rose nevertheless must disprove the assumptions she grew up with, and use Evan as proof, to herself and to those of her class, that there exists such a thing as 'natural aristocracy'.

Although Meredith's later novels show him to be highly conversant with Darwinian theory and the popular misconstructions of that theory, it is difficult to determine to what degree *Evan Harrington* is influenced by the recently published *Origin of Species*. Darwin's treatise was first published on 24th November 1859. All 1,250 copies were sold on the day of publication, and a second edition of 3,000 copies was published on 7th January 1860. Considering the stir that Darwin's work made, it seems highly unlikely that Meredith was not familiar with the treatise, or at least conversant with its language and argument. In the last number of *Evan Harrington* in *Once A Week*, published just less than a year after *Origin of Species*, the Countess de Saldar writes to her sister from Rome, 'I am not at all astonished that Mr. Raikes should have married [Rose's] maid. It is a case of natural selection' (p. 571). Darwin's language has crept in at the end of Meredith's novel, already showing signs of popular and literary misuse of the scientist's terms; the Countess probably means some form of sexual selection here. Certainly Rose Jocelyn, like one of Darwin's female birds of Paradise, practises sexual selection. Ferdinand and Evan must 'perform strange antics before her' – of fencing, horse-jumping, racing, dressing and conversing well, while she 'stand(s) by as spectator, at last [to] choose the most attractive partner'. But this 'sexual selection' has a long pre-Darwinian tradition. In Rose's case it is translated from the language of the scientific treatise to the language of courtly romance and the chivalric tournament. Rather than connecting her with females of other species watching the whirling and bellowing of male alligators or the altercations of male stag beetles, Meredith decorously keeps Rose within a human sphere. She is the courtly lady standing by as spectator over the jousting field while her knights battle for her favour.

Fatal competition for a woman belongs to another era, an era which Evan admires and which is represented for him by the print of 'the Douglas and the Percy' on his bedroom wall. It belongs to a time of knights and chivalric tournament, not (the Eglinton tournament and its imitations aside) to the world of the Victorian country house. Rose signals that she too looks to a more chivalrous and dangerous age when she presides over a competition, giving as a prize to the winner what her cross little cousin describes as her 'stupid, dirty old pocket handkerchief' (p. 257). Rose gives Laxley and Evan the starting signal for the race and jump by waving the sought-after hankie in the air like any medieval damsel watching her knights joust, perhaps to the death. And the jump over 'Break-Neck Leap' is almost to the death. Laxley's horse refuses to make the jump, but Evan's complies, throwing him and leaving him badly wounded. Again the handkerchief comes into play as Rose, fearing Evan is dead, 'held a gory handkerchief to his temple with one hand, and with the other felt for the motion of his heart' (p. 259).

Meredith deflates the high-flown language and incident by turning to the mock-heroic with the last words of the chapter, 'But heroes don't die, you know'. But the touch of humour cannot remove entirely the impression that Rose's feverish need to prove Evan the fittest, the superlative, is a desperation which endangers her lover's life. Even if the heroics of Evan and Rose are slightly ridiculed it is the fact that they believe in the same obsolete code of honour that brings them together; when Evan finally decides to leave Beckley to take up his father's debts and tailoring, he goes to Rose to claim the one thing that according to this code he feels he has the right to – the pocket handkerchief which was his prize. This humble claim from 'a squire of low degree' results in a declaration of love between Evan and Rose, and their engagement.

Rose yearns for the superlative in Evan, and must show to herself and to others of her class that his natural aristocracy is superior to Ferdinand's well-documented pedigree. Ferdinand's prospective title is a sticking point for Rose's family. Rose's father is a mere baronet, and Meredith describes their home, Beckley, as a 'third-rate English mansion'. The Jocelyns themselves are described as 'upper-middle class' rather than aristocratic. Liberal as Lady Jocelyn and Sir Franks are, they respect title and old estates. Perhaps it is his title which enables the Jocelyns to turn a blind eye to Laxley's peculiar lack of charm and boorish manners toward their guest, Evan.

Rose's parents, and particularly Lady Jocelyn are certainly less susceptible than many to a blind reverence for old family and title. As the Countess writes to her sister of the Jocelyns' family tree and rank:

> Lord Elburne is the fourteenth of his line – originally simple country squires. They talk of the Roses, but we need not go so very far back as that. I do not quite understand why a Lord's son should condescend to a Baronetcy. Precedence of some sort for his lady I suppose. I have yet to learn whether she ranks by his birth, or his present title. If so, a young Baronetcy cannot possibly be a *gain*. One thing is *certain*. She cares very little about it. She is *most eccentric*. (p. 177)

The Countess cares a great deal for rank and title, is in her element among the Portuguese aristocracy, and careful of her title among the English. She instructs her sister to address all letters to her at Beckley as 'de Saldar de Sancorvo. That is our title *by rights*, and it may as well be so in England. English *Countess* is certainly best' (p. 176). Lady Jocelyn may care little for rank, but she cares enough that she would do her best to prevent Rose marrying a tailor's son, even though, or perhaps because, her own family background is in trade. She will not absolutely forbid the marriage (she hardly seems to have the emotional energy for that), and she gracefully accepts it when it seems inevitable. However, before Rose's marriage she sends her to Elburne House, her mother-in-law's bastion of pride in old family and title. Rose feels particularly confused and shamed in this environment by her love of a tailor's son who is (falsely) accused of the dishonourable and ungentlemanly forgery of a letter. (In fact it was the Countess, working her mysterious Machiavellian tactics, who had forged the letter to discredit Rose's admirer Laxley.) Lady Jocelyn may rise philosophically above the dirty work of class snobbery which will affect Rose at Elburne House, but she is shrewd enough to know what she is doing by sending her daughter there.

With her scorched sensitivity to her trading-class background, the Countess Louisa is acutely aware of the Jocelyns' sore spot over their own ancestry. If class snobbery is latent in Sir Franks and Lady Jocelyn, their children, Harry and Rose, have inherited it in a more virulent form. Early in the novel Rose exclaims of shopkeepers in general: 'Oh! I can't bear that class of people. I always keep out of their way. You can always tell them' (p. 38). But Rose's snobbery cannot 'tell' the Countess or Evan, to whom this comment is partly addressed.

The Jocelyns have a tenuous hold on their estate; Sir Franks has it for a life tenure only, and it depends upon his mother-in-law's will and whim whether or not it will stay in his family. This estate, which should stand as a sign of old family, has been bought only recently with new money from trade. Since Sir Franks is a baronet, his children will inherit no title, and they are at risk of not inheriting the estate. The family is on the lowest level of the aristocratic hierarchy, and in danger of slipping into the middle classes.

Confronting the snipocracy, Rose reacts viscerally when she watches herself with repugnance pronounce the word 'snip' before the mirror. Aside from its connotations of desexualization, the word makes her feel ugly and soiled by reminding her of the trading class in her own blood. By the removal of a generation, and the schooling, travel, estate and associations of her aristocratic upbringing, she has always felt superior to her mother's family background in trade. Her love for Evan sets her on the difficult path of questioning her own class snobbery. Rather than rejecting Evan because of his background, Rose in a sense chooses to cover it from her eyes and the eyes of society in an instinctive and daring move to assimilate and secure Evan – and as quickly as possible – with a position in her own class. She seeks patronage for Evan from her uncle. This established method among the aristocracy to keep their class the ruling class was being challenged by the middle classes at the time *Evan Harrington* was written. As Robin Gilmour writes:

The Government of India Act 1853 established the principle of competition for the Indian Civil Service, and a year later the Northcote-Trevelyan Report on the Organization of the Permanent Civil Service advocated competitive examinations and promotion by merit ... This movement for reform was implicitly (and sometimes explicitly) an attack on aristocratic dominance: competition would overthrow the old pattern of 'interest' whereby the government and diplomatic services, the church, the army and the navy provided a refuge for younger sons and dependants of noble families.[28]

The paradox inherent in Rose's action is that while she turns to an aristocratic system of patronage which opposes open competition to those outside her class, she seeks competition as a way to prove Evan worthy of her class and herself when she constantly forces challenges between him and Laxley. She wishes others to see him as *de facto* a member of her own class, but for herself the new spirit of competition, which allows the middle classes to compete with the aristocracy, serves not as a method of reform, but as a way for Evan to prove that he has 'natural aristocracy' and breeding. Rose is no social reformer; rather than reject her class and its reverence for title, she wishes to appropriate Evan for her class and for herself.

Rose demands that Evan and Laxley undergo physical rather than scholarly or intellectual tests to prove themselves worthy of her. This may be in part because Evan's subtlety of thought and intellect are evident in his quiet diplomacy and conversation, but there may be a vestige also of that aristocratic snobbery which dictates that it does not do for a man of title to be too much of a scholar. Intense study or intellectual fireworks are considered a superfluity, a bit of an embarrassment, and should be left to the tutors and governesses. It is worth noting that John Raikes and Evan have had the same schooling, but it is John rather than Evan who takes up a paid position as tutor to Juliana Bonner, at Evan's suggestion. Evan has the more gentlemanly position of unpaid secretary to Rose's diplomat uncle. Meredith evinces a certain snobbery here; just as we never see Evan with a pair of shears in his hands when he must work in Mr. Goren's tailor shop, we never see him as anything but a guest at Beckley. In contrast, John Raikes is continually pilloried for his classical scholarship. He is depicted as a buffoon, and while Evan marries Rose, Raikes is destined to marry Rose's maid, and to take over the tailor shop.

BEASTS OF THE COUNTRY ESTATE

Rose's love for Evan means that she must find an alternative definition for 'gentleman' than the one she was brought up to believe. In 1860, Ruskin wrote in his chapter 'Of Vulgarity' in *Modern Painters* of the primary definition of a 'gentleman':

Its primal, literal, and perpetual meaning is 'a man of pure race'; well-bred, in the sense that a horse or dog is well-bred.[29]

In his efforts to convince his readership of his theories of Natural Selection, Darwin in *Origin of Species* repeatedly refers to man's breeding of various domestic animals; if man can improve a species over a few generations by selecting and breeding certain advantageous characteristics, what can nature not do over the millenia? As Darwin argues, it is simply a matter of transferring what man has practised and believed true of the breeding of his animals to all living things, including man. On her family estate, Rose is surrounded by the language of breeding and pedigree, both in her own family, and with regard to the horses and dogs which are bred and trained there. In addition to her love of courtly romance, perhaps another factor in Rose's arguably 'scientific' and certainly methodical approach to the sexual selection and proof of her partner is her familiarity with the breeding of thoroughbred dogs and horses. A knowledge of the pedigrees of these 'noble' animals seeps into her instinctive testing of Evan.

In her book *The Animal Estate*, Harriet Ritvo asserts that among domestic animals the horse and dog were considered 'noble' in the Victorian period:

> Britons of all ranks were known for their love of horses. The affluent kept high-spirited thoroughbreds; those who followed the plow preferred horses to other draft animals, no matter how strong or cheap to maintain. Popular natural history writers routinely characterized the horse as 'noble', and sometimes as nobler than the class of humans generally charged with its care. In part this epithet, embodied in a flood of paintings and prints beginning in the early eighteenth century, reflected the traditional association of horseflesh with aristocratic sport.[30]

The relationship between the nobility of the horse and the nobility of those who can properly appreciate, manage, and care for this animal is stressed in the incidents of the 'Break-Neck Leap' chapter and their aftermath. Meredith's theme seems to be that the true pedigree of the man can be told by the way he manages a thorough-bred animal.

Lady Jocelyn makes the association of man and beast at the opening of the chapter, when she spies the local squire, George Uploft, riding on a ridge of the downs. He sees the Beckley riders below him and instigates a chase for fun, pretending to be a fox by gathering his coat-tails to form a brush and waving it at them. The Countess and Lady Jocelyn watch the race:

'And who may the poor hunted animal be?' inquired the Countess.
'George Uploft,' said Lady Jocelyn, pulling out her watch. 'I give him twenty minutes . . . he hasn't a chance . . . The squire keeps wretched beasts'. (p. 252)

George Uploft is certainly not a 'noble' creature; he is depicted as 'a fat-faced, rotund young squire – a bully where he might be, and an obedient creature enough where he must be' (p. 251). The Countess describes him as a 'poor brute flying from his persecutors', and the inference is that if there is a metaphorical relationship between human hierarchy and that of the animal kingdom, then George Uploft is one of the lower, hunted creatures. It is fitting that such a poor specimen of manhood should ride a 'wretched beast' rather than one of Beckley's noble beasts.

At 'Break-Neck Leap' neither Laxley nor his horse have sufficient 'pluck' to take the jump. 'Pluck', with its connotations of upper-class sport and public school games, is the quality that Rose is determined to test when she sets Evan and Ferdinand against each other. While Evan lies senseless from his fall in the opening of the following chapter, horse and man become indistinguishable in the language of the Jocelyns who stand around him:

Lady Jocelyn sat upright in her saddle, giving directions about what was to be done with Evan and the mare, impartially.
'Stunned, and a good deal shaken, I suppose; Lymport's knees are terribly cut,' she said ... Seymour added, 'Fifty guineas knocked off her value!' One added, 'Nothing worse I should think;' and another, 'A little damage inside, perhaps'. Difficult to say whether they spoke of Evan or the brute. (p. 260)

It is the final straw for the Countess when she hears Lady Jocelyn say;

'Franks [her husband] will be a little rusty about the mare.'
'We are not cattle!' exclaimed the frenzied Countess, within her bosom. Alas! it was almost a democratic outcry they made her guilty of; but she was driven past patience. (p. 261)

Aside from its comic purpose, it is difficult to gauge Meredith's attitude to this calm failure to discriminate between man and beast. At this juncture Lady Jocelyn coldly comments of the Countess that she 'does not ruffle easily', but we must feel that her brief 'frenzy' is quite understandable. A distinctive feature of the upper classes or nobility was held to be this *sang froid*: Disraeli encapsulates this quality of noble blood in *Sybil* when Mowbray Castle is attacked by a 'mob' of working people: 'When they perceived the castle this dreadful band gave a ferocious shout. Lady de Mowbray showed blood; she was composed and courageous' (p. 471). It seems that the Countess has 'shown blood' of an inferior sort, revealing in her democratic cry her trading-class background. Meredith evidently admires Lady Jocelyn, whom he describes as 'a veritable philosopher ... [who] permitted her fellows to move the world on as they would, and has no other passions in the contemplation of the show than a cultured audience will usually exhibit.' Meredith is apparently enamoured of that proverbially English stiff upper lip, a quality which both Rose and Evan exhibit; in the carriage with the wounded Evan, 'Rose, to judge by her face was as calm as glass', but Meredith allows her to exhibit for the reader what is going on beneath the surface when she tightly clasps Mrs. Evremonde's hand 'once for a fleeting instant' (p. 261). And Evan, replying to Lady Jocelyn's, 'Not killed this time!' responds with the perfect comment of the gentleman/cavalier, 'At your ladyship's service tomorrow' (p. 263). At times the

Countess's frenzy and Machiavellian plotting, translated from the Portuguese court to Beckley, are a necessary and welcome antidote to the 'cultured philosophy' and elegant good-breeding of Rose, Evan and Lady Jocelyn.

Lady Jocelyn, sitting 'upright in her saddle' and directing the care of the wounded is truly 'Amazonian'; a woman capable of remaining calm in a battle charge and, like her daughter, worthy to lead. Indeed, giving thought to the animal as well as the human is seen as a true sign of the ability to lead and to rule. Harriet Ritvo writes that for the Victorians, 'The animal kingdom, with humanity in a divinely ordained position at its apex, represented, explained and justified the hierarchical human social order'.[31] Care for the welfare of the animal would be analagous to the care for the 'lower orders' of the human hierarchy. In the crisis of battle, and supposedly in a just government, he who can spare a thought for both the great and small is the worthy leader. Thus Evan too is depicted in a crisis of his own affairs, as thinking of his horse's feed when he visits Jack Raikes at an inn:

'Did I order the feeding of the horse?' said Jack rising and yawning. 'No, I forgot him. Who can think of horses now?'
'Poor brute!' muttered Evan, and went out to see to him. (p. 222)

Like Evan's care for his horse, his help to the maid Polly Wheedle's pregnant sister when he has much else on his mind indicates that he is able to manage and justly treat the 'lower orders', whether they be of the animal or servant breed. Apparently his ability to keep his head and think of those who are supposedly below him places him among a natural aristocracy worthy to rule, or to lead England in battle. As in Tennyson's 'The Charge of the Light Brigade' there is thought for both man and horse: 'Storm'd at with shot and shell/While horse and hero fell – '.[32] Ironically in that poem it is the leaders who 'have blunder'd' in ordering the charge – sacrificing horse and man. As does Tennyson's poem, *Evan Harrington* questions the right of a hereditary aristocracy to lead. Indeed, inquiries into the incompetence of the leaders in the Crimean War were partly what led to the administrative reforms, and the opening of the Civil Service to proof of merit by competitive examination rather than patronage, as discussed earlier. In his anxiety to give his hero every advantage, Meredith seems to be in a quandary as to whether Evan will be raised into the upper classes by proof of his natural aristocracy in fair competition, or by the old system of patronage (through Rose's efforts) usually reserved for the younger sons of the aristocracy. Finally Evan has it both ways because Meredith himself cannot help admiring and envying the patronage and society of the upper classes, even as he feels himself naturally aristocratic and deserving of a place among them.

DISEASED LITTLE HEROINES

In Rose's unconscious relating of the breeding of her horses and dogs to the breeding of the man she wishes to marry, and through the relating of the nobility of horses in a hierarchy of animals to the nobility of those who can manage and breed them well, it is clear how closely allied are physical and moral breeding in *Evan Harrington*. A negative case of this lies in the portrayal of the 'little cripple' heiress, Rose's cousin Juliana Bonner. Juliana hails from the trade side of Rose's family. The Countess describes her and her relation to the Jocelyns:

> Her age must be twenty. You would take her for ten. In spite of her immense expectations, the Jocelyns hate her. They can hardly be civil to her. It is the poor child's temper. (p. 182)

Juliana is physically defective, and unlike the imperturbable Jocelyns, she often in her illness and frustration gives way to frenzies of temper and hysterical crying. In love with Evan and madly jealous of Rose, she has difficulty hiding her emotions from the Jocelyns:

> As the tears came thick and fast, she jumped up to lock the door, for this outrageous habit of crying had made her contemptible in the eyes of Lady Jocelyn, and an object of pity to Rose. Some excellent and noble natures cannot tolerate disease, and are mystified by its ebullitions. (p. 377)

Rose may indeed feel pity for her cousin, but she also takes part in a cruel family conspiracy which ignores Juliana's intelligence and need for love. If Juliana inherits Mrs Bonner's fortune, the Jocelyns require that their obtuse son Harry be immediately ready to marry her. They know that Harry does not care for his cousin, but Juliana represents the money and estate which they need to continue living as landed gentry.

Juliana is perhaps the most ambivalently portrayed character of the novel. We feel sympathy for her as she is drawn to her mirror, in hopes that she might find in her wasted features something which Evan may find attractive. Her love for Evan excites sympathy as well, especially as she believes him guiltless of the forgery which forces him to leave Beckley in disgrace, when even Rose doubts him. But the depth of her love and belief in him are called into question when we see her plotting to betray him, because she cannot bear his love for her cousin. The Countess belittles the nature of Juliana's love when she tells her sister Caroline, 'she is enamoured of his person. These little unhealthy creatures are always attracted by the person. She thinks it to be Evan's qualities. I know better' (p. 506). (It is interesting to note that the Countess calls Juliana a 'creature'; again the animal metaphor reveals the status of the human individual in the novel.) The Countess's voice can always be doubted by the reader, and we can believe her to be false and uncharitable to Juliana here. But a few chapters later, when Juliana is on her death-bed, the narratorial voice steps in to corroborate the Countess's assumptions:

The Countess was right in her judgement of Juliana's love. Juliana looked very little to his qualities. She loved him when she thought him guilty, which made her conceive that her love was of a diviner cast than Rose was capable of. Guilt did not spoil his beauty to her; his gentleness and glowing manhood were unchanged; and when she knew him as he was, the revelation of his high nature simply confirmed her impression of his physical perfections. (p. 521)

The validity of Juliana's love is undermined by her admiration of the merely physical; the question we might then ask is, how different is she from Rose in this? In her testing of Evan's physical prowess, Rose also conflates her lover's 'high nature' with his 'physical perfections'; she does recognize his moral nature, but it is so closely bound up with his physical heroism that it becomes almost impossible to imagine Rose loving Evan as a cripple. There is an element in Meredith's writing – his love of heroism, physical competition and strength – which supports Lady Jocelyn's attitude of contempt and impatience with those who, like Juliana, are weak or diseased. We are encouraged to believe that Rose's love is stronger and more real than Juliana's. By the end of the novel Rose's love wins by a rather cruel case of 'natural selection'; Juliana is killed off in chapter forty-two mainly as a plot device by which she can leave everything in her will to Evan, and through this bring Rose and her lover together. The beautiful and healthy must breed with each other. Meredith himself, with his handsome features and belief in heroically long walks (thirty miles a day in the Alps after his first wife left him), must have regarded himself as one example of a blessed and healthy species; his treatment of Juliana reveals that though he may pity her, she has no chance in his book of breeding Evan's children, or even of surviving.

Juliana is very conscious that she is of 'lower birth' than Rose, coming as she does from the trade side of the family tree. Although Meredith is at pains to prove that Evan, a child of trade, can still be naturally aristocratic, Juliana does not get such sensitive treatment; her nature is compared to that of the 'lower orders', to the servant class, in the following passage. Juliana has heard how a maid at Beckley,

> proclaimed of Evan, to a companion of her sex, that, 'he was the only gentleman who gave you an idea of how he would look when he was kissing you.' Juliana cherished that vision likewise. Young ladies are not supposed to do so, if menial maids are ... Bear in mind that she was not a healthy person. Diseased little heroines may be made attractive, and are now popular; but strip off the cleverly woven robe which is fashioned to cover them, and you will find them in certain matters bearing a resemblance to menial maids. (p. 522)

Here Meredith is not claiming, as Hardy does of the dairymaids at Talbothays in their love for Angel Clare, that all women have a common sexuality – or in Hardy's words, 'the differences which distinguished them as individuals were abstracted by this passion, and each was but portion of one organism called sex'.[33] Rose's sexuality is distinguished from that of menial maids and diseased heroines, partly because her physical desire for Evan is never referred to directly. Apparently menial maids *are* of a lower order – and perhaps a lower nature – and there is something cruel and degrading to Juliana in the treatment of her sexuality in this passage. The narrator strips Juliana naked, both metaphorically and physically by removing 'the cleverly woven robe' from her undergrown and diseased body, and seems to find her somewhat contemptible and repugnant. The 'diseased little heroines' such as Little Nell in *The Old Curiosity Shop* (1840–1), or Little Eva in Beecher Stowe's *Uncle Tom's Cabin* (1852), are loved for their moral goodness and stature, despite (and within this sentimental tradition partly because of) their physical illness. An interesting comparison with Juliana is a much later heroine, James's Milly Theale of *The Wings of the Dove* (1902), who has a gentle nature, and like Juliana leaves her riches to the man she loves. But Meredith seems to reject the idea that a physically debilitated heroine may have a high moral nature; this would be simply the 'cleverly woven robe' of the sentimental artist's imagination, 'fashioned to cover' – what? an equally diseased nature? Meredith comes disturbingly close to a kind of Social Darwinism; Juliana's physical defects are apparently a fairly accurate mirror of her moral defects, and in lumping the diseased heroine with 'menial maids', he implies that the servant classes are somehow of a degenerate or debased nature as well.

METAPHORICAL TAILORS

In his emulation of the 'gallant Percy', Evan turns to a code which predates the less noble code of the aristocracy or gentry of his own day. In writing the semi-autobiographical *Evan Harrington*, Meredith also turns to a fiction which, however recent, predates the more common stories which are associated with tailors in his own day. Margaret Tarratt has written upon links between *Evan Harrington* and Carlyle's *Sartor Resartus* (1833–4); of the latter she writes:

The tailor is the piercing eye, the man who cannot be deceived by the social pretensions of his 'betters'. He is the creator of the basic symbols used by Society to indicate and support the hierarchical structure. As such his knowledge and skill place him in the position of Shelley's poet, and the analogy ... is also reversed when poets and moral teachers become a 'Species of Metaphorical Tailors'.[34]

It is true that Evan 'cannot be deceived by the social pretensions of his "betters"', especially when they take the form of Laxley or Harry Jocelyn. But the link with *Sartor Resartus* is especially important because it helps Meredith remove Evan from the actual trade of the tailor shop, and to turn him into a 'metaphorical tailor'. Tarratt does not comment upon the more contemporary literary works and political pamphlets which dealt with the much-publicised plight of tailors and seamstresses in a literal and unmetaphorical treatment – works such as Thomas Hood's 'The Song of the Shirt' (published in *Punch* in 1843), Kingsley's *Alton Locke, Tailor and Poet* (1850), or his political pamphlet of 1849, 'Cheap Clothes and Nasty'. Meredith had been an admirer of Charles Kingsley's writing, and had sent his first published book of poetry to him to be reviewed, with a letter praising Kingsley's first novel *Yeast* (1848). Certainly Meredith would have been aware of Kingsley's works, and of the other numerous works in art and literature which dealt with the plight of journeymen tailors and seamstresses. In the late 1830s, Meredith's father had gone to London after the bankruptcy of his tailor shop in Portsmouth to become a journeyman tailor. Although Meredith did not move to the capital with his father he must have known something of the humble and probably very difficult circumstances in which he was working.

Although *Evan Harrington* may be considered Meredith's most autobiographical work, the 'autobiography' is removed by one generation back to the time of his grandfather and father. The experience of tailordom in the novel is distanced by time and the metaphor of *Sartor Resartus*; it is no work of social realism or reform. Although his novel does question to a certain extent the right of the hereditary aristocracy to rule, Meredith is not concerned here with giving a voice to the weak or poor. It is a natural aristocracy of the fit and strong that he champions, but this does not mean that he has no reverence for a hereditary aristocracy. Like Evan, Meredith seems to have 'inherited a feeling for rank'. He admires the modesty in Evan by which,

he never took Republican ground in opposition to those who insulted him ... nor compared the fineness of his instincts with the behaviour of titled gentlemen. Rather he seemed to admit the distinction between his birth and that of a gentleman, admitting it to his own soul, as it were, and struggled simply as men struggle against a destiny. (p. 290)

For Meredith it is a private struggle of the single strong and worthy man to raise himself in rank – not a social or revolutionary struggle against an existing hierarchy.

Norman Kelvin has written of the misconceptions surrounding Meredith's political leanings:

The generation of critics writing after Meredith's death in 1909 created for the public a monolithic, liberal-Radical Meredith, one who was always on the side of 'progress' and radical democracy. Meredith was such a person in 1848, and showed signs of becoming one again near his death. But in between – in his most fruitful years – his political and social ideas varied from decade to decade, and seldom, if ever did he show any real commitment to democratic idealism.[35]

In the mid-nineteenth century, memories of radical tailors associated with early unionization, Chartism and radicalism would still have resonated in the popular imagination. Meredith avoids these associations in his characterization of Evan; indeed, he assiduously preserves his hero from the tailor shop altogether. Like so many of Meredith's heroes, Evan is no radical working man, but a cultivated gentleman among the aristocracy.

The Countess distances herself from her background with a noble Portuguese pedigree, and the language and tactics of Continental fiction; Evan distances himself by hearkening back to the code of the noble Percy line as a desired model. Meredith too distances himself from the pain and shame of his own pedigree, both by removing the story from himself by a generation, making the tailordom of the novel mostly metaphorical, and choosing to write, not a radical novel of suffering journeymen tailors, but a novel of titled ladies and gentleman on an English country estate.

The next chapter takes as its focus Meredith's *The Egoist*. In this novel Meredith returns to the country estate setting even more claustrophobically than in *Evan Harrington*. In this later novel there is no hint of the tailor-gentleman; Sir Willoughby Patterne is the titled master of Patterne Hall. His pedigree however is also under threat, not from an outsider of the trading class, but from within: from within his own class, through the women he wishes to marry; from within his family tree, through his cousins; from within himself, through an egoism which threatens to send him degenerating swiftly backwards on his family tree to a primitive ancestor.

CHAPTER FIVE

Pedigree, sati and the widow in Meredith's 'The Egoist'

> 'True to My Dust? ... True to My Name!'
> George Meredith, *The Egoist*, p. 57.

In his poem, 'The Pedigree', Hardy provides two different images for the genealogical tree, images which ultimately are in conflict. He writes first of the 'long perspective' of the straight line, leading back to some origin, to 'the primest fuglemen of my line'. This is the image that family patriarchs keep before them as they record their family history in gilt-edged tomes. Fascination with the remote ancestor is at work upon various fictional *paterfamiliae* from the eighteenth century through to the twentieth: there is, for example, Sir Walter Elliot in Jane Austen's *Persuasion*, who turns to the pages of the baronetage for comfort; there are the numerous pedigree-proud fathers of nineteenth-century fiction, including the father of Basil, in Wilkie Collins's early novel of that name, Squire Hamley of Gaskell's *Wives and Daughters*, or Consul Johann Buddenbrook in Thomas Mann's *Buddenbrooks*. The other, opposing image for the pedigree in Hardy's poem is more problematic than a straight line back to early ancestors; it is described, as the man scans his own pedigree at night:

And the hieroglyphs of this spouse tied to that,
With offspring mapped below in lineage,
Till the tangles troubled me,
The branches seemed to twist into a seared and cynic face.[1]

If the first image could describe the male head of the family looking back to his 'fuglemen', it may be that the second could give attention to some female concerns in viewing a mapped lineage. Although women are necessary breeders of the patrilineal descent, in this system they are not directly part of the line. On a pedigree the woman's name usually appears away from the line after a dash next to the husband's name, or to the side and underneath her parents. As wife or daughter, she is peripheral or collateral to the patrilineal; her perspective on the pedigree may be concerned less with the linear perspective of 'distant fuglemen' and more with the complex branches and offshoots spreading from the line, representing marriages and offspring.

For many women in fiction who are entering upon a marriage engagement and who are therefore preparing to perform their part in continuing a pedigree, the 'tangles' of family alliance are troubling. In Mann's *Buddenbrooks* (1901) for instance, Tony becomes fascinated one morning upon reading her father's meticulously-kept pedigree, and finally seduced by it, she writes her own betrothal into the blank space under her name. It is the betrothal to the man who will 'fit' into the family history and not the man she would have chosen for love. The tangles and ties of the family tree hold her to what she feels is a kind of inevitable destiny of the patrilineal, and in that moment she does not fight it.

This chapter focusses in part upon a female protagonist who does decide to fight the destiny of the family tree onto which she is being grafted against her will. Clara Middleton, the heroine of George Meredith's *The Egoist*, is engaged to the handsome, wealthy and charming Sir Willoughby Patterne. But during a pre-wedding holiday, sequestered on Willoughby's country estate, Clara realizes to her horror that she has developed an intense aversion to her betrothed. Her increasingly desperate attempts to disengage herself with dignity from Willoughby are complicated by the fact that Willoughby will not release her from the solemn vow of betrothal that he has elicited from her; as he puts it, 'they were plighted, they were one eternally, they could not be parted.'[2]

Willoughby Patterne's egoism extends from himself to his family line: just as he regards his own person as the origin and focus of all thought to those around him, so his view of his genealogy is that of a line originating with himself and continuing in a line of small copies or patterns of himself. Willoughby rarely speaks of his ancestors; his concern is with the line coming after him, and, repeatedly invoking his 'duty to his line' he sets about the task of finding and keeping a suitably healthy and beautiful breeder to propagate it. He sees his pedigree as a line stemming from himself rather than a family tree laden with the branches of collateral kin. But there are shadow pedigrees which disturb the linearity of Willoughby's vision. These are the possible family lines which Willoughby could forge with three different women in the novel: with Constantia, who to the surprise of the county has fled Willoughby just prior to their marriage, and of whom we hear only indirectly; with

Laetitia Dale, who has admired Willoughby from her humble position in a cottage on his estate since she was a young girl; and with Clara. During the course of the novel, and particularly in the farcical last chapters, it is impossible to predict whether Willoughby will finally mate with Clara or Laetitia or neither. The fortunes and the propagatrix of his future pedigree are left up in the air as the women discover his egoism and resist being grafted on to a family tree which is so centered in the male line and in a male ego. In conversation with her twelve-year-old admirer, Crossjay, a young cousin of Willoughby's, Clara comes to the conclusion that the loss of her surname to Willoughby may entail a loss of herself:

'But, Miss Middleton, when you're married you won't be Clara Middleton.'
'I certainly shall, Crossjay.'
'No, you won't, because I'm so fond of your name!'
She considered, and said: 'You have warned me, Crossjay, and I shall not marry.' (p. 298)

Clara realizes that by changing her last name to 'Patterne' she will lose, as Crossjay unconsciously intimates, not only her maiden name, but something of her essential identity as Clara Middleton. The patrilineal system of recording genealogy leads to the loss of the woman's ancestry and the history of her family name in the records. Constantia, Clara and Laetitia all in their turn resist this assimilation and the literal and symbolic loss of their name and separate identity, by resisting the Patterne pedigree. Meredith's privileging of their stories, in his presentation of them while they still hold their maiden names and identities, enables him to present a model of matrilineal narrative that is alternative to the 'pattern' of Willoughby's line.

Not only does Meredith undermine the patrilineal perspective of genealogy, but also the patrilineal narrative, which traditionally follows the adventures of a hero of noble descent. Unaristocratic Patternes, as well as women, abound in *The Egoist*, disturbing the linearity of 'begetters, dwindling backward each past each/ All with the kindred look'.[3] Meredith puts forward an alternative non-linear image of genealogy in the beginning of the first chapter of *The Egoist*. His introduction of the Patternes of Patterne Hall reveals all the complications and knotty branchiness of the family tree:

There was an ominously anxious watch of eyes visible and invisible over the infancy of Willoughby, fifth in descent from Simon Patterne of Patterne Hall, premier of this family, a lawyer, a man of solid acquirements and stout ambition, who well understood the foundation-work of a House, and was endowed with the power of saying No to those first agents of destruction, besieging relatives. He said it with the resonant emphasis of death to younger sons. For if the oak is to become a stately tree, we must provide against the crowding of timber. Also the tree beset with parasites prospers not. A great House in its beginnings lives, we may truly say, by the knife ... Pauper Patternes were numerous when the fifth head of the race was the hope of his county. A Patterne was in the Marines. (pp. 6–7)

The metaphor for the genealogy of the Patternes turns from that of the bricks and mortar of foundation-work, to a house under siege, to the oak in a crowded wood, to a tree beset by parasites, to a tree in need of pruning. As J. Hillis Miller has noted, the word 'pedigree' is itself a metaphor, derived from the Old French *pied de grue*, or crane's foot, which resembles the shape of a genealogical tree.[4] The passage may in fact be partly inspired by Darwin's equally metaphorical passage in *On the Origin of Species*, describing 'the struggle for existence':

The missletoe is dependent on the apple and a few other trees, but can only in a far-fetched sense be said to struggle with these trees, for if too many of these parasites grow on the same tree, it will languish and die. But several seedling missletoes, growing close together on the same branch, may more truly be said to struggle with each other. As the missletoe is disseminated by birds, its existence depends on birds; and it may metaphorically be said to struggle with other fruit-bearing plants, in order to tempt birds to devour and thus disseminate its seeds rather than those of other plants.[5]

In these passages, metaphor collapses into metaphor, until the signification of 'pedigree' seems to become infinitely collapsible into yet another trope, another perspective. The novel enacts this deconstruction as the numerous and shifting permutations and possibilities of Willoughby's pedigree slip into each other from one chapter to the next; in his anxiety to reproduce himself, in his 'duty to his line', he invests himself completely in the idea of a new line as each of the three women reject him. When Constantia Durham discards him, she becomes immediately 'extinct' to Willoughby as he saves face by immediately wooing Laetitia. The morning after Willoughby has discovered Constantia's elopement with an officer, Laetitia, unknowing, asks after Miss Durham. Willoughby replies, 'Durham? ... there is no Miss Durham to my knowledge' (p. 24). She simply ceases to exist, and Willoughby allows the county to invest themselves imaginatively, as they had with Constantia, in the idea of Laetitia Dale as the mistress of Patterne Hall. But Willoughby is still harping on his pedigree; 'He had his eyes awake. His duty to his House was a foremost thought with him, and for such a reason he may have been more anxious to give the slim and not robust Laetitia to Vernon than accede to his personal inclination' (pp. 18–9). Laetitia may not be robust and healthy enough to breed his offspring, so he leaves her for a grand tour to America and returns to meet the healthy and beautiful Clara Middleton. Just as the confused county gentry must adjust themselves to a new mistress of Patterne Hall as the fortunes of Constantia, Laetitia, Clara and Laetitia (again) rise and fall, so Willoughby adjusts himself to a new version of his pedigree, believing, and ensuring that the county believes, in a retrospective narrative in which he never loved the previous woman, or even ceasing to believe that she existed. His ordered and 'scientific' approach to the future of his line (he invokes a Darwinian language of heredity and sexual selection) is rendered farcical and eventually meaningless by his abrupt and total reversals as each woman rejects him. The equally abrupt changes in metaphor by which Meredith describes the Patterne pedigree in the above passage from the opening of chapter one may give a sense that, behind all those alternating tropes signifying pedigree, there may be nothing. The baroque elaborateness of metaphor upon metaphor may be a facade hiding the fact that pedigree itself is not simply a line or trunk of a noble or privileged family, but can be infinitely inclusive of daughters, wives, younger sons, poorer unaristocratic branches of the tree, 'cousins' to the nth degree, and so on until in its all-inclusiveness it contains the entire human race, and without limits, loses all meaning.

However, in the terms of kinship and narrative, Meredith is not writing a novel about the human race, but about a few people staying on an English country estate. Within this limited space Willoughby's rapidly alternating future pedigree, and the importance of the minor branches of his family tree to the novel's plot, question the linearity of perspective that Willoughby holds of his ancestors and descendants. This disturbance of linear perspective questions the idea of pedigree sufficiently to make it a fairly meaningless term by the end of the novel. Pedigree peters out both metaphorically and literally; Willoughby finally marries the faded Laetitia to save face before the county and probably to save his sanity, but he knows that in this he may have sacrificed his future pedigree; 'Haply also he had sacrificed more: he looked scientifically into the future: he might have sacrificed a nameless more' (p. 585).

The originating point of a family line could be any one of the branches of the family tree, depending upon the angle or viewpoint that the reader of the pedigree takes. Each branch, or crane's ligament, could be the new premier of another family line. Fiction works in a similar manner; a novel has a protagonist, but the minor characters have their own stories to tell, and it is the choice of the author to suppress some stories and privilege others. In much Victorian fiction, and especially the works of Dickens, Trollope, and George Eliot, there is a heightened awareness of the life stories of the minor characters. Subplots proliferate, and often become entangled with the main plot, resembling and often representing the branchiness of a family pedigree.

The beginning of chapter one – 'There was an ominously anxious watch of eyes visible and invisible over the infancy of Willoughby, fifth in descent from Simon Patterne of Patterne Hall' – places the noble line immediately before the reader, leading to expectations of a traditional narrative following the fortunes of the noble heir. But the titles of the following three chapters are in turn, 'Constantia Durham', 'Laetitia Dale', and 'Clara Middleton', departing from the noble line into a disruptive matrilineal narrative. Equally, 'cousins' disrupt both the narrative focus on the noble line, and the line of Willoughby's succession. Crossjay Patterne and Vernon Whitford are both removed from the direct line of Patterne inheritance; they are from poor and lesser branches of Willoughby's pedigree. But they are important characters in the novel, and they both succeed in ruining Willoughby's plans for the future of his line: Crossjay by accidentally overhearing Willoughby's proposal to Laetitia when he is still engaged to Clara, and Vernon by becoming the man that Clara decides to marry.

Crossjay is the son of Lieutenant Crossjay Patterne, a poor but heroic cousin of Willoughby's who is trying to support a large and hungry family. Vernon Whitford, Willoughby's cousin and personal secretary takes responsibility for the boy, educating and supporting him. Years before, when Willoughby had come into his majority, he had 'cut' young Crossjay's father. Having heard of the Marine's heroic act overseas, Willoughby deigns to acknowledge this poor relation with an invitation to Patterne Hall. When the Lieutenant comes to call on Willoughby, arriving in a torrential rainstorm, Willoughby spies his approach from the terrace and, unwilling to acknowledge as his relative a drenched man who bears the appearance of 'a bankrupt tradesman absconding; no gloves, no umbrella' (p. 9), he sends the message that he is 'not at home,' and the man has no choice but to return the way he came, plodding another ten miles in the rain. Here Meredith describes Willoughby as 'supremely advanced at a very early age in the art of cutting' (p. 10). But no matter how much Willoughby cuts or prunes his family tree, he cannot help becoming entangled in its branches; Willoughby's cousins, Crossjay and Vernon, unconsciously weave their stories in with his own, possibly causing the downfall of the Patterne succession.

So, 'cousins', those 'besieging relatives' that Willoughby's founding ancestor cut off so summarily, besiege Willoughby in ways that he could never have expected. By the time Willoughby comes into his majority, the cutting and pruning process on the family tree has already been executed very effectively by his ancestors. Remote founders of an old House are not expected to have a great deal of subtlety or finesse; they cut and hack away in a barbarous fashion, whether it be literally at the limbs of infidels in Crusading wars, or at the outstretched palms of mendicant relatives. However, Willoughby is a student of Science, and believes in progress and 'civilization'. But of his social cutting of Lieutenant Patterne the narrator ominously states that the 'imps' of comedy 'perceived in him a fresh development and very subtle manifestation of the very old thing from which he had sprung' (p. 10). This 'very old thing' is not the lawyer Simon Patterne who founded the family five generations ago; behind a mask of civilization, Willoughby is reverting to a much earlier ancestor on his family tree. In his 'prelude' to the novel, Meredith discusses how 'Science' (Darwinian theory) has led us to look very far back on our family tree to 'our o'er-hoary ancestry – them in the Oriental posture'. But Meredith looks to the Comic Muse, rather than science, to discover our early ancestors; he continues, 'Art is the specific. We have little to learn of apes, and they may be left' (p. 3). The Comic Muse deals not with apes, but with the human animal, and it is not necessary to look to apes to discover our barbarous ancestors; they can be found on a human line of descent. Willoughby has reverted to barbarity, and the novel's action is fuelled by the methods in which this barbarity is scantily clad in the robes of the civilized rituals of English country house society.

THE PREUX CHEVALIER

I saw a handsome man with wavy grey hair and short grey beard, in talk with a group of women with low necks and adoring looks. The man's profile was clear as a cameo, and his face had an intellectual refinement that was almost excessive, and not typically English ... Meredith wore the polite smile of an eighteenth-century *preux chevalier*, and was responding to the ladies' questions with witty little apothegms and paradoxes ... But his manner had not the ease of a man of the world, profound though was his insight into the world ... but his self-possession was, I thought, assumed; he was really shy and embarrassed, and trying to act up to what the ladies expected of him. (Julian Hawthorne on Meredith)[6]

In Chapter Four I argued that the hero of Meredith's *Evan Harrington* had found an alternative, psychological pedigree which helped him to overcome his shame and feelings of inferiority as a tailor on a country house estate. This pedigree was that of the English royal line of Percy, and Evan identified with 'that happy and glorious time', 'those days of knights and battles'. Willoughby also creates alternative, imaginative pedigrees for himself which obscure the fact that his ancestors were merely careful lawyers only five generations before.

The American writer Julian Hawthorne's observation of Meredith quoted at the opening of this section reveals Meredith acting out the part of *preux chevalier* or gallant knight, perhaps in much the same manner as his character Evan Harrington; both have a tailor ancestry to rise above. Willoughby also reverts to a previous historical era which enables him psychologically to rise above a pedigree which, although not embarrassing, he may feel is not quite good enough for him. Rather than the gallant knight, he sees himself as a gay cavalier of the Stuart court. Mrs. Mountstuart's epithet for him, 'He has a leg', only encourages this, as her phrase captures the imagination of the county ladies:

Dwell a short space on Mrs Mountstuart's word; and whither, into what fair region, and with how decorously voluptuous a sensation, do not we fly, who have, through mournful veneration of the Martyr Charles, a coy attachment to the Court of his Merrie Son, where the leg was ribboned with love-knots and reigned. Oh! it was a naughty court. Yet we have dreamed of it as the period when an English cavalier was grace incarnate. (p. 12)

Apparently Willoughby dresses the part as well: 'And the ladies knew for a fact that Willoughby's leg was exquisite; he had a cavalier court-suit in his wardrobe.' Rather than five generations of lawyers, Willoughby's leg at least can claim a literary and romantic genealogy of court poets: 'He has the leg of Rochester, Buckingham, Dorset, Suckling' (p. 13).

Willoughby wishes to distance himself from his crude forebears who carry the mercenary taint of professionalism. He achieves this distance partly by modelling himself as a gay cavalier before the county and partly by becoming renowned for his generosity towards 'cousins', those who in the eyes of his ancestors were impecunious 'besieging ancestors' who had to be lopped off the family tree. The county and Willoughby himself both believe in his 'good breeding', both in the sense of a pure pedigree, and in the ease of manners and the generosity that the phrase implies. But a closer look at the way he conducts himself, which is given to the reader, and to the three women in Willoughby's life – Constantia, Clara, and Laetitia – reveals that his generosity is merely the mask given to a ruthlessly possessive nature which could hearken back to the most barbaric of ancestors, perhaps much further back than Simon Patterne, the lawyer. Meredith warns us of this in the Prelude to the novel:

Aforetime a grand old Egoism built the House. It would appear that even finer essences of it are demanded to sustain the structure; but especially would it appear that a reversion to the gross original, beneath a mask and in a vein of fineness, is an earthquake at the foundations of the House. Better that it should not have consented to motion, and have held stubbornly to all ancestral ways, than have bred that anachronic spectre. (p. 6)

Willoughby's feudalism is of an opposite kind to that of his ancestors, who cut off 'besieging relatives'. He gathers a few aunts, cousins and tenants about him on his estate and parcels out a paternalistic generosity which renders them subservient and dependent.

THE 'NAUGHTY COURT' AND THE VICTORIAN COUNTRY HOUSE

Each member that Willoughby allows a place in Patterne Hall serves a feudal function. Vernon acts as his secretary. His two old spinster aunts serve as a reliable and unquestioning chorus to the county's praises and admiration of their youthful lord. The third 'spinster' lady, not so old, is the beautiful and poetic Laetitia Dale, a tenant on his estate with her ailing father. She quite literally sings her lord's praises, writing and reciting poetry about him at the grand party celebrating his majority.

Unlike Willoughby's spinster aunts, Laetitia is not past the age of child-bearing or sexual attractiveness. Indeed she is an attractive and marriageable woman, and the county favourite for Willoughby's wife when first introduced. This makes her 'spinsterhood' especially precious to Willoughby; he watches her change over the years from maiden to spinster, and believes all the time what is at first true of her – that she has sacrificed her sexuality and youth for him. For the young Laetitia, Willoughby is a county Hamlet, 'the glass of fashion and the mould of form'. Like the submissive Ophelia, she extracts hope from his tender words, and crushes it when she realizes he will never marry her. She is kept dangling over the years, until her chances of marriage are gone, secluded as she is on Willoughby's estate from contact with other men.

Willoughby's widowed mother, lying on her death-bed, confides to Laetitia that Willoughby calls her his 'Egeria', and exhorts her to live up to her namesake. In *Metamorphoses*, Ovid tells of Egeria, a nymph who is inconsolable after her husband's death. Retreating to a wood she weeps so much that Diana turns her into a mountain spring. Laetitia is to sacrifice herself in constancy to Willoughby, to be the self-immolating widow without having the privilege of being made a wife first. In this way, Willoughby desexualizes her, and a look at his household reveals that it is a collection of desexualized dependents who must centre their lives about him: there is the widowed mother, whom Willoughby extols to Clara because she stayed faithful to her husband's ashes; the spinster aunts; Laetitia, and finally Vernon Whitford. If Willoughby aspires to the manners of what Meredith describes as the 'naughty court' of Charles II, there is very little naughtiness in Willoughby's court of Patterne Hall; all the women must centre their fantasies and desires in him, or have none. Vernon Whitford is the only other man not of the servant class in Patterne Hall. Willoughby most often describes him as 'old Vernon', consistently presenting him to the world as a harmless scholastic bumbler, as dry and dusty as the books that Willoughby 'generously' makes available to him from the Patterne library. Willoughby's attempts to desexualize Vernon (which ultimately do not succeed) reveal the primitive, possessive aspects of his own sexuality; if it were possible under English law he would like to lay claim to the love of all women: 'He was of a vast embrace; and do not exclaim, in covetousness; for well he knew that even under Moslem law he could not have them all' (p. 162).

So, although Willoughby, unlike his ancestors, does gather a few 'besieging relatives' as loyal serfs about him, they are all neutered in some way by their contact with him. He ensures the centrality and strength of his family line and of himself more subtly than did his ancestors, by seeing to it that none of those who serve in his court will ever be able to produce cluttering branches to his family tree.

After Darwin, the contemplation of family ancestry, even if it could be traced back only five generations, would have conjured thoughts inevitably of a much further removed ancestry – the proverbial monkey. Indeed, Willoughby actually sees monkeys at a crucial moment in his courtship of Clara, when he tries to make her swear that if he dies she will be true to his ashes. She evades and refuses, making him desperate at the thought of a woman not absolutely 'pure' in her loyalty, a woman who could produce another family after he is gone, who could propagate a pedigree alternative to his. As says to her, 'It is no delusion, my love, when I tell you that with this thought upon me I see a ring of monkey faces grinning at me; they haunt me. But you do swear it! ... That you will be true to me dead as well as living!' (p. 58).

Willoughby is monkey-haunted, haunted by those who in his eyes let themselves regress upon the evolutionary ladder. Purity in women is essential to evolutionary order and progress in his eyes, and of course this is particularly true of patrilinear inheritance; if the women are not pure and faithful, then the blood lines will be brought to a chaos of uncertainty and mixture. As he says to Clara, 'especially in women, distinction is the thing to be aimed at. Otherwise we are a weltering human mass. Women must teach us to venerate them, or we may as well be bleating and barking and bellowing' (p. 60).

SEXUAL SELECTION AND THE MARRIAGE MARKET

Willoughby has courted Clara with an energy both bewildering and flattering to her, partly for the glory of winning over many rivals, but also because he wants to possess her quickly, before she becomes shop-soiled by the 'pack' of men who surround her in the marriage market. He goes about winning her 'scientifically':

The superlative is magnetic to her. She may be looking elsewhere, and you will see – the superlative will simply have to beckon and away she glides. She cannot help herself; it is her nature, and her nature is the guarantee for the noblest races of men to come of her. In complimenting you, she is the promise of superior offspring. Science thus – or it is better to say – an acquaintance with science facilitates the cultivation of aristocracy (p. 43).

Willoughby prides himself upon his scientific knowledge, and he is well-versed in the language of Darwinian theory, and specifically of sexual selection. Darwin's treatment of sexual selection in the *Origin of Species* is clearly influential upon Meredith's *Evan Harrington*, and this is understandable; this aspect of Darwinian theory lends itself most naturally to novels concerning courtship and 'mating rituals'. Darwin gave sexual selection a fairly brief treatment in the *Origin*; it is in his 1871 *The Descent of Man, and Selection in Relation to Sex* that the discussion of sexual selction is prevalent, comprising over two-thirds of the work. Appearing eight years after the publication of *The Descent*, *The Egoist* resonates with its influence.

Willoughby's description of sexual selection is fairly true to Darwin's *Descent*, particularly in the county baronet's theme that it is the aristocracy who are in every way the best, the 'noblest races of men' to come from woman's choice. Although this view may seem to approach Social Darwinism, it was nevertheless Darwin's view. As Jonathan Smith notes in his study of sexual selection in *The Egoist*, Darwin considered 'the aristocracy a special case. In the rest of human society sexual selection, viewed solely in physical terms, no longer operates: the battle for women has ceased, and class concerns have become paramount. But aristocratic men, and particularly eldest sons like Willoughby, are free to select middle-class women like Clara for their health and beauty.'[7] As Darwin writes in *The Descent*:

Many persons are convinced, as it appears to me with justice, that our aristocracy, including under this term all wealthy families in which primogeniture has long prevailed, from having chosen during many generations from all classes the more beautiful women as their wives, have become handsomer, according to the European standard, than the middle classes.[8]

It is interesting and somewhat paradoxical that the physical sexual selection which Darwin claims is now limited to the animal world is yet carried on among that class of humanity which considers itself very far superior to apes, the lower classes, and other sorts of 'animals'. Darwin's 'special case' of the aristocracy could be seen as his unconscious rendering of what Meredith describes in *The Egoist* as a 'reversion to the gross original, beneath a mask and in a vein of fineness' (p. 6).

In Willoughby's assessment of sexual selection in the above passage from chapter five of the novel, it is the woman who chooses the male, and this is consistent with Darwinian theory. Darwin, however, again makes a special case of the aristocracy: it is the primogenitive males who may select a woman from 'all classes' for their wives. Whatever Willoughby believes about the influence of his physical charms upon Clara, the latter formulation is more consistent with Willoughby's practice: Clara is selected. As Willoughby says to Mrs Mountstuart of his choice, 'I would ... have bargained for health above everything, but she has everything besides – lineage, beauty, breeding; is what they call an heiress, and is the most accomplished of her sex' (p. 45).

In 'bargaining' for Clara's health, Willoughby reveals his investment in both evolutionary theory (with her health 'the survival of the Patternes was assured') and the marriage market, in which he bargains for her before she becomes shop-soiled. Aside from Darwin's noting of the possibility of a special case for the aristocracy, sexual selection was generally regarded as an early practice, obsolete in human courtship rituals. Equally, for Victorian anthropologists and ethnologists, the 'marriage market' was a practice consigned to long ago or to primitive societies such as that of ancient Babylon: it had no bearing upon nineteenth-century Christian English marriage. In his study of Victorian anthropology George Stocking maintains that Victorian sociocultural evolutionists, all saw the evolutionary process culminating in a monogamous family resembling that of mid-Victorian Britain.'[9] Whereas Victorian anthropologists such as John McClennan, whose influential *Primitive Marriage* was published in 1865, made little or no connection, metaphorically or otherwise, between primitive courtship and marital practices and those of contemporary English society, Meredith's *The Egoist* is inundated with such connections and comparisons. *The Egoist* employs specifically orientalist metaphors indicating that the marital practices of Oriental 'primitive' cultures are thriving metaphorically in English society. Before considering more closely Meredith's comparison of English and Oriental cultures, it is helpful to explore briefly just how much currency Meredith's comparative 'anthropological' stance had in the 1870s. Was it a stance taken with ease? Was it simply popular currency to speak of, for example, the 'marriage market' as a phenomenon equally at home in the cultures of contemporary England and the Orient? Attempts to excavate popular attitudes and idioms of the past are notoriously difficult, and in this case a move across genres from the novel to painting and art criticism may be illuminating. *The Egoist* is permeated with the language of the marriage market, and specifically of the 'primitive' oriental marriage market; therefore a closer look at one of the most popular paintings of the 1870s which takes this market as its subject may give some clues as to how new or radical Meredith's comparative cultural stance was at this time.

THE BABYLONIAN MARRIAGE MARKET

Edwin Longsden Long's painting *The Babylonian Marriage Market* was exhibited at the Royal Academy in 1875, four years before the publication of *The Egoist*. The enormous popularity and warm critical reception of the picture gained Long his Associateship of the Royal Academy. Long took his subject from George C. Swayne's history of *Herodotus* (1870), and his entry for the painting in the Royal Academy catalogue is from Swayne's description of the Babylonian marriage market. Both

Figure 9 Edwin Longsden Long, *The Babylonian Marriage Market*, exhibited at the Royal Academy, 1875.

Swayne's account and Long's use of it give significant insights into contemporary attitudes to the 'marriage market'. Swayne describes the 'wife-auction, by which they managed to find husbands for all their young women':

> The greatest beauty was put up first, and knocked down to the highest bidder; then the next in order of comeliness – and so on to the damsel who was equidistant between beauty and plainness, who was given away gratis. Then the least plain was put up, and knocked down to the gallant who would marry her for the smallest consideration, – and so on until even the plainest was got rid of to some cynical worthy who decidedly preferred lucre to looks ... The Babylonian marriage market might perhaps be advantageously adopted in some modern countries where marriage is still made a commercial matter. It at least possesses the merit of honesty and openness, and tends to a fair distribution of the gifts of fortune.[10]

Where are these 'modern countries where marriage is still made a commercial matter'? Surely there is a touch of irony in Swayne's comment here, especially when one considers the widespread treatment of marriages for money or status in the nineteenth-century novel from Edith in Dickens's *Dombey and Son* to Trollope's Lady Glencora, and in numerous paintings of the day such as William Quiller Orchardson's *Mariage de Convenance* (1884). It is possible that George Swayne, and through Swayne, Edwin Long, are using the Babylonian marriage market as a mirror held up to Victorian society. Certainly Long's painting is tantalizing in its employment of mirroring effects. The girl in the left foreground holds up a mirror to view herself before she ascends the selling platform, but in effect the whole painting is a mirror, reflecting the viewer back to him or herself. As viewers of the painting our gaze is drawn to the back of the woman on display, as she draws away her veil for the Babylonian men, and our gaze is reflected in that of those men – viewers inside and outside the painting are focussed on the same woman. Some of the women in the painting who are waiting backstage in the foreground stare out directly at the viewer, in their gaze bringing a consciousness to the viewer of being included in the scene, and also a consciousness of his or her own gaze, which considering the theme and plan of the painting, cannot help but be voyeuristic.

According to the *Academy* the painting was 'the town-talk of a season' and large crowds thronged around it during the exhibition.[11] How many among those crowds sensed in the mirroring effects of the painting a mirroring of their own society it would be hard to say; however John Ruskin's comments on the work in *Academy Notes* demonstrate the formation of at least the beginnings of a subtle, comparative cultural stance in response to the painting. Ruskin begins his analysis of Long's *Marriage Market* by asserting that it is 'a painting of great merit, and well deserving purchase by the Anthropological Society'. But Ruskin is not, in this suggestion, simply pointing to the 'Oriental' detail, and the 'varieties of character in the heads' displayed in the different Babylonian figures; he writes later in the article of the anthropological merits of the work: 'As a piece of anthropology it is the natural product of a century occupied in carnal and mechanical science.'[12] Ruskin is not writing an account here of ancient Babylon, but is averting the anthropological gaze away from distant primitive or ancient societies towards modern English and European society. His final comments make this abundantly clear, and are specifically concerned with the institution of the 'marriage market':

as the most beautiful and marvellous maidens were announced for literal sale by auction in Assyria, are not also the souls of our most beautiful and marvellous maidens announced annually for sale by auction in Paris and London, in a spiritual manner, for the spiritual advantage of a position in society? (p. 20)

William Michael Rossetti, writing in the *Academy*, also noted that the painting's success lay partly in its combination of 'antique fact and modern innuendo'.[13]

Long's painting and the responses to it do reveal an 'anthropological' stance which turns to examine the customs and rituals of the English marriage market as well as the Babylonian. These are comparative cultural stances which are subtly, tentatively put forward. Although in *The Egoist* George Meredith's writing style is sometimes indirect, even obscure, his metaphorical comparisons between Oriental and English marriage customs are forthright and clear. The novel is so punctuated with Oriental metaphors that the cultural comparisons are blatantly obvious in spite of Meredith's 'obscurity': for example, Willoughby regrets the possibility of losing Laetitia's 'adoring worship' because 'the soft cherishable Parsee is hardly at any season other than prostrate' (p. 157); Clara's father has to remind himself after a few glasses of Willoughby's port, 'yet we are not turbaned Orientals, nor are they inmates of the harem. We are not Moslem' (p. 235); and Willoughby has to remind himself (often) that he can only have one wife, 'he knew that even under Moslem law he could not have them all' (p. 162). Even Willoughby's gestures begin to take on an 'Oriental' rhythm: 'Swaying his head, like the Oriental palm whose shade is a blessing' (p. 176), as he futilely tries to escape a primitive 'o'er-hoary ancestry – them in the Oriental posture' (p. 2).

Meredith's novel is obviously full of many of the orientalist assumptions of nineteenth-century anthropology and popular myth, but his writing diverges from this new Victorian science in that he, like Ruskin, Rossetti, and (perhaps) Edwin Long, is willing to turn the anthropological gaze in upon his own society. This he does through a plethora of oriental metaphors, but the one which is the most pervasive, and the most significant to a discussion of the egoist's interrelated anxieties over marriage, death and the family line, is the theme of the widow and the Hindu ritual of 'suttee' or 'sati' in the novel.[14]

CONTAGIOUS WORDS

Certain words in *The Egoist* hold an almost incantatory power: the word 'egoist' itself acts powerfully upon Clara Middleton when Willoughby unwittingly ends an anecdote saying, 'Beware of marrying an Egoist, my dear' (p. 115). His absolute blindness to the fact that he has just described himself confounds Clara, and the word itself begins to act upon her, gradually giving her a way to formulate her aversion to her betrothed. Knowing that he is an egoist releases her from the fear that she is, as her father, the county and Willoughby would describe her, simply irrational and quixotic in her wish to be released from her engagement. The word 'egoist' reverberates throughout the novel, spreading in a linguistic contagion: Clara calls herself an egoist, then in thinly-veiled terms describes men in general as egoists to Laetitia Dale. Laetitia then catches the word from Clara, and it seems to enter her – perhaps encapsulating her nagging disillusionment with Willoughby – giving her repressed anger a name and then a voice. Expressing the word to Laetitia, Clara apologizes, saying, 'I have not your power to express ideas', but Laetitia replies, 'Miss Middleton, you have a dreadful power' (p. 191). The word then seems to incubate inside Laetitia, until she finally voices it, crying out in the climactic scene of her acceptance of Willoughby; 'Privation has made me what an abounding fortune has made of others – I am an Egoist' (p. 618).

The Irishman Horace de Craye, who comes to Patterne Hall later in the novel to prepare for his role as Willoughby's best man, is another character whose words, like Clara's, have a 'dreadful power'. Willoughby, threatened by the introduction of a sexual rival into his well-guarded court, is ill at ease with de Craye's wit and linguistic facility. He attempts to desexualize the Irishman by treating his stories, jokes and 'prattle' as if they were the language of a child, and this is related to the prevailing regard of Ireland as an 'infant' nation in need of indulgent and fatherly treatment, discussed in earlier chapters. But, like the political subversiveness hinted at in de Craye's comic forebear, the Irish fortune-hunter, de Craye's language holds a power that is highly subversive in Willoughby's dominion. Willoughby tries to combat his Irish friend's linguistic seductions by treating him as a man from a primitive, barbarous culture, from whom sense cannot be expected. De Craye turns this tactic on its head by using language which subtly associates Willoughby with what was popularly regarded as the 'primitive', 'barbarous' ritual of sati.

The first direct reference to sati occurs at Mrs. Mountstuart's disastrous dinner party, although the novel is riddled with oblique references to the custom. We only hear about what was said at the dinner retrospectively, mainly through Clara, and it is she who relates de Craye's comment on sati to Mrs. Mountstuart, revealing that unconsciously she has registered something powerful in de Craye's seemingly innocuous joke:

'You did not hear him? He took advantage of an interval when Mr. Capes was breathing after a paean to his friend, the Governor – I think – of one of the Presidencies, to say to the lady beside him: "He was a wonderful administrator and a great logician; he married an Anglo-Indian widow, and soon after published a pamphlet in favour of Suttee".'
'And what did the lady say?'
'She said: "Oh!' (p. 423).

The lady to whom Horace appears to address this snippet treats it with utter incomprehension, because it was really addressed to Clara. Clara understands only that there is something in the reference to sati which impinges on her relationship to Willoughby, a something which she cannot yet define or formulate. Horace merely plants the word in the middle of the dinner table carefully within Clara's hearing, to take fruit if it falls on a fertile mind. It is de Craye's mischievous reference to sati that occasions Clara's first formulation of her projected marriage as an immolation. His joke reveals to her also that he acknowledges her unwillingness to approach the altar as bridal sacrifice. She begins to make a connection between her own future as seemingly privileged British bride, and the fate of the Hindu widow.

HINDU WIDOW AND BRITISH BRIDE

After much Parliamentary debate, sati was outlawed in India in 1829. By this time the practice had become a favourite topic for indignant letter-writers to the government and the press; they almost always denounced the practice as either 'primitive', 'barbarous' or both. A barrage of petitions, official accounts and statistics were published in Parliamentary papers, which made their way, along with gruesome eye-witness accounts, into both the British and Anglo-Indian press. But the law forbidding sati did not put an end to the newspaper accounts and to popular interest in the practice. A survey of nineteenth-century British periodicals reveals articles on the ritual, and on the degraded position of the Hindu widow, well into the 1880s. As well as the interest in the plight of the Hindu widow, and the factual accounts of sati in the periodicals and government reports, some Victorian novelists, such as Wilkie Collins, Trollope, and Charlotte Bronte, appropriated the Hindu ritual as a way to describe metaphorically the position of the British widow, whose severe mourning costume and lengthy period of mourning were often denounced (albeit rather jokingly) as a type of sati. Indeed, sati seems to have held a morbid fascination for the Victorians, and Meredith was no exception. Twice in his notebooks he records a joke involving the practice which he then puts into the mouth of Horace de Craye in *The Egoist*. A number of his novels, including *Beauchamp's Career* and *Diana of the Crossways*, make reference to the practice, but it is *The Egoist* which is inundated with sati and which employs it most comprehensively as a metaphor, not only for the British widow, but also for the British bride.

Willoughby wishes for complete devotion and constancy from both Laetitia and Clara. He realizes that he cannot have two wives, as 'the law governing princes and pedestrians alike' forbids it (p. 20). But that does not stop him from trying to garner the wifely devotion of both. An early description of Laetitia's devotion, after she discovers Willoughby's engagement to Constantia Durham, is the first oblique reference to sati in the novel. Laetitia will 'burn' her life and hopes for Willoughby, without ever becoming his wife:

> so submissive was she, that it was fuller happiness for her to think him right in all his actions than to imagine the circumstances different ... It is a form of passion inspired by little princes, and we need not marvel that a conservative sex should assist to keep them in their lofty places. What were there otherwise to look up to? We should have no dazzling beacon-lights if they were levelled and

treated as clod earth; and it is worth while for here and there a woman to be burned, so long as women's general adoration of an ideal young man shall be preserved (p. 22).

Through their constancy and unswerving loyalty, women have become 'a conservative sex', and their husbands may be sure of their faithfulness. This assurance means that the patrilineal line of descent and primogeniture are upheld, and ensures that the inherited land and wealth remain in the family, the foundation of a conservative society.

To a modern reader, the convoluted tactics, alliances and soul-searching involved in Clara's efforts to disengage herself from Willoughby may seem highly unnecessary. But as Vernon tells Clara at the train station when she has decided to flee Patterne Hall, 'You have beauty and wit; public opinion will say, wildness: indifference to your reputation will be charged on you, and your friends will have to admit it' (p. 328). The greatest obstacle in Clara's path to freedom is that she will be labelled 'inconstant', 'flighty', or a 'jilt' in changing her mind about marrying Willoughby. She fears appearing inconsistent to the world and especially to her father. To Dr. Middleton, 'mutability is but another name for the sex, and it is the enemy of the scholar' (p. 63). The mutability of women is an enemy to more than the scholar; it is one step away from faithlessness and inconstancy in marriage. To be labelled a jilt in Victorian society was a serious charge, and is the basis of the great fear of 'inconsistency' instilled into Clara by her father, Willoughby, and conservative society, and which makes it so difficult for her to break her solemn oath of engagement. Inconsistency of purpose, a criticism so often levelled at women, is considered a possible precursor to inconstancy. The first leads to a lack of respect for the woman – she is 'flighty' and doesn't know her mind. The latter leads to her loss of name and her possible expulsion from society. Perhaps Clara thinks less of this, however, and more of a need to be thought intellectually consistent and reasonable: Meredith writes, 'for her sex's sake, and also to appear an exception to her sex, this reasoning creature desired to be thought consistent' (p. 212).

Clara tries to look upon Willoughby with the eyes of society, in an attempt to regain her affection for him. She tries to place him in that lofty position of one of the 'princes of men', but the more she aims to regard him with the generally accepted view, the more she knows that she cannot, like Laetitia Dale, 'burn' her individuality for him. She feels her own self, separate from his constantly reiterated 'I', too much.

Figure 10 Richard Redgrave, *Preparing to Throw Off her Weeds*, exhibited at the Royal Academy, 1846.

Willoughby wishes to persuade Clara that as lovers they must happily forget the world, so that in marriage they become, 'so entirely one, that there never can be a question of external influences'. Clara inwardly rejects Willoughby's 'poetry of the enclosed and fortified bower' and curiously phrases her own dismissal of it:

She would not burn the world for him; she would not, though a purer poetry is little imaginable, reduce herself to ashes, or incense, or essence, in honour of him, and so, by love's transmutation, literally be the man she was to marry. (p. 54)

Marriage becomes associated with mourning and death here as Clara begins to see her marriage with Willoughby as a form of sati, an ultimately consuming sacrifice. Because Willoughby demands that both her legal and spiritual identity become one with his, Clara sees that marriage would be a period of mourning for her consumed, dead self which has become not only one flesh, but forced into one mind with an egoist from whom she feels alienated and repelled. She registers deeply that to marry Willoughby – not to be widowed by him – would be to reduce herself to ashes. We begin to see with Clara that Willoughby takes his views on constancy in marriage to a much greater extreme than civilized English society would like to admit. This becomes clearer when we look at Willoughby's almost horrified distaste for widows who remarry.

At an early point in the novel Mrs. Mountstuart, a widow, asks Willoughby if there is any truth to the rumour that he was almost 'snared' by 'a brilliant young widow of our aristocracy... The mention of the widow singularly offended him, notwithstanding the high rank of the lady named. "A widow!" he said. "I?". And again he repeats, 'A widow!" straightening his whole figure to the erectness of the letter I' (p. 19).

Willoughby cannot bear the idea of widows who remarry; he extols his mother because she never did, attempting to persuade Clara to swear yet another oath, aside from her 'solemn vow' of engagement, that she will, 'be inviolate? – mine before all men, though I am gone: – true to my dust?... True to my name!' (p. 57). Having only recently gained Clara's vow of engagement Willoughby makes a mental leap to elicit from her a vow of faithful widowhood if he should die after they marry. As an English gentleman who covets his reputation in the county as a model of civilization and enlightened thought, Willoughby can hardly ask Clara to burn upon his funeral pyre. Yet as the references to sati accumulate and gain momentum Clara registers that, spiritually, this is what her future husband will require of her. Of his mother Willoughby exclaims to Clara:

'She dies Lady Patterne! It might have been that she... But she is a woman of women! With a father-in-law [stepfather]! Just heaven! Could I have stood by her bedside then with the same feelings of reverence? A very little, my love, and everything gained for us by civilization crumbles; we fall back to the first mortar-bowl we were bruised and stirred in' (p. 60).

Invoking 'civilization' in this passage, Willoughby reveals his barbarous nature. He enjoins Clara to vow to be 'a saint in widowhood' because he wishes to ensure his immortality through her not only by her breeding his offspring, but also by her immortalization of his memory; the world will look at her and say, 'He lives in the heart of his wife' (p. 57). For Willoughby this upholds his idea of civilization, but it is a subtle form of widow-sacrifice which, as the anthropologist Edward Tylor had recently written in *Primitive Culture* (1871), was common to many 'primitive' societies:

Widow sacrifice is found in various regions of the world in a low state of civilization, and that fits with the hypothesis of its having belonged to the Aryan race while yet in an early and barbarous condition. Thus the prevalence of a rite of suttee like that of modern India among ancient Aryan nations settled in Europe – Greeks, Scandinavians, Germans, Sclavs – may be simply accounted for by direct inheritance from the remote common antiquity of them all.[15]

Responses to the practice of sati in nineteenth-century periodicals, Parliamentary reports, and letters make it clear that the writers were pointing to a practice which they understood to be greatly distanced from any practice in their own society. Sati was a primitive ritual prevalent in a geographically distanced culture. The quotation from Tylor brings the practice closer to British shores; now widow-sacrifice may only be removed in time, because 'civilized' European nations (and Scandinavians, who have common ancestors with the British) may have the barbarous and primitive practice of widow-sacrifice in their own past. Meredith uncovers the ways in which Willoughby reverts to an earlier, barbarous type: supposedly the quintessence of the educated, civilized English gentleman he nevertheless demands that his wife not only become the proverbial 'angel of the hearth' but a 'saint in widowhood'. Meredith lays bare this English gentleman's approval of quiet, unbloody widow-sacrifice, and Willoughby's 'reversion to the gross original, beneath a mask and in a vein of fineness' sets him back on the evolutionary ladder.

Anthropology began to come into its own as a science in the nineteenth century. The Ethnological Society of London first met in 1843 after breaking away from the Aborigines Protection Society, the latter name of course encapsulating the imperialist connection between 'primitive' society and its infantilization, its need for 'protection'. As

George Stocking writes, even the Aborigines Protection Society was by the 1840s moving away from the project of protection: 'the printed statement of the Society's object was changed in 1842: rather than 'protecting the defenceless', it would 'record the[ir] history', and a resolution was passed to the effect that the best way to help aboriginals was to study them.'[16] Rather than protection and instruction, the project of the modern anthropologist, to observe cultures rather than teach them civilization, gradually began to emerge in the 1840s, and to develop through the century. While most nineteenth-century anthropologists limited their field studies to distant, primitive cultures, with no reference to the practices of their own, the project of the nineteenth-century novelist was equally 'anthropological' in the sense that for authors such as Jane Austen, George Eliot, or Elizabeth Gaskell the delimited area of a small village or county town was the area under close observation; all the social rituals of tea-drinking, visiting, courtship, gift-exchange, mourning and the rites of passage are recorded. But it was Meredith who was perhaps more consciously aware of the anthropological possibilities for the novelist of British society, and he went further in his writing than most other Victorian novelists, and certainly than most anthropologists of his day, to put forward a culturally comparative perspective. In his sustained use of the sati metaphor in *The Egoist*, Meredith achieves a perspective which was beginning to evolve at this time, as can be seen in the responses to Edwin Long's painting, discussed earlier.

When Willoughby exclaims to Mrs Mountstuart, 'A widow. I!', he clearly shows how absurdly incongruous he finds this juxtaposition. That he should mate and carry on the Patterne line with a second-hand woman is inconceivable to him. As egoist he sees himself as the centre of all attention, care and thought on his estate; the world is a swinish multitude which may be dismissed. He is central to his pedigree as well, the current head of a line of descendants in his own image; entanglement of this linearity with the pedigree of a previous husband is unthinkable. The sense of 'I' and of his sexual power to carry on a 'pure' pedigree are inseparable. When he 'straight(ens) his whole figure to the erectness of the letter "I'; his figure becomes associated with the erect tool with which he will forge the continuation of the Patterne pedigree.

It is not only Clara Middleton whose pre-marital consciousness plays with thoughts of immolation and bride/widow sacrifice; Willoughby also finds his unconscious anxieties centring around this metaphor. He too is disturbed by the sacrifices he may have to make if he marries, worrying that Laetitia will not keep her vestal flame burning for him. Willoughby's physical sense of himself as a fine specimen of erect English manhood is essential to his rather vague idea of a more abstract spiritual self, as in a soul, or a memory of himself carrying on after death. Contemplating a possible loss of Laetitia's love if he takes another bride, we can see the real physicality, the morbidity, of Willoughby's fears of being forgotten and replaced:

> She might have buried it [the secret of the old days between them], after the way of woman, whose bosoms can be tombs, if we and the world allow them to be; absolutely sepulchres, where you lie dead, ghastly. Even if not dead and horrible to think of, you may be lying cold, somewhere in a corner. Even if embalmed, you may not be much visited. And how is the world to know you are embalmed? You are no better than a rotting wretch to the world that does not have peeps of you in the woman's breast, and see lights burning and an occasional exhibition of the services of worship. There are women – tell us not of her of Ephesus! – that have embalmed you, and have quitted the world to keep the tapers alight, and a stranger comes, and they, who have your image before them, will suddenly blow out the vestal flames and treat you as dust to fatten the garden of their bosoms for a fresh flower of love. (pp. 38–39)

Willoughby's confusion of the physical and the spiritual, and his insecurities concerning sexuality, self, mortality and memory are all in this passage. The woman of Ephesus, from a story in Petronius' *Satyricon*, was another widow willing to sacrifice herself for her husband's memory. Her method of self-immolation was to be starvation in her husband's tomb rather than burning. However this widow's span of faithfulness does not last the night's vigil; she is finally seduced at her husband's tomb by a soldier who is keeping guard over the bodies of some crucified criminals. The relatives of one of the executed steal a body from the cross while the soldier is making love to the widow, and the widow replaces the stolen body with her husband's so that her new love will not be court-martialled. The blunt physical replacement of one body with another horrifies Willoughby, who places so much emphasis on his own physical attractiveness and superiority with women.

MOURNING AND WEDDING: TWO VICTORIAN PAINTINGS

Many of the accounts of sati in the English periodicals combined a horror of the practice with an admiration for the widow victim of the ritual. English periodicals were replete with articles championing the causes of victimized Englishwomen, whether they were ill-paid, maltreated governesses, seamstresses, factory workers, 'Magdalens' or so-called 'redundant women'. These victimized Englishwomen all came under the rubric of the 'Woman Question' as it was frequently termed. The articles on the plight of the Hindu widow reveal that the popularity of the 'Woman Question' extended itself outside Britain to her Indian colonies. The sympathy and occasional admiration for the Hindu widow may also reflect attitudes to English women, and specifically to the English widow. As the epigraph to one eye-witness account of a sati from the 1840s reads:

> Of woman's strength, and woman's nobleness,
> And all that she can bear and all her gentleness.[17]

All women, including the Hindu and the English, are represented here as quietly suffering victims, able to bear their burdens with dignity and nobility. The constant woman, whether she be a sati or not, is sentimentalized. The stereotype of women as victims or sufferers is particularly convenient for Willoughby in his relations with Laetitia Dale: she is dignified in his eyes by embodying his image of the constant woman, his 'Egeria'. In many accounts of sati in the nineteenth century this admiration for the Hindu widow (especially the young and attractive widow) who sacrifices herself has parallels with what I would argue is a sentimentalization of the young widow in English culture. In entreating Clara to be 'true to [his] dust, true to [his] name!', Willoughby sentimentalizes his fiancée in her imagined future role as his faithful 'relict'. As his anxiety over Laetitia's possible disloyalty to his memory is cast in terms of a sexual, physical replacement by another man in the 'widow of Ephesus' passage quoted above, so his fears over Clara's possible marriage to another after his death manifest themselves in a similar manner. He expresses his disgusted terror of the sensuality of those men who will sully her in replacing him: he tells Clara that after his death, 'You would be surrounded; men are brutes; the scent of unfaithfulness excites them, overjoys them. And I helpless!' (p. 58). Willoughby's presumptive fear of his widow's remarriage blinds him to the fact that his fiancée is preempting any such circumstance in her determination to escape the wedding. His terror of sexual replacement is central to the comedy of *The Egoist*; through Willoughby, Meredith lampoons both the sentimentalizing of those women who will 'burn the world' for their men, and the pedestal-building for the young, faithful widow, which he observed in Victorian society.

Two Victorian paintings which portray opposing images of the widow, the comic and the sentimental, and which both reveal this anxiety over the remarriage of the widow which Meredith addresses, are Richard Redgrave's *Preparing to Throw Off her Weeds* (exhibited Royal Academy, 1846, see fig. 10) and a watercolour by a minor artist, E. K. Johnson, entitled *A Young Widow* (1877, see fig. 11). A close analysis of these paintings serves to clarify the nexus of English mourning and wedding rituals which Meredith brings together through the metaphor of sati in *The Egoist*.

In Redgrave's painting, a young widow has been in deep mourning, then in modified or half-mourning for about two years. As Susan Casteras notes, she is now in the final phase of the mourning socially required for the widow and is returning to brighter colours (traditionally as in this painting, lilac or grey). Evidence of the traditonal *vanitas* motif lies in the maid holding up the mirror to her mistress. A key to the narrative of this painting is the hat-box in the corner which contains a bridal bonnet and orange blossom.[18] The widow is not simply throwing off her weeds but is preparing for another marriage, and her vulgar hastiness goes against all social decorum. Orange blossom, for example, represents virginity and is unsuitable for a widow's wedding, but the widow of Redgrave's painting prepares her trousseau in flagrant dismissal of the etiquette books of the day. Mrs John Sherwood, writing in 1884 in her *Manners and Social Usages* sets down the rules for the widow-bride:

A widow should never be accompanied by bridesmaids or wear a veil or orange blossom at her marriage ... It is proper for her to remove her first wedding ring, as the wearing of that cannot but be painful to the bridegroom ... she should not indulge in any of the signs of the first bridal.[19]

Redgrave's painting in its original form, as it was exhibited at the Royal Academy, showed a young officer, presumably her fiancé, entering from a door on the left of the painting. In the centre background above the dressing room screen the portrait of the former husband, keeping an eye on the proceedings, is just discernible.

Redgrave's painting aroused considerable journalistic comment when exhibited, critics almost unanimously dismissing the subject matter as 'vulgar'. The art journal *The Critic* announced that the painting 'went too far for good taste in the lady who, it should be remembered, is yet attired in mourning.'[20] And *The Art Union* demurred, feeling that the 'the engagement of the widow is indelicately announced by the hasty entrance of the officer, which is assuredly ill-timed and ill-judged; and the treatment otherwise is toned with vulgarity.'[21]

The painting now hangs in the Sheepshanks Collection at the Victoria and Albert Museum, and it was the great Victorian collector John Sheepshanks who is believed to have asked Redgrave to paint over the image of the soldier/fiancé before he added the painting to his collection.[22] The reactions to this painting reveal much about the anxiety surrounding the position of the young, available widow in Victorian society. Redgrave's widow is attractive and sexually experienced, and clearly she is not going to be faithful to her husband's ashes. Its 'vulgarity' lies in the abrupt juxtaposition of mourning and wedding rituals, the black crêpe and orange blossom, reminiscent of Hamlet's reply to Horatio's observations upon the juxtaposition of his friend's 'father's funeral' and 'mother's wedding': 'Thrift, thrift, Horatio. The funeral baked-meats/Did coldly furnish forth the marriage tables'. The risqué tone of Redgrave's painting is emphasised by placing the scene in the private space of the widow's dressing room. That room contains the presence of two men (in the original version) who should never meet; the image of the dead husband in the portrait and the now-erased image of the husband-to-be. The incongruity both of the mourning and wedding rituals and of these two men clearly grates on a Victorian sensibility.

The second painting, *A Young Widow* by E. K. Johnson, offers a sentimentalized version of the faithful relict. This widow could serve as an illustration of Willoughby's preferred vision of Clara after his decease, and it is this sanctification of woman sacrificed to the memory of the male that Meredith attacks. In Johnson's painting, the young widow has taken her wedding dress out of its box and is wistfully remembering her bridal day. Although Queen Victoria went into severe mourning for ten years after Albert's death, and remained in some degree of mourning for the rest of her life, Susan Casteras has remarked that 'Victorian painters seemed far more fascinated by the widow who was young, attractive and vulnerable, a potent formula to excite pathos.'[23] Clearly the image of Johnson's widow follows this formula. As in Redgrave's painting, Johnson's watercolour exhibits a jarring juxtaposition of mourning and wedding to dramatic effect. However, the tone in this later painting is not one of *vanitas* or social satire, but of pathos and sentimentality, depicting the tragedy of a young widow, her lost hopes of love and the further implications of lost hopes of fulfilled sexuality and motherhood. The rich sheen of her wedding dress and its voluminous folds and furbelows contrast with her almost clerical or monastic

Figure 11 E. K. Johnson, *A Young Widow*, 1877.

mourning wear; the inference seems to be that she will now devote herself to a life of celibacy and devotion to the memory of her dead husband.

With the rather uncanny effect of a trick photograph, this painting, if looked at from another mental perspective, could be interpreted very differently; it leaves itself open to the possibility that the young widow is wistfully regarding the wedding dress and thinking not of that past wedding day, but of her chances of wearing the dress again. In this light her musing face takes on an expression of anticipation and calculation rather than tender nostalgia. Obviously this is not the original intention of the painting, but perhaps this alternative interpretation does acknowledge a certain tension or ambivalence in the image. Once thought of, it is hard to dispel because the juxtaposition of a young beautiful widow with a wedding dress may almost inevitably demand thoughts of her marriage. This tension, even anxiety, cuts across the painting's sentimental intentions. It is related to the anxiety which obliged Redgrave to erase the image of the soldier/fiancé entering the widow's dressing room, and the sensibility which dismissed that painting as vulgar. Both Redgrave's and Johnson's paintings show the woman as survivor, and both portray the woman in conjunction with mourning and wedding clothes. In that space of difference, between mourning and wedding, black and white, is shaded in the shadowy figure of a man – either the recently-deceased husband or the perhaps still unknown future husband – who, like the painted-out figure of the fiancé in the Redgrave painting, waits in the wings to meet the shadowy portrait of the dead husband in his lady's private chamber. Part of the uneasiness surrounding these two paintings and other contemporary paintings of young widows is the fear of the blunt physical substitution of one man by another, and that the dead man will be replaced and forgotten in the mind of the supposedly faithful widow after his death. Willoughby's horror of the 'widow of Ephesus' hangs over these two paintings: the same fears of that lady's body-swapping of dead husband for dead criminal to aid a very much alive lover inspire the negative criticism of Redgrave's painting, and the comforting negation of the Ephesian widow in Johnson's portrait of the constant woman.

As I have discussed, the two adjectives most frequently intoned when discussing the practice of sati in the nineteenth-century British and Anglo-Indian press were 'primitive' and 'barbarous'. Meredith, although certainly not equating the Hindu ritual and British rituals surrounding women in marriage, does make the point that those indignant denouncers of 'primitive' practices in foreign countries should be less complacent about the civilization of their own British rituals. His writing turns the anthropological gaze away from the Empire and back into the heart of English social life. Talking with Viscountess Milner in 1904, Meredith spoke of what he saw as the barbarity of British attitudes surrounding extra-marital love:

And then there is that absurd law of possession, as if a man had any 'rights' over a woman after he had lost her regard. There is a great risk in such flying in the face of society, because, of course, according to society's rules, people are thrown absolutely on each other in such a union. But with nature and books surely a well-mated couple would be happy? ... I study people, as you know, and I think if a man and a woman found perfect harmony – that rare thing! – they would be absolutely wrong, and going against truth and right living, to keep apart. It is not an *adventure* to be rashly thought of, but it should be more tolerated than it is. Our civilisation is very barbarous.[24]

Meredith is speaking in 1904. Times have changed since 1879 and the writing of *The Egoist*, when he would have been vilified for excusing an extra-marital affair. Clara is trying to escape a vow of engagement, not of marriage, but in her efforts to extricate herself she supports Meredith's judgment that 'our civilization is very barbarous'.

The novel's action is almost entirely circumscribed within the limits of a country house estate; the rather claustrophobic atmosphere is relieved by Clara's 'flight in wild weather' to the railway station. Like the torrential rainstorm which coincides with her flight, Clara's 'dreadful power' with language tends to clear the air, and her name, as Hillis Miller notes, is associated with 'clarification'.[25] She is the only character in the novel who understands a direct rather than metaphorical connection between Willoughby and the primitive. In conversation with Clara, Laetitia initially 'supposed she was listening to discursive observations upon the inequality in the relations of the sexes', but soon realizes that Clara is thinly veiling her assessment of Willoughby. As Clara says; 'women who are called coquettes make their conquests not of the best of men; but men who are Egoists have *good* women for their victims; women on whose devoted constancy they feed; they drink it like blood' (p. 191). This is the most direct and violent image for Willoughby's primitive nature provided in the novel; Clara likens him to a blood-drinking cannibal. His obsession with 'blood', or lineage, and with the total possession of the woman who will provide that blood, makes the rituals of engagement and marriage in the hands of an English egoist appear frighteningly barbarous, disturbingly close to the literal 'savage' rather than the metaphorical.

Meredith brings the accusation of barbarity to English shores and into that supposed bastion of civilization, the country house estate. While he would not perhaps wish Clara to burn upon his pyre, Willoughby's desexualization of his dependants on his estate, his decree of extinction to those who wish for independence, and his desire that all women in his 'enclosed and fortified bower' should remain eternally faithful to him, question the practices of the civilized British male. Through Willoughby's example, British rituals are likened to those of a despotic prince surrounded by the typically 'primitive' court which offers bride-price, and includes eunuchs, a harem and wives committed to widow-sacrifice.

Sexual jealousy and a desire to be remembered after death are 'primitive' feelings common to most. Meredith observes Willoughby's 'barbarous' impulses, and it is because Willoughby hides these common human instincts from the world and from himself 'beneath a mask and in a vein of fineness', that he becomes both ridiculous and dangerous. If he can produce a 'pure' pedigree to come after him which will never be adulterated by his wife's second marriage, he can feel that he has conquered his sexual rivals who will compete for his prize after he is gone, and also that in some way, through his wife's loyalty, and the continuation of his line, he has conquered death.

He may view pedigree as a straight line carrying his ego into the future, but for Willoughby, as well as for the night observer of a pedigree in Hardy's poem of that name, 'the branches seemed to twist into a seared and cynic face', hinting that he is 'merest mimicker and counterfeit'. This cynic face observes how Willoughby, in believing himself superior to his ruder lawyer ancestors of five generations before him, finds himself imitating ancestors far ruder, far more remote on a primitive family tree.

CHAPTER SIX

Pedigree and forgetting in Hardy

'If Mem'ry o'er their Tomb no Trophies raise'
(Thomas Gray, 'Elegy, Written in a Country Church-Yard')

PREFACE: PEDIGREE AND NARRATIVE IN HARDY'S WRITING

A late poem of Thomas Hardy's, 'On an Invitation to the United States', exhibits a peculiar symbiosis between the first and second stanzas which reveals much about Hardy's concerns in his writing. In the first stanza Hardy refuses the invitation because, 'since Life has bared its bones' to him, he 'shrinks to see a modern coast' where the inhabitants have no history, no tragedy, no 'centuried years' behind them. The 'new regions' of America 'claim them[selves] free' of the burden of centuries of memory, but it is precisely this burden, passed down through the generations, which serves as a crucial catalyst for narrative in Hardy's writing. I give the second stanza in full:

> For, wonning in these ancient lands
> Enchased and lettered as a tomb,
> And scored with prints of perished hands,
> And chronicled with dates of doom,
> Though my own Being bear no bloom
> I trace the lives such scenes enshrine,
> Give past exemplars present room,
> And their experience count as mine.[1]

Obviously Hardy is privileging the inhabitants of the Old World; Native Americans had left their own chronicles of doom, tears, and tragedy upon the regions of their own ancient land, but Hardy is no Fenimore Cooper. His writing is 'enchased' like the tomb of the poem, in that it keeps itself within a setting, frame or limit, and this limit is not Britain, or even England, but for the most part the regional limit of Wessex. His writing does stray upon occasion outside these limits to London or even as far as the Continent, but as may be seen in the two novels which are to be focussed upon in these final chapters, *A Pair of Blue Eyes* and *The Well-Beloved*, a straying too far from geographical and cultural limits often entails a doomed chain of missed connections and a sense of frustration, futility. Rather than an expansion of mind and spirit, travelling outward often leads to a narrowing of choices and a stifling repetition.

The symbiotic relationship between the two stanzas of the above poem is clear in that in the first stanza 'Life has bared its bones' to Hardy, but the poet's response in the second stanza is to flesh out those bare bones through his particular type of story-telling. His writing takes bare bones – in tombs or in the skeletons of 'perished hands' – and gives them life. The 'ancient lands' are 'enchased and lettered as a tomb'; Hardy takes a date on a tomb or a quirk in a pedigree and enchases it – places it in a setting, surrounds it in detail – and thereby 'letters' it.

Hardy uses this image of 'dry bones' from 'On an Invitation to the United States' again in a group of stories most obviously derived from the concept of pedigree: *A Group of Noble Dames* finds its narrative inspiration in the county genealogies. The frame story to this collection is a meeting of 'one of the Wessex Field and Antiquarian Clubs'. The eclectic group of antiquarians, from all walks of life, improvise on a wet afternoon by 'fleshing out' the old pedigrees of Wessex. They tell stories of various noble ladies, and the quirks which occur in their pedigrees through marriage or misalliance. The narrator describes the club as unusual in its 'inclusive and intersocial character':

> indeed remarkable for ... Wessex, whose statuesque dynasties are even now only just beginning to feel the shaking of the new and strange spirit without, like that which entered the lonely valley of Ezekiel's vision and made the dry bones move.[2]

It is this 'strange spirit without' of modern progress and social mobility which makes possible the meeting of such an eclectic group of men. This eclecticism is emphasised by the fact that none of the members are named; all are identified either by profession or by some personal characteristic: the local historian, the old surgeon, rural dean, sentimental member, crimson maltster, man of family, etc. The reference to Ezekiel is interesting because in the Biblical passage the bones actually come to life when the prophet, as commanded by God, proclaims:

> Dry bones, hear the word of the Lord. This is what the Sovereign Lord says to these bones: I will make breath enter you, and you will come to life. I will attach tendons to you and make flesh come upon you and cover you with skin. (Ezekiel 27: 4–6)

It is the word of the Lord which gives the bones breath and life, and, analogously, the various narrators of *A Group of Noble Dames* breathe life into the skeletons of these noblewomen through their words, their story-telling. If, in the first stanza of 'On an Invitation to the United States' Hardy feels that 'Life has bared its bones' to him, then he recovers something of that fading life in the second stanza by taking into his own existence the lives of 'past exemplars ... and their experience count as mine.' Pedigree, and the narratives it conjures up, give flesh to the bare bones of a mere life-span.

Hardy seems almost to fear, or to be exhausted by, the newness of the United States. His poem which declines an invitation there reveals a conception of America similar in some ways to that of Henry James, a writer who did, however, make the Atlantic crossing both in his life and in his novels upon numerous occasions. Henry James writes in his *Hawthorne* (1879):

> History, as yet, has left the United States but so thin and impalpable a deposit that we can very soon touch the hard substratum of nature ... A large juvenility is stamped upon the face of things.[3]

James quotes Hawthorne's response to the difficulties of writing American stories, a response which would seem to confirm Hardy's reasons for declining the 'invitation';

> No author, without a trial, can conceive of the difficulty of writing a romance about a country where there is no shadow, no antiquity, no mystery, no picturesque and gloomy wrong, nor anything but a commonplace prosperity, in broad and simple daylight, as is happily the case with my dear native land.[4]

Hawthorne could claim one of the longest pedigrees conceivable for an American of European descent, tracing his genealogy on American soil to a Major William Hathorne, one of the early Puritan settlers. Certainly in novels such as *The Scarlet Letter* (1850) and *The House of the Seven Gables* (1851), Hawthorne uses his old American pedigree as inspiration for his New England narratives.

It is interesting that Henry James employs a geological metaphor to describe the state of history in the United States: the workings of geological time upon landscape often serve as crucial metaphors in Hardy's writing. The marks left by ancient rivers, seas, glaciers and other traces of geological time are of course just as apparent in America as in Europe, but James views the landscape of human history almost as a *tabula rasa*, covered only with a 'thin deposit'; for him as for Hardy, it is the Old World which has the 'deep soil' essential for history and narrative.5

While Henry James writes metaphorically of soil and deposits, he is hardly likely to muddy his hands with the literal material in his writing. The rich loam around Marlott; the flinty frozen earth of Flintcombe Ash in *Tess*; the digging and tree-planting in *The Woodlanders*; the rock face to which Henry Knight clings for his life: for Hardy the case is quite different, and the layers of soil and stone in his writing work on a literal and figurative level as the very substance of place and time. The various soils and rock mark out the land, designate *region* which is so significant to Hardy, and they are also the materials which symbolize different time-scales. The earth and stone are worked by human hands in a single life-span such as Tess's or Marty South's, by the hands of many generations of workers in genealogical time, and are in themselves the products of sedimentary and igneous processes in geologic time. Again and again in Hardy's work, narrative is built upon a foundation which is palpable, material and layered with seams of generational and geological history. It is often some object tangibly historical which initiates his narratives; such objects may be as varied as a 'lettered tomb', the Durbeyfield spoon exhibiting the d'Urberville arms, old furniture smoothed by generations of handling, geological or ancient remains on the landscape, or a pedigree. Even a 'gentleman's second-hand suit' in the poem of that name has hidden stories to tell of its dancing days, and a lady's abandoned sunshade, which, again compared with 'bare bones', evokes stories about what the woman was like and what she thought under the sunshade:

> Noonshine riddles the ribs of the sunshade
> No more a screen for the weakest ray;
> Nothing to tell us the hue of its dyes,
> Nothing but rusty bones as it lies
> In its coffin of stone, unseen till today.

And in the last stanza:

> Is the fair woman who carried that sunshade
> A skeleton just as her property is,
> Laid in the chink that none may scan?
> And does she regret – if regret dust can –
> The vain things thought when she flourished this?[6]

The skeletal sunshade inspires conjectural narratives about her regrets, her vanities; was she a 'woman with a story'? Even a 'gentleman's second-hand suit' – which could claim a history of at most two generations – could tell some stories of its 'ancestry' and its possible 'descendants'; had its owner fallen upon hard times, or given up his dancing days? Would the suit be redeemed and, if not, what stories would it tell of its next generation of owner? Even one or two generations of ownership may breed a proliferation of possible, alternative stories.

Then there are those objects of an older pedigree, those which conjure the vision of 'Begetters, dwindling backward each past each' ('The Pedigree'). These are old things such as the 'relics of householdry' of his poem 'Old Furniture'; common, familiar objects such as the household clock, an old viol, or a tinder box. These things are so commonplace, that it takes an idiosyncratic perspective to see what lies behind them. Hardy sees,

> the hands of the generations
> That owned each shiny familiar thing
> In play on its knobs and indentations,
> And with its ancient fashioning
> Still dallying:[7]

Hardy's fascination with time-scales and layering transforms even living things into mere signifiers of repetition in the poem 'A Second Visit': in a characteristic moment of *déja vu* in which everything is already belated, a man comes upon a country scene which appears not to have changed since he visited some years ago. In the last stanza however, he realizes:

> But it's not the same miller whom long ago I knew,
> Nor are they the same apples, nor the same drops that dash
> Over the wet wheel, nor the ducks below that splash,
> Nor the woman who to fond plaints replied, 'You know I do!'[8]

The ducks and the apples, at least, are remote descendants of those he saw years before, and this generational repetition heightens the poignancy inherent in the object; things look the same, but circumstances and the viewer have changed irrevocably.

Entries in Hardy's notebooks from 1865 and 1866 give further evidence of his almost obsessive need to juxtapose the time-scale of human generation with greater and lesser time-scales. This, from 1866:

June 6. Went to Hatfield. Changed since my early visit. A youth thought the altered highway had always run as it did. Pied rabbits in the Park, descendants of those I knew. The once children are quite old inhabitants. I regretted that the beautiful sunset did not occur in a place of no reminiscences, that I might have enjoyed it without their tinge.[9]

He wishes to escape this reminiscence-tinged perspective, imparted by the sense that everything is subject to, or trapped by, generational repetition. These 'generations' may be those of ducks, apples, old furniture, pied rabbits, and even cows' flanks, as in *Tess of the D'Urbervilles*: 'wooden posts rubbed to a glossy smoothness by the flanks of infinite cows and calves of bygone years, now passed to an oblivion almost inconceivable in its profundity' (p. 134). In his poem 'Afterwards' Hardy wrote in a fictively posthumous fashion of himself that 'He was a man who used to notice such things.' He acknowledges his idiosyncratic perspective, and an eye that can see an 'inconceivable ... profundity' in cows' flanks is clearly of a peculiar cast. Few objects, animate or inanimate, escape his attention to repetition, lineage, and the opposing concepts of regeneration and 'cancelled cycles'. But the fulcrum of the greater and lesser time-scales which Hardy juxtaposes is the human time-scale. Its importance is clear in this notebook entry from the close of December 1865: '– To insects the twelvemonth has been an epoch, to leaves a life, to tweeting birds a generation, to man a year.'[10] The time-scale of man encompasses and dwarfs those of other creatures. In both *A Pair of Blue Eyes* and *The Well-Beloved*, as will be discussed, man's genealogical time is juxtaposed with geological time. Whereas a year in a man's life may encompass whole epochs for an insect, a geological moment dwarfs generations of a human pedigree.

Particularly evocative for Hardy are those objects which are at once familiar but which also bespeak a noble pedigree, such as the D'Urberville tombs, old stonework, paintings and tombs. Often the traceability of their pedigrees, through which the present is connected with the past, is under threat or has vanished completely. Just as Tess is now a Durbeyfield, rather than a D'Urberville, so the stones of many old houses are now found dispersed in fences or roads, as in the poem 'A Man' in which a 'noble pile' is pulled down:

But evil days beset that domicile;
The stately beauties of its roof and wall
Passed into sordid hands. Condemned to fall
Were cornice, quoin, and cove,
And all that art had wove in antique style.[11]

Both common and noble old things can claim a 'pure' pedigree, 'purity' in this sense signifying the pedigree's traceability back to an origin or early ancestor. The 'new and modern spirit without' which is 'shaking' Wessex disperses and dilutes purity of lineage. With reference to the common things, we can think of the objects in 'Old Furniture' which have remained in the same family and the same house for generations, and then remember the scene in *Tess of the D'Urbervilles* in which the Lady-Day migration takes place. The labourers have begun to move every year, taking their goods with them. In the Durbeyfield case, they have no new home to go to, because they have lost the life-hold on their house.

Their household effects are left exposed on the street in Kingsbere, the home of their noble lineage. These common objects, which have a closer, more familiar 'pedigree' to Tess than do her ancestors' tombs, look incongruous and meaningless when wrested from their domestic context:

> Tess gazed desperately at the pile of furniture. The cold sunlight of this spring evening peered invidiously upon the crocks and kettles, upon the bunches of dried herbs shivering in the breeze, upon the brass handles of the dresser, upon the wicker cradle they had all been rocked in, and upon the well-rubbed clock-case, all of which gave out the reproachful gleam of indoor articles abandoned to the vicissitudes of a roofless exposure for which they were never made.[12]

Mrs. Durbeyfield and Tess can find no room at any affordable inn in Kingsbere. They finally uncover the old four-poster bed which has been abandoned by their driver under the churchyard wall, and pull the curtains around it to make a tent in which the children may sleep, for that night at least:

> Over the tester of the bedstead was a beautiful traceried window, of many lights, its date being the fifteenth century. It was called the D'Urberville Window, and in the upper part could be discerned heraldic emblems like those on Durbeyfield's old seal and spoon.

Here the old four-poster representing the common Durbeyfield lineage (also the site of Durbeyfield sexual relations and continuation of their line) is brought together with the stained glass window representing the D'Urberville line. The juxtaposed lineages have both become, to use a favourite quotation of Hardy's from Shelley's 'Prometheus Unbound', 'the melancholy ruins of cancelled cycles'.[13]

The idea of a pure pedigree, then, does not only pertain to a noble ancestry. The intermarriages occurring in small, isolated areas such as Little Hintock in *The Woodlanders*, or the Isle of Slingers in *The Well-*

Beloved can produce just as pure a pedigree as that which produced the Habsburg jaw.

In spite of Hardy's popular reputation as a writer of rural life and manners, some critics have denounced him as a snob who in both his personal life and in his writing privileged the noble pedigree – or at least the respectable upper-middle-class pedigree – of his family. Hardy did take pride in those of his ancestors who had some claim to fame or respectability, no matter how remote they were, and this is evident when in the early chapters of the *Life* he writes of the family history:

> It was a family whose diverse Dorset sections included the Elizabethan Thomas Hardy who endowed the Dorchester Grammar School, the Thomas Hardy captain of the *Victory* at Trafalgar, Thomas Hardy an influential burgess of Wareham.[14]

Robert Gittings writes in *Young Hardy* that Hardy,

> omits almost totally all his other close relatives, uncles, aunts, and very numerous cousins. The touchstone throughout seems to have been social class. Labourers, cobblers, bricklayers, carpenters, farm servants, journeymen, joiners, butlers have no place in Hardy's memoirs ... Hardy himself did not want to record the lives of his lower-class relatives.[15]

In his *Annals of the Labouring Poor*, historian Keith Snell is yet more damning of Hardy's 'snobbery'. He argues that Hardy distanced himself so much from his background that he created an unreal picture of the lot of the Wessex labourer. Snell claims that in many cases Hardy condescends to the 'Hodge' that he had actually defended and claimed to know in his essay 'The Dorsetshire Labourer', and he argues that Hardy plays down the tensions between farmer and labourer in his novels.[16] Like Ethelberta in Hardy's 1876 novel *The Hand of Ethelberta*, Hardy was a writer in London, and to some extent may have felt the same instinct for social survival that she felt when she kept her immediate family literally and figuratively 'below stairs'. But Ethelberta's ambivalence, regrets and struggles, and the difficult price that she had to pay, are after all Hardy's creations. It is likely that he not only felt the ambivalence that she did, but in writing a story so close to home he quite openly revealed his own struggle and the fact that he too had relatives whom his new acquaintances among the upper-class literati would only recognize below stairs. Gittings's assessment, and in particular Keith Snell's arguments, are persuasive. It is important, however, to balance a condemnation of Hardy as social climber forgetful of his past with the pressures of his class context in Victorian London society, and also with other evidence in his writings which demonstrates that he not only acknowledged but admired his 'humbler' forebears. Ethelberta may hide her mother downstairs in the guise of her cook, but Hardy is quite open in his 'autobiography' about his mother Jemima, who grew up in very poor circumstances; 'She resolved to be a cook in a London club-house; but her plans in this direction were ended by meeting her future husband, and being married to him at the age of five and twenty.'[17]

Hardy may have been uncomfortable about his unsophisticated family background when among his cosmopolitan acquaintances and friends, but in his poetry and novels he did not hide his pedigree. He associates himself with the labouring Durbeyfield family when he writes of his own in the *Life*; 'They had all the characteristics of an old family of spent social energies',[18] which is precisely how Angel Clare regards degenerated families of old lineage in *Tess*. Hardy's openness, and actual pride in this lineage of labourers and artisans is especially evident in the poetry. The poem 'A Man', quoted earlier, is dedicated to 'H. of M.' – either Hardy's father or grandfather. The poem tells the story of his relation who was hired, without knowing the nature of the work beforehand, to dismantle an Elizabethan house. Upon realizing that the job entailed the destruction of the beautiful mansion, he refused the job. His act of principle meant hunger and hardship:

> Hunger is hard. But since the terms be such –
> No wage, or labour stained with the disgrace
> Of wrecking what our age cannot replace
> To save its tasteless soul –
> I'll do without your dole. Life is not much!
>
> Dismissed with sneers he backed his tools and went,
> And wandered workless; for it seemed unwise
> To close with one who dared to criticize
> And carp on points of taste:
> Rude men should work where placed, and be content.

This last line is unmistakably bitter towards those who would label his proud relative 'rude'. His father or grandfather is an itinerant labourer, hired for a temporary job. He is also his own man who makes a judgement on aesthetic grounds and pays the price. Rather than trying to hide his ancestry here, Hardy is quite obviously proud of it. As an author he had to make changes in his novels to which he was aesthetically averse, to please his readership, satisfy nervous editors and 'Mrs

Grundy'. Just as his ancestor refused to please the 'tasteless soul' of the age by pulling down the great house, Hardy, embittered by his critics, in 1895 finally refused to write any more novels. 'A Man' was written in 1901, after Hardy had made this decision to write only poetry; it affirms his kinship of resistance.

Whether humble or noble, pedigree and the repetitions it involves are important inspirations to Hardy's writing. He saw both under threat from the forces of modern progress; from trends such as increasingly standardized education which both encouraged social mobility and spurred migration from any given locality, resulting in less intermarriage and less local attachment. Although a lover of old things and old families, he writes in the 1883 essay 'The Dorsetshire Labourer' that these modern forces cannot and should not be halted for mere romantic or artistic sentiments:

> But the artistic merit of their old condition is scarcely a reason why they should have continued in it when other communities were marching so vigorously towards uniformity and mental equality ... It is too much to expect them to remain stagnant and old-fashioned for the pleasure of romantic spectators.[19]

Progress must not be stopped, and yet there is ambivalence in 'The Dorsetshire Labourer' – an aesthetic regret at the passing of an old order.

The Lady-Day migrations of agricultural workers, and the loss of the lease-hold on their family home, lead the destitute Durbeyfield family back to Kingsbere, to sleep (quite literally) among the tombs of their D'Urberville ancestors. This return to the ancestral burial place in *Tess of the D'Urbervilles* is an ironic reversal of the movement at this time away from the ancestral home. This movement was an aspect of the rapidly increasing agricultural migration of country dwellers escaping the grinding poverty of rural areas in order to work in the city. Those who did move away from their ancestral village tended to look back nostalgically to their family home, especially those later on in the century whose parents or grandparents had left the countryside; the distancing of one or two generations did much to remove the memory of the cruel hardships of agricultural life, and to idealize the rural community and the 'joys' of nature. In the poetry and literature of the nineteenth century a focus of this nostalgia often lay in the depiction of the country or village churchyard. The graveyard could be viewed as the last bastion of pedigree for those families who had left their village, a place to which they could return to read their genealogical record on the tombstones.

Indeed, for the poor who had no written or emblazoned pedigree, the graves were frequently the sole written record of their ancestry. Without these records, there was only oral tradition to combat the possibility that the blood-lines, alliances and the stories associated with them would fade from memory. I turn now to a discussion of some of the anxieties over death and forgetting that are embodied in literary and artistic depictions of the graveyard, and in the public outrage concerning overcrowded graveyards in the early and mid-nineteenth century.

NARRATIVE PLOT AND FAMILY PLOT IN THE VICTORIAN GRAVEYARD

The village churchyard was hallowed in the poetry, painting and novels of the Victorian era as a place of peaceful community between the living and the dead. But this communal sensitivity is clearly felt much earlier as, for instance, in Gray's 'Elegy Written in a Country Church-Yard' (1750), and in Wordsworth's 'Essay Upon Epitaphs' (1810). Wordsworth writes:

A village church-yard, lying as it does in the lap of nature, may indeed be most favourably contrasted with that of a town of crowded population; and sepulture therein combines many of the best tendencies which belong to the mode practised by the ancients, with others peculiar to itself. The sensations of pious cheerfulness, which attend the celebration of the sabbath-day in rural places, are profitably chastised by the sight of the graves of kindred and friends, gathered together in that general home towards which the thoughtful yet happy spectators themselves are journeying. Hence a parish church, in the stillness of the country, is a visible centre of a community of the living and the dead; a point to which are habitually referred the nearest concerns of both.[20]

Of the associations and connections between the family names in the country churchyard, Wordsworth claims:

As in these registers the name is mostly associated with those of the same family, this is a prolonged companionship, however shadowy; even a Tomb like this is a shrine to which the fancies of a scattered family may repair in pilgrimage; the thoughts of the individuals, without any communication with each other, must oftentimes meet here. – Such a frail memorial then is not without its tendency to keep families together; it feeds also local attachment, which is the tap-root of the tree of Patriotism.[21]

Wordsworth connects different types of human association, the family and the nation, through the interim step of 'local attachment'. Sensitivity to the distinctiveness of one's locality or region inspires communal feeling which, according to Wordsworth, expands into an attachment to the nation. It is with this 'local attachment' or regionality, and its relation to family lines and narrative structure, that I shall concern myself in these final chapters on Hardy's writing. As re-creator of 'Wessex', Hardy, after Scott, is the novelist most often associated with regionality in the nineteenth-century British novel. (Although this is of course debatable in the case of Scott, as his Scottish novels are just as much 'national' as they are 'regional'. Indeed this is the point to be decided at the heart of novels such as *Redgauntlet* and *Waverley*.) In many of Hardy's novels and poems, a sense of 'local feeling' or attachment to region is mapped onto the rather more abstract or spiritual topographical space of 'God's Acre' – the burial ground. The names and family connections which appear on a family tomb or on the graves of generations of the same family in a country churchyard, provide a family history of sorts. As Nigel Llewellyn writes in *The Art of Death*: 'Since the sixteenth century antiquaries and historians such as Leland, Camden, Hearne and Aubrey have used inscriptions on English [funerary] monuments as sources of data for family and county histories.'[22]

But the movement of workers from the country to the city in the nineteenth century meant that these migrants were no longer buried in the family plot. The move to the city resulted not only in an overcrowding of the city of the living, but in the city of the dead as well. In the 1830s and 40s there was public outrage over official reports on the state of city necropoli, and particularily those of London. In his book, *Gatherings from Graveyards* (1839) G. A. Walker drew attention to an article in the *Quarterly Review* which stated that, 'many tons of human bones every year are sent from London to the North, where they are crushed in mills constructed for the purpose, and used as manure.'[23] Walker, whose work is supposed to have influenced the Parliamentary enquiry of 1843 into methods of interment, writes:

Decently to dispose of the dead, and vigilantly to secure their remains from violation, are among the first duties of society; our domestic endearments – our social attachments – our national prepossessions, respect and sanctify the resting places of our forefathers.[24]

Commercial undertakers resold coffins or used them for firewood, and those visiting the grave of a loved one in a city cemetery could not be sure whether the bones of the beloved were lying under the gravestone or enriching the soil of some northern field. It is understandable then that a nostalgia for the peace and sanctity of the country churchyard grew as the nineteenth century advanced. Hardy's particular concern at the overcrowding in city cemeteries is mainly with the loss of family and communal associations, as is clear in the following passage from his short story, 'The Son's Veto' (1894). It is a story which opposes the ties of family and community in the country with the barrenness of a London suburb:

> Mr. Twycott had never rallied, and now lay in a well-packed cemetery to the south of the great city, where, if all the dead it contained had stood erect and alive, not one would have known him or recognized his name.[25]

Henry Alexander Bowler's Pre-Raphaelite painting, *The Doubt; 'Can These Dry Bones Live?'* (exhibited at the Royal Academy, 1855, see fig. 12) is one of a number of Victorian paintings which exhibits this nostalgia for the country churchyard. A young woman leans in contemplation over the gravestone of 'John Faithful', regarding his exhumed remains of skull and bone. The doubt over the possible resurrection and after-life of the bones is expressed in the woman's furrowed brow. This religious doubt is answered, according to Michael Wheeler, with:

> a surplus of signs of hope of resurrection over signs of death: the message of the inscriptions on the two gravestones in the foreground ('I am the Resurrection and the Life' (John 11:25) and 'Resurgam') is reinforced by two symbols of new life and resurrection – the germinating chestnut on the flat stone, and the butterfly which sits on the skull.[26]

The still, peaceful moment in the country churchyard of the painting seems to agree with Wordsworth's edicts for the ideal burial place:

> when death is in our thoughts, nothing can make amends for the soothing influences of nature, and for the absence of those types of renovation and decay, which the fields and woods offer to the notice of the serious and contemplative mind.[27]

In Bowler's painting the 'soothing influences of nature' are represented in sharp realistic detail; the effect of sun through leaves, the trailing ivy, almost every blade of grass is crisply set forth. The young woman also, with details such as the lace on her contemporary style of dress, and the lines in her face, is realistically presented. In the midst of all this realism, what is the viewer of the painting to make of the skull and bones lying on top of the gravestone? Michael Wheeler comments on their role in the painting: 'the stark reality of the exhumed bones is not erased, or

Figure 12 Henry Alexander Bowler, *The Doubt; 'Can These Dry Bones Live?'*, exhibited at the Royal Academy, 1855.

explained away, but rather held in tension with the hope of resurrection offered by John 11 on the gravestone.'[28]

Michael Wheeler provides a religious interpretation for the disturbing, jarring effect of the exhumed bones within this painting; the bones, even if starkly real, are yet symbolic. The representation of a human skeleton, or of a skull and bones, has been employed in paintings and funerary monuments for centuries to symbolize the nearness of death in life – the theme of *Et in Arcadia Ego* – or the close community of the living and the dead. This is certainly an important level of interpretation of Bowler's painting, and it is also the case that the Pre-Raphaelites did return to the symbolic motifs of earlier artistic traditions, particularly the medieval, in their works. Nevertheless this cannot entirely account for the strangeness of seeing the skull and bones placed within the intense realism of this Victorian painting. It is unusual, and was disturbing to some contemporary reviewers, to see this representation of death, which usually functions on a symbolic level, placed within a Victorian artistic tradition which does not seem entirely commensurate with the *Et in Arcadia Ego* motif; because although this painting is a well-known example of the Pre-Raphaelite style, it also has much in common with the popular 'Keepsake' paintings which commonly depicted attractive young women in sentimental, pretty situations (i.e. not bending over a partly exhumed grave). Perhaps it was the disparity between the symbolic and realistic levels of the skull and bones (as well as sexism) which led a contemporary reviewer from the *Art Journal* to comment that a man would have been more appropriate at the centre of the painting; a clash of artistic traditions left a sense that something did not quite fit in Bowler's work. A consideration of why the bones in this painting are so jarring, why they seem so disturbingly out of place, may reveal that there are other tensions and resonances here aside from the admittedly prominent one of religious doubt and the question of resurrection.

Bowler's painting was exhibited at the Royal Academy in 1855, at the height of public outrage over the exhumation and disposal of corpses in city churchyards. If for a moment we concentrate upon the skull and bones as actual, literal remains rather than just symbolic, then an interpretive trace which may have existed for Victorian viewers but which is now lost to us may perhaps be recovered; an alternative, more literal interpretation of this 'problem painting' may lie in the anxiety that the last bastion of eternal rest – the country churchyard – is showing signs of grave-disturbance. To those Victorian city-dwellers who had moved away from an ancestral village (or whose parents or grandparents had moved), this meddling with the buried could hamper alarmingly their nostalgic sense that their family history and a community of the living and the dead lay, still intact, in their ancestral churchyard. As G. A. Walker wrote, violation of the grave meant that 'the identity of relationship is destroyed' between the dead and the living.[29] Once the body has been disinterred, and consequently disconnected from the narrative of the gravestone, there can be no meaning or purpose in a visit to the grave. The signified is disassociated from signifier, the language of epitaph no longer has a referent, and the continuity of the family line between the living and the dead is arrested, rendered meaningless. The possibility of return to the country churchyard to trace family origins and history there is destroyed when the graves are disturbed. Blood-lines are cut, and with the passing of a few generations the city-dweller will come to the countryside as a tourist, with little or no memory of family or communal origin there.

In Bowler's painting, the bones are still associated with the gravestone of 'John Faithful'. But lying unburied, they are exposed to the danger of being lost or removed. The young woman is a privileged viewer who can still, in the moment of the painting, make the connection between John Faithful and his remains. In the conjunction of the name 'John Faithful' with her rapt contemplation of his remains there may lie other possible narratives apart from the religious or the sociological aspects of this 'problem picture'. In the predominant religious interpretation, John Faithful is faithful to the Lord. But the woman's youth, attractiveness and intense contemplation of the grave gives rise to a possible secular, sentimental or romantic narrative. Who was John Faithful to her; a faithful lover? Of course, the woman's costume is mid-Victorian, and the grave informs us that Faithful died in 1791. Literally, he could not have been her lover, but the romantic possibilities of 'faithful' and the young woman still resonate around the religious interpretation. Bowler's painting invites various interpretations because it stills a number of narrative alternatives within its frame; the gravestone tells a story which is framed by the narrative frame and then by the literal frame of the entire painting (and Bowler further extended this narrative *mise en abyme* by entitling the work with words based on the opening to Ezekiel 37, and intending the painting as an illustration to Tennyson's *In Memoriam*).

Like Wordsworth, Gray and county historians, Thomas Hardy was very much aware of the narrative potential and power of gravestones. As in Bowler's painting, gravestones in his writing often serve as a narrative within the narrative. They tell stories within the frame of his novels and poems, stories which are crucially connected to the frame story. In his tales of the gravestone, the churchyard becomes the site, not of a harmonious community of the living and the dead, but of disconnection, either of lovers or of families.

The gravestone, as in that of Bowler's painting, partly reveals the tale of its occupant, but often leaves much of its familial or romantic history to conjecture. Hardy often writes the narrative inspired by the gravestone, the story which it could not tell. As in his poem 'In Death Divided', this is often a narrative of severance, of disruption:

> I shall rot here, with those whom in their day
> You never knew,
> And alien ones who, ere they chilled to clay,
> Met not my view,
> Will in your distant grave-place ever neighbour you.

And, in stanza 4:

> The simply-cut memorial at my head
> Perhaps may take
> A rustic form, and that above your bed
> A stately make;
> No linking symbol show thereon for our tale's sake.[30]

Hardy provides those 'linking symbols' for his 'tale's sake' in much of his writing which links lovers' histories and family lines. Often however, he connects the linking symbols of graves with his tale, only to destroy the connections and to reveal the futility of hoping for any permanence to the stories behind the inscriptions on tombs. In *Far From the Madding Crowd*, for instance, Troy selects an expensive gravestone for Fanny; one which, according to the stone-cutter, is warranted 'to resist rain and frost for a hundred years without flying.'[31] But the grave is placed under a grotesque gargoyle on the church tower, and the waterfall from its spout after the night's rain destroys the flowers that Troy sentimentally planted on her grave. In future years the stone and its inscription will be worn away, and the only memorial of Fanny as beloved of Troy will be obliterated. Hardy's description of the violence of the water spout upon her grave may even imply that one day her very remains will be disinterred by its force.

As in Bowler's painting, the peace of the country churchyard cannot guarantee a quiet resting place, and Wordsworth's belief in the 'soothing influences of nature' in the country churchyard pales in comparison with the violent and obliterative 'vengeance' of the gargoyle. Troy's determination to make Fanny's grave a place of lasting remembrance is futile. No monument to her name can compensate for the fact that Troy did not join his name with hers in marriage, or for the fact that the possibility of carrying on her memory through children is ended with their dead baby who lies in the grave illegitimate and nameless. After Troy is shot dead, Bathsheba orders that he be buried with Fanny, and she inscribes his name on Fanny's grave. Bathsheba's catharsis is to write the story of her husband's relationship with the girl, but as is so often the case in Hardy's work, the tale is still incomplete because Bathsheba cannot go so far as to write their baby's name on the grave. In Hardy's early novel, *A Pair of Blue Eyes*, and his late novel *The Well-Beloved*, monuments, whether graves or statues, are created as memorials to stave off a forgetting of the life stories of the dead, and to stave off a sense of disconnection between the family and community of the living and the dead. As the son of a stone-mason, and as an architect specializing in church restoration, Hardy's experiences gave him a peculiar perspective on these stone memorials.

THOMAS HARDY AND CHURCH RESTORATION

Hardy was a young architect with literary aspirations when in 1865 he took on an unusual and macabre assignment for his employer, Arthur Blomfield. In the *Life*, Hardy relates how this came about:

Mr Blomfield (afterwards Sir Arthur) being the son of a late Bishop of London, was considered a right and proper man for supervising the removal of human bodies in cases where railways had obtained a faculty for making cuttings through the city churchyards, so that it should be done decently and in order. A case occurred in which this function on the Bishop's behalf was considered to be duly carried out. But afterwards Mr Blomfield came to Hardy and informed him with a look of concern that he had just returned from visiting the site on which all the removed bodies were said by the company to be reinterred; but there appeared to be nothing deposited, the surface of the ground lying quite level as before. Also that there were rumours of mysterious full bags of something that rattled, and cartage to bone mills. He much feared that he had not exercised a sufficiently sharp supervision, and that the railway company had got over him somehow. 'I believe those people are all ground up!' said Blomfield grimly.[32]

Shortly after this, Blomfield was asked to supervise 'the carrying of a cutting by the Midland Railway through Old St. Pancras Churchyard, which would necessitate the removal of many hundreds of coffins, and bones in huge quantities.'[33] This time Blomfield was determined that the bones, so unceremoniously moved from their eternal bedchambers, would find a decent resting place, and he asked Hardy to attend the railway works every evening in the autumn and winter, to keep an eye on the proceedings. Many years later, in 1890, Hardy wrote in *A Group of Noble Dames* of 'dear, delightful Wessex, whose statuesque dynasties are even now only just beginning to feel the shaking of the new and strange spirit without, like that which entered the lonely valley of Ezekiel's vision and made the dry bones move.'[34] Certainly Hardy was not quite thinking of the 'shaking of the new and strange spirit' as a *train*, but the railway was, as he witnessed every evening, clearly making the 'dry bones move'.

As an architect in the 1860s, Hardy was active in two very different evocations of a 'new and strange spirit' of progress and change; one of commerce and industry in the form of the railway, and the other a religious force, a new zeal in the Church of England for church restoration. Each of these very different activities involved disruption of that seemingly last bastion of changelessness – that is, a disturbance of the grave, that 'eternal' resting place from which people do not expect to be moved, at least until the Day of Judgement.

Church restoration was Hardy's principal work as an architect. The removal of walls and particularly the repaving of the old church floors with their ledger stones marking the graves underneath involved a disturbance and confusion of who was buried where. In the *Life* Hardy writes that through his restoration work he was 'passively instrumental in destroying or altering' much old architecture 'beyond identification – a matter for his deep regret in later years.'[35] At another point he remembers, 'seeing the old font of —Church, Dorchester, in a garden, used as a flower vase, the initials of ancient godparents and churchwardens still legible upon it. A comic business – church restoration.'[36] If this 'altering beyond identification' both of architecture and of graves caused him regret, it also became a fascination in his writings – both in the poetry and the novels. Mixed-up graves, lost family names on gravestones, inform his idiosyncratic delight in what he called 'satires of circumstance'. Sometimes the plight of the buried elicits a tragic tone, as in the poem 'I Found Her Out There', one of the 'Poems of 1912–13', in which he imagines his first wife Emma's body underground, buried in the wrong place, far away from her beloved Cornwall:

> Yet her shade, maybe
> Will creep underground
> Till it catch the sound
> Of that western sea
> As it swells and sobs
> Whence she once domiciled
> And joy in its throbs
> With the heart of a child.[37]

But, just as often, there is a satirical or tragi-comic tone as in this poem of 1882, 'The Levelled Churchyard', which deals directly with church restoration:

> O passenger, pray list and catch
> Our sighs and piteous groans,
> Half-stifled in this jumbled patch
> Of wrenched memorial stones!
>
> We late-lamented, resting here
> Are mixed to human jam,
> And each to each exclaims in fear,
> 'I know not which I am!'

And the fourth stanza:

> Where we are huddled none can trace,
> And if our names remain,
> They pave some path or porch or place
> Where we have never lain![38]

In so much of his writing, it seems as if Hardy cannot leave graves alone; like a zealous church restorer he is always disturbing the bones, shifting the gravestones, and all the time there is his sense of regret at the loss of the names of the buried, and the life stories that went with their names. The desire to restore the names and stories of those who are buried is illustrated continually in his interest in the tales of old people speaking of their contemporaries. He often spoke with old country people, and visited the Chelsea Hospital to chat with soldiers who remembered Waterloo. One characteristic story, retold in the *Life*, demonstrates Hardy's preoccupation with a recuperation of lost names and lost stories. He was told,

> by a very old country-woman he met, of a girl she had known who had been betrayed and deserted by a lover. She kept her child by her own exertions, and lived bravely and throve. After a time the man returned poorer than she, and wanted to marry her; but she refused ... The young woman's conduct in not caring to be 'made respectable' won the novelist-poet's admiration, and he wished to know her name; but the old narrator said, 'Oh, never mind their names: they be dead and rotted by now.'[39]

Hardy's wish to connect the name with the story of one 'dead and rotted' informs writing which often concerns itself with characters whose stories are on the brink of being forgotten, and who lived in times just beyond the reach of his memory. Hardy later made use of the above story in both fiction and verse (for example in the short story 'For Conscience's Sake', and less directly in *Tess*).

Hardy's writings run the entire spectrum of family records in graves from noblemen to the meanest of commoners. The tombs of Tess's ancestors in Kingsbere for instance bespeak her ancient pedigree, but the best she can do for her own child is an unhallowed grave marked only with the name 'Keelwell's Marmalade' on the jar of flowers she places over it. Her child, as in the poem 'The Levelled Churchyard', can only expect to be 'mixed to human jam' with the suicides, unbaptised children, and drunkards buried in this unblessed corner of the churchyard.

PEDIGREE AND THE TOMB: A PAIR OF BLUE EYES

In his early, and most autobiographical novel *A Pair of Blue Eyes* (1873), Hardy combines the elements of church restoration, disturbance of graves, and pedigree. A young architect, Stephen Smith, comes from London to a remote parish on the Cornish coast to restore the ancient crumbling church at Endelstow. There he falls in love with the vicar's daughter, Elfride Swancourt. Elfride has been loved before, unrequitedly, by a young farmer now dead, whose mother, the lonely Widow Jethway, blames Elfride for his death.

Unbeknownst to Elfride and her father, Stephen is not a London man, but originally from the next village, where his parents still live. In the churchyard, Elfride and Stephen secretly plan their marriage, and Stephen confesses to her that his is not a noble pedigree, as the vicar would like to believe. He tells her, 'My father is John Smith, Lord Luxellian's master-mason, who lives under the park wall by the river.'[40] This he tells her while they are sitting together on Felix Jethway's tomb. At first Elfride is reluctant to sit over the remains of her former admirer, but Stephen draws her to him, and, as in so many things, she passively acquiesces. The tomb is a natural place to sit; most of the other graves are simple upstanding headstones. Widow Jethway has commemorated the name of her only son in an expensive tomb of white marble. Differing from all the other gravestones which are hewn from the 'dark blue slabs from local quarries', Jethway's tomb stands out in the moonlight in several crisis scenes of the novel.

Stephen and Elfride's discussion on the tomb centres around pedigree, a subject which fascinates Elfride's father who keeps a copy of Burke's *Landed Gentry* to hand:

'My mother curtseyed to you and your father last Sunday,' said Stephen, with a pained smile at the thought of the incongruity. 'And your papa said to her, "I am glad to see you so regular at church, *Jane*."' ... 'Contrast with this ... your father's belief in my "blue blood", which is still prevalent in his mind. The first night I came he insisted upon proving my descent from one of the most ancient west-county families, on account of my second Christian name; when the truth is, it was given me because my grandfather was assistant gardener in the Fitzmaurice-Smith family for thirty years.' (pp. 107–8)

The vicar can address Stephen's mother simply as 'Jane' because in his eyes she is not of a notable enough family to remember the last name – she is not gentry or of 'blue blood'. (Hardy's narrator makes a similar distinction in the novel; Stephen is always referred to by his first name, but Elfride's second love, Henry Knight is always called by his last name or as 'Mr. Knight'.)

When Stephen discovers that he is sitting on the tomb of Elfride's former admirer, the discussion turns from preceding ancestors to preceding lovers. Elfride is able to resign herself to 'the overwhelming idea of her lover's antecedents', but Stephen is disturbed momentarily that there was someone in Elfride's life before him. However, with the assurance of Elfride's love this soon passes from his mind.

Jethway's tomb haunts the narrative, and is returned to again and again: as Elfride plays the organ in church and realizes she is falling in love with Henry Knight, Stephen's 'successor' in love, she looks up from Knight to see, 'From the gallery window the tomb of Mrs Jethway's son was plainly visible'; as Stephen waits for Elfride in the churchyard after his return from India he is almost literally haunted by the tomb:

Turning the corner of the tower, a white form stared him in the face. He started back, and recovered himself. It was the tomb of young farmer Jethway, looking still as fresh and as new as when it was first erected. (p. 262)

While Stephen is away in India hoping to earn enough to marry Elfride, Henry Knight has come to Endelstow and gradually usurped Stephen's place in her heart. Another scene takes place near Jethway's tomb. Knight browbeats Elfride into a confession of her former 'lovers'. Unlike Stephen, Knight cannot reconcile himself to his romantic antecedents. He reprimands her; 'I hardly think I should have had the conscience to accept the favours of a new lover whilst sitting over the poor remains of the old one', and 'in moody meditation, [he] continued looking towards the tomb, which stood staring them in the face like an avenging ghost' (p. 342).

There are many other returns and repetitions involving Jethway's tomb in the novel, and in later chapters, repetitions involving the tomb of the noble Luxellian family. It may seem odd that the tombs in a remote village churchyard punctuate this novel about a young woman's experience of love and her broken engagements. Knight's sullen comments to Elfride about accepting the favours of a new lover while sitting above the 'poor remains' of the old one give an indication of why mourning and wedding are so persistently juxtaposed in this novel. *A Pair of Blue Eyes* is concerned with what it means to become mere 'poor remains'. To Knight, Felix's bodily remains are 'poor' because they are to be pitied as they are all that is left of one who has been replaced, superseded by another man. This fear of being forgotten is a central anxiety of the novel. Tombs do not merely signify death here, but also, what is perhaps much worse, they signify the forgetting rather than the remembrance of the deceased, and in that forgetting, a death of love.

What is at stake here for Knight is a fear that he will not be the first and only of Elfride's lovers, but will instead be added to an unsung 'pedigree' or line of lovers, becoming one day forgotten like the 'poor remains' of Felix Jethway. Knight's fear of being forgotten, of becoming an empty shell of love, can be seen on a geological scale in the well-known cliff-hanging episode, midway through the novel. Knight faces death as he hangs from a cliff, waiting to be rescued by Elfride. The moments that he hangs suspended give him an opportunity to contemplate the shelf of slaty rock against which his face is pressed. It is layered with the impressions of trilobites, molluscs and other shells of former life:

> opposite Knight's eyes was an imbedded fossil, standing forth in low relief from the rock. It was a creature with eyes. The eyes, dead and turned to stone, were even now regarding him. It was one of the early crustaceans called Trilobites. Separated by millions of years in their lives Knight and this underling seemed to have met in the place of their death.... Zoophytes, mollusca, shell-fish, were the highest developments of those ancient dates. The immense lapses of time each formation represented had known nothing of the dignity of man. They were grand times, but they were mean times too, and mean were their relics. He was to be with the small in his death. (p. 240)

The impersonality of the trilobite's dead eyes impress upon Knight his own smallness in geological time and perhaps also in the layers of memory of those he knows and loves. His own body will become a shell, to be forgotten in layers of time among a multiplicity of other lovers. As Mary Jacobus writes of this scene:

the threat which Hardy faces is the mind's own effortless spawning of images, the imaginative autonomy which must be buried in the interest of maintaining the realist illusion ... Arbitrariness invades the world of the novel, threatening individual consciousness and laying waste the present.[41]

In the sphere of love, Knight needs to maintain the illusion of constant and exclusive devotion between lovers; he needs to keep at bay an 'effortless spawning of images' of other possible lovers and to believe that he and Elfride were created exclusively for each other. He confesses to Elfride that she is the first woman he has ever kissed and his idealistic fiction of true love demands that she be in the same position toward him. This is destroyed when he stares at the tomb of Felix Jethway, and begins to feel that he is just one of a row of lovers in her life.

Of these lovers, Felix Jethway is the one about whom we know the least. Elfride does not mourn over Felix's grave – he left little impression upon her in life or death – and the only mourner who knows his full story is his mother. A lonely widow, she is the last left of his pedigree to tell his story and to commemorate him, but she is silenced when killed by the falling tower of the church which has been knocked down in the restoration process. As church restorer, Stephen, Elfride's second 'lover' is indirectly responsible for the death of the only woman who can tell the story of her first. And Knight, the third in line, is the one who discovers the widow under the rubble and unknowingly lays her body on her son's tomb, which she had come to visit. There is nothing marked on Felix's grave which could tell the story of his love for Elfride, and if it were not for the widow's letter to Knight, warning of Elfride's supposed ill-usage of her son and of her aborted elopement with Stephen, the last of the story would have died with the widow. From unpretentious farming stock, Jethway's only written pedigree is that on his tombstone, and with the death of his mother the story behind his name and its family connections is lost.

In the preface to *A Group of Noble Dames*, Hardy wrote of the relationship of pedigrees to narrative:

the careful comparison of dates alone – that of birth with marriage, of marriage with death, of one marriage, birth or death with a kindred marriage, birth or death – will often effect [a] transformation and anybody practised in raising images from such genealogies finds himself unconsciously filling into the framework the motives, passions and personal qualities which would appear to be the single explanation possible of such extraordinary conjunction in times, events, and personages that occasionally marks those reticent family records.[42]

In contrast to the unpedigreed single grave of Felix Jethway, is the Luxellian family tomb in the neighbouring churchyard. Chapters 26 and 27 of the novel take place mainly inside this tomb which is being set in order for a new inmate, the recently-deceased Lady Luxellian. (At the end of the novel we learn that Elfride finally marries the noble widower to become the next Lady Luxellian.) Old William Worm, one of the labourers preparing the tomb, tells stories of the tomb's various inhabitants as he shifts the coffins about. The close proximity of the family members buried in the same tomb emphasizes their kinship relations to each other, and the stories that were bred by their proximity in life. In the following chapter the tomb becomes the accidental meeting place for three whose proximity in life structures the story of *A Pair of Blue Eyes* – Elfride, Stephen and Knight. Elfride has almost joined her pedigree to both of these men in marriage, having once been engaged to Stephen and now engaged to Knight. William Worm relates the story of Elfride's grandmother, also named 'Elfride', who was a Luxellian and who is buried in the tomb. She had run away with the singing master and died giving birth to the heroine's mother. Worm, appropriately named for tomb tales, comments upon the female Luxellian line: 'That trick of running away seems to be handed down in families, like craziness or gout. And they two women be as alike as peas' (p. 278), meaning Lady Elfride Luxellian and her grandaughter, Elfride Swancourt. Of course, William does not know to what extent these Elfrides will actually repeat each other; he does not know of Elfride's cancelled elopement with Stephen, or that in the future the present Elfride will become another 'Lady Elfride Luxellian', and die as she did, giving birth to a first child.

In the mind of this old villager it is difficult to distinguish between these various incarnations of an 'Elfride'. The two women begin to merge into one another in the layers of his memory, which is of a wider scope than that of the young Stephen, Knight or Lord Luxellian. Knight's fear when confronted with the trilobite's dead and impersonal eyes, that he 'would be with the small in his death' is connected to his fear that he will be forgotten in the time of one generation – in Elfride's life – by becoming a forgotten layer in her memory, one of a row of lovers. William Worm's conflation of the two Elfrides emphasizes this forgetting; even in one generation the similar stories of lovers begin to merge and get lost in one another.

As discussed in the Preface to this chapter, Hardy was repeatedly drawn to the comparison of various time-scales, and this juxtaposition of geological time and human time is a frequent concern in his writings. In a diary entry of 1873 (the year of publication of *A Pair of Blue Eyes*), he notes after a visit to Tintern Abbey, 'A wooded slope visible from every unmullioned window. But compare the age of the building with that of the marble hills from which it was drawn!', and in the *Life* he comments upon this entry, 'this shortcoming of the most ancient architecture by comparison with geology was a consideration which frequently worried Hardy'.[43] A notebook entry from September 1877 again shows Hardy wrestling with time-scale, attempting to allay this 'worry': 'An object or mark raised or made by man on a scene is worth ten times any such formed by unconscious Nature. Hence clouds, mists and mountains are unimportant beside the wear on a threshold, or the print of a hand.'[44] One would think from these last words that it must have been Hardy, and not his fictional Henry Knight, who had been rescued from the terrifying contemplation of the 'fan of time' opened up in the geological layers in the Cliff without a Name. This cliff is so terrifying partly because it has no name; all the surrounding cliffs have some mark of the human upon them in that they have been given names. Hardy, like Knight, struggles to allay the fear of the arbitrariness and immensity which makes the human insignificant when placed in the perspective of geological time. In the notebook entry from 1877, Hardy privileges the human generational time scale, which leaves 'the print of a hand', as he does in his poem 'Old Furniture', 'I see the hands of the generations/That owned each shiny familiar thing/In play on its knobs and indentations'.

In *A Pair of Blue Eyes* the mark of the human is slowly but decisively erased. Some graves are left untended and forgotten, others cannot yield up the stories of their buried, and always in the background there are those graves which are destroyed by church restoration. Even in the human time of a William Worm, the Luxellian tomb conflates the stories of the two Elfrides buried there, erasing their individuality. Geological time is frightening and alienating in its vastness, but even within genealogical time, the human trace is at risk of being misread or forgotten. A silting process is beginning in the Luxellian tomb which will place Elfride, if not quite yet among the geological layers, then as a tiny layer among the many layers of the Luxellian succession. She is, after all, the second wife of the lord, and the reason that she, Stephen and Knight met in the Luxellian tomb to begin with was because it was being prepared for the *first* Lady Spenser Hugo Luxellian. Future visitors to the tomb will see two Lady Elfride Luxellians there, both having died in childbirth, and with time no-one will be able to distinguish between them or their separate stories.

Henry Knight and Stephen Smith must experience what it is to become one in a row of lovers in one woman's life and memory. In one of the last scenes of the novel they travel in the same train from London to Cornwall, both intending to propose to Elfride. They do not realize that the strange dark carriage which has been attached to the train since London is a hearse containing her body. Discovering her death upon arriving in Endelstow station, they still compete with each other over which of them was the lover to whom the dead Elfride had kept faith in her heart while living. Each needs to be the one that she remembered at her end. When they shelter from the rain in a smithy they learn that they have both been usurped by another. There they read her new coffin plate which marks that she died, 'Elfride, Wife of Spenser Hugo Luxellian, Fifteenth baron Luxellian' (p. 398). Again and again they read it together, 'as if animated by one soul'. The sudden knowledge that she died the wife of another and that they have joined the 'poor remains' of Felix Jethway in a row of seemingly forgotten lovers, brings them together; they seem to merge into one another, their differences put aside, and act for the remaining pages of the novel with one will, walking 'side by side' away from her tomb.

The final scene of the novel takes place, in one of Hardy's characteristic repetitions, with Elfride, Knight and Stephen together again in the Luxellian tomb. This time, of course, Elfride is being entombed, and there is another man mourning over her. Her husband, Lord Luxellian, grieves, 'kneeling on the damp floor, his body flung across the coffin, his hands clasped, and his whole frame seemingly given up in utter abandonment to grief' (p. 403). Knight and Stephen retreat, feeling themselves to be 'intruders'. As Knight says: 'We have no right to be there. Another stands before us – nearer to her than we!' (p. 403). As her husband, Luxellian is the only one of Elfride's lovers who has the 'right' to mourn in the public eye. He may abandon himself to grief and go through all the official customs of mourning – placing her in his family tomb – because of all the men gathered in the tomb he is the only one who gave her his name. The names on the tomb will tell a story that will endure for some generations at least, of the relationship of Luxellian and Elfride – a story which we only hear the rudiments of, told indirectly by Elfride's maid, Unity. Stephen and Knight's connections with her, which form the story of the novel will have no marker and no permanence at all in written history because neither of their names has been officially engraved with hers by marriage on a pedigree or tombstone.

As Elfride's husband, Luxellian is sanctioned by society as her official mourner; he wears black mourning, sends out black-bordered funeral cards, orders a black funeral carriage to carry his wife's body, and generally marks his grief with that definite colour of death. The cult of death in Victorian society recognized, perhaps unconsciously, that black was a sign both of catharsis and of power. John Harvey comments on the 'great paradox of black': 'For black is a negative quality, the absence of colour: considered *as* a colour, which one chooses to wear, it is the sign of denial and loss. Yet self-denial can also give power, and authority over un-denied selves'. Black, according to Harvey, may make one 'a person to be heeded with reverence and awe', regarded as a person of 'impressive, intense inwardness'.[45] One of the final images of *A Pair of Blue Eyes* is that of Lord Luxellian, 'the dark form of a man, kneeling on the damp floor' grieving over Elfride's coffin. He is 'still young', 'graceful' and is praying half aloud, unconscious of the presence of Stephen and Knight. Although Lord Luxellian hardly figures at all as a character, his black mourning presence at the close of the novel has a dignity and power which Elfride's previous lovers cannot claim. Knight's and Stephen's grief is marked by grey, and in much of Hardy's writing this colour represents a painful neutrality – an inability to mourn fully, cathartically. His poem of 1867, 'Neutral Tones' is coloured by grey; it concerns the inability to mourn a lost love because of a forgetting of that love in indifference;

> We stood by a pond that winter day,
> And the sun was white, as though chidden of God,
> And a few leaves lay on the starving sod;
> – They had fallen from an ash, and were grey.[46]

Neither Knight nor Stephen is indifferent to Elfride – both men are grief-stricken at her death. But they are not allowed the definite black of mourning, because for different reasons they were not definite enough in their love of Elfride to marry her when the opportunity arose. Grey becomes a more disturbing colour of death than black, because it is, like the awful neutrality in the smile of the woman in the above poem, 'the deadest thing/Alive enough to have strength to die', not yet quite dead, not quite put out of its misery. Black mourning allows for a public and private 'abandonment to grief'; mourning costume is both a public and private marker: it makes a public declaration of bereavement and of relationship, and is also a sign that the mourner be set apart, granted privacy. The social signs of mourning allow for the attempt to exhaust grief through catharsis. Knight and Stephen feel they have no right to such catharsis. They are not sanctioned to tell the story of their relation with Elfride, or to have it acknowledged and understood publicly. Grief must fester within them, and to the world they must appear as indifferent, neutral or 'grey' lovers and mourners. Reading Elfride's coffin-plate, the revelation that she dies the wife of another, they first realize the grey area they inhabit as her former lovers. It is then that, 'the quiet sky asserted its presence overhead as a dim grey sheet of blank monotony' (p. 398). The greyness of their world asserts itself again in the final sentence of the novel; 'And side by side they retraced their steps down the grey still valley to Castle Boterel' (p. 403). Earlier in the novel it is Elfride's indifference to Stephen which is foreshadowed by grey as she rides away from him after their cancelled elopement:

And the pony went on, and she spoke to him no more. He saw her figure diminish and her blue veil grow grey – saw it with the agonizing sensations of a slow death. (p. 150)

The next time they meet, years later, Elfride is engaged to another; the death presaged by the fading of blue into grey in the above passage is her foreshadowed death of love for Stephen, a 'slow death' of forgetting and grey indifference.

In a journal entry of January 1897, Hardy made a note of the relation of the senses and memory:

Today has length, breadth, thickness, colour, smell, voice. As soon as it becomes *yesterday* it is a thin layer among many layers, without substance, colour or articulate sound.[47]

This statement seems to work against the very way in which Hardy writes; his sensual recall seems to capture past moments in a vivid present. As Gillian Beer writes, commenting upon this journal entry; 'His writing seeks the palpable. It is in the present moment that human knowledge is realised and human happiness is experienced.'[48] The struggle is to hold the moment in an eternal tangible present in the face of the knowledge that, through death or forgetting, the moment is being overwhelmed by the past. Nowhere is this more evident than in his elegaic 'Poems of 1912–13' in which he tries to recapture his first meetings with Emma Gifford in Cornwall. Colour and voice especially encourage sensual recall in these poems; Emma's voice calls to him, haunts him from the grave (in 'The Haunter', 'The Voice', 'His Visitor'). The colours she is remembered by – her 'nut-coloured hair', and 'air blue gown', and 'the opal and the sapphire of that wandering western sea' which is her element – are evoked in these poems. For Hardy, sensual detail (particularly colour) is inextricably bound up with the kind of memory that is constant and loyal. Vivid, strong colours become his hues of mourning, and unlike the 'neutral tones' of grey which encroach upon Stephen and Knight's grief, Hardy's elegaic colours struggle against both black and grey to keep Emma's memory presently visible. In the Luxellian tomb Stephen and Knight can remember when they had all met there, 'before she had herself gone down into silence like her ancestors, and shut her bright blue eyes forever' (p. 403). Elfride has no voice for them, and her colour – the blue of her eyes – is now shut from them. For Knight and Stephen her colours and voice threaten to become 'a thin layer among many layers' just as she joins the layers of her ancestors, and just as they feel, however mistakenly, that they have been placed together in layers of her forgotten former lovers.

Elfride's corpse is brought to her ancestral tomb in a very modern conveyance – the railway carriage. According to Julian Litten, funerary railway carriages had become quite common by mid-century:

One enterprising cemetery, the London Necropolis Company ... had an arrangement between 1854 and 1941 with the London and Southwestern Railway to use their track from Waterloo to transport coffins and mourners – by first or third class – in specially designed carriages.[49]

Ironically the railway, whose construction Hardy had seen disturbing and destroying graves in 1865, had become a way of conveying people to their now questionably 'eternal' resting place. Within the story time of *A Pair of Blue Eyes* the railway reaches further and further out into the remote corners of Cornwall, and the 'new and modern spirit' which 'shakes' Wessex seems to make the processes of time move much faster. Railway time is very much evident in the novel; the meticulous timetabling of Stephen and Elfride's rail journey to London and back in their attempt to elope, and Elfride's flight by train to follow the estranged Knight. Geological and genealogical timescales in the novel bring about a gradual layering or silting process by which human lives are with time forgotten in layers of ancestors, romantic antecedents and memory. Railway time, its speed, schedules and connections, constitutes the third timescale at work in the novel. Compared with geological and genealogical scales, that of the railway compresses time dramatically and quickens the process of erasure, destruction and forgetting. Knight and Stephen become mere railway travellers in Elfride's life; they both allow the power and speed of the railway to carry them away from her irrevocably. Stephen weakly allows Elfride to board the return train to Cornwall, immediately upon arriving in London, rather than insisting that they go through with the elopement, and this leads to their permanent separation. Knight flees from Elfride by train to London, and when she desperately follows him, her father is close behind on the next train, coming to separate them.

Ease of train travel in this novel also means that the lovers are easily separated. They do not have the time and stasis forced upon them by which they might communicate, untangle their misunderstandings and establish a permanent connection with each other through marriage. Connections on the line take the place of human connections, and eventually lead to Stephen and Knight feeling that they have no real connection with Elfride and no right to mourn over her tomb. Luxellian, her husband, is bound by ancestral ties to Elfride's locality; he is no mere traveller in Elfride's life, but is fixed to his family estates, and eventually 'fixes' her in his ancestral home, finally having to bury her in his family tomb. The speed of railway time works against the possible pedigrees of both Knight and Stephen. They do not stay in Endelstow, and do not engrave her name onto their own family trees by marrying her. As a result, their stories in connection with her are at risk of being lost much more quickly. Hardy's telling of their stories is a way of recuperating the lost narratives of these 'wrong' or unofficial mourners. He has written of how geological and genealogical time can erase the stories of the dead. Railway time brings a sense of urgency to the plot. Narrative fiction becomes the only way to write the stories of Knight and Stephen, because their names and stories will not be evident on Elfride's grave, and will otherwise be lost and unknown to history.

CHAPTER SEVEN

Geology and genealogy: Hardy's 'The Well-Beloved'

> Let not a monument give you or me hopes,
> Since not a pinch of dust remains of Cheops.
> (Byron, *Don Juan*, Canto 1, stanza 219)

In his book, *The Art of Death*, Nigel Llewellyn writes of the role of funerary monuments in post-Reformation England:

To make concrete the ephemeral impressions of the funeral ceremony images were shaped in particular styles and materials, and effigies replaced the decaying natural body on funeral monuments to create permanent histories of the deceased. Those who remained – the bereaved – surrounded themselves with visual signs in their homes, in their costume and on their persons to sustain the memory and the very presence of the dead. This practice was not morbid but therapeutic.[1]

As discussed in the previous chapter, Wordsworth writes of the country churchyard as a place of 'community of the living and the dead'. A visit to the monument or grave of a family member is therapeutic partly because it connects the dead family member with his or her continuation on the family tree. In the country churchyard the 'soothing influences of nature' lie in their reminder to the living visitor of the process of regeneration. This regeneration is not only that of the surrounding trees and wildlife, with its spiritual analogy of the regeneration of the resurrected soul, but also of the continuing generations of the living souls who claim the same lineage with the deceased. In this view, death becomes not a negation of life, but part of it; the deceased represents a former generation in a continuing process of regeneration. The funerary monument which 'creat[es] permanent histories of the deceased' is also the material sign of a continuing family history.

The grave or monument is also the site of a therapeutic, cathartic process of mourning. It replaces the decayed natural body with its sign in stone, in the form of epitaph or effigy, of what that person was in life (or is, however fictitiously, remembered to be). This catharsis may allow regeneration to occur; the living may purge themselves of grief through mourning, and go on to live their lives, and to carry on the family line.

In much of Hardy's writing, this process of regeneration is ironically reversed. Statues, graves, and other *memento mori* inhibit or halt the process of regeneration, as in the following poem, 'The Children and Sir Nameless':

> Sir Nameless, once of Athelhall, declared:
> 'These wretched children romping in my park
> Trample the herbage till the soil is bared,
> And yap and yell from early morn till dark!
> Go keep them harnessed in their set routines:
> Thank God I've none to hasten my decay;
> For green remembrance there are better means
> Than offspring, who but wish their sires away.'
>
> Sir Nameless of the mansion said anon:
> 'To be perpetuate for my mightiness
> Sculpture must image me when I am gone.'
> – He forthwith summoned carvers there express
> To shape a figure stretching seven-odd feet
> (For he was tall) in alabaster stone,
> With shield, and crest, and casque, and sword complete:
> When done a statelier work was never known.
>
> Three hundred years hied; Church-restorers came,
> And, no one of his lineage being traced,
> They thought an effigy so large in frame
> Best fitted for the floor. There it was placed
> Under the seats for schoolchildren. And they
> Kicked out his name, and hobnailed off his nose;
> And as they yawn through sermon-time, they say,
> 'Who was this old stone man beneath our toes?'[2]

Church-restorers are again guilty of the obliteration of the names and family histories of the dead. But Sir Nameless is so very anonymous because he put all his hope for perpetuity in art, in his case, in a statue. The stone effigy replaces the living memorial of children, but children – the future generations – ironically complete the process of obliterating the name and history of Sir Nameless.

This substitution of stone memorial for the living is quite literally the case in Hardy's short story, 'Barbara of the House of Grebe' (1891), one of the tales collected in *A Group of Noble Dames*. Barbara's first husband

Edmond, a beautiful youth of low birth, is sent away for a year by her parents to gain education and social polish on the Continent, while Barbara waits for him at home. In Italy, he suffers a horribly disfiguring accident when his face is burnt in a fire, and upon his eventual return to England, Barbara is so horrified by his appearance that the youth decides to torment her no longer. He leaves her, eventually to die, and after some years Barbara is married again, to the cold-blooded Lord Uplandtowers. When a statue of her first husband, sculpted in Italy before his accident, arrives at Barbara's new home, she is overcome with regret and guilt at her treatment of Edmond. In an inversion of the Pygmalion myth, she begins to worship the dead image of her first husband, visiting the statue at night, rather than her living husband's bed. The eroticism of the following scene indicates that Hardy's ironic reversals make the hope of regeneration as dead as the stone of this *memento mori*. Barbara's husband secretly observes her at night:

Arrived at the door of the boudoir, he beheld the door of the private recess open, and Barbara within it, standing with her arms clasped tightly around the neck of her Edmond, and her mouth on his. The shawl which she had thrown around her nightclothes had slipped from her shoulders, and her long white robe and pale face lent her the blanched appearance of a second statue embracing the first.[3]

In this case the lover is being petrified, and Lord Uplandtowers recognizes the infertility of his wife's embrace of a *memento mori*: 'This is where we evaporate – this is where my hopes of a successor in the title dissolve – !'[4] In this story the process of regeneration, the continuation of the family line is literally at risk of dying out because the *memento mori* becomes the site, not of cathartic mourning, but of death-in-life.

The possibility of regeneration, of continuing blood-lines, seems equally hopeless at the close of *A Pair of Blue Eyes*. It seems probable that the Luxellian genealogy will end with Elfride, who died in miscarriage, and the grief-stricken Knight and Stephen who close the novel seem to have surrendered themselves to a mourning which is not cathartic, but which is described as 'grey' and 'still', a 'blank monotony'; it is a barren, sterile end to the novel, leaving little prospect of renewal. Paradoxically, however, even genealogy is sterile in this novel, and, as I will argue, this is the case in a number of Hardy's works; Elfride's name and individuality merges with three generations of Elfrides, her mother and grandmother of the same name. The barrenness of this repetition over the generations is what led Tess to exclaim to Angel Clare that she does not want to study history, 'Because what's the use of learning that I am one of a long row only'; to retain at least the illusion of individual will, she thinks it best to remain ignorant of those who have come before her on the D'Urberville line. Her sentiments could, with equal pertinence and force, have been uttered by Elfride of her matrilineal Luxellian legacy, if Hardy's earlier heroine had had the insight and tragic knowledge of the later.

Another generational repetition across the female line, similar to that of *A Pair of Blue Eyes*, is found in Hardy's late novel, *The Well-Beloved*, which tells the story of three generations of women, all named Avice Caro, and how they merge into one woman in the eyes of the sculptor Jocelyn Pierston, who loves all three. In Pierston's case, statues of his own creation become involved with both the geological and genealogical layers of his native island. These time-spans dwarf his own life-span, and his statues – his only offspring – make a mockery of his attempts at marital union and sexual consummation. Like Barbara of the House of Grebe, he is a 'petrified' and infertile lover, and his mythology of love turns the women he loves to stone.

Pierston is a successful London sculptor, the son of a quarry-owner on the Isle of Slingers. In a variation of the Pygmalion myth he places his sculpture between himself and love as a fictive mediating or controlling device to mitigate his 'thralldom' to love, but pays for this stratagem by becoming enthralled instead by his artistic fiction about love. This artistic fiction takes the form of a spirit whom he names his 'well-beloved'. He falls in love with the women who are endowed with this spirit – a spirit which is in the habit of flitting randomly from the body of one woman to another, leaving the former vehicle a 'corpse', 'as if her soul had shrunk and died/And left a waste within'.[5]

The vacant sadness Jocelyn experiences when confronted with the successive empty shells of each former 'well-beloved' is related to Knight's fear in *A Pair of Blue Eyes* when confronted with the empty shells of molluscs in the slaty rock of the Cliff without a Name. The anxiety over being forgotten, of joining an arbitrary universe in a forgotten layer of memory pervades Hardy's work. It is the impulse behind elegy, the inscriptions on tombs, and the creation of monuments, or, as in the case of Pierston, of statues. For Pierston, the departure of the well-beloved leaves behind nothing but a lifeless shell, without colour, substance or voice to call him to her.

Jocelyn attempts to control this fear of the arbitrariness of love and the forgetting that accompanies its passing, by sculpting stone images of his 'well-beloved'. His artistic medium is taken from the 'stratified walls of oolite' from the quarries of his native isle. In London, it is again the stone which forms a bridge between Pierston and his island home, just as the Pebble Bank of the Isle of Slingers connects the 'island' to the mainland; 'he haunt[s] the purlieus of the wharves along the Thames, where the stone of his native rock was unshipped from the coasting craft that had brought it thither. He would ... contemplate the white cubes and oblongs, imbibe their associations, call up their *genius loci* whence they came, and almost forget that he was in London'.[6] The geological layers of this stone serve his art, and also serve to connect him with the genealogical layers of the intermarrying families of his birthplace.

Hardy modelled the Isle of Slingers on Portland, and the similarity of the names of Pierston and Portland is evident, both being made up of part land and part sea – in fact comprising the pier or port which is the very threshold of land and sea. The Isle is not actually an island, but a peninsula of 'treeless rock', connected to the mainland by a 'long thin neck of pebbles' (p. 28). The geological state of the island/peninsula describes Pierston's state at the opening of the novel. He has not visited his home for years, and in London his only contact with the island is through the rock he sculpts. Just as the 'island' is connected to the mainland by a thin strand of rock, so Jocelyn is tenuously connected to his home by that same rock. He is first described in the novel, upon returning to visit the Isle after an absence of a few years, as a 'person who differed from the local wayfarers ... The pedestrian was what he looked like – a young man from London and the cities of the Continent. Nobody could see at present that his urbanism sat upon him only as a garment (p. 28). Like the Isle's geologically and geographically 'betwixt and between' state, Jocelyn also is caught between two modes of existence – no longer simply a native islander and yet not completely cosmopolitan. Through education and the polish it has given him, through his father's money (earned in the stone quarries of the island) and by virtue of being an artist and a bachelor, Jocelyn is able to elude the classifications and responsibilities that society might place upon him. In London he is a liminal figure: 'he was floating in society without any soul-anchorage or shrine that he could call his own' (p. 63).

Upon this first return to the island, his childhood sweetheart, Avice Caro sees through his urbane veneer and recognises him as a native. Greeting him unrestrainedly with a kiss, there is a moment of awkward surprise as Jocelyn readjusts himself to the open simplicity of island ways, and there is 'some constraint in the manner in which he returned her kiss' (p. 29). This uncertainty on his part presages Jocelyn's future plight. Becoming engaged to Avice on this island holiday, he is never entirely sure whether or not the well-beloved spirit has taken up its abode in her frame. He leaves the island intending to return to marry her, but by chance meets another woman, to whom, he believes, the well-beloved has been transferred. Jocelyn never returns to marry Avice, and subsequently spends the rest of his life pursuing 'her' through three genealogical layers – the first Avice, her daughter and her granddaughter. Over these three generations 'Avice Caro' becomes the most permanent, engrained version of his well-beloved. She is 'A/vice Caro' – the dear or beloved vice. (Hardy seems to suggest that the name 'Caro' meaning 'beloved' in Italian, is no coincidence: the Caros are probably descended from Roman colonists; 'The Caros, like some other local families, suggested a Roman lineage, more or less grafted on the stock of the Slingers. Their features recalled those of the Italian peasantry' (p. 89)). The pursuit of Avice Caro is the evil genius or 'vice' of Pierston's life, but also the desire which keeps both him and his art alive.

On the evening of his departure from the island, the evening which initiates his breaking faith with his childhood sweetheart, Avice does not keep her appointment to walk with him along the pebble bank to the train station. She fears that Pierston will adhere to the ancient island custom of premarital sex which was a traditional test of the bride-to-be's fertility. Avice's belief in the inbred customs of her forefathers prevents her going to Jocelyn, and leads to an encounter between him and another woman. For on the walk along the thin strand of pebbles to the mainland Jocelyn meets Marcia Bencombe – also an islander – but like Jocelyn, a liminal figure who has lived among fashionable London circles. While Avice stays fixed on her island, Jocelyn and Marcia walk the threshold of land and sea. Marcia's name, like Jocelyn's, evokes the threshold which defines them; it echoes the 'marches' – a boundary or 'tract of land on the border of a country, a disputed tract separating one country from another'.[7] Their liminality draws them together as much as the violent storm which forces them together to seek close shelter. As Jocelyn hangs Marcia's clothes to dry before the fireplace of a railway hotel he feels that, 'The Well-Beloved was moving house – had gone over to the wearer of this attire' (p. 48). Paradoxically, the empty shells of Marcia's clothing represent the new well-beloved, leaving Avice Caro the shell of his former love. However the rock of the island on the pebble bank which brought Jocelyn and Marcia together later splits them apart as they fight over loyalty to their respective quarry-owning fathers. Marcia's father is a wealthy quarry-owner who had tried to ruin his smaller counterparts on the island, Jocelyn's father included. After an argument with Jocelyn, Marcia returns to her parents. Her father's 'antagonism to her union with one of his blood and name' and the fact that there is 'no issue' from their few days of cohabitation results in a permanent separation.

The novel is stratified with geological and genealogical layers. It is also 'layered' in itself: there are two quite different versions of *The Well-Beloved*; one which appeared in 1892 in the *Illustrated London News*, and the other in book form, published in 1897. In the more carefully respectable magazine version Marcia and Jocelyn elope to London, marry, argue and depart to separate continents agreeing never to meet again, or to reveal their marriage. In the 1897 version, they live together in London awaiting a marriage licence and then part – she back to the island and eventually to America, and he to search again for other incarnations of the well-beloved in London, as before.

The mutability of his well-beloved during the twenty years between the first and second part of the novel is such that Jocelyn struggles to fix the spirit in a 'durable shape', sculpted in stone. The fact that stone in the novel is always figured as the limestone of his native isle undermines Jocelyn's attempts to 'fix' the 'well-beloved' in sculpture: limestone is made up of millions of fossilized shells – like the dead shells of all the women in whom he has fleetingly seen the well-beloved. Hardy describes the stone in the opening of Chapter One, as 'the melancholy ruins of cancelled cycles';[8] the geological stratifications of the island rock undermine the art with which he tries to give life to the dead shapes of his artistic fiction.

'Substantial flesh' usurps his sculptures and the fleeting London incarnations of the spirit when he returns, twenty years after the beginning of the story, to the Isle of Slingers upon hearing of Avice the First's death. At her graveside by moonlight, Jocelyn sees the second Avice, the daughter of his former love. But to Jocelyn she appears to be the same Avice; the girl he watches is the same age as when he last saw her mother, and, because of the frequent intermarriage on the island, she looks almost exactly as her mother did and has the same last name (the first Avice had married into another branch of the Caro family). She is called 'Ann Avice Caro' – an Avice Caro – or simply another of the first for Jocelyn.

Upon discovering the death of the first Avice, Jocelyn realizes that it is her memory which has now been embodied with the spirit of the well-beloved; 'He loved the woman dead and inaccessible as he had never loved her in life' (p. 83). Upon seeing her daughter, the memory of Avice – now the well-beloved – assumes 'corporeal substance'. Jocelyn moves from London to the Isle of Slingers so that he can pursue the second Avice. He returns, not to his old home – the cottage of his dead father – but rents the grander 'Sylvania Castle' on the island. Again the island reflects Jocelyn's psychological state; Sylvania Castle is the one spot on the island marked by greenery, surrounded by a plantation of elms. Jocelyn is seeking a new chance in love, a spring in his life through his love for the second incarnation of Avice. But Hardy undermines Jocelyn's vernal mood, by turning our attention from the lover's view of the elms down to the island rock. The geological time-scale of the rock mocks Jocelyn's hope for a new season of love:

To find other trees between Pebble-bank and Beal, it was necessary to recede a little in time – to dig down to a loose stratum of underlying stone beds, where a forest of conifers lay as petrifications, their heads all in one direction, as blown down by a gale in the Secondary geologic epoch (p. 94).

If he were to look away from the greenery of the elms around Sylvania Castle, to dig down to the level of these petrified conifers, Jocelyn would see a geological reflection of what is happening to his love through his pursuit of the genealogical layers of Avice Caro. The evergreen conifers did finally die, and now only their stone impressions remain.

Returning to the cliff shore of the island one night, Pierston rediscovers his name engraved in stone with the first Avice Caro's, dating from their romance twenty years earlier: 'The letters were now nearly worn away by the weather and the brine. But close in quite fresh letters, stood "ANN AVICE", coupled with the name "ISAAC"' (p. 98). The sea and the process of time are gradually erasing Jocelyn's and Avice's linked names – turning their impression back into the layers of rock. The name of the second Avice is now coupled with another generation of Pierston (in the small pool of intermarried families on the island, Isaac's last name happens to be Pierston as well). Jocelyn fails to see that he is being displaced and erased by time, and that just as there is a genealogical succession of Avices, there are also newer generations of Pierstons who can love those Avices. He can belong to one generation only, not all three. As the petrified conifers have their distinct and proper place in the geological time scale, so does he in a genealogical division of that time scale.

The second Avice is described as 'impervious' to Jocelyn's attentions. Her indifference renders him 'as cold as stone' (p. 115). Twenty years later in the third and final cycle of Avices, this second Avice is no longer indifferent to Pierston. This time however she sees the wealthy, cultured sculptor as a suitable husband for her educated daughter. Jocelyn's courtship of this last Avice is always conducted in the evening, under the flattering rays of the moon. She becomes engaged to him, but at a decisive moment before the wedding she sees him for the first time by daylight and her visible shock at seeing his true age bared by the sun's rays prompts him to tell her of his courtship of both her mother and grandmother. Avice is tempted by the seeming timelessness of this man to ask if he were her 'great-grandmother's young man' as well. She looks at him, 'no longer as at a possible husband, but as a strange fossilized relic in human form' (p. 162). To the first Avice, Jocelyn was flesh and blood; the second can 'turn him to stone' with her indifference, and the cycle is completed in a petrification process by the third Avice, who actually places him *inside* the stone, into its geological layers as an empty shell to be dug up and wondered at – a 'fossilized relic' of a man.

Early in the novel, after the well-beloved has flown from the shape of Marcia Bencombe, Jocelyn is at great pains to explain to his friend Somers the myth of this spirit in his life:

the first embodiment of her occurred, so nearly as I can recollect, when I was about the age of nine. Her vehicle was a little blue-eyed girl of eight or so, one of a family of eleven, with flaxen hair about her shoulders, which attempted to curl, but ignominiously failed, hanging like chimney crooks only. (p. 51)

The little girl left the island and the boy Jocelyn thought that his 'well-beloved had gone forever ... But she had not. Laura had gone forever, but not my Beloved' (p. 52).

Jocelyn invokes two women who were 'immortalized' through art – Dante's Beatrice and Petrarch's Laura. Beatrice is indirectly present in the passage above, through its striking similarity to the opening of Dante's *La Vita Nuova*. Jocelyn recounts his past to his friend in what he calls his *Apologia pro vitâ meâ* (p. 53). Dante writes that his treatise is 'In the book of my memory':

Nine times the heaven of the light had revolved in its own movement since my birth and had almost returned to the same point when the woman whom my mind beholds in glory first appeared before my eyes. She was called Beatrice by many who did not know what it meant to call her this. She had lived in this world for the length of time in which the heaven of the fixed stars had circled one twelfth of a degree towards the East. Thus she had not long passed the beginning of her ninth year when she appeared to me and I was almost at the end of mine when I beheld her. She was dressed in a very decorous and delicate crimson, tied with a girdle and trimmed in a manner suited to her tender age.[9]

To ward off the arbitrariness of love, Jocelyn creates art to 'immortalize' and to fix in concrete form the aspect of his well-beloved. He clings to one name for his beloved – Avice Caro – because that will place him among the great artists, like Dante and Petrarch, with whom a woman's name will always be associated. Carrying on her name, he tries to ensure that his own name will last through time, placed in a pedigree of great, muse-inspired artists. The constancy of the artist and the lover are bound up in each other; both aspects of Jocelyn's mythology of art and love rely upon an adherence to the name and memory of the loved one, partly because by remembering he staves off the chance that he too may be forgotten. He ponders that his island muse may be none other than Venus herself, her spirit bound up in the well-beloved Avice; 'Tradition urged that a temple to Venus once stood at the top of the Roman road leading up into the isle; and possibly one to the love-goddess of the Slingers antedated this. What so natural as that the true star of his soul would be found nowhere but in one of the old island breed?' (p. 89).

Jocelyn encounters the great artistic force of his life – the spirit of the well-beloved – at the age of nine, the same age at which Dante met his Beatrice. In Jocelyn's description and in *La Vita Nuova* there is a similar artistic memory involved – the attention to colour and detail in the remembering of each inspirational little girl. It is the same artistic memory which appears in much of Hardy's writing and which I discussed in the previous chapter with particular reference to the 'Poems of 1912–13' and *A Pair of Blue Eyes*; in this attention to colour and other sensual detail associated with the woman, the lover/artist struggles to hold off the grey neutrality of forgetting. In fact, though both Dante and Pierston write of the woman as a 'vital spirit', each woman has a very tangible corporeal presence in memory – there is the flaxen hair failing to curl and the tie of a sash on a crimson dress.

Tombs, statues and elegies all serve as ways to keep at bay a loss of memory of the beloved and the gradual slipping away from passion into neutrality. Just as in Knight's and Stephen's inability to mourn Elfride in *A Pair of Blue Eyes*, there seems to be something about grey indifference which is worse than black death. This novel is imbued with quotations from Tennyson's elegy, 'In Memoriam A. H. H.', and Knight tellingly thinks of Tennyson's lines, 'O last regret, regret can die!' when he resolves to cut Elfride from his heart, and leave her (p. 338). Knight's and Stephen's mourning of Elfride may lack the definition of black, but it has a finality that Jocelyn's mourning never can have: for Jocelyn it is not the woman who has died, but his own love. Unlike the death of love, the arbitrariness of the actual death of the loved one lies outside the lover's control or responsibility. But a loss of passion, like Jocelyn's, which leaves the beloved like a 'mournful empty shape' living a kind of death-in-life, also involves the lover in a kind of death. This death is the realization that the heart can die toward someone in whom the lover has placed so much of himself. Part of the lover dies with the death of love.

Indifference can be as painful as the actual death of the beloved, as can be seen in both endings of *The Well-Beloved*. In the 1897 version Jocelyn loses his artistic faculty, which is connected with his faculty for love. With the coming of indifference he disperses all the stone images of the well-beloved which have been the products of a lifetime of his romantic and artistic passion. He marries Marcia, a former shell of the well-beloved, now described as an 'old crone'. In this marriage of supreme mundanity there are echoes of the death of love for his very first 'well-beloved': when he was nine he loved a little girl whose hair fell in 'chimney-crooks', and this 'defect ... was one of the main reasons of my Beloved's departure from that tenement' (p. 54); Marcia and Jocelyn finally marry because the chimneys in Marcia's cottage smoke, and her rheumatism makes Pierston's nearby cottage more comfortable! Pierston demonstrates that his artistic/romantic faculty is truly dead; 'The fever has killed a faculty which has, after all, brought me my greatest sorrows, if a few little pleasures' (p. 190). There is a relief to him in the death of his love but the anticlimactic ending of the 1897 novel is painful in its neutrality and disappointment – perhaps just as painful as the melodramatic ending of the 1892 novel.

In this earlier version the faculty that Jocelyn is threatened with losing is his sight, not his ability to feel passion and to translate it into art. Unfortunately, enough vision is left to him in the final moment of the novel for him to be confronted with the living spectre of an early incarnation of the well-beloved – his wife, Marcia, from whom he separated forty years before in London. She passes by a portrait on the mantelpiece of the last 'version' of Avice Caro:

> The contrast of the ancient Marcia's aspect, both with this portrait and with her own fine former self, brought into his brain a sudden sense of the grotesqueness of things. His wife was – not Avice, but that parchment-covered skull moving about his room. (p. 233)

Hardy's imaginative fascination with the grave did not always require a woman to be old to imagine her a walking death's-head as Marcia is here; he writes in a journal entry, 'A sweet face is a page of sadness to a man over thirty – the raw material of a corpse.' Seeing Marcia in this way, Jocelyn ends the novel in an 'irresistible fit of laughter, so violent as to be an agony, "O – no, no! I – I – it is too too droll – this ending to my would-be romantic history!"' (p. 233). Faced with the almost-dead aspect of his wife in the 1892 novel, Jocelyn feels similarly to Knight when faced with the dead gaze of the trilobite, that he is, as Knight feared, 'to be with the small in his death', the 'small' here being the 'droll', the ludicrous low-comedy close of a 'would-be romantic history'. His romantic history is robbed of passion and constancy until it has finally become, not the high art of Dante and Petrarch, but low farce. Indeed the whole of *The Well-Beloved* runs the risk of seeming merely an improbable farce; Jocelyn struggles to convince himself that his artistic fiction of the well-beloved is one of ennobled constancy to one spirit, but Hardy leaves it open to the reader to brand him as does his friend Somers, as simply 'fickle ... like other men, only rather worse' (p. 54).

Jocelyn needs to believe that the romantic history of his life will not end in an entrapment in layers of the unremembered fossils of past loves. In both endings of *The Well-Beloved* Jocelyn cannot sustain his artistic fiction and as a result his life and art are shattered: in the 1892 novel his mind is fragmented by the grotesqueness of his old love come back to haunt him, and in the 1897 novel he sinks into a passive death-in-life after the artistic/romantic faculties which kept him alive, fade away.

A contemplation of the individual human life-span contrasted with larger time scales can lead to a despair at the smallness and insignificance of the individual. These time scales can encompass the simple experience and remembered local history that William Worm has, the philosophical view of geology that the educated mind of Henry Knight entertains, or the cruel experience of a genealogical time span which finally leaves Jocelyn behind. In *Tess of the D'Urbervilles*, Tess refuses to contemplate these time spans which crush the individual life into insignificance. Her response to Angel Clare, when he asks her if she would like to study history, is that she 'doesn't want to know anything more about it than I know already':

'Because what's the use of learning that I am one of a long row only – finding out that there is set down in some old book somebody just like me, and to know that I shall only act her part; making me sad, that's all. The best is not to remember that your nature and your past doings have been just like thousands' and thousands', and that your coming life and doings'll be like thousands' and thousands'."[10]

Tess's response to her part in ancestry and history is very similar to the cry of the first Avice Caro in the 1892 version when she interrupts Jocelyn as he is burning love letters from his numerous former loves. She says to him, 'I am – only one – in a long, long row!' (p. 206). Avice means that she is only one in a long row of lovers, but she has her place in other lineages as well – romantic, artistic and genealogical. To be one of a long row of descendants or of a long line of trilobites begins to amount to much of the same thing. Love, in a single lifespan, produces the same fears of being forgotten and of being a mindless copy or proliferation of some other, as does a sense of place in ancestral or geological layers.

Loving three generations of Avice Caro, Jocelyn regards these women as three incarnations of the same woman; of the third he says, 'I do not require to learn her; she was learnt by me in her previous existences' (p. 151). His love not only robs each woman of her individuality, but metamorphoses her into a statue; the Avices are described upon different occasions as 'impervious', as 'speaking from a pedestal'. He assures the second Avice that he will 'deliver (her) up to (her) native isle without scratch or blemish' (p. 126), and that he knows 'the perfect and pure quarry she was dug from' (p. 118). When Marcia Bencombe returns to Jocelyn at the conclusion of the 1897 version she also is described as having been turned to stone:

> She stood the image and superscription of Age – an old woman, pale and shrivelled, her forehead ploughed, her cheek hollow, her hair white as snow. To this the face he once kissed had been brought by the raspings, chisellings, scourgings, bakings, freezings of forty invidious years – by the thinkings of more than half a lifetime. (p. 189)

Marrying for convenience and companionship, Jocelyn and Marcia spend their last years on their native Isle of Slingers. As a childless couple, they are quite exceptional on this 'isle'; the customary testing of fertility before marriage, the Portland 'trial marriage', resulted in a very low rate of childless marriages. The first Avice Caro's letter to Jocelyn explains that it is reluctance to go through with 'Island Custom' which is her reason for not meeting him on his last night on the island; 'But I have fancied that my seeing you again and again lately is inclining your father to insist, and you as his heir to feel, that we ought to carry out Island Custom in our courting – your people being such old inhabitants in an unbroken line'. Blood lines are kept pure and unbroken through the Island Custom and intermarriage. At the time of the novel's setting (beginning about 1850) the custom is, as Avice writes, 'nearly left off'. Trial marriages had been customary in other parts of Britain, but they lingered on in Portland, and Hardy, with his fascination with customs on the cusp of extinction, emphasizes the tradition in *The Well-Beloved*. He would have read an account of the Portland trial marriage and of the islanders' blood lines either in Smeaton's *A Narrative of the Building and a Description of the Construction of the Edystone Lighthouse with Stone* (1791), or in John Hutchins's *History and Antiquities of Dorset*. He was familiar with both works.[11]

Repeatedly in *The Well-Beloved* Hardy draws attention to the long history of intermarriage on the Isle of Slingers. The islanders have little social contact with the mainland (although this is beginning to change at the opening of the novel). On Pierston's initial return to the island/peninsula, he is reminded of 'the Caro family; the 'roan-mare' Caros, as they were called to distinguish them from other branches of the same pedigree, there being but half-a-dozen christian and surnames in the whole island' (p. 29). In the late eighteenth century John Smeaton described the Island Custom as it was explained to him when he visited Portland to further his building of the Eddystone lighthouse.

Smeaton admires the strength of the Portland quarrymen as he watches them cutting the huge stones, and inquires of his guide, 'where they could possibly pick up such a stout set of fellows.' The guide assures him that they are all islandmen, and that 'all our marriages here are productive of children':

'Our people here, as they are bred up to hard labour, are very early in a condition to marry and provide for a family; they intermarry with one another, very rarely going to the main land to seek a wife; and it has been the custom of the island, from time immemorial, that they never marry till the woman is pregnant. "But pray", says I, "does this not subject you to a great number of bastards? have not your Portlanders the same kind of fickleness in their attachments that Englishmen are subject to; and in consequence does not this produce many inconveniences?"' [12]

Apparently in Smeaton's time, and (according to Hutchins) long thereafter, there were very few illegitimate children born on the island, because an islandman well understood that if he reneged on his betrothal, 'he would be disgraced, and never more acknowledged by his countrymen.'[13] At one time, according to Smeaton's informant, Londoners came to the island, and, not understanding the island custom, were 'much struck and mightily pleased with the facility of the Portland ladies'.[14] The women of the island avenged their being 'inconvenienced' and 'arose to stone them out of the island'. Hutchins writes that 'the only disgrace on Portland is having no child.'[15]

In a novel which is set on an island where historically, 'every marriage is productive of children', Marcia and Jocelyn make an exceptionally impotent or infertile pair. This infertility is underlined by comparison with the consistent fertility of the first, second and (presumably) the third Avice Caro. Jocelyn later muses after the death of the first Avice that their lives would have been very different if she had met him on the night he left the island twenty years before:

Had she appeared the primitive betrothal, with its natural result, would probably have taken place; and, as no islander had ever been known to break the compact, she would have become his wife. (p. 85)

Marcia's few days' sojourn with Jocelyn in a London hotel after their elopement has no issue, and therefore, no consequences. After she leaves:

Jocelyn saw plainly enough that she owed it to her father being a born islander, with all the ancient island notions of matrimony lying underneath his acquired conventions, that the stone-merchant did not immediately insist upon the usual remedy for a daughter's precipitancy in such cases, but preferred to await issues. (p. 60)

There is no issue, and Marcia, although later married to Jocelyn, never has a child with him.

Although *Jude the Obscure* was Hardy's last novel, the radical and extensive revisions to *The Well-Beloved* were written after *Jude*, and were his final exception to his resolve to write no more novels. Edward Said has written of the role of genealogy and narrative in *Jude*:

Hardy's case in *Jude the Obscure* is, I believe, the recognition by a great artist that the dynastic principles of traditional narrative now seemed somehow inappropriate ... Both Little Father Time's name and his presence yield up further observations which, we may feel ... do great damage to the sacrament of ongoing human life. For the boy is neither really a son nor, of course, a father. He is an alteration in the course of life, a disruption of the archaeology that links generations one to the other.[16]

Similarly, in *The Well-Beloved*, Jocelyn Pierston is a 'disruption of the archaeology that links generations': as Hardy writes of him, '(his) inability to ossify with the rest of his generation threw him out of proportion with the time.' (Said's reference to the layering through time implicit in his term 'archaeology' is worked out as geological and genealogical layers in *A Pair of Blue Eyes* and *The Well-Beloved*.) Pierston is a genealogical 'disruption' because he could have been either the father of the second Avice or the grandfather of the third; instead, he bears no familial relationship as husband, father or grandfather to any of the three generations of island women. With Jocelyn's failure to unite himself with any of these women, 'the dynastic principles of traditional narrative' are not only 'inappropriate', as Said argues, but positively end-stopped. Not only is Jocelyn childless (and the literary child of a childless author), but his statues representing the 'well-beloved' – at once his 'lovers' and his artistic offspring – are 'dispersed' by his London agent. Of them he says to Marcia at the end of the novel: 'I don't feel a single touch of kin with or interest in any one of them whatever' (p. 189). His only 'kin' or family, which are made from the stone of his native isle, are committed to diaspora among art collections over the world. While the Portland stone in its raw state had for centuries left the island to become the walls and foundations of buildings on the mainland, Jocelyn's statues, because they had taken on the role of lovers or kin in his life, represent more than a simple dispersal of an art collection. They do not return with him to the native rock from which, like Jocelyn, they originated. Their dispersal represents both the islanders' move to the mainland, and the increasing exogamy beginning to occur on Portland; the novel concludes with the third Avice eloping with Marcia's stepson Henri Leverre, who is from Jersey. Jocelyn's attempts to marry any of the three Avices are as unproductive as is his final marriage to Marcia. The only hope for a continuation of the family line lies with the marriage of two from different islands, Avice and Henri. Henri's name implies that he is not only not a Portlander, but barely English.

Of regionalism in Hardy's novels George Wing writes:

As one novel follows another, mobility increases ... Characters and action move further and oftener from the centre of Wessex – occasionally outside of its borders as in the third novel, *A Pair of Blue Eyes* – and movement is often associated with an intensifying of sexual frustration and misapprehension.[17]

The sexual frustration which runs through *A Pair of Blue Eyes*, *The Well-Beloved* and *Jude*, results in a childlessness, a dying out of family lines. This failure of the 'dynastic principle' is connected to a dying out of regionalism in these novels. Hardy so often wrote of a threshold in time when the distinct customs and character of a region were yet intact, but about to be forgotten within the next generation or two. In previous chapters I have discussed how England's sense of herself as a unified island was undermined by the tensions of different cultures, would-be nations, or races within Britain, such as those produced by the Jews in England, or by Celtic cultures. Hardy is a writer who was and is regarded as quintessentially English. His concentration upon the regional, however, emphasizes that there are tensions and challenges to the idea of an essential 'Englishness', some of which may be found at the heart of his 'Wessex'. Regional differences may pull apart England's sense of herself as a unified, homogeneous island. These differences are presented at their most concentrated in Hardy's 'last' or penultimate novel. Setting this novel on an isle/peninsula which is almost separated from the English mainland, the 'Isle of Slingers' challenges not only the idea of Englishness, but also the very idea of the united British isles. Politically English, Hardy describes the Isle of Slingers as culturally, racially different and its difference is partly a result of and partly symbolized by its almost separate land mass. In his preface to *The Well-Beloved* Hardy describes the Isle of Slingers as a place which, 'has been for centuries immemorial the home of a curious and well-nigh distinct people, cherishing strange beliefs and singular customs, now for the most part obsolescent' (p. 25).

Jocelyn muses upon the connection between his 'race' and the woman he feels he could marry:

Hence in her nature, as in his, was some mysterious ingredient sucked from the isle; otherwise a racial instinct necessary to the absolute unison of a pair. Thus, though he might never love a woman of the island race, for lack in her of the desired refinement, he could not love long a kimberlin – a woman other than of the island race, for her lack of this groundwork of character. (p. 84)

Portland is neither quite an island, nor quite a peninsula; its thin bank of pebbles tenuously connecting it with England. It would seem that its cultural, and to Hardy, even 'racial' connections with the island of England are equally tenuous. Hardy is not the only writer to regard the Portlanders as a people as separate and distinct as the land mass they inhabit; when Smeaton asks his guide, 'Have not your Portlanders the same kind of fickleness in their attachments that Englishmen are subject to?', he distinguishes between Portlanders and the English. 'Fickleness' is one name for Pierston's artistic myth by which the spirit of the well-beloved flits randomly from one woman to another. Pierston, however, does not judge his 'fickleness' to be the same as that of an

Englishman. To him, the well-beloved is a spirit inspired by the ancient traditions of his isle. As he tells his friend Somers; 'We are a strange, visionary race down where I come from, and perhaps that accounts for it [for the well-beloved]' (p. 51). Somers, however, assesses Pierston's pursuit of love rather differently; 'Essentially all men are fickle, like you; but not with such perceptiveness' (p. 54). The theme of 'fickleness' (perhaps partly inspired by a reading of Smeaton), is central to *The Well-Beloved*, and whether we believe Pierston is fickle or enthralled by a spirit depends partly upon how much credence we give to his description of himself as one of a 'race' of people distinct, in both premarital and romantic practices, from the English. Smeaton reveals how truly alien and separate these islanders seem to him:

As I was struck with wonder at the construction of the Portland beach, I could not be wholly inattentive to an anecdote which occurred there, respecting an equal singularity in the manners and customs of the Portland Quarrymen: for at that time those of the South Sea islanders were entirely unknown to us.[18]

At the time of the writing of *The Well-Beloved*, the phrase 'South Sea islanders' would have conjured Gauguin-like visions of exotic, hot, distant islands. Smeaton (writing in 1791) presents the customs of Portland as if they are equally exotic and alien to the mainland English as those of Polynesia would have been one hundred years later. From Smeaton's time to Hardy's, that which is considered exotic or 'other' has moved to islands progressively further away than Portland, and Hardy acknowledges that alien and 'romantic' customs are becoming a thing of the regional past within England. As he writes in 'The Dorsetshire Labourer', those communities within England which had kept their regional customs and traditions, cannot be expected, 'to remain stagnant and old-fashioned for the pleasure of romantic spectators'. Regions lose their different, distinctive characters, to march, 'vigorously towards uniformity'.[19]

Hardy's depiction of Portland's geographical and 'racial' separateness, its insularity, places the regional in its most essential, rarefied form, undermining England's claim to encompass its own unified 'island race'. I began this book with a discussion of another island; Ireland, which throughout the nineteenth century was the troublesome exception to England's island unity. Certainly larger than Portland, and culturally, often linguistically, and, as many thought, 'racially' separate from England it was a rather big lump to swallow into a concept of a unified Britain. Hardy is not concerned with the representation of those more obviously alien groups within Britain which I have discussed in this study; he rarely includes characters of Celtic or Jewish extraction in his works. His depiction of difference within England, his challenging of England's sense of herself as a racially unified island is achieved through his narratives of regional difference, and even, as in the case of *The Well-Beloved*, of an 'island-race' distinct from the English, inhabiting nearby Portland. Because Hardy's 'Wessex' was (and is) seen as by definition English, Hardy's focussing upon how foreign and even alien the people and practices of the different regions of Wessex are strikes at the heart of England's sense of itself as a whole, and consequently of non-English nations as 'other'.

Regional difference is achieved partly through the intermarriage of families in a geographical area, and the passing down of customs and traditions through the generations of these families. Intermarriage serves to render a region distinct, by engraining its individual character. Paradoxically, in both *A Pair of Blue Eyes* and *The Well-Beloved*, intermarriage gives a region a distinctive character, but obliterates the distinctive character, the individuality of the regional inhabitant. William Worm's phrase for the likeness of Elfride and her grandmother, that the women 'be alike as peas', could equally be said of the three Avice Caros; intermarriage has made these women so physically alike as to appear merely repetitions of one another. In marrying a relative of her grandmother's, Elfride Swancourt becomes yet another generation of Elfride Luxellian. In this early novel, intermarriage results in a dead mother and child, and in *The Well-Beloved*, in infertility. Narrative ends with the end of the family line.

The Well-Beloved ends with the only hope of regeneration resting with a marriage to a non-islander or 'kimberlin'. Hardy's narratives of miscarriage (with Elfride) and impotency (with Pierston) put an end to the narrative of family lines. Without the ancient repetitions in the genealogical layers of old families, to which, like Angel Clare, 'lyrically, dramatically, and even historically, (he is) tenderly attached', it seems that Hardy can no longer write in the form of the novel.[20] The exogamous marriage of the third Avice will probably produce a family, another generation. But this generation is a step towards a mixture of family lines from different parts of Britain, a dispersal which will eventually produce a national uniformity, a lack of distinctiveness. Like the bodies in the crowded churchyard, they will be 'mixed to human jam'; family lines, the regions they represent, and the stories they inspire will no longer bear the mark of place. Hardy's pedigrees, which produce tensions of difference and distinction within England, die out, and with them his narratives which are linked so strongly to repetition and regeneration in the family line, die out as well. Enamoured as he is with 'the melancholy ruins of cancelled cycles', Hardy seems finally to have taken the decision to cancel his own narratives which rely so crucially upon cycles of generation.

Conclusion

At the opening of chapter two of *A Pair of Blue Eyes*, Stephen Smith, wearied by the journey from London to the coast of Cornwall, half-listens to a story of local genealogical history related by his driver. It is a story which encapsulates many of the issues surrounding pedigree and narrative in the nineteenth century, issues which cross and recross each other in this study of blood relations. The cart driver fancies himself as the local historian, and he tells the story of how Lord Luxellian, to whom Elfride is related and whom she eventually marries, gained his title centuries before:

'Well, his family is no better than my own, 'a b'lieve... Hedgers and ditchers by rights. But once in ancient times one of 'em, when he was at work, changed clothes with King Charles the Second, and saved the king's life.'

The king instructed Hedger Luxellian to come to court where he would be made a lord for his services:

'Well, as the story is, the king came to the throne; and some years after that, away went Hedger Luxellian, knocked at the king's door, and asked if King Charles the Second was in. "No, he isn't," they said. "Then, is Charles the Third?" said Hedger Luxellian. "Yes," said a young feller standing by like a common man, only he had a crown on, "My name is Charles the Third." And –'
'I really fancy that must be a mistake. I don't recollect anything in English history about Charles the Third,' said the other in a tone of mild remonstrance. 'O that's right history enough, only 'twasn't prented; he was rather a queer-tempered man, if you remember.'
'Very well; go on.'
'And, by hook or crook, Hedger Luxellian was made a lord, and everything went on well till some time after, when he got into a most terrible row with King Charles the Fourth –'
'I can't stand Charles the Fourth. Upon my word, that's too much.'

'Why? There was a George the Fourth, wasn't there?'
'Certainly.'
'Well, Charleses be as common as Georges. However I'll say no more about it ...' (p. 378)

This mythical sequence of royal Charleses is a comic presaging of the generational sequence of Elfride Luxellians in the tomb at the conclusion of the novel. But this passage also exhibits a number of the issues connecting genealogy and narrative which this study has aimed at exploring: the way in which stories inspired by pedigree contribute to a concept of shared community and nationhood; the fictionalization or invention of pedigree; myths of origin; oral versus written genealogies; the arbitrariness involved in the privileging of one family line over another in genealogy, narrative and society (it was an arbitrary decision of Charles the Second's to exchange clothes with the Luxellian ancestor; he could have chosen another hedger or ditcher ...), and the ease with which some names and family lines are lost to history.

The compelling power of generational sequence in narrative is demonstrated in the cart driver's need to produce a Charles the Third and Fourth. Such is his delight in repetition through family lines, that without Stephen's objections he might have continued the English royal line with Charleses to the nth degree. In Chapters One and Four I discussed Celtic royal lines, which were alternative to the English and based upon oral tradition. Stephen's cart driver creates his own oral tradition of a royal line, insisting that, 'that's right history enough, only 'twasn't prented'. His fictionalization of pedigree is comically preposterous because he has the confidence to create his own stories around the most authoritative, most documented pedigree of his country – that of the royal English line. This pedigree provides the framework of English history, and is essential to the English people's sense of themselves as part of a nation. Embedded in the cart driver's resistance to the authorized version of English history which Stephen propounds is Hardy's point that there are regional inhabitants within England (the cart driver living on the margins of Britain on the Cornish coast) who not only have customs and myths of origin which are separate from what is defined as 'English', but who have a very different (or certainly confused) version of the rudiments of the nation's history. If the nation is, as Benedict Anderson has defined it, an 'imagined community', and if as I have argued, a central part of this imagining consists of the stories surrounding genealogy and dynastic lines, then the cart driver is 'imagining' some nation other than England. This rather absurd example of separate myths of origin and of imagined or invented genealogies nevertheless accords with Hardy's fragmentation of the 'island race' of England into a diverse conglomeration of regions and separate peoples, or even, as in *The Well-Beloved,* into separate races, as with the intermarrying 'island race' on the Isle of Slingers. England is deconstructed into an archipelago of separate islands and regions, inhabited by distinct races who construct their own ancestral narratives.

The motto of the Aborigines Protection Society founded in 1837 was *ab uno sanguine,* but as I hope the previous chapters have made clear, this would have been a contentious claim as the nineteenth century advanced: Britain's empire expanded to include among her subjects 'primitive peoples', and these peoples were to be the study of the newly-developing science of anthropology, a science which was increasingly weighted towards regarding the human race not as 'of one blood', but as polygenist. Within Britain there were many who felt with much anxiety the need not only to deny blood relations with primitive tribes in far-flung corners of the Empire, but also to deny kinship with other peoples within Britain. Walter Scott wrote that for most Britons in the early nineteenth century, the Scottish Highlanders seemed as remote and alien a people as the 'Eskimos' or the 'Red Indian'; and the Irish and Jews were considered by many to be not only of different blood, but of a different species as well.

Some writers later in the nineteenth century turned the Victorian anthropological and ethnological study of primitive tribes on its head: whether we are all *ab uno sanguine* or not, we all have the potential to be 'red in tooth and claw'. Blood relations may become bloody indeed if at the heart of 'civilized' English society an heir to the aristocratic estate such as Willoughby Patterne becomes so sexually competitive, so egoistic, that he would sacrifice women and his blood relations on the altar of his ego and of his so-called 'duty' to continue his pedigree.

Meredith's 'hero' Sir Willoughby is terrified of degeneration, of the risk of slipping backwards on the evolutionary ladder in the direction of early man or ape. But in charting Willoughby's fears of this reversion Meredith hints in his preface at a tactic concerning early ancestry, 'our o'er hoary ancestry', that 'Science introduced us to': this is a tactic which this study has observed throughout the nineteenth century as a method of keeping at bay an uncomfortable recognition of those primitive ancestors within ourselves, and it involves an intense focus upon historical, invented, or imagined *human* genealogies rather than upon the prehistoric or evolutionary. As Meredith wrote, 'Art is the specific.

We have little to learn of apes and they may be left.' 'Art', according to Meredith, will deal with our origins, pedigree, and future blood lines: in Meredith's case it is art rather than science which is the more culturally significant in its treatment of blood relations. But in the nineteenth century as a whole both art and science are equally bound up in genealogy through the agency of narrative.

Today the genealogical model of origins, with its repeated generations and 'cancelled cycles', may be undergoing a change. Recent research analysing the genetic material in human blood cells from various test areas in the world has enabled Oxford University's Institute of Molecular Medicine to leap over the generations. Through these genetic fingerprints scientists have found 'blood relations' connecting the inhabitants of a fairly remote Oxfordshire village with Homo erectus, a relative of Homo sapiens living in Asia almost 400,000 years ago. As the *Sunday Times* reported,

> this weekend ... the astounded residents of Charlton-on-Moor ... were digesting the deeper ramifications of their genetic links with the present-day inhabitants of the windswept plains of Outer Mongolia and with their distant ancestor, Homo erectus. 'It's hard to believe,' said Eric Cooper, 62, whose father and grandfather lived in the same village all their lives. 'Mind you, it was always said that we were a bit of the wandering type.'[1]

Even today, when confronted with the advances of science into our ancestral origins, the response tends to be a *humanizing* one, and the process of transforming the difficult scientific facts to a digestible, comforting human level is accomplished through the imagination and specifically through stories: 'it was always said that we were a bit of the wandering type' is redolent both of stories about all those travels, and also sounds like the beginning of a story.

If the Oxfordshire villager can take his kinship with Homo erectus in his stride, it is because we have been prepared by the debates over origins in the nineteenth century to accept our early primitive or simian forebears. In the nineteenth century these relationships were not easy to accept, but were disturbing partly because of the fear that this primitive blood might still run in Victorian veins, and also because this ancestry might seem to bring Victorian Britons closer to contemporary 'primitive peoples' (many of whom became subjects of the British Empire at this time) whom they needed to feel were 'other' in order to define themselves as civilized and British. Hence the intensity of focus upon stories surrounding human, historical ancestry to build a consoling sense of familial, communal and national identity in nineteenth-century Britain.

But because stories constructed around genealogy are often works of invention or imagination, they are highly adaptable and flexible, as my study has demonstrated. If Scottish Highlanders were regarded as alien and as racially separate from the English as the 'Eskimo' or the 'Red Indian' at the beginning of the nineteenth century, about forty years later the English Queen Victoria was happy to claim kin with them, imaginatively and romantically inspired by Sir Walter Scott's narratives of Scottish culture and consanguinity, and also by her own participation in the imagined matrilineal inheritance of royal women in British history. This genealogy of royal women served as an inspirational imaginary pedigree for British women – another 'subgroup' in nineteenth-century Britain in need, like the Irish and Jews, of a defining ancestral narrative. These royal women served as role models for British women, helping them to negotiate and define their place in the public and private spheres of Victorian Britain. As both wife, mother and ruling monarch, Victoria was acutely aware of the tensions between these separate spheres, and I have argued that she chose her own role model from this popular genealogy of royal women. Her claiming kin, both literally and psychologically, with Mary Queen of Scots, underlines the power of imaginative genealogies, and how the inventions and stories surrounding pedigrees can have familial, gender and nationalist repercussions which connect and cross. This fabric of genealogical strands and significances is again seen in Benjamin Disraeli's romantic narratives surrounding his own Jewish ancestry, which he defended against anti-Semitism by championing it as naturally aristocratic. He fulfilled his genealogical tales of Eastern power and inspiration by writing, in effect, an Eastern romance for the Queen of England, crowning her his own imagined 'Queen of Sheba' but also the very real 'Empress of India'.

In the preface to his famous *Principles of Geology* (1830) Charles Lyell used the processes of human history as an analogy for the processes of natural history as revealed in the geological record of rock strata. In the later nineteenth century, Thomas Hardy oddly conflates the human and geological record, by describing a sedimentary model for genealogical stories, by which the individual is seemingly repeated over the generations, the repetitions going through a process of stratification in the tomb and in human memory to become mere 'layers among many layers'. Finally Hardy's genealogical narratives seem to metamorphose 'blood' into stone. The stone graves and memorials of his novels grad-

Conclusion 251

ually lose their historical records of epitaph, name and blood relations and become raw stone again. The childless Jude the stonemason and Pierston the sculptor in stone are reduced to a stony barrenness; they are 'the melancholy ruins of cancelled cycles' of both the genealogical and geological record.

A comic version of those 'cancelled cycles' of generation which Hardy wrote of at the end of the nineteenth century, which also serves as a later twentieth-century commentary on the Victorian and Edwardian values placed upon blood relation, is the Ealing comedy, *Kind Hearts and Coronets* (1949; the title adapted, appropriately, from the poetry of Tennyson, a poet who perhaps more than any other of his period has been made to represent extinct Victorian values).[2] Hardy's *A Pair of Blue Eyes* mourns three generations of Elfride who will with time be indistinguishable from one another; *The Well-Beloved* produces three seemingly identical generations of one woman, Avice Caro. In *Kind Hearts and Coronets*, one actor, Alec Guinness, plays successively the parts of all those who are in succession for the Dukedom. The aristocratic exclusiveness and inbreeding of nineteenth-century society, which could produce such an absolute repetition, is given a murderous blow by the hero, who hails from a minor branch of the family tree, and who has been 'cut' by his aristocratic blood relations because he is the product of his mother's unfortunate marriage to an Italian musician. As the hero murders each successive incarnation of Alec Guinness which stands in his way to the Dukedom, he crosses them off the blazoned family tree. Exogamy, foreign blood, quite literally kills off those repetitive cycles of inbred aristocrats, as the half-Italian hero proves the power of 'blood relations'. But those aristocratic victims are merely a blue-blooded version of the intermarrying and inbreeding which Hardy associated with the distinctiveness of region and 'race' within Britain, and which he claimed was, with exogamy and population movement, dying out at this period. The near-extinction of these narratives of pedigree is part of the urgency and compelling force of genealogy and narrative working at a profound level in both early and late nineteenth-century literature.

Notes

INTRODUCTION

1 Jeremy Paxman, 'Dear Mr. Paxman, I know you are Jewish but...', *Evening Standard*, 15 July 1993, 11. Jeremy Paxman is referring to the article by Jeremy Lester, 'Still No Peace for the Paxman', *Jewish Chronicle*, 9 July 1993, 16.
2 Auberon Waugh, 'Existential Anxiety', *Daily Telegraph*, 19 July 1993, 19.
3 Bernard Levin, 'Pedigree, what pedigree?', *The Times*, July 23 1993, 16.
4 Recent work on imaginative or invented constructions of nation include Benedict Anderson's *Imagined Communities: Reflections on the Origin and Spread of Nationalism* (1983; London, 1992); Eric Hobsbawm and Terence Ranger, (eds.), *The Invention of Tradition* (Cambridge, 1983); Homi K. Bhabha, ed., *Nation and Narration* (London, 1990); Jonathan Arac and Harriet Ritvo, (eds.), *Macropolitics of Nineteenth-Century Literature: Nationalism, Exoticism, Imperialism* (Philadelphia, 1991); Patrick Brantlinger, 'Nations and Novels: Disraeli, George Eliot, and Orientalism', *Victorian Studies*, 354 Spring 1992, 255–75.
5 Anderson, *Imagined Communities*, 6.
6 Arac and Ritvo, (eds.), *Macropolitics*, 6.
7 E. A. Freeman (1823–92), Anglo-Saxonist historian and frequent contributor to *The Saturday Review*. Matthew Arnold took Freeman to task in his 'On the Study of Celtic Literature' (1866).
8 Grant Allen, 'Are We Englishmen?', *Fortnightly Review* NS 28 (October 1880), 472.
9 Howard Weinbrot, *Britannia's Issue: the Rise of British Literature from Dryden to Ossian* (Cambridge, 1993), 559.
10 *Ibid.*, 477.
11 *Ibid.*, 571.
12 *Ibid.*, 8.
13 Rod Mengham, *Language* (1993; London, 1995), 4.
14 Allen, 'Are We Englishmen?', 487.
15 L. P. Curtis, *Anglo-Saxons and Celts: A Study of Anti-Irish Prejudice in Victorian England* (Bridgeport, CT, 1968).
16 As J. Hillis Miller notes in his essay, 'Prosopopoeia in Hardy and Stevens', in *Alternative Hardy*, Lance St. John Butler (ed.) (London, 1989), 117.

17 Oscar Wilde, 'A Woman of No Importance' in *Oscar Wilde: Complete Plays* (1893; Oxford, 1995), Act III, 134.
18 Jane Austen, 'The Beautiful Cassandra', in *The Juvenilia of Jane Austen and Charlotte Bronte*, Frances Beer (ed.) (Harmondsworth, 1986), 73–4.
19 These are narratological elements which are described at length in Vladimir Propp's seminal work of narratology, *Morphology of the Folktale*, rev. and ed. with a preface by Louis Wagner; new intro. by Alan Dundes (Austin, 1968).
20 Thomas Hardy, Preface to *A Group of Noble Dames*, F. B. Pinion (ed.) (1891; London, 1977), 209. J. Hillis Miller discusses the relationship between pedigree and narrative in the above passage in his essay 'Prosopopoeia in Hardy and Stevens' in Lance St. John Butler (ed.), *Alternative Hardy* (London, 1989), 113–114.
21 Oscar Wilde, *The Importance of Being Earnest: A Trivial Comedy for Serious People* (1895; London, 1969), 46–7.
22 *Ibid.*, 48.
23 *Ibid.*, 49.
24 Ernest Renan, *The Poetry of the Celtic Races*, tr. by W. G. Hutchison (ed.), (1896; Fort Washington, NY, 1970), 4–5.
25 Matthew Arnold, 'On the Study of Celtic Literature', *The Complete Prose Works of Matthew Arnold*, R. H. Super, (ed.), vol. 3 (Ann Arbor, 1962), 335.
26 *Ibid.*, 296–7.
27 W. H. Hutton, (ed.), *The Letters of William Stubbs* (London, 1904), 185–6.
28 Daniel Pick, *Faces of Degeneration: A European Disorder, c. 1848–c. 1918* (Cambridge, 1989), 177.
29 See Brian V. Street, *The Savage in Literature: Representations of 'Primitive' Society in English Fiction 1858–1920* (London, 1975).
30 Curtis, *Anglo-Saxons and Celts*, 38.
31 Benjamin Disraeli, *Tancred, or The New Crusade* (1847; London, 1881), 109.
32 Gillian Beer, *Darwin's Plots: Evolutionary Narrative in Darwin, George Eliot, and Nineteenth-Century Fiction* (1983; London, 1985), 10.
33 Anderson, *Imagined Communities*, 7.
34 Henry James, *Roderick Hudson*, ed., Geoffrey Moore (1875; Harmondsworth, 1986), 37.
35 Beer, *Darwin's Plots*, 37.
36 Mary Poovey, *Uneven Developments: The Ideological Work of Gender in Mid-Victorian England* (1988; London, 1989), 3.
37 Edward Said, *Beginnings: Intention and Method* (1975; New York, 1985), 138.
38 Louis Mink, 'History and Fiction as Modes of Comprehension', *New Literary History*, 1:3 Spring 1970, 557.
39 William Wordsworth, 'Essay Upon Epitaphs I', *The Prose Works of William Wordsworth*, W. J. B. Owen and Jane Worthington Smyser (eds.), (Oxford, 1974), 51.

1. ORAL AND WRITTEN GENEALOGIES IN EDGEWORTH'S 'THE ABSENTEE'

1 George Meredith, *Celt and Saxon* (1910; London, 1919), 6–7.
2 William Playfair, *British Family Antiquity: Containing the Baronetage of Ireland*, vol. 9 (London, 1811), xlii.
3 *An Act for the Union of Great Britain and Ireland* (London, 1799), repr. in *The Statutes: 1770–1821*, 3rd rev. ed., vol. II (London, 1950), 286.
4 Tobias Smollett, *The Expedition of Humphrey Clinker*, Peter Miles (ed.), (1771; London, 1993), 216.
5 Smollett, *Humphrey Clinker*, 195–6.
6 Fluellen assures the Irish Captain Macmorris that he is 'as good a man' as the Irishman, 'both in the disciplines of war, and in the derivation of my birth, and in other particularities' (*Henry V*, III.2.132–4). Speaking with the king, Fluellen concentrates on Henry V's Welsh blood, and reminds him of his genealogy; 'Your grandfather of famous memory, an't please your Majesty, and your great-uncle Edward the Plack Prince of Wales, as I have read in the chronicles, fought a most prave pattle here in France' (IV.7.96–99). An Irish, Scottish and Welsh captain appear in the play fighting for Henry, and at one point, Henry tells Fluellen that he is himself a 'Welshman', born in Monmouth. The Celtic elements are significantly represented in a play which deals with Britain's united front under a strong king against France.
7 See Edward D. Snyder, *The Celtic Revival in English Literature, 1760–1800* (1923; Gloucester, MA, 1965).
8 Richard Ormond and John Turpin, eds., *Daniel Maclise 1806–1870* (London, Arts Council of Great Britain, 1972), 100.
9 John Turpin, 'The Irish Background of Daniel Maclise', *Capuchin Annual* (Dublin, 1970), 192.
10 Edward Cooke, *Arguments For and Against a Union* (Dublin, 1798), 11–12.
11 Pemberton Rudd, *An Answer to the Pamphlet Entitled 'Arguments For and Against an Union etc.', in a Letter Addressed to Edward Cooke, Esq.* (Dublin, 1799), 9.
12 William Johnson, *Reasons for Adopting an Union Between Ireland and Great Britain* (Dublin, 1798), 4.
13 *Ibid.*, 1.
14 Meredith, *Celt and Saxon*, 44.
15 Anthony Trollope, *Castle Richmond* (1860; Oxford, 1989), 1.
16 See Chapter 47 of Smollett's *Roderick Random* (1748) in which Irish fortune-hunters are compared with 'Jesuits in disguise', agents of the Pretender, etc. If the Irish fortune-hunter was regarded as subversive to the marital/financial interests of English fortune-hunters, this subversiveness seems to have been linked to a political subversiveness and threat as well.
17 Playfair, *British Family Antiquity*, footnote to ix–x.
18 W. J. McCormack and Kim Walker, 'The Tradition of Grace Nugent', Appendix 2 of the World's Classics edition of Maria Edgeworth, *The Absentee*, W. J. McCormack and Kim Walker, (eds.) (Oxford, 1988), 276–281.
19 Richard Lovell Edgeworth and Maria Edgeworth, *Essay on Irish Bulls* (Lon-

don, 1802), 313–14.
20 Maria Edgeworth and others, *The Black Book of Edgeworthstown and Other Edgeworth Memoirs*, Harriet Jessie Butler and Harold Edgeworth Butler (eds.) (London, 1927), 4.
21 Edgeworth, 'The Black Book of Edgeworthstown', in *The Black Book of Edgeworthstown and Other Edgeworth Memories*, 175–6.
22 Sydney Owenson, Lady Morgan, *The Wild Irish Girl* (1806; New York and London, 1979), vol. 3, 16.
23 Terry Eagleton, *Heathcliff and the Great Hunger: Studies in Irish Culture* (London, 1995), 180.
24 Eagleton, *Heathcliff and the Great Hunger*, 183.
25 Maria Edgeworth, *The Absentee*, vols. 9 and 10 of Maria Edgeworth, *Tales and Novels* (London, 1832), vol. 9, 157. Subsequent references to *The Absentee* will be taken from this edition and referred to by volume and page number in the text.
26 *The Compact Edition of the Oxford English Dictionary* (Oxford, 1971), vol. 3, 2057, 4a.
27 McCormack and Walker, (eds.), introduction to *The Absentee*, xlii.
28 William Wordsworth, 'Preface to *Lyrical Ballads*' (1802) in *Lyrical Ballads*, ed. Michael Mason (London, 1982), 59.
29 Edgeworth and Edgeworth, *Essay*, 160–1.
30 Maria Edgeworth, Preface to Mary Leadbeater, *Cottage Dialogues Among the Irish Peasantry* (London, 1811), iii–iv.
31 Playfair, *British Family Antiquity*, footnote to ix.
32 W. J. McCormack, *Ascendancy and Tradition in Anglo-Irish Literary History From 1789 to 1939* (Oxford, 1985), 162.
33 Marilyn Butler, *Maria Edgeworth: A Literary Biography* (Oxford, 1972), 375.
34 McCormack and Walker give a detailed account of Edgeworth's employment of well-known Irish family names in her novel. Count O'Halloran may be partly based upon both Sylvester O'Halloran, an antiquarian discussed below, and upon, 'Lavall, Count Nugent (1777–1862) who became an Austrian commander and diplomat; he visited London in 1811 and 1812 to conduct negotiations with his allies, political descendants of those who had banished his ancestors' (McCormack and Walker, Introduction to *The Absentee*, xxv). This indirect reference to the family name of Nugent, and the clearing of Grace Nugent's name in the novel is politically significant in that many Nugents had been Jacobites. Thus Grace's prospective union with Colambre at the end of the novel both relies upon a clearing of her family name of the taint of illegitimacy, and clears her name of Jacobitism as she is marrying an Irish lord who is faithful to the English crown. Their union brings together two warring factions within Ireland.
35 McCormack and Walker, Notes, *The Absentee*, 304, and *The Dictionary of National Biography* (London, 1895), vol. 12, 57–8.
36 Sylvester O'Halloran, *A General History of Ireland, from the Earliest Accounts to the Close of the Twelfth Century*, vol. 1 (Dublin, 1778), ii–iii.

37 Maria Edgeworth, *Castle Rackrent* (1800; London, 1832), xiii.
38 Edgeworth and Edgeworth, *Essay*, 313–4.
39 McCormack, *Ascendancy and Tradition*, 162.
40 Playfair, *British Family Antiquity*, footnote to ix.

2. A MIRROR FOR MATRIARCHS: THE CULT OF MARY QUEEN OF SCOTS IN NINETEENTH-CENTURY LITERATURE

1 From a letter from Sir Thomas Lake to Viscount Cranbourne, 1 March 1604–5 (*HMC Salisbury (Cecil) MSS* (1605), part 17 London, 1938).
2 Arthur Penrhyn Stanley, Dean of Westminster, *Historical Memorials of Westminster Abbey* (London, 1868), 173.
3 Letter from Queen Elizabeth I to King James VI, 14 February, 1586–7, o.s. in, Agnes Strickland (ed.), *Letters of Mary, Queen of Scots: now first published with an historical introduction and notes*, new edition, 2 vols. (London, 1845), 272–3.
4 Linda Colley, *Britons: Forging the Nation 1701–1837* (1992; London, 1994), 272–3.
5 Helen Smailes, ' "In the End is My Beginning": The Cult of Mary, Queen of Scots in British History Painting', in *The Queen's Image* (Edinburgh, 1987), 57.
6 Viscount Esher (ed.), Preface to *The Girlhood of Queen Victoria: A Selection of Her Majesty's Diaries Between the Years 1832 and 1840* (London, 1912) vol.1, 32.
7 Queen Victoria, journal entry for Wednesday, 17 July, 1839. In Esher, (ed.), *The Girlhood of Queen Victoria*, vol. 2, 218–19.
8 *Ibid.*, vol. 2, 299–300.
9 Queen Victoria, *More Leaves from a Journal of a Life in the Highlands 1862–1882* (London, 1883), 172.
10 As, for example, in Joshua James Foster's dedication to the late Queen on the publication of his *The Stuarts, being illustrations of the personal history of the family (especially Mary, Queen of Scots) in the xvIth, xvIIth and xvIIIth century art* (London 1902).

> Her Majesty, the late Queen Victoria, having been pleased to accept the dedication of my book on miniatures, graciously permitted me to have access to the Art treasures of Windsor for this work also, in the subject of which her Majesty, herself of Stuart blood, took, as is well known, a deep interest.

11 Adrienne Munich, *Queen Victoria's Secrets* (New York, 1996), 46.
12 Queen Victoria's *Leaves from a Journal of Our Life in the Highlands 1848–61* appeared in 1868, and *More Leaves from a Journal of a Life in the Highlands 1862–1882*, appeared in 1883.
13 John Sutherland, *The Life of Sir Walter Scott* (Blackwell, 1995), 239.
14 *Black's Picturesque Tourist of Scotland* (1840; London, 1851).
15 Colley, *Britons*, 268.
16 Colley, *Britons*, 272.
17 Ruskin writes that the woman rules over the home, 'the place of Peace; the shelter, not only from all injury, but from all terror, doubt and division ... So far as she rules, all must be right, or nothing is. She must be enduringly, incorruptibly good; instinctively, infallibly wise'. (137–8). He continues, 'there is no putting by that crown; queens you must always be; queens to

your lovers; queens to your husbands and your sons; queens of higher mystery to the world beyond, which bows itself, and will for ever bow, before the myrtle crown, and the stainless sceptre of womanhood' (170). John Ruskin, 'Of Queens' Gardens', in *Sesame and Lilies* (1865, London, 1900).

18 Quoted in Munich, *Queen Victoria's Secrets*, 187.
19 As Cecil Woodham-Smith records, Queen Victoria disagreed with much of Agnes Strickland's biography, writing in the margins of the work, 'Not true' against many statements, as well as other censorious comments: 'when Miss Strickland was sent a copy of Queen Victoria's comments on this and other statements in her book, "the well-intentioned authoress"', writes Prince Albert, 'promptly had the whole edition recalled and destroyed.' Quoted in Cecil Woodham-Smith, *Queen Victoria: From her Birth to the Death of the Prince Consort* (New York, 1972), 31.
20 Agnes Strickland, *Queen Victoria from Her Birth to Her Bridal* (London, 1840), vol. 1, ix–x.
21 Colley, *Britons*, 268.
22 Some of the crimes which were imputed to Mary were adultery with Bothwell and conspiring with him in the murder of her second husband, Darnley; later in her life she was accused of plotting to murder Queen Elizabeth, for which she was executed by the English queen in 1587.
23 Sir Walter Scott, *The Abbot* (1820; Edinburgh, 1885), vol. 2, 4. All further references to this novel will be given by volume and page number within the text.
24 Sir Walter Scott was 'a great admirer and champion' of Sir William Allan: 'Under the influence of Scott he (Allan) pioneered (with Wilkie) the painting of major pictures from Scottish history' (Smailes and Thomson, *The Queen's Image*, 151). Indeed a precedent had been set for the close relationship between literary narrative, history and narrative painting when James Boswell commissioned Gavin Hamilton to paint *Mary Queen of Scots resigning her Crown* in the 1760s. Accompanied by a highly sympathetic inscription composed by Samuel Johnson, the painting was exhibited at the Royal Academy in 1776, 'the first major public manifestation of the pictorial cult of Mary, Queen of Scots' (*Ibid.*, 108). By the time Sir William Allan painted *The Murder of David Rizzio* in 1833, Roy Strong writes that Mary Stuart 'had already emerged as *the* heroine above every other from the British past ... [paintings by Scottish artists Allan, Hamilton, Opie] heralded an intense interest in the Queen of Scots for the rest of the century. Between 1820 and 1897, fifty-six works on this theme were exhibited at the Royal Academy, and these were just the top of a more sizeable iceberg. In addition, the cult proliferated through thousands of engravings after contemporary portraits and reconstructions of incidents from her life' (Roy Strong, *And When Did You Last See Your Father?: The Victorian Painter and British History* (London, 1978), 129, 133).
25 T. Mullet Ellis, *The Fairies' Favourite, or The Story of Queen Victoria Told for Children* (London, 1897), 30. Quoted in Adrienne Munich, *Queen Victoria's*

Secrets, 73.
26 Lou Taylor, *Mourning Dress: A Costume and Social History*, (London, 1983), 138.
27 Munich, *Queen Victoria's Secrets*, 54.
28 *Ibid.*, 27.
29 According to Hugh Trevor Roper, as he argues in his essay 'The Invention of Tradition: The Highland Tradition of Scotland' in Eric Hobsbawm and Terence Ranger (eds.), *The Invention of Tradition* (1983; Cambridge, 1992).
30 Munich, *Queen Victoria's Secrets*, 71.
31 Even Scott, who rarely describes sexuality in direct terms, comes close when inspired by Mary's 'unrivalled charms': 'again [she] let her slender fingers stray through the wilderness of the beautiful tresses which veiled her kingly neck and swelling bosom' (vol. 2, *The Abbot*, 13).
32 Antonia Fraser (ed.), Introduction to *Mary Queen of Scots: An Anthology of Poetry* (London, 1981), 19.
33 J. A. Froude, 'Elizabeth', in *History of England from the Fall of Wolsey to the Defeat of the Spanish Armada* (1856–70; London, 1883), vol. 12, 152.
34 J. A. Froude, *History of England*, vol. 4, 443.
35 Helen Smailes, *The Queen's Image*, 57.
36 A somewhat less chivalric assessment of Mary comes from John Sutherland's 1995 biography of Scott. Sutherland writes that Scott, 'like other romancers ... was drawn to Mary – the most glamorous of Scottish heroines – for her romantic associations. (It is significant that he makes her slightly younger and more sexually desirable than her actual age warrants.)' (*The Life of Sir Walter Scott* (Oxford, 1995), 237). This seems rather a harsh (and unchivalric) judgement of female age and sexuality, considering that Mary Stuart was, after all, only twenty-five years of age when she escaped from Lochleven, the time-frame of Scott's novel!
37 Agnes Strickland, *Lives of the Queens of Scotland and English Princesses Connected with the Regal Success of Great Britain* (Edinburgh and London, 1852) vol. 3, 3.
38 Strong, *And When Did You Last See Your Father?*, 133–4.
39 *Ibid.*
40 Sutherland, *The Life of Sir Walter Scott*, 238.
41 *Ibid.*, 239.
42 *Ibid.*, 239.
43 Walter Scott, *The Monastery* (1820; Edinburgh, 1885), vol. 2, 356.
44 Walter Scott, *Redgauntlet* (1824; Oxford, 1985), 16.
45 Antonia Fraser, *Mary Queen of Scots* (1969; London, 1995), 24.
46 Smailes and Thomson, *The Queen's Image*, 131.
47 *Ibid.*, 131.
48 Roland Barthes, 'Introduction to the Structural Analysis of Narratives', in *Image Music Text*, selected and translated by Stephen Heath (London, 1977), 94.
49 Agnes Strickland, *The Life of Mary Queen of Scots* (London, 1873), vol. 2, 58.
50 Fraser, *Mary Queen of Scots*, 411.
51 Charlotte M. Yonge, *Unknown to History* (1882; London, 1898), 539–540. All

Notes to pages 89–105 259

further references will be given in the text.
52 Both Lady Jane and Mary Stuart were executed because they posed a threat to dynasty and the similarity of their situations is interestingly reflected in the pictorial source for Delaroche's famous history painting, the *Execution of Lady Jane Grey* (National Gallery, London). Delaroche's model for this painting was John Opie's *The Execution of Mary Queen of Scots* for Bowyer's Historic Gallery based upon Humes's *History of England* (1796; reproduced in Bowyer's *Hume* 1806).
53 Felicia Hemans, *Records of Woman: with Other Poems* (Edinburgh and London, 1808), 14.
54 *Ibid.*, 3.
55 Fraser, *Mary Queen of Scots*, 547.
56 Colley, *Britons*, 273.
57 Agnes Strickland was so incensed at Froude's admittedly virulent and unbalanced attack upon Mary Stuart (particularly in his description of her execution) that she wrote a letter of criticism and complaint to *The Times*, thereby furthering the 'battle of the books' between the queen's defenders and detractors which began before her death and continues today.
58 Froude, *History of England*, vol. 12, 257.
59 Arthur Penrhyn Stanley, Dean of Westminster, *Historical Memorials of Westminster Abbey* (London, 1868), 173-4.
60 Froude, *History of England*, vol. 12, 256.
61 *Ibid.*, 257.
62 *Ibid.*, 258.
63 Colley, *Britons*, 272.
64 Stanley, *Historical Memorials*, 134.

3. PEDIGREE, NATION, RACE: THE CASE OF DISRAELI'S 'SYBIL' AND 'TANCRED'

1 Benjamin Disraeli, in Cecil Roth, *Benjamin Disraeli* (New York, 1952), 60.
2 Bishop William Stubbs, letter to R. Pauli, 6 June 1882, *The Letters of William Stubbs, Bishop of Oxford: Letters 1825–1901*, ed. W. H. Hutton (London, 1904), 185-6.
3 Isaiah Berlin, 'Benjamin Disraeli, Karl Marx and the Search for Identity', *Against the Current: Essays in the History of Ideas* (Oxford, 1981), 271-2.
4 Robert Blake, *Disraeli* (London, 1966), 194.
5 Quoted in Robert Blake, *Disraeli's Grand Tour: Benjamin Disraeli and the Holy Land 1830–1* (London, 1982), 126.
6 Benjamin Disraeli, *Coningsby* (1844; London, 1881), 219-20.
7 Benjamin Disraeli, *Lord George Bentinck: A Political Biography* (London, 1851), 322-3.
8 Blake, *Disraeli's Grand Tour*, 126.
9 Benjamin Disraeli, *Tancred: or The New Crusade* (1847; London, 1881), 150.
10 'Myth', *The Concise Oxford Dictionary of Literary Terms*, ed. Chris Baldick (Oxford, 1990), 143.

11 See, for example, Lucien Wolf, 'The Disraeli Family', *The Times*, 20 December 1904, 6; 21 December 1904, 12: Cecil Roth, *Benjamin Disraeli, Earl of Beaconsfield*, chapter 1; Robert Blake, *Disraeli*, 4.
12 Benjamin Disraeli, *Sybil, or The Two Nations* (1845; London, 1881), 76. All further quotations from *Sybil* will be taken from this edition and referred to by page number in the text.
13 Isaiah Berlin, 'Benjamin Disraeli', 252.
14 Christopher Harvie, *The Centre of Things: Political Fiction in Britain from Disraeli to the Present* (London, 1991), 41.
15 John Vincent, *Disraeli* (Oxford, 1990), 81.
16 W. R. Greg, 'Review of *Sybil* by Benjamin Disraeli', *Westminster Review*, September 1845, vol. 44, 141–52. Reproduced in R. W. Stewart (ed.), *Disraeli's Novels Reviewed 1826–1968* (Metuchen, NJ, 1975), 213.
17 Vincent, *Disraeli*, 94.
18 Isaiah Berlin, 'Benjamin Disraeli', 266.
19 Vincent, *Disraeli*, 94.
20 Eric Hobsbawm, 'Introduction: Inventing Traditions', *The Invention of Tradition*, Eric Hobsbawm and Terence Ranger (eds.), (Cambridge, 1983), 1–2.
21 Emir Fakredeen in Benjamin Disraeli, *Tancred, or The New Crusade* (London, 1881), 202. All further quotations from *Tancred* will be taken from this edition and referred to by page number in the text.
22 Benjamin Disraeli, 'On the Life and Writings of Mr. Disraeli by His Son', preface to Isaac Disraeli, *The Literary Character; or, the History of Men of Genius* (London, 1859), viii.
23 Robert Blake, *Disraeli*, 6.
24 Thomas Hardy, *Tess of the D'Urbervilles*, ed. and intro. P. N. Furbank (1891; London, 1975), 259.
25 Disraeli, *Coningsby*, 192.
26 Edward Henry Stanley, quoted in Stanley Weintraub, *Disraeli: A Biography* (London, 1993), 301–2.
27 Benjamin Disraeli, quoted in Weintraub, *Disraeli*, 364.
28 Quoted in John Vincent, *Disraeli*, 38.
29 Charlotte de Rothschild, letter to Louise de Rothschild, 10 September 1845. Quoted in Stanley Weintraub, *Disraeli*, 244–5.
30 Benjamin Disraeli, quoted in Weintraub, *Disraeli*, 364.
31 Disraeli, *Lord George Bentinck*, 314.
32 Patrick Brantlinger, 'Nations and Novels: Disraeli, George Eliot, and Orientalism', *Victorian Studies*, vol. 35, no. 3, Spring 1992, pp. 255–275. Patrick Brantlinger is responding in part in this essay to Homi K. Bhabha (ed.), *Nation and Narration* (London, 1990), and to Jonathan Arac and Harriet Ritvo (eds.), *Macropolitics of Nineteenth-Century Literature: Nationalism, Exoticism, Imperialism* (Philadelphia, 1991).
33 Brantlinger, 'Nations and Novels', 255.
34 *Ibid.*, 260.
35 Blake, *Disraeli*, 688.

4. 'A SORT OF ROYAL FAMILY': ALTERNATIVE PEDIGREES IN MEREDITHS'S 'EVAN HARRINGTON'

1. Charles Dickens, *Bleak House* (London, 1853), 169.
2. George Meredith, *Evan Harrington* (1860; London, 1914), 304–5. All further references to the novel will be taken from this edition and referred to by page number in the text.
3. Meredith, *Celt and Saxon*, 44.
4. George Meredith, 'Concession to the Celt', *The Fortnightly Review* 40, October 1896, 448–51.
5. Edward Clodd, 'George Meredith: Some Recollections', *The Fortnightly Review* 86, n.s., July 1909, 20.
6. Meredith, *The Egoist*, 611.
7. Algernon Sidney, *Discourses Concerning Government* (1698; New York, 1979), 197.
8. Viscountess Milner, *My Picture Gallery 1886–1901* (London, 1951), 74, 75.
9. Sir John Vanbrugh, *Aesop,The Complete Works of Sir John Vanbrugh*, eds. B. Dobree and G. Webb (London, 1927), vol 2, 33.
10. Lionel Stevenson, *The Ordeal of George Meredith* (New York, 1953), 33.
11. Prys Morgan, 'The Hunt for the Welsh Past in the Romantic Period,' in *The Invention of Tradition* eds Eric Hobsbawm and Terence Ranger (1983; Cambridge, 1992), 45.
12. Charles B. Dodson, Introduction, *Crotchet Castle, Nightmare Abbey*, and *The Misfortunes of Elphin* by Thomas Love Peacock (New York, 1971).
13. George Meredith, letter to Samuel Lucas, 3 October 1859, *The Letters of George Meredith*, ed. C. L. Cline, vol. 1 (Oxford, 1970), 43.
14. George Meredith, foreword to 'The Head of Bran the Blest,' in *The Poems of George Meredith*, ed. Phyllis B. Bartlett (New Haven, 1978), 175.
15. Prys Morgan, 'The Hunt for the Welsh Past', 45.
16. Viscountess Milner, 'Talks with George Meredith', *The National Review* 131, July-December, 1948, 453.
17. Meredith's father was once described by an acquaintance as 'A perfect gentleman and not the least like a tailor' (Stevenson, *Ordeal of George Meredith*, 4). Official documents concerning Meredith's grandfather, father and himself reveal much about this preoccupation with the title of gentleman; in 1796 Melchisidec Meredith described himself as 'gentleman' in the register of the Phoenix Lodge of Freemasons (*Ibid.*, 3), and upon his first marriage to Mary Ellen Nicholls, Meredith described his father as simply 'Augustus Meredith, Esquire', stating no profession. In 1901 Edward Clodd filled out census details for Meredith. Clodd writes, 'As to his occupation he declined to say "author", but asked me to write "has private means"' ('Some Recollections', 20). He clearly still subscribed to some extent to a code whereby a gentleman did not need to work to earn a living.
18. George Meredith, letter to Samuel Lucas, September 16 1860, *The Letters of George Meredith*, ed. C. L. Cline (Oxford, 1970), 63.
19. Norman Kelvin, *A Troubled Eden* (London, 1961), 19.
20. Clodd, 'Some Recollections', 20.

21 Lionel Stevenson, *Ordeal*, 4.
22 Robin Gilmour, *The Idea of the Gentleman in the Victorian Novel* (London, 1981), 28.
23 Ruskin, 'Of Vulgarity,' *Modern Painters*, vol. 5 (1860; London, 1904), 287.
24 Anthony Trollope, *Can You Forgive Her?* (1864; Oxford, 1982), 267.
25 Allon White, *The Uses of Obscurity: The Fiction of Early Modernism* (London, 1981), 86.
26 Charles Darwin, *The Origin of Species*, ed. J. W. Burrow (1859; London, 1985), 137.
27 George Meredith, *The Egoist* (1879; London, 1915), 71–2.
28 Gilmour, *The Idea of the Gentleman*, 4.
29 Ruskin, *Modern Painters*, 287.
30 Harriet Ritvo, *The Animal Estate: the English and Other Creatures in the Victorian Age* (1987; London, 1990), 19–20.
31 Ritvo, *The Animal Estate*, 15.
32 Lord Alfred Tennyson, 'The Charge of the Light Brigade' in *The Poems of Tennyson*, ed. Christopher Ricks, 3 vols. (1969; Harlow, 1987), vol. 2, 510.
33 Thomas Hardy, *Tess of the D'Urbervilles* (1891; London, 1976), 174.
34 Margaret Tarratt, ' "Snips", "Snobs", and "True Gentleman" in *Evan Harrington*', *Meredith Now*, ed. Ian Fletcher (London, 1971), 101.
35 Kelvin, *A Troubled Eden*, 13.

5. PEDIGREE, SATI AND THE WIDOW IN MEREDITH'S 'THE EGOIST'

1 Thomas Hardy, *The Complete Poems of Thomas Hardy*, ed. James Gibson (London, 1976), 460–1.
2 George Meredith, *The Egoist* (1879; London, 1915), 73. All further quotations from the novel will be indicated by page number in the text.
3 Hardy, 'The Pedigree', *Complete Poems*, 461.
4 J. Hillis Miller, 'Prosopopoeia in Hardy and Stevens', *Alternative Hardy*, ed. Lance St. John Butler (London, 1989), 117.
5 Charles Darwin, *The Origin of Species*, ed. J. W. Burrow (1851; Harmondsworth, 1985), 116.
6 Julian Hawthorne, quoted in Lionel Stevenson, *The Ordeal of George Meredith* (London, 1954), 235.
7 Jonathan Smith, ' "The Cock of Lordly Plume": Sexual Selection and *The Egoist*', *Nineteenth-Century Literature*, vol. 50, June 1995, 67.
8 Charles Darwin, *The Descent of Man, and Selection in Relation to Sex*, ed. Paul H. Barrett and R. B. Freeman, vols. 21–2 of *The Works of Charles Darwin* (London, 1989), 610.
9 George W. Stocking, *Victorian Anthropology* (New York, 1987), 204.
10 George C. Swayne, *Herodotus* (Edinburgh and London, 1870), 36–7.
11 Quoted from the *Academy*, in Jeannie Chapel, *Victorian Taste: The Complete Catalogue of Paintings at the Royal Holloway College* (Egham, 1982), 109.
12 John Ruskin, *Notes on Some of the Principal Pictures Exhibited in the Rooms of the*

Royal Academy, 1875 (London, 1875), 18.
13 William Michael Rossetti, quoted from the *Academy*, in Chapel, *Victorian Taste*, 109.
14 'Suttee' is the anglicization of the Hindi word 'sati', which refers to the obsolete Hindu practice in which a widow burns herself upon her husband's funeral pyre. Both words may refer to the ritual itself or to the woman who performs, or suffers, the ritual. In the course of this chapter I shall tend to use 'sati' rather than 'suttee' as the former is now in common parlance.
15 Edward Tylor, *Primitive Culture: Researches into the Development of Mythology, Philosophy, Religion, Language, Art and Custom*, vol. 1 (London, 1871), 421.
16 Stocking, *Victorian Anthropology*, 244.
17 R. Hartley Kennedy, 'The Suttee: Narrative of an Eye-Witness', *Bentley's Miscellany*, 13 (1843), 241.
18 Susan P. Casteras and Ronald Parkinson (eds.), *Richard Redgrave 1804–1888* (New Haven and London, 1988), 91.
19 Quoted in Phillis Cunnington and Catherine Lucas, *Costumes for Births, Marriages and Deaths* (London, 1972), 116.
20 'The Royal Academy', *The Critic*, 3 (May 1846), 622–3.
21 'The Royal Academy', *The Art-Union*, 8 (June 1846), 177.
22 Casteras and Parkinson. *Richard Redgrave*, 124.
23 Susan P. Casteras, *The Substance and the Shadow: Images of Victorian Womanhood* (New Haven, 1982), 35.
24 Milner, 'Talks with George Meredith', p. 455. Meredith gives a sanguine version of extra-marital union in *Lord Ormont and his Aminta* (1894) and a gloomy version in *One of Our Conquerors* (1891).
25 J. Hillis Miller, '"Herself Against Herself": The Clarification of Clara Middleton', in *The Representation of Women in Fiction*, eds. Carolyn G. Heilbrun and Margaret R. Higonnet (Baltimore, 1983), 98–123.

6. PEDIGREE AND FORGETTING IN HARDY

1 Thomas Hardy, 'On an Invitation to the United States', *The Complete Poems of Thomas Hardy*, ed. James Gibson (London, 1976), 110.
2 Thomas Hardy, *A Group of Noble Dames*, ed. F. B. Pinion (1891; London, 1977), 246.
3 Henry James, *Hawthorne*, ed. and introduced by Tony Tanner (1879; London, 1967), 23.
4 Nathaniel Hawthorne, quoted in James, *Hawthorne*, 54.
5 James, *Hawthorne*, 23
6 Thomas Hardy, 'The Sunshade', *Complete Poems*, 490.
7 Hardy, 'Old Furniture', *Complete Poems*, 485–6.
8 Hardy, 'A Second Visit', *Complete Poems*, 892.
9 Thomas Hardy, *The Life and Work of Thomas Hardy*, ed. Michael Millgate (1984; London, 1989), 56.
10 Hardy, *Life and Work*, 56.

11 Hardy, 'A Man', *Complete Poems*, 153–4.
12 Thomas Hardy, *Tess of the D'Urbervilles*, ed. and intr. P. N. Furbank (1891; London, 1975), 385.
13 Hardy, *The Well-Beloved* (London, 1975), 28.
14 Hardy, *Life and Work*, 9.
15 Robert Gittings, *Young Thomas Hardy* (1975; Harmondsworth, 1980), 18.
16 K. D. M. Snell, 'Thomas Hardy, Rural Dorset and the Family', Chapter 8 of *Annals of the Labouring Poor* (Cambridge, 1985).
17 Hardy, *Life and Work*, 12.
18 *Ibid.*, 9.
19 Thomas Hardy, 'The Dorsetshire Labourer', *Longman's Magazine*, vol. 2, July, 1883, 2–3.
20 William Wordsworth, 'Essay Upon Epitaphs, I', *The Prose Works of William Wordsworth*, eds. W. J. B. Owen and Jane Worthington Smyser, vol. 2 (Oxford, 1974), 55.
21 Wordsworth, 'Essay Upon Epitaphs, III', 93.
22 Nigel Llewellyn, *The Art of Death: Visual Culture in the English Death Ritual, c.1500 – c.1800* (London, 1991), 131.
23 G. A. Walker, *Gatherings from Graveyards; Particularly Those of London ...*, (London, 1839), 380.
24 *Ibid.*, 188.
25 Thomas Hardy, 'The Son's Veto', *Life's Little Ironies*, ed. F. B. Pinion (London, 1977), 38.
26 Michael Wheeler, *Death and the Future Life in Victorian Literature and Theology* (Cambridge, 1990), 59.
27 Wordsworth, 'Essay Upon Epitaphs, I', 54.
28 Wheeler, *Death and the Future Life*, 61.
29 Walker, *Gatherings from Graveyards*, 188.
30 Hardy, 'In Death Divided', *Complete Poems*, 320–1.
31 Thomas Hardy, *Far from the Madding Crowd*, intr. John Bayley; ed. Christine Winfield (London, 1975), 320.
32 Hardy, *Life and Work*, 45.
33 *Ibid.*, 46.
34 Hardy, *A Group of Noble Dames*, 246.
35 Hardy, *Life and Work*, 35.
36 *Ibid.*, 129.
37 Hardy, 'I Found Her Out There', *Complete Poems*, 342–3.
38 Hardy, 'The Levelled Churchyard', *Ibid.*, 157–8.
39 Thomas Hardy, *Life and Work*, 162–63.
40 Thomas Hardy, *A Pair of Blue Eyes*, ed. Ronald Blythe (1873; London, 1975), 107. All further references from this novel will be referred to by page number in the text.
41 Mary Jacobus, 'Hardy's Magian Retrospect', *Essays in Criticism*, 32:3, July 1982, 264.
42 Hardy, *A Group of Noble Dames*, 209.

43 Hardy, *Life and Work*, 96.
44 *Ibid.*, 120.
45 John Harvey, *Men in Black* (London, 1995), 46.
46 Hardy, *Collected Poems*, 9.
47 Hardy, *Life and Work*, 302.
48 Gillian Beer, *Darwin's Plots: Evolutionary Narrative in Darwin, George Eliot and Nineteenth-Century Fiction* (1983; London, 1985), 244.
49 Julian Litten, *The English Way of Death* (London:, 1991), 120.

7. GEOLOGY AND GENEALOGY: 'THE WELL-BELOVED'

1 Nigel Llewellyn, *The Art of Death: Visual Culture in the English Death Ritual, c. 1500–c. 1800* (London, 1991), 134.
2 Hardy, *Complete Poems*, 627.
3 Thomas Hardy, 'Barbara of the House of Grebe', *Wessex Tales and A Group of Noble Dames*, ed. F. B. Pinion (London, 1977), 269.
4 *Ibid.*, 270.
5 Hardy, 'The Well-Beloved', *Complete Poems*, 135.
6 Thomas Hardy, *The Well-Beloved*, ed. Edward Mendelson; introduced by J. Hillis Miller (1897; London, 1976), 28. All further references from this novel will be given by page number in the text.
7 *The Shorter Oxford English Dictionary*, ed. Lesley Brown, 2 vols. (Oxford, 1993), 1694, 'March' 1.
8 From Shelley's *Prometheus Unbound*, Act 1, 11. 288–9. These are favourite poetic lines of Hardy's which he uses often, including in *Tess of the D'Urbervilles* to describe the fallen generations of the d'Urberville line.
9 Dante Alighieri, *La Vita Nuova*, trans. Barbara Reynolds (1290–4; Harmondsworth, 1969), 29.
10 Hardy, *Tess of the D'Urbervilles*, 153–4.
11 Henry Knight refers to Smeaton in *A Pair of Blue Eyes*, telling Elfride, who has written an Arthurian romance, that to hear 'that a young woman has taken to writing is not by any means the best thing to hear about her'. When Elfride asks what *is* the best thing to hear he replies, 'to hear no more about her. It is as Smeaton said of his lighthouse: her greatest real praise, when the novelty of her inauguration has worn off, is that nothing happens to keep the story of her alive.' Elfride's fear of 'stories' damaging to her reputation, her own wish to write stories, and the merging and final inevitable loss of her own story in the merging with her grandmother's and mother's, come together in Knight's comment on Smeaton.
12 John Smeaton, *A Narrative of the Building and a Description of the Construction of the Edystone Lighthouse with Stone*, Book 2 (London, 1791), Chapter 3, footnote to 65.
13 John Hutchins, *The History and Antiquities of the County of Dorset*, vol. 2 (1861–70; East Ardsley, 1973), 811.
14 Smeaton, *Narrative*, Book 2, footnote to 65.

15 Hutchins, *History and Antiquities*, vol. 2, 809.
16 Edward Said, *Beginnings: Intention and Method*, (1975; New York, 1985), 138.
17 George Wing, 'Hardy and Regionalism', *Thomas Hardy: The Writer and His Background*, ed. Norman Page (London, 1980), 85.
18 Smeaton, *Narrative*, Book 2, 65.
19 Hardy, 'The Dorsetshire Labourer', 262–3.
20 Hardy, *Tess of the D'Urbevilles*, 195.

CONCLUSION

1 Steve Connor, 'Asian Genie in the Oxford Gene Bank', *The Sunday Times*, Sunday, 16th March 1997, 5.
2 Robert Hamer, *Kind Hearts and Coronets* (Ealing Studios, 1949).

Bibliography

Allen, Grant, 'Are We Englishmen?', *The Fortnightly Review*, NS 28 (October 1880), 472–87.
An Act for the Union of Great Britain and Ireland. Reprinted in *The Statutes. 1770–1821*, vol. 2 (1779). London, His Majesty's Stationery Office, 1950.
Anderson, Benedict, *Imagined Communities: Reflections on the Origin and Spread of Nationalism*, 1983; London, Verso, 1992.
Arac, Jonathan and Ritvo, Harriet (eds.), *Macropolitics of Nineteenth-Century Literature: Nationalism, Exoticism, Imperialism*, Philadelphia, University of Pennsylvania Press, 1991.
Arnold, Matthew, 'Irish Catholicism and British Liberalism', *The Fortnightly Review*, NS 24 (July 1878), 26–45.
  'On the Study of Celtic Literature', in R. H. Super (ed.), *The Complete Prose Works of Matthew Arnold*, vol. 3, Ann Arbor, University of Michigan Press, 1962.
Aronson, Theo, *Victoria and Disraeli: The Making of a Romantic Partnership*, London, Cassell, 1977.
Austen, Jane, *The Beautiful Cassandra*, in Frances Beer (ed.), *The Juvenilia of Jane Austen and Charlotte Bronte*, Harmondsworth, Penguin, 1986.
Baldick, Chris (ed.), *The Concise Oxford Dictionary of Literary Terms*, Oxford University Press, 1990.
Barthes, Roland, 'Introduction to the Structural Analysis of Narratives', in Stephen Heath, (ed. and trans.), *Image Music Text*, London, Fontana Press, 1977.
Beer, Gillian, *Darwin's Plots: Evolutionary Narrative in Darwin, George Eliot and Nineteenth-Century Fiction*, 1983; London, Ark, 1985.
  George Meredith: A Change of Masks, London, Athlone Press, 1970.
Berlin, Isaiah, 'Benjamin Disraeli, Karl Marx and the Search for Identity', in Henry Hardy, (ed.), *Against the Current: Essays in the History of Ideas*, Oxford, Clarendon Press, 1981.
Bhabha, Homi K. (ed.) *Nation and Narration*, Cambridge University Press, 1983.
Bjork, Lennart A. (ed.), *The Literary Notebooks of Thomas Hardy*, 2 vols., London Macmillan, 1974.
Black's Picturesque Tourist of Scotland, Edinburgh, Adam and Charles Black, 1840, 1851.

Blake, Robert, *Disraeli*, London, Eyre and Spottiswoode, 1966.
 Disraeli's Grand Tour: Benjamin Disraeli and the Holy Land 1830–31, London, Weidenfeld and Nicolson, 1982.
Blewitt, Octavian, *Murray's Handbook for Travellers in Central Italy*, London, 1850.
Bowen, Desmond, *The Protestant Crusade in Ireland, 1800–70: A Study of Protestant-Catholic Relations Between the Act of Union and Disestablishment*, Dublin, Gill and Macmillan, 1978.
Brantlinger, Patrick, *Rule of Darkness: British Literature and Imperialism, 1830–1914*, Ithaca, Cornell University Press, 1988.
 'Nations and Novels: Disraeli, George Eliot, and Orientalism', *Victorian Studies* 35, 3 (1992), 255–75.
Bronfen, Elisabeth, *Over Her Dead Body: Death, Femininity and the Aesthetic*, New York, Routledge, 1992.
Bullen, J. B., *The Expressive Eye: Fiction and Perception in the Work of Thomas Hardy*, Oxford, Clarendon Press, 1986.
Butler, Harriet Jessie and Butler, Harold Edgeworth (eds.), *The Black Book of Edgeworthstown and Other Edgeworth Memories 1585–1817*, London, Faber and Gwyer, 1927.
Butler, Marilyn, *Maria Edgeworth: A Literary Biography*, Oxford, Clarendon Press, 1972.
Casteras, Susan P., *The Substance or the Shadow: Images of Victorian Womanhood*, New Haven, Yale Center for British Art, 1982.
— Parkinson, Ronald (eds.), *Richard Redgrave 1804–1888*, New Haven, Yale University Press, 1988.
Chapel, Jeannie, *Victorian Taste: the Complete Catalogue of Paintings at the Royal Holloway College*, London, Royal Holloway College, 1982.
Clodd, Edward, 'George Meredith: Some Recollections', *The Fortnightly Review* NS 86 (July 1909), 19–31.
Colley, Linda, *Britons: Forging the Nation 1701–1837*, 1992; London, Pimlico, 1994.
Cooke, Edward, *Arguments For and Against a Union*, Dublin, 1798.
Cosslett, Tess, *The 'Scientific Movement' and Victorian Literature*, Brighton, The Harvester Press, 1982.
Cunnington, Phillis and Lucas, Catherine (eds.), *Costumes for Births, Marriages and Deaths*, London, Adam and Charles Black, 1972.
Curtis, L.P., *Anglo-Saxons and Celts: A Study of Anglo-Irish Prejudice in Victorian England*, (Conference on British Studies at the University of Bridgeport, CT), New York University Press, 1968.
Dante, Alghieri, *La Vita Nuova*, trans. Barbara Reynolds, 1290–4; London, Penguin, 1969.
Datta, V. N., *Sati: A Historical, Social and Philosophical Enquiry into the Hindu Rite of Widow-Burning*, New Delhi, Manohar, 1988.
Darwin, Charles, *The Descent of Man, and Selection in Relation to Sex*, Paul H. Barrett, and R.B. Freeman (eds.), of *The Works of Charles Darwin*, vols. 21–2 London, William Pickering, 1989.
 The Origin of Species, Burrow, J. W. (ed.), 1859; Harmondsworth, Penguin,

1985.

Davey, Richard, *The Sisters of Lady Jane Grey*, London, Chapman and Hall, 1911.

Disraeli, Benjamin, *A Vindication of the English Constitution*, London, 1835.

Contarini Fleming, a Psychological Romance, London, 1832, 1853.

Lord George Bentinck: A Political Biography, London, 1851.

'On the Life and Writings of Mr. Disraeli by his Son', Preface to Isaac Disraeli, *The Literary Character: or, the History of Men of Genius*, London, 1859.

Whigs and Whiggism, Hutcheon, William (ed.), London, John Murray, 1913.

Dodson, Charles B., Introduction to Thomas Love Peacock's *Crotchet Castle, Nightmare Abbey*, and *The Misfortunes of Elphin*, New York, Holt, Rinehart and Winston, 1971.

Eagleton, Terry, *Heathcliff and the Great Hunger: Studies in Irish Culture*, London, Verso, 1995.

Edgeworth, Maria, Preface to Mary Leadbeater, *Cottage Dialogues Among the Irish Peasantry*, London, 1811.

— and others, *The Black Book of Edgeworthstown and Other Edgeworth Memoirs*, Harriet Jessie Butler, and Harold Edgeworth Butler (eds.), London, Faber and Gwyer, 1927.

Edgeworth, Richard Lovell and Edgeworth, Maria, *Essay on Irish Bulls*, London, 1802.

Ellis, T. Mullet, *The Fairies' Favourite, or The Story of Queen Victoria Told For Children*, London, Ash Partners, 1897.

Esher, Viscount (ed.), *The Girlhood of Queen Victoria: A Selection of Her Majesty's Diaries between the Years 1832 and 1840*, London, John Murray, 1912.

Flint, Kate (ed.), *The Victorian Novelist: Social Problems and Social Change*, London, Croom Helm, 1987.

Foster, Joshua James, *The Stuarts, being illustrations of the personal history of the family (especially Mary, Queen of Scots) in the XVIth, XVIIth, and XVIIIth century art*, London, 1902.

Foster, R. F., *Modern Ireland: 1600–1972*, 1988; Harmondsworth, Penguin, 1989.

Fraser, Antonia, *Mary Queen of Scots*, 1969; London, Mandarin Paperbacks, 1995.

(ed.), *Mary Queen of Scots: an anthology of poetry*, chosen and with an introduction by Antonia Fraser, London: Eyre Methuen, 1981.

'Mary Queen of Scots and the Historians', *Royal Stuart Papers* 7, Ilford, The Royal Stuart Society, 1974.

Froude, J. A., *History of England from the Fall of Wolsey to the Defeat of the Spanish Armada*, 12 vols., 1856–70; this edition, London, 1883.

Garrett, Peter K., *The Victorian Multiplot Novel: Studies in Dialogical Form*, New Haven, Yale University Press, 1980.

Gilmour, Robin, *The Idea of the Gentleman in the Victorian Novel*, London, George Allen and Unwin, 1981.

Girouard, Mark, *The Return to Camelot: Chivalry and the English Gentleman*, New Haven, Yale University Press, 1981.

Gittings, Robert, *The Older Thomas Hardy*, London, Heinemann, 1975.

Young Thomas Hardy, London, Heinemann, 1975.

Godkin, J., 'The Irish Land Question', *The Fortnightly Review* 1 (July 1865), 385–401.

Goode, John, '*The Egoist*: Anatomy or Striptease?', *Meredith Now*, Ian Fletcher (ed.), London, Routledge, 1971.

Thomas Hardy: The Offensive Truth, Oxford, Basil Blackwell, 1988.

Greg, W. R., 'Review of *Sybil* by Benjamin Disraeli', *Westminster Review* 44 (September 1845), 141–52.

'Why Are Women Redundant?', *National Review* 14 (1862), 434–460.

Hardy, Thomas, *The Complete Poems of Thomas Hardy*, James Gibson (ed.), London, Macmillan, 1976.

'The Dorsetshire Labourer', *Longman's Magazine* 2 (July 1883), 252–69.

The Life and Work of Thomas Hardy, Michael Millgate (ed.), London, Macmillan, 1989.

The Personal Notebooks of Thomas Hardy, R. H. Taylor (ed.), London, Macmillan, 1978.

Hare, Augustus J. C., *The Life and Letters of Maria Edgeworth*, 2 vols. London, 1894.

Harvie, Christopher, *The Centre of Things: Political Fiction in Britain from Disraeli to the Present*, London, Unwin Hyman, 1991.

Hallam, Henry, *Constitutional History of England*, London, 1827.

Harvey, John, *Men in Black*, London, Reaktion Books, 1995.

Hemans, Felicia, *Records of Woman: With Other Poems*, Edinburgh and London, 1808.

Heywood, Valentine, *British Titles*, London: Adam and Charles Black, 1953.

Hobsbawm, Eric and Ranger, Terence (eds.), *The Invention of Tradition* 1983; Cambridge University Press. 1992.

Hughes, W. J., *Wales and the Welsh in English Literature from Shakespeare to Scott*, Wrexham, Hughes, 1924.

Hutchins, John, *The History and Antiquities of the County of Dorset*, vol. 2. William Shipp, and James Whitworth Hodson (eds.), 1861–70; 3rd edn, intro. R. Douch, East Ardsley, Classical County Histories, 1973.

Jacobus, Mary, 'Hardy's Magian Retrospect', *Essays in Criticism* 32, 3 (July 1982), 258–279.

James, Henry, *Hawthorne*, Tony Tanner (ed.), London, Macmillan, 1967.

Johnson, William, *Reasons for Adopting an Union Between Ireland and Great Britain*, Dublin, 1798.

Kelvin, Norman, *A Troubled Eden: Nature and Society in the Works of George Meredith*, Edinburgh, Oliver and Boyd, 1961.

Kennedy, R. Hartley, 'The Suttee: Narrative of an Eye-Witness', *Bentley's Miscellany* 13 (1843), 241–56.

Lake, Sir Thomas, 'Letter to Viscount Cranbourne, March 1, 1604–5', *HMC Salisbury (Cecil) MSS [1605]* part 17, London, HMSO, 1938.

Lester, Jeremy, 'Still No Peace for the Paxman', *Jewish Chronicle*, 9 July 1993, 16.

Levin, Bernard, 'Pedigree, What Pedigree?', *The Times*, 23 July 1993, 16.

Litten, Julian, *The English Way of Death*, London, Robert Hale, 1991.

Llewellyn, Nigel, *The Art of Death: Visual Culture in the English Death Ritual, c. 1500–c.1800*, London, Reaktion Books in Association with the Victoria and Albert Museum, 1991.

Lodge, David, '*The Woodlanders*: A Darwinian Pastoral Elegy', *Working with Structuralism: Essays and Reviews on Nineteenth- and Twentieth-Century Literature*, London, Routledge, 1981, 79–94.

Lyell, Charles, *Principles of Geology*, London, 1830.

Major, Norma, *Chequers: The Prime Minister's Country House and its History*, London, Harper Collins, 1996.

Mani, Lata, 'Contentious Traditions: The Debate on *Sati* in Colonial India', *Cultural Critique* 7 (Fall 1987).

McCormack, W. J., *Ascendancy and Tradition in Anglo-Irish Literary History From 1789–1939*, Oxford, Clarendon Press, 1985.

McCormack, W.J. and Walker, Kim, Introduction to Maria Edgeworth, *The Absentee*, Oxford University Press, 1988, ix–xlii.

'The Tradition of Grace Nugent", Appendix 2 to Maria Edgeworth, *The Absentee*, 276–81.

McLennan, J. F., *Primitive Marriage*, London, 1865.

Mengham, Rod, *Language*, 1993; London, Fontana, 1995.

Meredith, George, 'Concession to the Celt', *The Fortnightly Review* NS 40 (October 1896), 448–51.

Letter to Samuel Lucas, 3 October, 1859. Letter 50 in *The Letters of George Meredith*, C. L. Cline (ed.), Oxford, Clarendon Press, 1970, 43.

Letter to Samuel Lucas, 30 September, 1860. Letter 78 in C. L. Cline (ed.), 63.

The Notebooks of George Meredith, Gillian Beer, and Margaret Harris (eds.), Institut fur Anglistik und Amerikanistik, Universität Salzburg, 1983.

The Poems of George Meredith, Phyllis B. Bartlett (ed.), New Haven, Yale University Press, 1978.

Miller, J. Hillis, *Ariadne's Thread: Story Lines*, New Haven, Yale University Press, 1992.

Fiction and Repetition, Cambridge Harvard University Press, 1982.

' "Herself Against Herself": The Clarification of Clara Middleton', *The Representation of Women in Fiction*, Carolyn G. Heilbrun, and Margaret R. Higonnet (eds.), Baltimore, Johns Hopkins University Press, 1983, 98–123.

'Prosopopoeia in Hardy and Stevens', *Alternative Hardy*, Lance St. John (ed.), London, Macmillan, 1989.

Millgate, Michael, *Thomas Hardy: A Biography*, London, Oxford University Press, 1982.

— (ed.), *The Life and Work of Thomas Hardy, by Thomas Hardy*, 1984; London, Macmillan, 1989.

Milner, Viscountess, *My Picture Gallery 1886–1901*, London, John Murray, 1951.

'Talks with George Meredith', *The National Review* 81 (July–December 1948).

Mink, Louis, 'History and Fiction as Modes of Comprehension', *New Literary History* 1, 3 (Spring 1970), 541–58.

Morgan, Prys, 'From a Death to a View: The Hunt for the Welsh Past in the Romantic Period', *The Invention of Tradition*, Hobsbawm and Ranger (eds.), 43–100.
Munich, Adrienne, *Queen Victoria's Secrets*, New York, Columbia University Press, 1996.
O'Halloran, Sylvester, *A General History of Ireland, from the Earliest Accounts to the Close of the Twelfth Century*, 2 vols., Dublin, 1778.
Ormond, Richard and Turpin, John (eds.), *Daniel Maclise 1806–1870*, London, Arts Council of Great Britain, 1972.
Owenson, Sydney, Lady Morgan, *The Wild Irish Girl*, 3 vols., 1806; New York and London, Garland, 1979.
Paxman, Jeremy, '"Dear Mr. Paxman, I Know You Are Jewish But..."', *Evening Standard*, 15 July, 1993, 11.
Peacock, Thomas Love, *The Misfortunes of Elphin*, London, 1829.
Pick, Daniel, *Faces of Degeneration: A European Disorder, c. 1848–c.1918*, Cambridge University Press, 1989.
Playfair, William, *British Family Antiquity: Containing the Baronetage of Ireland*, vol. 9, London, 1811.
Poovey, Mary, *Uneven Developments: The Ideological Work of Gender in Mid-Victorian England*, 1988; London, Virago, 1989.
Propp, Vladimir, *Morphology of the Folktale*, 2nd edn, Louis Wagner (ed.), 1928; Austin, University of Texas Press, 1968.
Queen Victoria, *Leaves from a Journal of Our Life in the Highlands 1848–61*, London, 1868.
More Leaves from a Journal of a Life in the Highlands 1862–1882, London, 1883.
Renan, Ernest, *The Poetry of the Celtic Races, and other Studies*, trans. with intr. and notes by W. G. Hutchinson, 1896; Port Washington, NY, Kennikat Press Scholarly Reprints, Series in Irish History and Culture, 1970.
Ritvo, Harriet, *The Animal Estate: The English and Other Creatures in the Victorian Age*, Cambridge, MA, Harvard University Press, 1987.
Roth, Cecil, *Benjamin Disraeli, Earl of Beaconsfield*, New York, Philosophical Library, 1952.
Rudd, Pemberton, *An Answer to the Pamphlet Entitled Arguments for and Against a Union In a Letter Addressed to Edward Cooke Esq.*, Dublin, 1799.
Ruskin, John, *Notes on Some of the Principal Pictures Exhibited in the Rooms of the Royal Academy, 1875*, London, 1875.
'Of Queens' Gardens', *Sesame and Lilies*, 1865; London, 1871.
'Of Vulgarity', *Modern Painters*, vol. 5, 1860; London, George Allen, 1904.
Said, Edward, *Beginnings: Intention and Method*, 1975, New York, Columbia University Press, 1985.
Orientalism, 1978 Harmondsworth, Penguin Books, 1985.
Scott, Sir Walter, *Sir Walter Scott's Journal*, vols. 1 and 2, Edinburgh, David Douglas, 1890.
Chivalry, an entry by Scott for the *Encyclopaedia Britannica*, in *The Miscellaneous Prose Works of Sir Walter Scott, Bart*, Edinburgh, Robert Condell, 1834, vol. 6,

Bibliography 273

3–126..

Sherwood, Mrs. John, *Manners and Social Usages*, London, 1884.

Smailes, Helen and Thomson, Duncan, *The Queen's Image*, Edinburgh, The Scottish National Portrait Gallery, 1987.

Smeaton, John, *A Narrative of the Building and a Description of the Construction of the Edystone Lighthouse with Stone*, London, 1791.

Smith, Jonathan, ' "The Cock of Lordly Plume": Sexual Selection and *The Egoist*', *Nineteenth-Century Literature*, 50, (June 1995).

Smollett, Tobias, *The Expedition of Humphry Clinker*, Peter Miles (ed.), 1771; London, J. M. Dent, 1993.

Snell, K. D. M., *Annals of the Labouring Poor: Social Change and Agrarian England, 1660–1900*, Cambridge University Press, 1985.

Snyder, Edward D. *The Celtic Revival in English Literature, 1760–1800*, 1923; Gloucester, MA, Peter Smith, 1965.

Spenser, Edmund, *A View of the Present State of Ireland*, vol. 4 of *The Complete Works of Edmund Spenser*, c.1596; London, Eric Partridge, 1934.

Stanley, Arthur Penrhyn, Dean of Westminster, *Historical Memorials of Westminster Abbey*, London, 1868.

Stevenson, Lionel, *The Ordeal of George Meredith*, New York, Charles Scribner's Sons, 1953.

Stewart, R.W. (ed.), *Disraeli's Novels Reviewed, 1826–1968*, Metuchen, NJ, The Scarecrow Press, 1975.

Stocking, George W., Jr., *Victorian Anthropology*, 1987; New York, The Free Press, 1991.

Street, Brian V., *The Savage in Literature: Representations of 'Primitive' Society in English Fiction 1858–1920*, London, Routledge and Kegan Paul, 1975.

Agnes Strickland, *Letters of Mary, Queen of Scots: now first published with an historical introduction and notes*, 2 vols., new edn, London, 1845.

The Life of Mary Queen of Scots, 2 vols., London, 1873.

Lives of the Queens of Scotland and English Princesses Connected with the Regal Succession of Great Britain, Edinburgh and London, 1852.

Queen Victoria from her Birth to her Bridal, 2 vols., London, 1840.

Strong, Roy, *And When Did You Last See Your Father?: The Victorian Painter and British History*, London, Thames and Hudson, 1978.

Stubbs, Bishop William, *Letters of William Stubbs, Bishop of Oxford, 1825–1901*, Hutton, W.H. (ed.), London, Archibald Constable, 1904.

Sutherland, John, *The Life of Sir Walter Scott*, Oxford, Blackwell, 1995.

Swayne, George C., *Herodotus*, Edinburgh and London, 1870.

Tanner, Tony, *Adultery in the Novel: Contract and Transgression*, Baltimore, Johns Hopkins University Press, 1979.

'Colour and Movement in *Tess of the D'Urbervilles*', in *Hardy: The Tragic Novels*, London, Macmillan, 1975.

Tarratt, Margaret, "Snips", "Snobs", and the "True Gentleman" in *Evan Harrington*', in Ian Fletcher (ed.), *Meredith Now*, London, Routledge. 1971.

Taylor, Lou, *Mourning Dress: A Costume and Social History*, London, Allen and

Unwin, 1983.
'The Royal Academy', *The Art Union* 8 (June 1846), 177.
'The Royal Academy', *The Critic* 3 (May 1846), 622–3.
Thompson, E., *Suttee*, London, 1928.
Thompson, E. P., *The Making of the English Working Class*, 1963; New York, Vintage, 1966.
Trollope, Anthony, *Castle Richmond*, Oxford University Press, 1989.
Trotter, David, *The English Novelist in History, 1895–1920*, London, Routledge, 1993.
Turpin, John, 'The Irish Background of Daniel Maclise', *Capuchin Annual*, 1970, 186–94.
Tylor, Edward B., *Primitive Culture: Researches into the Development of Mythology, Philosophy, Religion, Language, Art and Custom*, 2 vols., London, 1873.
Vanbrugh, Sir John, *Aesop, The Complete Works of John Vanbrugh*, eds. B. Dobree and G. Webb, London, 1927.
Vincent, John, *Disraeli*, Oxford University Press, 1990.
Walker, George Alfred, *Gatherings from Graveyards; Particularly those of London: with a Concise History of the Modes of Interment among Different Nations, from the Earliest Periods. And a Detail of Dangerous and Fatal Results Produced by the Unwise and Revolting Custom of Inhuming the Dead in the Midst of the Living*, London, 1839.
Waugh, Auberon, 'Existential Anxiety', *Daily Telegraph*, 19 July 1993, 19.
Weinbrot, Howard, *Brittania's Issue: the rise of British Literature from Dryden to Ossian*, Cambridge University Press, 1993.
Weintraub, Stanley, *Disraeli: A Biography*, London, Hamish Hamilton, 1993.
Wheeler, Michael, *Death and the Future Life in Victorian Literature and Theology*, Cambridge University Press, 1990.
White, Allon, *The Uses of Obscurity: The Fiction of Early Modernism*, London, Routledge, 1981.
White, Hayden, 'The Value of Narrativity in the Representation of Reality', in W. J. T. Mitchell, *On Narrative*, The University of Chicago Press, 1981, 1–23.
Wilde, Oscar, *The Importance of Being Earnest: A Trivial Comedy for Serious People*, 1895; London, Dawsons of Pall Mall, 1969.
Williams, Raymond, *The Country and the City*, New York, Oxford University Press, 1973.
Wing, George, 'Hardy and Regionalism', in Norman Page (ed.), *Thomas Hardy: the Writer and His Background*, London, Bell and Hyman, 1980.
Wolf, Lucien, 'The Disraeli Family', *The Times*, 20 December 1904, 6 and 21; December 1904, 12.
Wood, Christopher, *Victorian Panorama: Paintings of Victorian Life*, London, Faber, 1976.
Woodham-Smith, Cecil, *Queen Victoria; From her Birth to the Death of the Prince Consort*, New York, Alfred A. Knopf, 1972.
Woolf, Virginia, 'The Niece of an Earl', *The Common Reader*, repr. in *Collected Essays*, vol. 1, London, The Hogarth Press, 1966, 219–23.

'The Novels of George Meredith' and 'On Re-reading Meredith', *The Common Reader*, repr. in *Collected Essays*, vol. 1, 224–32.

Wordsworth, William, 'Essay Upon Epitaphs I, II, III', repr. in W. J. B. Owen and Jane Worthington Smyser (eds.), *The Prose Works of William Wordsworth*, vol. 2, Oxford, Clarendon Press, 1974.

'Preface to Lyrical Ballads' (1802 version), in Michael Mason (ed.), William Wordsworth, *Lyrical Ballads*, London, Longman, 1992.

Index

Aborigines Protection Society   185–6, 248
Academy, The   177–8
Act of Union (of Great Britain and Ireland)   13, 23–4, 27–31, 52
Aeneas   5–6, 93, 135
Aladdin   *116*, 118
Albert of Saxe-Coburg and Gotha, Prince Consort   59–62, 64–6, 190
Allan, David   63, 257n. 24
Allan, William   63, 257n. 24
Allen, Grant
   'Are We Englishmen?'   5, 8
Anderson, Benedict   4, 19, 247
Anthropological Society of London   17, 178
Arac, Jonathan   4, 127
Arnold, Matthew
   'On the Study of Celtic Literature'   14–16
Art Journal, The   209
Art Union, The   189–90
Ashkenazi   119
Austen, Jane   34, 186
   'The Beautiful Cassandra'   10–11
   Mansfield Park   98
   Persuasion   163
   Sense and Sensibility   39

Babel, Tower of   6–7
Babington Plot   87
Babylon   175–8
Babylonian Marriage Market, The   175–9, *176*
Balmoral   59, 65
Barthes, Roland   85
Battle of Langside   82
Bedouin   103, 121
Beer, Gillian   19–20, 223
Bennett, Arnold   12
Benthamites   108
Bentinck, George
   Disraeli's biography   104, 126
Berlin, Isaiah   102, 106, 108

Bess of Hardwicke (*see* Shrewsbury, Elizabeth, Countess of)
Bhabha, Homi   127
Black Book of Edgeworthstown, The   33–5
Black's Picturesque Tourist of Scotland   60
Blake, Robert   103–4, 119
Blomfield, Arthur   212
Bonaparte, Napoleon   5
Bowler, Henry Alexander
   The Doubt: 'Can These Dry Bones Live?'   207–11, *208*
Brantlinger, Patrick   127
Bronte, Charlotte   181
Brutus   5
Buckingham, George Villiers, second duke of,   170
Burke, Edmund   46
Burke, John
   Landed Gentry   215
Burns, Robert   57
Butler, Harriet Jessie   33
Butler, Harold Edgeworth   33
Butler, Marilyn   44
Byron, George Gordon, sixth baron   105

Canova, Antonio
   Monument to the Stuarts, Rome   59
Carlyle, Thomas
   Sartor Resartus   160
Caroline of Brunswick (wife of George IV)   60–1, 68–71
Carpenter, William
   The Israelites Found in the Anglo-Saxons   6
Castelnau *see* Mauvissiere, Castelnau de
Casteras, Susan   189–90
Cavendish, Elizabeth   89
Chambers, Robert
   Vestiges of the Natural History of Creation   18
Charles I, King of England   2, 170
Charles II, King of England   170, 172, 246
Charlotte, Princess   61–3

276

Index

Charlotte, Queen Consort to George III 60–1
Chartism 103, 105–7, 161
Chatterton, Thomas 132, 135
church restoration 212–15, 227
Clodd, Edward 132, 141
Colley, Linda 56, 60–3, 70, 96, 100
Collins, Wilkie 181
  Basil 163
Conroy, John 57–8
Cooke, Edward
  Arguments For and Against a Union 27–8
Cooper, James Fenimore 195
Cornhill Magazine, The 14
Critic, The 189
Cromwell, Oliver 2, 30
Curtis, L. P. 8, 17

Daily Telegraph 1
Dante Alighieri 237
  La Vita Nuova 234–5
Darnley, Henry Stuart, Lord 58, 66, 89
Darwin, Charles 167, 169, 172
  The Origin of Species 17–18, 148–9, 153, 166, 173
  The Descent of Man, and Selection in Relation to Sex 173–4
Davies, Edward
  Mythology and Rites of the Druids 135
de Clare, Richard 25
de Lara family 105, 119
Dickens, Charles
  Bleak House 130
  Dombey and Son 177
  The Old Curiosity Shop 159
  Oliver Twist 12
  A Tale of Two Cities 94
Disraeli, Benjamin 2, 3, 12, 16, 140
  Coningsby 103–4, 120, 122, 124–5, 128
  Sybil 3, 12, 103, 105–18, 124, 128, 155
  Tancred 3, 16, 18, 103, 106, 109, 115, 118–29
Disraeli, Isaac 118–9
Disraeli, Mary Anne Lewis 124–5
Donizetti, Gaetano
  Maria Stuart 57
Dorset, Charles Sackville, sixth earl of, 170
Duff-Gordon, Janet 132, 134–5, 140–1

Eagleton, Terry 36, 38–9
Edgeworth, Maria 2, 3, 12
  Castle Rackrent 43, 44–6
  The Absentee 3, 12, 16, 29, 30–53, 102, 127, 130, 134
  Essay on Irish Bulls 32, 38, 42, 45–6
  Ormond 39

Edgeworth, Richard Lovell 32, 33
Egeria 172, 188
eisteddfod 15
Eliot, George 186
Elizabeth I, Queen of England 54, 56–8, 82–3, 87–8, 96–7, 257n. 22
Ephesus, woman of 187–8, 192
Esher, Viscount 58
Ethnological Society of London 17, 185
Evening Standard 1
Ezekiel, Book of 196–7, 210

Fielding, Henry
  Tom Jones 12
  Joseph Andrews 12
Fortnightly Review, The 5, 130
Fraser, Antonia 65, 74, 86
Freeman, Edward Augustus 5
Frith, William Powell
  L'Adieu de Marie Stuart (1892) 85
Froude, J. A. 66, 98–100, 259n. 57

Gaskell, Elizabeth 186
  Wives and Daughters 163
Genesis, Book of 6–7
George IV, King of England 59, 69
Gifford, Emma *see* Hardy, Emma
Gilmour, Robin 144, 152
Gissing, George 12
Gittings, Robert 202
Glendower, Owen 134
Gobineau, Count Arthur de 17
Goethe, Wolfgang von 37
Gomer 6
Government of India Act (1853) 152
Gray, Thomas
  'The Bard' 25
  'Elegy Written in a Country Church-Yard' 195, 205, 210
Greg, William Rathbone 107
Grey, Lady Jane 88, 259n. 52
Grey, Lady Katherine 88–9
Grey, Lady Mary 88–9
Guest, Lady Charlotte 135–6
  The Mabinogion 136
Guinness, Alec 251

Hague, The 97
Hallam, Henry
  Constitutional History of England 58
Hamilton, Gavin 63, 257n. 24
Hardy, Emma 213, 223–4
Hardy, Jemima 203
Hardy, Thomas 4, 11, 85–6, 121, 195–251
  'Barbara of the House of Grebe' 227–9

Hardy, Thomas (*cont.*)
  'The Dorsetshire Labourer' 202, 204, 243
  Far From the Madding Crowd 211–12
  'The Gentleman's Second-Hand Suit'
    198–9
  A Group of Noble Dames 11, 196, 227–9
  The Hand of Ethelberta 202
  Jude the Obscure 240–1
  'Old Furniture' 199
  'On an Invitation to the United States'
    195–7
  A Pair of Blue Eyes 18, 196, 198, 200, 212,
    215–25, 241, 244, 246–7, 251
  'The Pedigree' 163–4, 194, 199
  'A Second Visit' 199
  'The Sunshade' 198–9
  Tess of the D'Urbervilles 120, 198, 200–1,
    203–4, 215, 228–9, 237–8
  The Well-Beloved 196, 200–2, 212, 229–45,
    248, 251
  The Woodlanders 198, 201
Harvey, John 222
Harvie, Christopher 106
Hawthorne, Julian 169–70
Hawthorne, Nathaniel 197
Helen of Waldeck 96
Hemans, Felicia
  Records of Woman 89–90
Hennessy, William 94–6, *96*
Henry VII, King of England 133
Henry, VIII, King of England 83, 110
Herdman, Robert
  Mary, Queen of Scots' Farewell to France (1868)
    85
Hindu widow 180–1, 188
Hobsbawm, Eric 113
Home Rule 13, 27–8, 130–1
Hood, Thomas
  'The Song of the Shirt' 160
Hutchins, John 239

Illustrated London News, The 232
Inquisition, Spanish 119

Jacobite 36, 38, 45, 71, 74, 82
Jacobus, Mary 217–18
James I, King of England 36, 54–6, 58, 89,
  97, 99
James II, King of England 59
James, Henry
  Roderick Hudson 20–1
  The Wings of the Dove 159
  Hawthorne 197–8
Jerusalem 104, 120–1, 123–4
Jewish Chronicle, The 1

Johnson, E. K.
  A Young Widow 189–92, *191*
Johnson, William 28

Kelvin, Norman 140–1, 161
'Kensington System' 57–8
Kind Hearts and Coronets 251
Kinglake, Alexander William 134
Kingsley, Charles
  Alton Locke 135, 160
  'Cheap Clothes and Nasty' 160
  Yeast 160
Knox, John
  *First Blast of the Trumpet Against the Monstrous
    Regiment of Women* 75

La Laboureur 86–7
Lawrence, T. E. 122
Leadbeater, Mary
  Cottage Dialogues 43
Lee, Sophia
  The Recess 57
Leopold, Prince, Duke of Albany 96
Levin, Bernard 1, 2
Litten, Julian 224
Llandudno 15
Llewellyn, Nigel 206, 226
Lochleven 60, 72, 75–8, 85
Long, Edwin Longsden
  The Babylonian Marriage Market 175–9, *176*,
    186
Lucas, Samuel 133, 136, 140
Lyell, Charles 17, 250
Lyndhurst, Lord (John Singleton Copley) 14

Macklin, Charles 29
Maclise, Daniel
  The Marriage of Eva and Strongbow 25, 27, 32,
    52
Macpherson, James 7, 35, 135 *see also* Ossian
McClennan, John
  Primitive Marriage 175
McCormack, W. J. 39, 41, 44, 46
Mann, Thomas
  Buddenbrooks 163–4
'Marie Stuart style' (of mourning headdress)
  64, 94
Martin, John
  The Bard 25, 32
Martineau, Harriet
  The Anglers of the Dove 57
Mauvissière, Castelnau de 86
Maxse, Violet *see* Milner, Violet Maxse,
  Viscountess
Melbourne, William Lamb, 2nd Viscount

(Prime Minister 1834, 1835–41) 58
Mengham, Rod
  The Descent of Language 8
Meredith, Arthur Gryffydh 135
Meredith, Augustus 139, 141–3, 160, 261
Meredith, George 2, 4, 8, 24
  Beauchamp's Career 181
  Celt and Saxon 23, 28, 52, 130
  'Concession to the Celt' 130–1
  Diana of the Crossways 181
  The Egoist 4, 133, 148, 162, 163–94, 248–9
  Evan Harrington 4, 130–62, 173
Meredith, Louisa (Louisa Read) 138
Meredith, Melchisidec 141
Milesians 103
Millais, Sir John Everett 136
Miller, J. Hillis 166, 192
Milner, Violet Maxse, Viscountess 133, 134, 139–40, 193
Mink, Louis 21–2
Moore, George 12
Morgan, Prys 135
Morgan, Lady, *née* Sydney Owenson
  The Wild Irish Girl 29, 34–9
  O'Donnel 38
Morganwg, Iolo
  The Myvyrian Archailogy of Wales 136
Munich, Adrienne 59, 64–5

Newman, John Henry, Cardinal 100
Noah 6
Northcote-Trevelyan Report 152

O'Carolan, Turlough 32
O'Connell, Daniel 27
O'Halloran, Sylvester
  General History of Ireland 45
Once a Week 136, 149
Orchardson, William Quiller
  Marriage de Convenance 177
  Marriage de Convenance – After! 93, 177
Ormond, Richard 25
Ossian 7, 82, 135 *see also* Macpherson, James
Ovid
  Metamorphoses 172
Oxford Movement 100
Oxford, University of
  Chair of Celtic Studies, 14–15
  Institute of Molecular Medicine 240

Pale, the English 41
Palestine 16, 102, 120
Parnell, Charles Stewart 27
Paxman, Jeremy 1, 2
Peacock, Jane Gryffydh 135, 136

Peacock, Thomas Love 135–6
  The Misfortunes of Elphin 135
Percy family 143–4, 161, 170
Percy, Thomas, Bishop of Dromore
  Reliques of Ancient English Poetry 135
Petrarch 234–5, 237
Petronius
  Satyricon 187
Pick, Daniel 16
Playfair, William
  British Family Antiquity 23, 30, 32, 34, 40, 44, 53
Poovey, Mary
  Uneven Developments 21
Portland 4, 230, 238–45 *passim*
Pre-Raphaelites 207, 209
Pughe, William Owen
  Myvyrian Archailogy of Wales 136
Punch 18, *116–7*
  cartoons from 118, 160
Pygmalion myth 228–9

Quarterly Review 206

Ranger, Terence 113
Redgrave, Richard
  Preparing to Throw Off Her Weeds *183*, 189–92 *passim*
Renan, Ernest
  La Poesie des Races Celtiques 14, 19
Ritvo, Harriet 4, 127, 154, 156
Rizzio, David (*also* Riccio) 58, 85
Rochester, John Wilmot, second earl of, 170
Ross, Henry 140
Rossetti, William Michael 178, 179
Rothschild, Baroness Charlotte de 125
Rothschild, Evelina de 243
Rothschild, Baron Lionel de 121
Royal Academy 132, 175, 177, 189, 207–9 *passim*
Rudd, Pemberton
  An Answer to the Pamphlet Entitled 'Arguments For and Against a Union etc.' 28
Ruskin, John
  Notes on the Royal Academy 177–8
  'Of Queens' Gardens' 61, 256–7
  'Of Vulgarity' 145, 153

Said, Edward 21, 240–1
St Omer (Jesuit college, N. France) 41
sati 4, 179–94 *passim*
Schiller, Friedrich
  Maria Stuart (1800) 57
Scota 16, 102

Scott, Walter 2, 3, 34, 36, 38, 42, 59, 65, 86, 88, 92, 123, 248, 257n. 24
  The Abbot 57, 60, 63, 66, 67, 68–83 *passim*, 91, 98–100, 206, 258n. 31
  'Health to Lord Melville' 69–70
  The Monastery 71–4 *passim*
  'The Lady of the Lake' 60
  Minstrelsy of the Scottish Border 135
  Redgauntlet 74, 82, 206
  Waverley 71, 206
Scythians 103
Semiramis (Queen Victoria as) 103
Sephardi 119
Severn, Joseph
  The Abdication of Mary, Queen of Scots 66, 79
Seymour, William (husband to Arabella Stuart) 89
Shakespeare, William 9, 37, 134
  Hamlet 171, 190
  Henry V 25
  Henry VI 81
Sheba, Queen of 102–3, 105, 118, 250
Sheepshanks, John (and the Sheepshanks collection at the Victoria and Albert Museum) 190
Shelley, Percy Bysshe 201, 232, 245
Sheridan, Richard 29
Sherwood, Mrs John
  Manners and Social Usages 189
Shrewsbury, Elizabeth, Countess of (Bess of Hardwicke) 87, 88, 90, 92–4
Shrewsbury, George Talbot, Earl of, 87
Sidney, Algernon
  Discourses concerning Government 133
Sinai 121, 123
Smailes, Helen 66
Smeaton, John 239, 242–3, 265
Smith, Jonathan 174
Smollett, Tobias
  The Expedition of Humphry Clinker 24
Snell, Keith 202
Social Darwinism 149, 159
Spenser, Edmund 18
Stanley, Arthur Penrhyn, Dean of Westminster
  Memorials of Westminster Abbey 99, 101
Stanley, Edward 122
Stevenson, Lionel 134, 142
Stocking, George 175, 186
Stowe, Harriet Beecher
  Uncle Tom's Cabin 159
Strickland, Agnes 55, 67
  works listed 62
  The Life of Mary Queen of Scots 62, 86, 259

Queen Victoria from Her Birth to Her Bridal 61–2
Strong, Roy 67–8
Stuart, Arabella 88–90, 93, 99
Stuart, Charles (Darnley's younger brother and son-in-law to Bess of Hardwicke) 89
Stuart, Charles Edward 59–60, 82
Stuart, Mary, Queen of Scotland 3, 54–101 *passim*
  cult of, 57, 66–7, 100
  paintings of, 63–4, 79, *84*, 85, *95*
  secret pregnancy at Lochleven 86
  execution of, 98–100
Stubbs, William, Bishop of Oxford 16, 102
Suckling, John 170
Sunday Times 249
Sutherland, John 60, 69–72, 258n. 36
suttee *see* sati
Swayne, George C.
  Herodotus 175, 177
Swinburne, Algernon Charles 57
Syria 104, 121

Taliesin 135–6
Tarratt, Margaret 160
Taylor, Lou 64
Taylor, Tom 134
Tennyson, Alfred 156, 210, 235, 251
Thackeray, William Makepeace 134
The Times 1, 2
Titania (Queen Victoria as) 103
Torah 106, 127
Tractarianism 100
Trollope, Anthony 145, 177, 181
  Castle Richmond (1860) 29
Troyes, Chretien de 137
Turpin, John 25, 27
Tylor, Edward
  Primitive Culture 185

Vanbrugh, John
  Aesop 134–5
Victoria, Queen of England 3, 57–66, 94, 96, 102, 108, 190
  claiming Stuart ancestry 59–60
  relationship with Disraeli 102–3, *116*, *117*, 118, 128–9
  Scottish travels 59–60
  widow's weeds 64–5
Victoria and Albert Museum 190
Vincent, John 106, 108, 110, 115
Villa Real family 119

Walker, G. A. 206, 209

Walker, Kim 41
Wallis, Henry 132
Waugh, Auberon 1, 2
Weinbrot, Howard 5–8
Westall, Richard 83, 85
   The Departure of Mary Queen of Scots to France When a Child 84
   The Flight of Mary Queen of Scots into England 83, *84*
Westminster Review 107
Wheeler, Michael 207–8
White, Allon 132, 147
widows 38, 48, 50, 64–6, 172, 179–94 *passim*
widows' weeds 64–5, 94, 181, 189
Wild Geese 45

Wilde, Oscar 9, 12, 13
Wildman, Major John Wildman 114
Wilkie, David 63, 257
Wood, Mrs Henry
   East Lynne 91
Wordsworth, William 42, 57, 210, 226
   'Essay Upon Epitaphs' 22, 205–7

Yonge, Charlotte 2
   Unknown to History 3, 11, 12, 57, 66, 68, 86–101 *passim*
Young England 107, 112, 114, 120
Young England trilogy (*Coningsby, Sybil, Tancred*) 103–29 *passim*
Young Pretender *see* Stuart, Charles Edward

CAMBRIDGE STUDIES IN NINETEENTH-CENTURY
LITERATURE AND CULTURE

GENERAL EDITOR
GILLIAN BEER, *University of Cambridge*

Titles published

1. The Sickroom in Victorian Fiction: The Art of Being Ill
by Miriam Bailin, *Washington University*

2. Muscular Christianity: Embodying the Victorian Age
edited by Donald E. Hall, *California State University, Northridge*

3. Victorian Masculinities: Manhood and Masculine Poetics
in early Victorian Literature and Art
by Herbert Sussman, *Northeastern University*

4. Byron and the Victorians
by Andrew Elfenbein, *University of Minnesota*

5. Literature in the Marketplace: Nineteenth-Century British
Publishing and the Circulation of Books
edited by John O. Jordan, *University of California, Santa Cruz*
and Robert L. Patten, *Rice University*

6. Victorian Photography, Painting and Poetry
The Enigma of Visibility in Ruskin, Morris and the Pre-Raphaelites
by Lindsay Smith, *University of Sussex*

7. Charlotte Brontë and Victorian Psychology
by Sally Shuttleworth, *University of Sheffield*

8. The Gothic Body
Sexuality, Materialism, and Degeneration at the *Fin de Siècle*
Kelly Hurley, *University of Colorado at Boulder*

9. Rereading Walter Pater
by William F. Shuter, *Eastern Michigan University*

10. Remaking Queen Victoria
edited by Margaret Homans, *Yale University*, and Adrienne Munich, *State University of New York, Stony Brook*

11. Disease, Desire, and the Body in Victorian Women's Popular Novels
by Pamela K. Gilbert, *University of Florida*

12. Realism, Representation, and the Arts in Nineteenth-Century Literature
by Alison Byerly, *Middlebury College*

13. Literary Culture and the Pacific: Nineteenth-Century Textual Encounters
by Vanessa Smith, *King's College, Cambridge, Vermont*

14. Professional Domesticity in the Victorian Novel:
Women, Work and Home by Monica F. Cohen

15. Victorian Renovations of the Novel
Narrative Annexes and the Boundaries of Representation
by Suzanne Keen, *Washington and Lee University*

16. Actresses on the Victorian Stage
Feminine Performance and the Galatea Myth
by Gail Marshall, *University of Leeds*

17. Death and the Mother from Dickens to Freud
Victorian Fiction and the Anxiety of Origins
by Carolyn Dever, *New York University*

18. Ancestry and Narrative in Nineteenth-Century British Literature
Blood Relations from Edgeworth to Hardy
by Sophie Gilmartin, *University of London*